DK SMITHSONIAN HANDBOOKS

FOSSILS

SMITHSONIAN
HANDBOOKS
FOSSILS

CYRIL WALKER
& DAVID WARD

Photography by
COLIN KEATES ABIPP

A Dorling Kindersley Book

LONDON, NEW YORK, MUNICH,
MELBOURNE, and DELHI

Editors Susie Behar, Jonathan Metcalf
Art Editors Peter Cross, Clive Hayball
Production Caroline Webber
US Editor Charles A. Wills

Scientific Editors Cyril Walker, David Ward

Contributors Dr. Andy Gale, David Sealey, Dr. Paul Taylor,
Dr. Richard Fortey, Dr. Brian Rosen, Sam Morris, Dr. Ed Jarzembowski,
Dr. Neville Hollingworth, Steve Tracey, Dr. Chris Duffin, David Ward,
Dr. Angela Milner, Cyril Walker, Andy Currant, Miranda Armour-Chelu,
Robert Kruszynski, Dr. Jerry Hooker, Mark Crawley

Consultants Dr. Chris Cleal,
Dr. Peter Forey, Dr. Andrew Smith, David Sealey
US Consultants Elana Benamy and Ted Daeschler,
The Academy of Natural Sciences, Philadelphia

Illustrations Will Giles, Sandra Pond

First American Edition, 1992
Reprinted with corrections in 2000
Second American Edition, 2002
10 9 8 7 6 5 4

Published in the United States by
Dorling Kindersley, Inc.
375 Hudson Street
New York, NY 10014

A Cataloging-in-Publication record
is available from the Library of Congress
ISBN 0-7894-8984-8

Reproduced in Singapore by Colourscan
Printed and bound by South China Printing Company in China

see our complete product line at
www.dk.com

CONTENTS

INTRODUCTION • 6
Authors' Introduction 6
How This Book Works 9
What is a Fossil? 10
Modes of Preservation 12
Geological Time Chart 14
Where To Look 16
Collecting Fossils 18
Preparing Your Collection 20
From Hobby to Science 22
Fossil Identification Key 24

INVERTEBRATES • 32
Foraminifera 32
Sponges 33
Bryozoa 36
Worms 40
Trace Fossils 42
Problematica 43
Graptolites 45
Corals 50
Trilobites 56
Crustacea 66
Chelicerata 73
Insects 76
Brachiopods 79
Bivalves 94
Scaphopods & Chitons 114
Gastropods 115
Nautiloids 134
Ammonoidea 141
Ammonites 145
Belemnites & Squids 161
Crinoids 166
Echinoids 175
Asteroids 186
Ophiuroidea 189
Blastoids 190
Cystoids 191
Carpoids 193

VERTEBRATES • 194
Agnathans 194
Placoderms 196
Chondrichthyans 198
Acanthodians 208
Osteichthyans 209
Amphibians 221
Anapsid Reptiles 225
Diapsid Reptiles 231
Dinosaurs 245
Synapsid Reptiles 255
Birds 258
Mammals 263

PLANTS • 286
Algae 286
Early Land Plants 289
Hepatophytes 290
Sphenopsids 290
Ferns 292
Lycopods 294
Pteridosperms 295
Bennettites 300
Progymnosperms 300
Cordaitales 301
Conifers 301
Ginkgos 307
Dicotyledonous
Angiosperms 307
Monocotyledonous
Angiosperms 311

Glossary 312
Index 317
Acknowledgments 320

AUTHORS' INTRODUCTION

Fossil collecting is a fascinating hobby that has grown considerably in popularity over the last few decades. Its appeal is understandable; it combines the excitement of discovery with the practical skills of collecting and preparing specimens and the academic challenge of identifying fossil finds. There are few other branches of science in which a beginner may make a contribution to the knowledge of our planet's remarkable prehistory.

In 1910, Sir Robert Falcon Scott embarked on his historic but tragic expedition to the South Pole. On his return from the Pole, Scott and four companions met their death in freak weather conditions. Out of this tragedy came an important scientific discovery: among the personal belongings of the dead explorers, a fossilized seed fern, *Glossopteris,* was found. The existence of this seed fern proved conclusively that the frozen wastes of Antarctica were once part of a fertile continent. Scott had recognized the scientific importance of the fossil plant.

TRACHYPHYLLIA (CORAL)

plants and animals, but also rocks, minerals, and man-made artifacts such as coins. It is now used to refer to the naturally buried (and fortuitously preserved) remains of organisms that lived on Earth, long before historic times.

FROM COINS TO BONES

Originally the word "fossil" (derived from the Latin word *fossilis,* meaning "to be dug up") referred to anything that had been buried. It included not only the petrified remains of

DIPLOMYSTUS (FISH)

YEARS OF SPECULATION

Fossils have intrigued people for generations. Greek philosophers regarded them as rather strange, natural phenomena, that formed in the earth, in a similar way to a stalactite or crystal. Martin Luther (1483–1546) believed that fossil finds on mountain tops were evidence of the biblical Flood. In his notebooks, Leonardo da Vinci (1452–1519) suggested that fossils were the petrified remains of once-living organisms. His views, heretical for his era, were withheld until his notebooks were published in the 19th century. The true nature of fossils slowly became apparent in the 17th and 18th

HEMICIDARIS
(SEA URCHIN)

CLASSIFICATION

Fossils are usually referred to by their two-part scientific name, although a few have popular or informal names as well. For instance, the oyster *Gryphaea* is often called a "Devil's Toenail" and brachiopods are known as "lamp shells." These names have their uses, but lack the precision needed in science; more importantly, they are not internationally accepted and can be confusing. The usual form is to give the scientific name, usually written in italic, followed by the name of the author (the person who first described the species). The first part is the genus, the second part, the species. If the author's name is in brackets, it means that the species has, at a later date, been moved to a different genus. When correctly used, a scientific name

centuries. This was aided by the publication of books figuring collections of fossils, and by a wider understanding of natural history. One key observation was that different types of rocks contain different fossils. This fact was of considerable help in the production of the first geological maps and led to the modern sciences of paleontology (the scientific study of fossils) and stratigraphy (the study of rock strata). Today, paleontology is concerned only with the remains of animals and plants that lived more than 10,000 years ago.

FIELD TRIP

The authors, David Ward (right) and Cyril Walker (left), in the southern Sahara, examining an exciting fossil find: a scatter of dinosaur bones. Some of the bones found can be seen on page 248.

refers only to a single type of organism and can be understood by scientists all over the world. The basic unit of classification is the species. There are many and various definitions, but essentially all members of a species look similar and are able to interbreed. One or more species may be grouped into a genus, linked by features they share. This, along with the family (a group of genera) and the order (a group of families) makes up the pedigree or family tree of an organism. All the stages above "species" are artificial, a man-made classification, and they tend to change depending on current opinion. This can be frustrating to both beginner and specialist alike.

CRINOID STEM

AMBER (FOSSILIZED PLANT RESIN)

AIMS AND LIMITATIONS

This book is intended to assist the collector by illustrating a broad range of fossils, from those most likely to be found, to some of the more spectacular, but less common. The fossils were chosen from the Natural History Museum, London, UK, one of the largest and most diverse collections in the world. Microscopic specimens have not been included. While many are fascinating and visually stunning, their

study is quite specialized. Most major groups of fossils are included, from worms to dinosaurs, from ammonites to man, and from all geological ages and continents. The description of each fossil has been written by experts who work on the many different types of fossil included. Technical terms have been kept to a minimum, but where this has proved difficult, they have been explained in a comprehensive glossary (see pp.312–316).

Many fossils, particularly the larger reptiles and mammals, are only occasionally found whole. This poses a problem in terms of identification. In such cases, small parts of the skeleton have been illustrated.

It would be impossible to show a photograph of every type of fossil. However, the range and diversity of specimens contained in this book should enable the collector to find a photograph and description of something sufficiently close to attempt a preliminary identification.

CALLIOSTOMA (GASTROPOD)

HOMO HABILIS (HOMINID SKULL)

HOW THIS BOOK WORKS

The main body of the book is divided into three parts: invertebrates, vertebrates, and plants. Within each major division, the main groups are introduced. The genus is the starting point of identification. Usually a typical or relatively common species of the described genus is illustrated. Identifying features are clearly highlighted in annotation. Occasionally, an unusual specimen, but one that makes an interesting point, has been chosen. Each photograph is accompanied by a reconstruction of a typical species of the organism in life. Some of the reconstruction details, such as the color, are educated guesswork. This annotated example shows a typical page.

name of the order to which the fossil belongs •

name of the family to • which the fossil belongs

informal name of • the fossil

Order CROCODYLIA | Family METRIORHYNCHIDAE | Informal name Marine crocodile

genus name •

METRIORHYNCHUS

main text • describing the main identifying characteristics of the genus

The metriorhynchid family is the most specialized of all known crocodiles and is perhaps the only archosaur group to become fully aquatic. Changes in its original habit are clearly reflected in its skeleton, for the forelimbs were transformed into paddles, the neck was shortened, the tail is bent downward at the end to support a large caudal fin, and the body armor lost. In contrast to their more terrestrial crocodilian cousins, the skull is long and lightly built – this was another requirement for a fully aquatic mode of life.

information • about the habitat and mode of life of the genus

• HABITAT Species of *Metriorhynchus* were particularly common in the Jurassic seas of Europe, where they hunted for fish and squidlike animals which shared the same habitat. It may be that they only came to land to lay their eggs, in the manner of modern turtles. It is also possible that they hauled themselves onto sand banks to bask after hunting for fish.

general • information pertaining either to the genus or to the particular specimen featured

• REMARK The metriorhynchids belong to the primitive mesosuchian suborder of crocodiles, which appeared in the Triassic but finally became extinct in the earliest part of the Tertiary, some 60 million years ago.

• nostril

• long snout

METRIORHYNCHUS LAEVE Andrews; Oxford Clay; Late Jurassic; UK.

• neural spine

articulation •

• caption giving the species name, author, lithological unit (when known), geological age, and country of origin of the specimen. If the species has been moved to a different genus after it had been named, then the author's name appears in brackets. Abbreviations used in this caption are: sp.=species; cf.=compares favorably with

annotation • highlighting the main identifying features of the genus

eye sockets •

flat-faced • articulation

VERTEBRA

• plain bone surface

• label giving information on the fossil or part of fossil featured

large temporal • opening

abbreviations used in this band are: E.=Early; M.=Middle; L.=Late; Carb.= Carboniferous

• jaw articulation

SKULL

Typical length 10 ft (3 m)

• illustration showing a typical species of the fossil genus in life. Under the illustration is a measurement which gives an indication of the organism's size

Range M.–L. Jurassic | Distribution Europe, S. America | Occurrence

geological range • of the genus

• geographical distribution of the genus

• the number of symbols indicates the frequency with which the fossil occurs (one=rare; five=common)

WHAT IS A FOSSIL?

FOSSILS ARE THE REMAINS of long-dead plants and animals that have partly escaped the rotting process and have, after many years, become part of the Earth's crust. A fossil may be the preserved remains of the organism itself, the impression of it in the sediment, or marks made by it in life (known as a trace fossil). For fossilization to occur, rapid burial, usually by water-borne sediment, is required. This is often followed by chemical alteration, where minerals may be added or removed. The replacement by and/or addition of minerals usually aids preservation.

FOSSIL DUNG
Trace fossils are true fossils. This dropping (below left) is probably from an extinct shark. It is usually difficult to relate these coprolites to the animal that produced them.

REPTILE FOOTPRINT
While difficult to identify to a particular species, fossil footprints (above) can provide valuable information about the organism's behavior, such as speed, weight, and mode of life.

MUMMIFIED FROG
Mummification – the natural drying of an organism – has meant that the frog (right) has progressed part of the way toward becoming a fossil. To ensure proper preservation, it must become entombed in a medium that would guard against further decomposition.

HORSE TOOTH
This cheek tooth (below) looks like that of a modern horse, but is actually a fossil. Over the centuries, its organic tissue has been replaced by strengthening mineral salts, ensuring its preservation.

BANDED FLINT
Flints (right) are sometimes mistaken for fossils. During formation, flint can be deposited in bands. With a little weathering and staining, these flints can resemble fossil corals, mollusks, worms, and trilobites.

FOOT-SHAPED
Cretaceous flints come in many forms; this one resembles a human foot (below). Some flints are crustacean burrow infills; if so, they are regarded as trace fossils.

BIRDS' NEST
The birds' nest (above) is not a fossil; it is a modern nest that has been petrified in a spring.

CLAY BOTTLE
Objects as mundane as a collapsed clay bottle (above) are sometimes mistaken for fossils.

HOW FOSSILIZATION OCCURS

Fossilization is, at best, a risky process which relies on a chain of favorable circumstances. The vast majority of the plants and animals that have ever lived have completely disappeared without trace, leaving no fossil record. With rare exceptions, it is only the skeletal or hard parts of an organism that become fossilized. This often occurs when the organism decaying in the sediment alters the local conditions and promotes the incorporation of mineral salts within its structure, a process known as mineralization. This chemical change often enables the fossil to become more resistant than the surrounding sediment.

FOSSILIZATION
After death an organism may slowly disintegrate (a) or become buried in soft sediment (b). However, it may be disturbed or digested by sediment-feeding organisms, or current or wave activity may re-expose it (c). As the sediment compacts and the complex chemical reactions of diagenesis occur, the potential fossil may be dissolved (d). But if the sediment is sufficiently consolidated, a mold may be formed (e). Percolating mineral solutions may infill the mold, creating a cast (f). Some enter the sediment relatively unaltered by mineralization (g). If buried and subjected over time to increased temperature and pressure, sedimentary rocks become softened and distorted (metamorphosed), and ultimately destroyed (h). As rocks are folded, uplifted, and eroded, buried fossils may be exposed on the surface (i).

WATER COLUMN

SOFT SEDIMENT

CONSOLIDATED SEDIMENT

METAMORPHIC ROCK

MODES OF PRESERVATION

TO BECOME preserved as a fossil, some of the normal processes of decay must be permanently arrested. This usually involves isolating the organisms that cause decay from the air or water, and then filling any voids in the hard tissue with additional minerals. The vast majority of fossils are, therefore, found in fresh-water or marine sediments, where oxygen-deprived silt or clay has buried the organism soon after death. If the sediment conditions remain favorable *(see pp.10–11)*, the organism may be preserved as a fossil. In the case of mummification, the arrest of decay is only temporary; a mummified organism will begin to decay as soon as it is exposed to air once again.

Under exceptional circumstances, soft-tissue details may be preserved. Insects in amber and mammoths in ice or tar are well-known examples. In both cases, the living organism has been caught in the sticky substance (tar or resin) which has then been fossilized, ensuring preservation. If limestone, phosphate, or pyrite is deposited in the sediment surrounding a decaying plant, it forms a "tomb" that may preserve very fine details of the organism. Silicified or otherwise petrified wood can produce spectacular color effects, although the cell preservation itself is often poor.

TRAPPED IN AMBER
Amber, the fossilized resin of a plant or tree, sometimes preserves not only the external, but also the internal, structure of an organism. Insects, spiders (above), frogs, and lizards may be preserved in this way.

SILICIFICATION
This is a form of "petrification." Silicified wood (left) can often be found in both terrestrial and freshwater deposits, usually sands and silts. Weathering volcanic ash usually supplies silica, which is gradually incorporated into partially decayed wood. Generally, the cell structure of silicified wood is quite poorly preserved; however, the presence of iron and other minerals can produce some really spectacular coloring.

PHOSPHATIZATION
Bones and teeth (above), *which normally dissolve on the sea bed or leach out of the sediment, are more likely to be preserved if large quantities of phosphates are present. Phosphatic deposits are a source of well-preserved fossils and are often mined commercially*

MUMMIFICATION
The dry sterile atmosphere of a cave has preserved this moa foot (above) *with some soft tissue intact; usually bones are only preserved in a fragile state. Mummification is only a pause in disintegration and is not true fossilization.*

FREEZING
This Siberian mammoth's hair (right) *was preserved in permafrost until recently. Once thawed, the flesh will decay unless action is taken, but the hair is relatively durable.*

TAR AND SAND
A mixture of tar and sand has embalmed this beetle (left). *This could be stable for thousands, but not millions, of years.*

LIMESTONE TOMB
The completeness of this fragile crinoid, entombed in limestone (left), *suggests that the calcareous nodule encasing it formed soon after death.*

PYRITIZATION
The shell and chambers of this ammonite (right) *were replaced by iron pyrite. This is often unstable in moist air, so it must be stored in very dry conditions.*

GEOLOGICAL TIME CHART

THE PLANET EARTH was formed 4,600 million years ago, with life present for at least 3,850 million years. Although multicellular life appeared more than 1,000 million years ago, remains from that period are scarce. The first organisms with hard parts, allowing fossils to become relatively common, appeared about 550 million years ago. Geological time is divided into Periods, usually named after the area in which the rocks from that period were first described: for example, Jurassic is named after the Jura Mountains between France and Switzerland; Devonian after the rocks in Devon, UK. Although estimates of their actual age may vary quite dramatically, these periods provide a framework within which rocks and fossils can be correlated worldwide.

Fish

Amphibians

Dinosaurs

Birds

Reptiles

Mammals

Vertebrates

Echinoderms

Brachiopods

Man

Chelicerates

Insects

Crustaceans

Bivalves

Gastropods

Modern Cephalopods

Worms

Invertebrates

CHART KEY
The symbols on the chart indicate the different groups of plants and animals, both vertebrates and invertebrates, some living, some long extinct. The blue radial lines show their presumed relationships. The color bands represent the conventional geological periods, stretching from the Precambrian (4,600 million years ago) to the present (Recent) time.

WHERE TO LOOK

YOU CAN FIND FOSSILS in many places where sedimentary rocks, such as clays, shales, and limestones, are exposed. Exposures of hard rock weather afresh very slowly after collecting and can be disappointing. Artificial exposures, such as road cuts or quarries, can be much more productive. Exposures of softer rocks can be good sites, provided they have not been too badly altered by metamorphism. Inland sections in sands and clays tend to degrade rapidly and become overgrown. Here temporary exposures are valuable, along with continually eroding river or coastal sections.

Establishing the age of the rocks, with the aid of a geological map, will give you an idea of what sort of fossils to expect. Most libraries have geological guides, but remember that they may be out of date: many an hour has been spent looking for quarries that have been infilled and had houses built on them.

A visit to a local museum is often useful, but up-to-date information from other collectors is better. Consider joining a natural history society or a rock and mineral club. They can often gain access to private localities. Most geological societies have a code of conduct relating to collecting, which it is advisable to follow. Wherever you decide to collect fossils, get permission from the authorities.

COASTAL SITES
Wave-washed cliffs and foreshore exposures (above) *are good places to search for fossils. Be aware of the state of the tide when you are climbing headlands. Wear a hard hat to protect you from small stones dislodged by startled seabirds, but remember it will not protect you from larger falling rocks.*

QUARRIES
Supervised parties are usually allowed to collect fossils in quarries (left), *but individuals may be discouraged. Check beforehand whether there are places, usually around active faces, that are out-of-bounds. Hard hats are a normal requirement. The staff often know where the best specimens may be found.*

TRILOBITE
Concoryphe (left), *an eyeless deep-water genus, was found in a hard Cambrian mudstone.*

ARID TERRAINS
Although erosion is slow in deserts (below) and badlands, the large areas of exposure that exist can more than compensate.

NATIONAL PARKS
Hammering rocks is often discouraged in areas of natural beauty and is illegal in most national parks (above), so please be sensitive. In this way fossils will still be there for future generations.

RUGGED TERRAIN
Fossils are often concentrated along particular bedding planes; the combination of a potentially interesting area and well-stratified rocks make an ideal hunting ground (below).

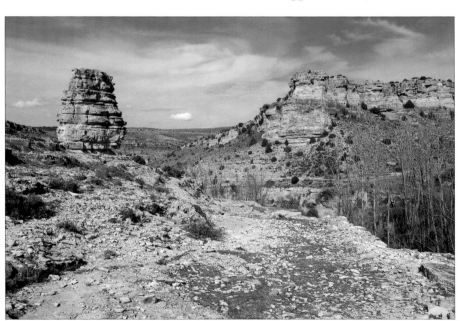

COLLECTING FOSSILS

COLLECTING FOSSILS is a very relaxing and intellectually stimulating hobby, but it is one that can often be frustrated by not having suitable field equipment. It is clearly impossible to cater for all eventualities, but the tools shown below form a basic selection that covers most situations. However, it is always better to leave a fossil in the field than to try to dig it out in a hurry with the wrong tools; this could damage a valuable scientific find.

Occasionally, equipment for plastering is required. You use this to protect fragile fossils before you remove them from the rock. Clean the fossil and expose it as much as possible. Cover it with layers of a separator (wet paper or cling film), followed by layers of plaster bandage. Once the plaster has been set, you can lift the fossil out of the rock face, and then repeat the process on the underside.

Your safety should be a primary concern. Hard hats, goggles, and gloves are essential. Finally, before you set out on an expedition, ask other collectors who are familiar with the area you intend to visit exactly what tools you will need.

SAFETY EQUIPMENT

Rocks can be sharp and dangerous. A hard hat is essential if collecting near high rock faces. Goggles will shield your eyes from dust and stones, and gloves will protect your hands.

• compass

• map

• long tape measure

MAP AND COMPASS
A geological map and a compass will help you find fossil localities. Take a long tape measure to record the level of the bed in which you find fossils.

NOTEBOOK AND CAMERA
Record field notes, such as locality, type of rock, and fossils seen, in a sturdy notebook, in waterproof ink. A photograph can also prove invaluable.

• notebook and pens

• hand lens

• camera

FIELD TOOLS
For extracting fossils from hard rocks, a sturdy mallet and several guarded chisels are essential equipment. A pick-ended geological hammer is useful on most types of rock. Soft sediments are best tackled with a trowel or a spade.

mallet

geological hammer

trowel

guarded chisels

SIEVE
Use a sieve to separate fossils from sands and gravels. Usually one or two different meshes are needed, to avoid losing small fossils.

PLASTERING
Protect fragile fossils in a plaster jacket before removing them from the rock. This prevents them from shattering.

plaster bandages

small brush

large brush

plastic sieve

SPADE
When you are searching for fossils in soft sediments, such as sands, silts, and clays, a narrow-bladed spade, rather than a conventional geological hammer, is the most useful tool for clearing an area around the fossil.

Preparing Your Collection

UNLIKE MOST OUTDOOR activities, fossil collecting does not end when you return from a field trip. A freshly collected specimen usually needs cleaning to remove any adherent matrix. This can be a very simple procedure, such as dusting sand off a specimen, or, it may involve using dilute acids to remove fossils encased in hard rock. For example, you will need acid to remove fossilized teeth from an unconsolidated matrix of shell debris. This is a tricky process that should first be attempted with the guidance of an expert.

Fragile fossils can be strengthened with a dilute solution of consolidant. Use a glue that can be removed, so that a joint can be repositioned later. Plastic boxes are ideal for storing small fossils. Open plastic trays suit larger specimens (cardboard may give off vapors harmful to fossils). Use glass vials or microscope slides to house very small specimens.

Each fossil should be labeled. A good method of labeling fossils is to give each fossil a number, corresponding to a card in a card-file index. The label or card should include the following data: the name, the lithological unit, and the rock's geological age. This should be followed by the locality, its map reference, the county or state, and the date it was collected. A fossil without these details is of little scientific value.

Cleaning Fossils
Use a variety of large and small brushes and dental probes to clean the specimen, and to remove small fragments of rock. Chip off more resistant matrix with a lightweight hammer and chisel or with an engraving tool. Handle small or fragile specimens very carefully, preferably with fine forceps. It is a good idea to protect them with a consolidant, so that they will not break up when they are handled or transported.

brushes

forceps

dental probes

engraver

sieve

dilute acid

sharks' teeth

Sieving
Use a stack of stainless steel or brass sieves to separate samples containing small fossils, such as sharks' teeth, into different sizes. Brass sieves are soft and damaged by seawater, and so are not suitable for use in the field.

Organic Acids
Use dilute organic acids, e.g. vinegar, to remove the surplus matrix from a calcareous specimen. Practice the procedure on an unimportant fossil first, to avoid damaging a valuable specimen.

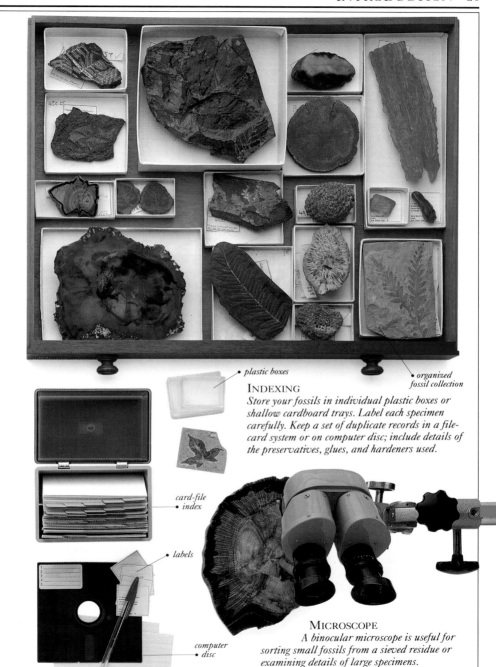

plastic boxes •

• organized
fossil collection

INDEXING
*Store your fossils in individual plastic boxes or
shallow cardboard trays. Label each specimen
carefully. Keep a set of duplicate records in a file-
card system or on computer disc; include details of
the preservatives, glues, and hardeners used.*

card-file
• index

• labels

computer
• disc

MICROSCOPE
*A binocular microscope is useful for
sorting small fossils from a sieved residue or
examining details of large specimens.*

FROM HOBBY TO SCIENCE

B EGINNERS NORMALLY START by collecting any fossil that comes their way. This is not a bad idea, as there is a lot to learn about the hobby. After a while, however, most collectors specialize in a particular group of fossils, such as trilobites, ammonites, or plant fossils, or perhaps an age or locality.

Initially, most collectors tend to regard fossils merely as objects that are attractive in their own right, a pleasure to admire and own. With time and experience the specimens themselves become less important and collectors soon realize that their true value lies in the scientific information they represent. Donating specimens to a local or national museum collection is one way a fossil collector can repay any help that he or she has received from museum staff in the past; most museums rely very heavily on the generosity of amateur collectors.

It is no exaggeration to say that paleontology is one of the few sciences to which an amateur is able make a significant contribution to the state of knowledge – indeed, this is probably one of its major attractions as a hobby.

NATIONAL MUSEUMS
These often have an identification service and good regional and national exhibits of fossils (left), allowing collectors to make their own determinations. Only the best of a vast collection is on display, so try not to be discouraged if your fossils don't quite match in quality. The museum shop will usually have a good selection of books on fossil identification.

LOCAL MUSEUMS
Most museum curators are happy to give advice, discuss the local geology, and help identify problem specimens (right). Their knowledge and enthusiasm have inspired many young collectors to pursue geology as a career. Local museums can also put you in touch with the nearest geological society.

EASY FIND
Shark's teeth are a favorite among fossil collectors. In rocks of the right age, they are quite easy to find.

ERYOPS
MEGALOCEPHALUS
COPE

Most fossil collectors dream of finding something new. This need not be a large and spectacular specimen, like a dinosaur; it is more often a small and apparently insignificant fossil. The skill, for the amateur paleontologist, lies in recognizing something unusual. If it is a new species, a description is published in a scientific journal, accompanied by a photograph and details of the locality; a procedure that can take several years. The specimen must then be housed in a museum collection. This ensures that all those interested are able to study it. A private collection is not acceptable because it is not open to the public. Parting with a prize specimen can be difficult, but it is necessary if the full potential of the discovery is to be realized.

MUSEUM EXHIBIT
This giant amphibian (above) is from the Permian of Texas, USA. Magnificent specimens like this, reconstructed by paleontologists, are a feature of natural history museums worldwide.

BUYING FOSSILS

You can purchase small fossils, such as mollusks and trilobites, quite cheaply in rock and mineral shops or at fossil exhibitions. Fish, reptiles, and dinosaurs are also sold on the open market, but usually for considerable sums of money. This means that large vertebrate fossils are often placed out of the price range of most museums, and are therefore, sadly, lost to the public.

REFERENCE BOOKS
Libraries may house old illustrated monographs. Paleontology is one of the few branches of science in which something written more than a century ago can still be relevant.

FOSSIL IDENTIFICATION KEY

THE FOSSIL RECORD is so vast that to give adequate coverage in a book of this size is impossible. Nevertheless, typical examples of the more common groups of fossils have been illustrated here. In this way, even if a particular genus is not illustrated, a similar organism will be shown. On the next eight pages, visual examples of each major group of fossils are given, along with a concise description and the pages of the book where the group is covered in detail. When attempting an identification, it is vital to relate the range of any fossil to the rock in which your particular specimen is found; for instance, you do not find trilobites in the Cretaceous, or mammals in the Devonian. A look at the geological time chart on pages 14–15 will help you with this. The key is divided into three sections: invertebrates, vertebrates, and plants.

INVERTEBRATES

FORAMINIFERA

Small (some microscopic), multi-chambered, calcareous objects; either round, discoidal, or ovoid. Usually present in large numbers, they can be rock forming.
Range Cambrian–Recent

Page: 32

Test of
NUMMULITES

WORMS

Burrows, tracks, or calcareous tubes; usually spiral, cemented to objects. Can be confused with teredinid tubes *(p.111),* scaphopods *(p.114),* or corals *(p.50).*
Range Cambrian–Recent

Tube of
PROLISERPULA

Tube of
ROTULARIA

Pages: 40–41

SPONGES AND BRYOZOANS

Composed of calcite or silica, or as an outline on a bedding plane. Shaped more like a plant than an animal; irregular, often branching, treelike; size variable. Sponges are generally thick walled, with a featureless or coarsely ornamented surface. Bryozoa are usually thin walled with a delicate pore network; they can encrust other fossils or pebbles. They can be confused with corals *(p.50)* or calcareous algae *(pp.286–287).*
Range (sponges) Cambrian–Recent
Range (bryozoa) Ordovician–Recent

Skeleton of
RHIZOPOTERION

Pages: 33–39

Skeleton of
RAPHIDONEMA

Skeleton of
CONSTELLARIA

TRACE FOSSILS AND PROBLEMATICA

These encompass tracks, trails, borings, and burrows. Generally they are radiating, feeding, or tubular burrow structures made by worms, arthropods, echinoids, mollusks, or they are walking tracks of arthropods. Terrestrial shallow lake sediments may show regularly spaced depressions made by "footprints." The systematic position of problematicans is uncertain because they are either poorly preserved or they resemble no modern fossil group.
Range Precambrian–Recent

Trace of CHONDRITES

Footprint of TETRAPOD

Pages: 42–44

Imprint of SPRIGGINA

GRAPTOLITES

These are impressions on rocks resembling watch springs, fretsaw blades, or meshwork. "Teeth" may be on one or both sides of stipe which may be single or multiple. Graptolites may be confused with some plant remains *(pp.286–311)*, or bryozoa *(p.37–41)*, or an oblique section of crinoid stem *(p.168).*
Range Ordovician–Carboniferous

Skeleton of RETIOLITES

Pages: 45–49

Skeleton of DIDYMOGRAPTUS

Skeleton of PHYLLOGRAPTUS

CORALS

Shapes are very variable: hornlike, tubelike, or treelike. The skeleton is calcareous. There are one or many calices; each individual calice is divided by a series of radial plates giving a starlike appearance. Calices may be closely abutted or laterally fused in meandering chains (like brain coral, *p.54).* The size of the colony can vary from less than a centimeter to several meters. They can be confused with encrusting bryozoa *(p.36),* calcareous algae *(p.286),* serpulid worm tubes *(p.40),* or sponges *(p.33).*
Range Ordovician–Recent

Colony of COLPOPHYLLIA

Pages: 50–55

Colony of FAVOSITES

Calice of TRACHYPHYLLIA

ARTHROPODS

Arthropods have segmented bodies with a differentiated anterior end. The body is covered by a cuticle, or shell, that acts as an external skeleton (exoskeleton). The exoskeleton is sometimes strengthened by calcium carbonate or calcium phosphate. Arthropods have a variable number of appendages (legs), specialized into locomotory, sensory, or feeding elements. Molting is a common feature of arthropods – otherwise their growth would be constrained by the external cuticle. Arthropods include the trilobites, the Crustacea (crabs, lobsters, barnacles, and shrimps), the chelicerates (king crabs, scorpions, and spiders), and the Uniramia (millipedes and insects).

TRILOBITES
These have a flattened, min-eralized, calcium carbonate shell, and are preserved in three dimensions, or as an impression. The eyes are often fragmented. The thorax may segment.
Range Cambrian–Permian

Internal mould of
OLENELLUS

Pages: 56–65

Exoskeleton of
PHACOPS

CHELICERATES
The body is divided into a fused head, thorax, and abdomen. They can be con-fused with some trilobites and insects. Rarely found as fossils.
Range Cambrian–Recent

Imprint of
MESOLIMULUS

Pages: 73–75

Body of
DOLOMEDES

CRUSTACEA
Usually the ornamented phosphatic carapace is preserved; sometimes limb fragments, calcareous plates, or bivalve shells, are found.
Range Cambrian–Recent

Imprint of
HYMENOCARIS

Pages: 66–72

Exoskeleton of
ARCHAEOGERYON

INSECTS
These are divided into head, thorax, and abdomen. The adults have six legs, and sometimes wings.
Range Devonian–Recent

Exoskeleton of
HYDROPHILUS

Pages: 76–78

Imprint of
PETALURA

BRACHIOPODS

The shells have two sym-metrical, calcareous, or chiti-nous, dissimilar valves. One valve usually bears a hole (pedicle foramen), through which it is attached to the substrate. They are common in older rocks, often in large "nests" of a single species.
Range Cambrian–Recent

Pages: 79–93

Shell of
GONIORHYNCHIA

Shell of
LINGULA

Shell of
TEREBRATULA

MOLLUSKS

Mollusks are a very diverse group that includes the chitons, scaphopods, bivalves, gastropods, and cephalopods. Nearly all mollusks have calcium carbonate shells; only a few genera of gastropods, cephalopods and nudibranchs lack this. The soft body is rarely preserved, so mollusks are classified by their shell structure. Most are marine; only a few families of bivalve and gastropod have entered fresh water. Some gastropods have become air breathing and colonized the land. They can be filter feeders (most bivalves), herbivores (some gastropods), carnivores (gastropods, cephalopods). One major group, the ammonoids, became extinct at the end of the Cretaceous.

BIVALVES

Two valves, similar in shape but each asymetrical; exceptions are oysters and rudists. May be loose in the sediment or cemented to a firm substrate. May be confused with brachiopods *(pp.79–93)* and corals *(p.50)*.
Range Cambrian–Recent

Pages: 94–113

Shell of
CRASSATELLA

Cast of
WHITEAVESIA

CHITONS AND SCAPHOPODS

Chitons: ridged, tilelike plates.
Scaphopods: curved; tapering.
Range (Chitons) Cambrian–
Recent *Range* (Scaphopods)
Ordovician–Recent

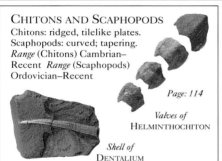

Page: 114

Valves of
HELMINTHOCHITON

Shell of
DENTALIUM

GASTROPODS

Single asymmetrical, spiral, unchambered calcium carbonate shell.
Range Cambrian–
Recent

Pages: 115–133

Shell of
ECPHORA

Shell of
ARCHIMEDIELLA

NAUTILOIDS

Straight, curving, or loosely or lightly coiled calcium carbonate shells, divided into a chambered phragmocone and a living chamber. The chambers are connected by a tube (siphuncle).
Range Cambrian–Recent

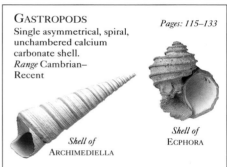

Cast of
ORTHOCERAS

Pages:
134–140

Section of
UNKNOWN NAUTILUS

AMMONOIDS

Similar to nautiloids but with a ventral siphuncle. Chambers give rise to a complex suture. Ribs and tubercles are common.
Range Devonian–Cretaceous

Pages: 141–160

Cast of
MANTELLICERAS

BELEMNITES AND SQUIDS

These have a solid, tapering, crystalline calcium carbonate guard, partially enclosing a chambered phragmocone.
Range Jurassic–
Recent

Pages:
161–165

Guard of
BELEMNITELLA

ECHINODERMS

The echinoderms include the echinoids (sea urchins), holothuroids (sea cucumbers), asteroids (starfish), crinoids (sea lilies), as well as the extinct blastoids, cystoids, and carpoids. All have five-rayed symmetry, except for some echinoids and carpoids. They possess a complex water vascular system that operates a network of multi-functional tube feet. All are restricted to fully marine environments and thus act as marine indicators. Most possess solid calcite skeletons that fall apart on death; crinoidal debris can be so abundant as to be rock forming *(see p.168)*. Some irregular echinoids *(see Micraster p.185)* have evolved in a manner which makes it possible for them to be used as zone fossils.

CRINOIDS
Comprise a columnar stem, head (or calyx), and arms (pinnules); some species are stemless. On death, they usually disintegrate to isolated calyx ossicles and round, pentagonal, or star-shaped, crystalline-calcite stem segments.
Range Cambrian–Recent

Pages: 166–174

Calyx of
MARSUPITES

Calyx of
CYATHOCRINITES

ECHINOIDS
The shell or test is composed of thin, loosely cemented, calcite plates. The test may be sub-spherical and have five-rayed symmetry, or heart shaped, or dorsoventrally flattened with a bilateral symmetry (characterized by irregular echinoids). Plates bear spines that may be short and bristlelike or large and club shaped.
Range Ordovician–Recent

Test of
HEMICIDARIS

Pages: 175–185

Test of
HEMIASTER

ASTEROIDS
These are five-sided, with margins edged with solid calcitic blocks (ossicles). Occasionally preserved as whole, articulated specimens; more usually found as isolated ossicles.
Range Ordovician–Recent

Pages: 186–188

Cast of
TROPIDASTER

OPHIUROIDS
These small, individual ossicles are common in sieved residues; articulated specimens are rare. The central disk of calcite plates has five, snakelike arms. They are common in deep-water sediments.
Range Ordovician–Recent

Page: 189

Skeleton of
PALAEOCOMA

BLASTOIDS
Usually intact, compact calyx.
Range Ordovician–Permian

Page: 190

Calyx of
PENTREMITES

CYSTOIDS
Short stem, calyx of many small irregular plates.
Range Cambrian–Permian

Pages: 191–192

Calyx and stem of
LEPADOCRINITES

CARPOIDS
Stem short, asymmetrical calyx of small polygonal plates, no arms.

Range Cambrian–Devonian

Page: 193

Calyx of
COTHURNOCYSTIS

VERTEBRATES

FISH

Fish are a very diverse group of marine and freshwater vertebrates. The group includes the jawless agnathans, the armored placoderms, the cartilaginous sharks, rays, and chimeroids, the spiny acanthodians, and the modern bony fish. All fish possess segmented body musculature, a brain, spinal cord, notochord, terminal mouth, hollow gut, and pharyngeal perforations (usually known as gills). Paired sense organs for smell, sight, balance, and electric fields are also characteristics common to all. The body is usually covered with scales or denticles that may fuse into armored plates. They all have paired pelvic and pectoral fins, unpaired dorsal and anal fins, and a post-anal tail.

AGNATHANS

Jawless and covered with fine scales. The head may be encased in an armored shell of fused scales.
Range Late Cambrian–Late Devonian

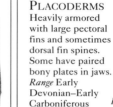

Head shield of PTERASPIS

Pages: 194–195

PLACODERMS

Heavily armored with large pectoral fins and sometimes dorsal fin spines. Some have paired bony plates in jaws.
Range Early Devonian–Early Carboniferous

Pages: 196–197

Skeleton of BOTHRIOLEPIS

CHONDRICHTHYANS

Skeletons of sharks, rays, and chimeroids are rarely preserved articulated. Usually teeth, tooth plates, placoid scales, fin spines, and calcified vertebrae are found. Sharks' teeth have enameloid crowns.
Range Late Silurian–Recent

Pages: 198–207

Tooth of PTYCHODUS

Tooth of STRIATOLAMIA

ACANTHODIANS

Found as isolated scales, teeth, and ornamented fin spines. Fin spines can be confused with those of a shark. Teeth lack enamel.
Range Late Silurian–Early Permian

Page: 208

Skeleton of DIPLACANTHUS

OSTEICHTHYANS

These are found as teeth, bones, scales, fin spines, and otoliths.
Range Late Silurian–Recent

Otolith of CENTROBERYX

Scales of LEPIDOTUS

Pages: 209–220

AMPHIBIANS

The bones are solid or hollow; the skull is composed of fused bony plates. The teeth are simple with no roots. Vertebrae may be unitary or multipartite and have neural canals. Limb bones may bear a variable number of digits.
Range Late Devonian–Recent

Pages: 221–224

Skeleton of RANA

REPTILES

ANAPSIDS
Bones are solid; skulls are without secondary openings.
Range Early Carboniferous–Recent

Pages: 225–230

Carapace of TRIONYX

DIAPSIDS
Limb bones are usually hollow. Teeth are enameled with single long root, set in sockets or fixed to jaws; skulls may be massive and ornamented (crocodiles) or lightly built and loosely ornamented (snakes). Dermal armor, when present, is usually ornate.
Range Late Carboniferous–Recent

Teeth of LEIODON

Pages: 231–244

Skull of DIPLOCYNODON

DIAPSIDS (DINOSAURS)
Bones are solid, or thick walled and hollow. Skull is lightly built with fixed quadrate bones; enamelled teeth lie in deep sockets. Hip socket is perforated; head of thigh bone is angled inward.
Range Late Triassic–Cretaceous

Jaw of DASPLETOSAURUS

Skull of HETERODONTOSAURUS

Pages: 245–254

Tooth of JOBARIA

SYNAPSIDS
Bones are solid, vertebrae biconcave, neural canal is present. Skull is often massive. Teeth differ.
Range Late Carboniferous–Jurassic

Pages: 255–257

Skull of CYNOGNATHUS

BIRDS

Skull is light, teeth are usually absent. Limb bones are hollow and thin-walled, sternum is keeled, ankle bones are fused, tail is reduced, vertebrae are saddle shaped with neural canal.
Range Late Jurassic–Recent

Limb bone of AEPYORNIS

Pages: 258–262

MAMMALS

Limb bones are hollow (except in seals and manatees), often gracile and thin walled; epiphyseal plates present. Teeth are enamel-covered, and multifaceted; some have bony roots; incisors, canines, premolars, and molars present. Skull may bear horns or antlers. Lower jaw is a single bone.
Range Late Triassic–Recent

Pages: 263–285

Tooth of TETRALOPHODON

Skull roof of BISON

PLANTS

ALGAE

Preserved as microscopic single-celled plants, banded stromatolitic masses, calcified structures, or thin impressions.
Range Precambrian–Recent

Pages: 286–288

Colony of
MASTOPORA

EARLY LAND PLANTS AND HEPATOPHYTES

Present as small, upright, branching, leafless, aerial shoots, or low thallus with ovoid spores; no true roots.
Range Late Silurian–Recent

Pages: 289–290

Thallus of
HEXAGONOCAULON

SPHENOPSIDS

Vertical stems emerge from underground rhizomes. The main stem is jointed, and pith filled with leafed stems.
Range Early Devonian–Recent

Pages: 290–291

Frond of
ASTEROPHYLLITES

FERNS, LYCOPODS, AND PTERIDOSPERMS

The fronds of ferns and pteridosperms are divided into multiple leaflets. In lycopods the leaves are spirally arranged. Spores are borne on the underside of leaves in ferns; in cones in the leaf axil in lycopods. Pteridosperm fronds bear a single seed.
Range Late Silurian–Recent

Stem of
LEPIDODENDRON

Pages: 292–299

Leaflets of
DICROIDIUM

Stem of
OSMUNDA

BENNETTITES AND CYCADS

Foliage grows from large trunk. Cones are in center of crown or leaf bases; flowers are present.
Range Triassic–Recent

Page: 300

Flower of
WILLIAMSONIA

CONIFERS

Woody trunks, often rich in resin; leaves are needle-like, spirally arranged. Male and female reproductive structures present on a single tree; seeds in cones.
Range Late Carboniferous –Recent

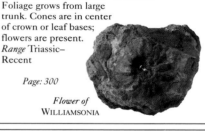

Cone of
PICEA

Pages: 301–306

ANGIOSPERMS

Preserved as wood, leaves, and, very rarely, flowers, where both male and female organs may be present. Seeds are large; leaves are deciduous, (some) broad, with a radiating network of veins, or relatively narrow with parallel veins.
Range Cretaceous–Recent

Leaf of
ARALIOPSOIDES

Pages: 307–311

Trunk of
PALMOXYLON

INVERTEBRATES

FORAMINIFERA

F ORAMINIFERANS ARE SMALL, single-celled organisms belonging to the kingdom Protista. Some species secrete a shell, called a test, made of calcium carbonate or (less commonly) chitin. Others construct a test by sticking together particles of sand and debris. Most species live in the sea:

planktonic foraminiferans float in the surface waters of the oceans, their dead tests drifting down to the sea bed; benthonic foraminiferans live in or on the sea bottom. Both types occur in large numbers, and rocks may form from their remains. The few large species live in warm, shallow waters.

Order FORAMINIFERIDA	Family NUMMULITIDAE	Informal name Nummulite

NUMMULITES

Circular in outline and biconvex, this large foraminiferan is made up internally of small chambers arranged in a spiral.
• **HABITAT** *Nummulites* was abundant in the shallow, warm seas of the ancient Tethys Ocean.
• **REMARK** Nummulitic lime-stone was used in the building of the Egyptian pyramids.

tiny internal • chambers

• circular biconvex form

NUMMULITES GHISENSIS (Ehrenberg); Nummulitic Limestone; Eocene; Egypt.

Typical diameter ⅗ in (1.5 cm)

Range Paleocene–Oligocene	Distribution Europe, M. East, Asia	Occurrence ⊙⊙⊙⊙⊙

Order FORAMINIFERIDA	Family ALVEOLINIDAE	Informal name Alveolinid

ALVEOLINA

Oval in shape and often large in size, this creature is made up internally of numerous small chambers, which in life may have housed symbiotic algae.
• **HABITAT** *Alveolina* lived on the sea bed in warm, shallow waters.
• **REMARK** Where locally abundant, *Alveolina* some-times formed limestones.

BLOCK OF ALVEOLINA LIMESTONE

ALVEOLINA ELLIPTICA; Kithar Series; Eocene; India.

• *oval shape*

Typical diameter ¼ in (4 mm)

Range Eocene	Distribution Europe, M. East, Africa, Asia	Occurrence ⊙⊙⊙⊙⊙

SPONGES

S PONGES ARE PRIMITIVE, sedentary, aquatic animals. Water passes in through their many surface pores to the central cavity of the saclike body, and out through larger holes. The skeleton, where present, is made up of needlelike spicules, and is either calcareous, siliceous, or horny. Sponges occur as fossils from Cambrian times onward and were abundant in the Cretaceous. Stromatoporoids are also believed to be sponges, but archeocyathids are now thought to be an independent phylum.

Order LYSSAKIDA	Family DICTYOSPONGIIDAE	Informal name Glass sponge

HYDNOCERAS

The thin-walled, vase-shaped *Hydnoceras* is a fine example of a glass sponge, with an open structure of spicules forming a rectangular meshwork. Bulbous swellings appear along the longitudinal ridges.
• **HABITAT** Living glass sponges are found only in deep water, but they were once common at all depths.
• **REMARK** This fossil is a cast in sandstone, preserving the filling of the skeleton but not the skeleton itself. The meshwork is clearly visible, but not the spicules themselves.

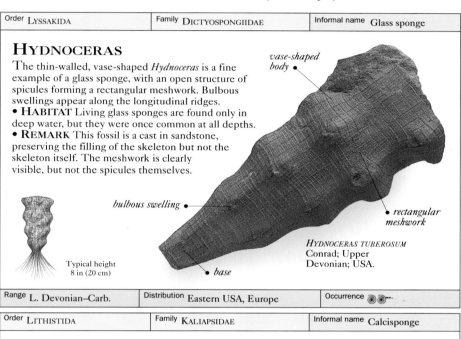

vase-shaped body

bulbous swelling

rectangular meshwork

Typical height 8 in (20 cm)

base

HYDNOCERAS TUBEROSUM Conrad; Upper Devonian; USA.

Range L. Devonian–Carb.	Distribution Eastern USA, Europe	Occurrence

Order LITHISTIDA	Family KALIAPSIDAE	Informal name Calcisponge

LAOSCIADIA

This flat, mushroom-shaped sponge, common in the Late Cretaceous, is a lithistid, a kind of demosponge characterized by a compact, complex structure with many chambers. The skeleton consists of a rigid interlocking framework of four-rayed spicules.
• **HABITAT** These siliceous sponges lived in depths of water varying from 330–1,300 ft (100 to 400 m).

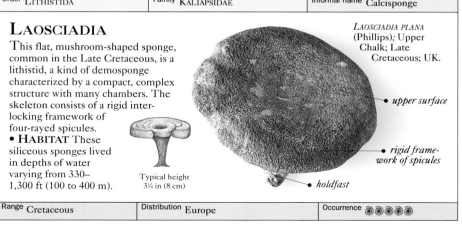

LAOSCIADIA PLANA (Phillips); Upper Chalk; Late Cretaceous; UK.

upper surface

rigid framework of spicules

Typical height 3¼ in (8 cm)

holdfast

Range Cretaceous	Distribution Europe	Occurrence

Order LYCHNISKIDA	Family VENTRICULITIDAE	Informal name Glass sponge

RHIZOPOTERION

This generally funnel-shaped genus is one of the glass sponges, or hexactinellids, which are very different in organization from other sponges found as fossils. Their siliceous skeletons have an open structure of spicules, with four to six rays mutually at right angles, forming a rectangular meshwork. Within the glass sponges, ventriculitids form an important group, of which *Rhizopoterion* is a member. They vary in form, but all are characterized by the form of their spicules, as well as by walls pierced by an irregular array of slotlike inhalant and exhalant canals. Their bases have a holdfast of radiating "roots," and they range in shape from tall, narrow vases to flat, open mushrooms.

• **HABITAT** Glass sponges, such as *Rhizopoterion* lived on muddy substrates down to a depth of 20,000 ft (6,000 m) or more.

• **REMARK** As indicated by its usual (but incorrect) name, *Ventriculites infundibuliformis*, this species is generally funnel shaped. It occurs commonly in the Late Cretaceous (Chalk) of Europe.

RHIZOPOTERION CRIBROSUM (Phillips); Upper Chalk; Late Cretaceous; UK.

top •

• side wall

• rectangular exhalant canals

• open mesh-work of spicules

Typical height 4 in (10 cm)

Range Cretaceous	Distribution Europe	Occurrence ⊛⊛⊛⊛⊛

Order PHARENTRONIDA	Family LELAPIIDAE	Informal name Calcisponge

RAPHIDONEMA

This genus belongs to the separate class of calcisponges, in which the skeleton is made of calcareous, rather than siliceous, spicules. *Raphidonema* is irregularly cup shaped and very variable in size. Generally, the interior is smooth, while the exterior is covered with rounded knobby projections.

• **HABITAT** This calcareous sponge lived in warm, shallow waters.

• **REMARK** This is the most common sponge found in the famous Faringdon Sponge Gravels at Faringdon, Oxfordshire, in the United Kingdom.

RAPHIDONEMA FARRINGDONENSE (Sharpe); Faringdon Sponge Gravels; Early Cretaceous; UK.

• main exhalant opening

• side wall

knobby • outside surface

Typical height 3¼ in (8 cm)

Range Triassic–Cretaceous	Distribution Europe	Occurrence ⊛⊛⊛⊛⊛

| Order STROMATOPOROIDEA | Family ACTINOSTROMATIDAE | Informal name Stromatoporoid |

ACTINOSTROMA

Actinostroma is a typical calcareous, reef-building, bloblike stromatoporoid. Although enigmatic, the genus is thought by some to be the ancestor of modern sclero-sponges. When studied in thin section, it shows a fine structure of thin, concentric layers and radial pillars.

• **HABITAT** This genus commonly lived on, and formed, reefs.

• **REMARK** These organisms were important rock formers, particularly in the Silurian and Devonian.

Typical height
4¾ in (12 cm)

concentric growth layers •

irregular shape •

ACTINOSTROMA CLATHRATUM
Nicholson; Middle
Devonian; UK.

| Range Cambrian–E. Carb. | Distribution Worldwide | Occurrence ⊚⊚⊚⊚⊚ |

| Order ARCHEOCYATHIDA | Family METACYATHIDAE | Informal name Archeocyathid |

METALDETES

Metaldetes is a widely distributed example of the group of marine animals known as archeocyathids. Although sponges and archeocyathids are unrelated, the latter have a similar calcareous (but non-spicular) skeleton. *Metaldetes* has a basically a single- or double-walled cone perforated by numerous pores. The central cavity is empty, as in sponges. It is not known how the soft tissue was organized.

• **HABITAT** These small creatures lived in reefs in warm, shallow seas.

• **REMARK** Most archeocyathids are found silicified in hard limestones, and are known from the Early Cambrian of South Australia, Siberia, Sardinia, and Antarctica.

• outer wall

empty central • cavity

septum • (partition)

Typical height
2 in (5 cm)

inner wall •

METALDETES TAYLORI (Bedford);
Early Cambrian;
South Australia.

| Range Cambrian | Distribution Worldwide | Occurrence ⊚⊚⊚⊚⊚ |

BRYOZOA

BRYOZOANS ARE colonial animals which resemble miniature corals but are more closely related to brachiopods. They range from the Ordovician to the present day. Most bryozoans live on the sea bed and secrete calcareous skeletons. Bryozoan colonies vary in shape – some are sheetlike encrustations on shells and stones, whereas others grow as small trees or netlike fronds. Each colony consists of a few to thousands of connected individuals (zooids). Each zooid has a tubular or box-shaped skeleton.

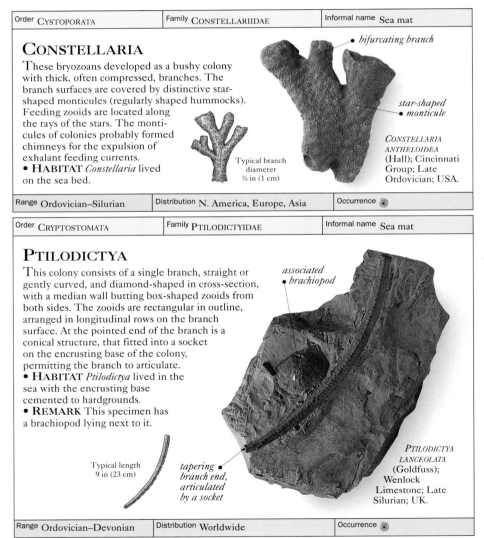

Order CYSTOPORATA	Family CONSTELLARIIDAE	Informal name Sea mat

CONSTELLARIA

These bryozoans developed as a bushy colony with thick, often compressed, branches. The branch surfaces are covered by distinctive star-shaped monticules (regularly shaped hummocks). Feeding zooids are located along the rays of the stars. The monticules of colonies probably formed chimneys for the expulsion of exhalant feeding currents.
• **HABITAT** *Constellaria* lived on the sea bed.

bifurcating branch

star-shaped monticule

Typical branch diameter ⅜ in (1 cm)

CONSTELLARIA ANTHELOIDEA (Hall); Cincinnati Group; Late Ordovician; USA.

Range Ordovician–Silurian	Distribution N. America, Europe, Asia	Occurrence ⊛

Order CRYPTOSTOMATA	Family PTILODICTYIDAE	Informal name Sea mat

PTILODICTYA

This colony consists of a single branch, straight or gently curved, and diamond-shaped in cross-section, with a median wall butting box-shaped zooids from both sides. The zooids are rectangular in outline, arranged in longitudinal rows on the branch surface. At the pointed end of the branch is a conical structure, that fitted into a socket on the encrusting base of the colony, permitting the branch to articulate.
• **HABITAT** *Ptilodictya* lived in the sea with the encrusting base cemented to hardgrounds.
• **REMARK** This specimen has a brachiopod lying next to it.

associated brachiopod

Typical length 9 in (23 cm)

tapering branch end, articulated by a socket

PTILODICTYA LANCEOLATA (Goldfuss); Wenlock Limestone; Late Silurian; UK.

Range Ordovician–Devonian	Distribution Worldwide	Occurrence ⊛

Order FENESTRATA	Family FENESTELLIDAE	Informal name Lace corals

FENESTELLA

This erect, netlike colony is formed of narrow, regularly spaced, branches linked by dissepiments. The zooids are arranged in two rows along the branches, with apertures opening on only one side of the planar, folded, or conical colonies. The dissepiments lack zooids. Spinose outgrowths have been developed, especially near the colony base, and were sometimes barbed.

• **HABITAT** *Fenestella* and similar reticulate bryozoans lived by filtering food from self-generated water currents, which flowed in one direction through the holes in the colony.

branches linked • by dissepiments

limestone matrix •

Typical colony height 2 in (5 cm)

FENESTELLA PLEBEIA McCoy; Carboniferous Limestone; Early Carboniferous; UK.

• oldest part of colony

• rootlike spines

Range Silurian–Permian	Distribution Worldwide	Occurrence ◉

Order CYCLOSTOMATA	Family CAVIDAE	Informal name Sea mat

CERIOCAVA

This is a bushy colony with bifurcating cylindrical branches up to 2 in (5.5 cm) in diameter. The branch surfaces are covered with a honeycomb of polygonal (typically hexagonal) zooidal apertures, many sealed by lids. Long, sack-shaped polymorphic zooids for larval brooding are occasionally found.

• **HABITAT** This bryozoa formed low colonies on the sea floor, filtering food from the surrounding water.

cylindrical branches •

soft matrix •

CERIOCAVA CORYMBOSA Lamouroux; Bathonian; Middle Jurassic; France.

Typical branch diameter ⅛ in (3 mm)

• fractured end of branch

Range Jurassic–Cretaceous	Distribution Europe	Occurrence ◉

Order CYCLOSTOMATA	Family MULTISPARSIDAE	Informal name Sea mat

REPTOCLAUSA

This encrusting colony is characterized
by having long ridges aligned parallel to the
direction of its growth. Ridge flanks and
crests are occupied by feeding zooids
with subcircular apertures. Smaller,
indistinct, nonfeeding, polymorphic
zooids form the smooth-surfaced
valleys between the ridges. These
zooids lack apertures.
• **HABITAT** These colonies
were relatively robust, and
capable of living on rolling
stones and shells in turbulent
marine conditions.

*ridges on
• colony surface*

*sediment
trapped
between
• ridges*

*sheetlike colony •
spreading over pebble*

*exposed surface •
of dark gray pebble*

Typical colony
diameter
1½ in (4 cm)

*REPTOCLAUSA
HAGENOWI* (Sharpe); Faringdon
Sponge Gravel; Early Cretaceous; UK.

Range Jurassic–Cretaceous	Distribution Europe, Asia	Occurrence ◉◉

Order CHEILOSTOMATA	Family SERTELLIDAE	Informal name Lace corals

SCHIZORETEPORA

This is a colony of complex
folded fronds pierced by oval
fenestrules. Feeding zooids
opened on one side of the
fronds. They had apertures
with sinuses. Defensive poly-
morphs (avicularia) are scattered over all branch surfaces.
Schizoretepora is one of several
similar genera that require
careful microscopic study for
accurate identification.
• **HABITAT** *Schizoretepora*
lives on the sea bed.

corrugated fronds

*zooids opening on
• branch surface*

*SCHIZORETEPORA
NOTOPACHYS*
(Busk); Coralline
Crag; Pliocene;
UK.

Typical colony diameter
1½ in (4 cm)

perforations •

*cross sections
of broken branches*

Range Miocene–Recent	Distribution Worldwide	Occurrence ◉

Order Not Applicable	Family Not Applicable	Informal name Bryozoan limestone

BRYOZOAN LIMESTONE

Some limestones consist predominantly of fragments of the calcareous skeletons of bryozoan colonies. Many different bryozoan species may be present, often accompanied by broken mollusk shells and barnacles.

• **HABITAT** Bryozoan limestones are especially common in the shallow-water deposits of the Cenozoic Era. Today, they can be found forming in subtropical to cold-water environments, but bryozoan limestones are rarer in the tropics, where coral limestones are found in great abundance.

echinoid fragment

pieces of reticulate bryozoans

branch fragments

Width of rock specimen
4½ in (11 cm)

bryozoan encrusting a shell

BRYOZOAN LIMESTONE; Miocene; South Australia.

Range Jurassic–Recent	Distribution Worldwide	Occurrence 🌑🌑🌑🌑🌑

Order CHEILOSTOMATA	Family CLEIDOCHASMATIDAE	Informal name Sea mat

HIPPOPORIDRA

The thick, multilayered colonies encrust gastropod shells. The feeding zooids have frontal walls pierced by marginal pores, and apertures with a sinus. Atop the monticules are larger zooids, and scattered between the monticules are avicularia with pointed rostra.

• **HABITAT** Recent *Hippoporidra* live symbiotically with hermit crabs, providing the crabs with excellently camouflaged homes. Although the crabs are not preserved as fossils, paleontologists believe the bryozoan colony form is diagnostic of their past presence.

monticule

gastropod shell completely enveloped

apex

larger zooids on monticule

hermit crab aperture

HIPPOPORIDRA EDAX (Busk); James River Formation; Pleistocene; USA.

Typical length ¾ in (2 cm)

outer lip

Range Miocene–Recent	Distribution Europe, N. America, Africa	Occurrence 🌑

WORMS

WORM IS A GENERAL NAME applied to representatives of various soft-bodied invertebrate groups. They include the platyhelminthes, nematodes, nemertines, acanthocephalans, annelids, and some hemichordates. Most are unknown or very rare in the fossil record. However, some members of the polychaeta group of segmented worms secrete a dwelling tube made of durable calcite, which is often found attached to fossil shells or pebbles. These are common fossils in certain Mesozoic and Cenozoic rocks.

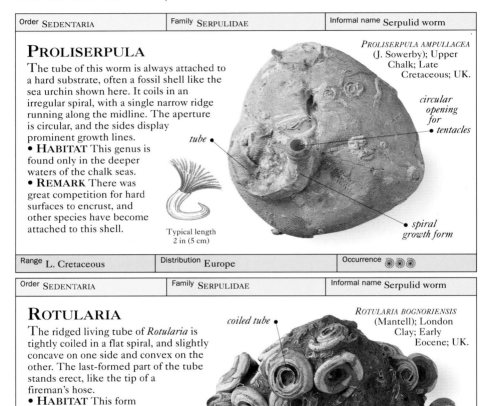

Order SEDENTARIA	Family SERPULIDAE	Informal name Serpulid worm

PROLISERPULA

The tube of this worm is always attached to a hard substrate, often a fossil shell like the sea urchin shown here. It coils in an irregular spiral, with a single narrow ridge running along the midline. The aperture is circular, and the sides display prominent growth lines.
• **HABITAT** This genus is found only in the deeper waters of the chalk seas.
• **REMARK** There was great competition for hard surfaces to encrust, and other species have become attached to this shell.

PROLISERPULA AMPULLACEA (J. Sowerby); Upper Chalk; Late Cretaceous; UK.

circular opening for tentacles

tube •

spiral growth form

Typical length 2 in (5 cm)

Range L. Cretaceous	Distribution Europe	Occurrence

Order SEDENTARIA	Family SERPULIDAE	Informal name Serpulid worm

ROTULARIA

The ridged living tube of *Rotularia* is tightly coiled in a flat spiral, and slightly concave on one side and convex on the other. The last-formed part of the tube stands erect, like the tip of a fireman's hose.
• **HABITAT** This form was free-living on sandy substrates in a shallow marine environment. The dense aggregation of individuals in this specimen was probably caused by storm waves.

coiled tube •

ROTULARIA BOGNORIENSIS (Mantell); London Clay; Early Eocene; UK.

Typical diameter ⅝ in (1.5 cm)

• *concave face*   • *convex face*

Range Eocene	Distribution Europe	Occurrence

Order SEDENTARIA	Family SERPULIDAE	Informal name Serpulid worm

SERPULA

The tube of this serpulid worm is elongated and rounded in cross section, tapering slowly to a fine point. It may be gently curved or sharply bent, with a relatively thin wall ornamented by irregular growth lines. It has a rounded aperture.
• **HABITAT** This genus is not cemented to its substrate but is not mobile, burying itself partially in sandy sediment.

SERPULA INDISTINCTA (Fleming); Carboniferous Limestone; Early Carboniferous; Northern Ireland.

narrow part of tube, formed first •

• limestone matrix

• rounded aperture

Typical length 2 in (5 cm)

• growth lines

Range Paleozoic–Recent	Distribution Worldwide	Occurrence

Order SEDENTARIA	Family SERPULIDAE	Informal name Serpulid worm

GLOMERULA

GLOMERULA PLEXUS (J. Sowerby); Upper Chalk; Late Cretaceous; UK.

The narrow, rounded tubes of *Glomerula* grew in an irregular, twisting fashion. Tubes from different individuals intertwined, so that the whole group eventually resembled a badly rolled ball of broken string. In proportion to the thick wall of the tube, the aperture is actually quite narrow.
• **HABITAT** A large number of individuals made up a single group, which lived unattached on the sea bed. This intertwined habit allowed it this freedom.
• **REMARK** Like most serpulids, *Glomerula* fed by filtering particles of organic debris and plankton from the sea.

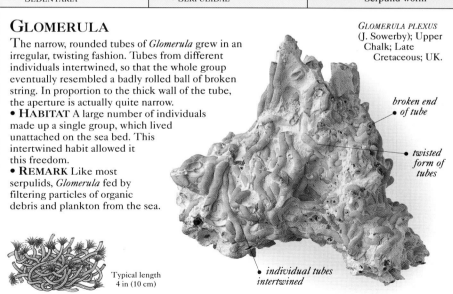

broken end • of tube

• twisted form of tubes

Typical length 4 in (10 cm)

• individual tubes intertwined

Range E. Jurassic–Paleocene	Distribution Worldwide	Occurrence

TRACE FOSSILS

TRACE FOSSILS ARE the remains of structures made by animals, preserved in sedimentary rock. They include tracks, trails, borings, and burrows. Since different organisms are able to make the same trace, trace fossils are classified by their shape, rather than by their constructor. Ichnogenera and ichnospecies, from the Greek word *ichnos* (trace), are the usual classifications, but fossils may also be classified by their cause, e.g., feeding, crawling, dwelling, and hence fodinichnia, repichnia, dominichnia.

Order Unclassified	Family FODINICHNIA	Informal name Trace fossil

CHONDRITES

This small burrow superficially resembles a plant root, as it comprises a central tube, from the base of which numerous, subdividing branches radiate. The animal most likely to have constructed these burrows is a nematode (roundworm).
• **HABITAT** *Chondrites* is found in marine sediments and is especially common in sediment formed in conditions of reduced oxygen.

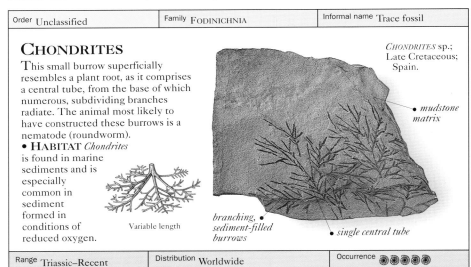

CHONDRITES sp.; Late Cretaceous; Spain.

• *mudstone matrix*

Variable length

branching, sediment-filled burrows •

• *single central tube*

Range Triassic–Recent	Distribution Worldwide	Occurrence ⬤⬤⬤⬤⬤

Order Unclassified	Family REPICHNIA	Informal name Trace fossil

CRUZIANA

This trace has a two-lobed structure with a central groove – the hardened infill of a double groove excavated on the sea floor. The lobes are covered with scratch marks made by the legs of the excavating organism, usually a trilobite.
• **HABITAT** *Cruziana* is most common in marine sediments from the Paleozoic era.

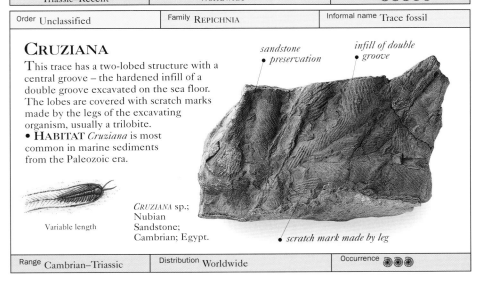

sandstone • *preservation*

infill of double • *groove*

Variable length

CRUZIANA sp.; Nubian Sandstone; Cambrian; Egypt.

• *scratch mark made by leg*

Range Cambrian–Triassic	Distribution Worldwide	Occurrence ⬤⬤⬤

PROBLEMATICA

S OME FOSSILS CANNOT be placed into major groups of animals or plants with any certainty. Often this is because they represent only a small, obscure part of an organism, but there are others, from strata of the Late Precambrian age, that have completely preserved forms. These have been variously classified as worms, soft coral, jellyfish, etc. However, the true identity of these ancient fossils remains a subject of controversy – some may even be trace fossils – and they are best treated as Problematica.

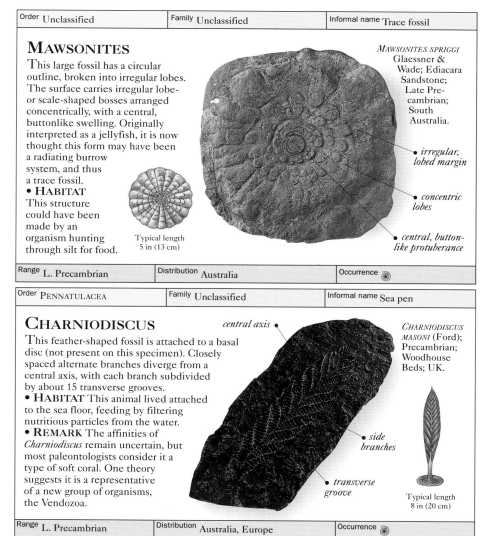

| Order Unclassified | Family Unclassified | Informal name Trace fossil |

MAWSONITES

This large fossil has a circular outline, broken into irregular lobes. The surface carries irregular lobe- or scale-shaped bosses arranged concentrically, with a central, buttonlike swelling. Originally interpreted as a jellyfish, it is now thought this form may have been a radiating burrow system, and thus a trace fossil.
• **HABITAT** This structure could have been made by an organism hunting through silt for food.

Typical length
5 in (13 cm)

MAWSONITES SPRIGGI Glaessner & Wade; Ediacara Sandstone; Late Precambrian; South Australia.

• *irregular, lobed margin*

• *concentric lobes*

• *central, button-like protuberance*

| Range L. Precambrian | Distribution Australia | Occurrence ⬡ |

| Order PENNATULACEA | Family Unclassified | Informal name Sea pen |

CHARNIODISCUS

central axis •

This feather-shaped fossil is attached to a basal disc (not present on this specimen). Closely spaced alternate branches diverge from a central axis, with each branch subdivided by about 15 transverse grooves.
• **HABITAT** This animal lived attached to the sea floor, feeding by filtering nutritious particles from the water.
• **REMARK** The affinities of *Charniodiscus* remain uncertain, but most paleontologists consider it a type of soft coral. One theory suggests it is a representative of a new group of organisms, the Vendozoa.

CHARNIODISCUS MASONI (Ford); Precambrian; Woodhouse Beds; UK.

• *side branches*

• *transverse groove*

Typical length
8 in (20 cm)

| Range L. Precambrian | Distribution Australia, Europe | Occurrence ⬡ |

Order Unclassified	Family Unclassified	Informal name Unclassified

SPRIGGINA

The body of *Spriggina* is elongated, tapering to a point at the rear, similar to a tail. The broader front end is rounded and consists of a narrow, crescent-shaped arc. The rest of the body is divided along its length by a central line, and transversely into short, broadly V-shaped segments.
• **HABITAT** *Spriggina* lived in a shallow, sandy, marine habitat.
• **REMARK** This form was first thought to be a worm, then an early arthropod or part of a new group, neither plant nor animal.

SPRIGGINA FLOUNDERSI Glaessner; Ediacara Sandstone; Late Precambrian; South Australia.

pointed "tail" end

crescent-shaped "head"

V-shaped segments

Typical length 2¼ in (7 cm)

Range L. Precambrian	Distribution Australia, Africa, Russia	Occurrence

Order CONULARIIDA	Family CONULARIIDAE	Informal name Conularid

PARACONULARIA

This shell is conical and four-sided, but rhombic in cross section. Each of the four sides carries upwardly arched, closely spaced growth lines, and at each of the four corners is a shallow V-shaped groove. The shell itself is thin, made up of phosphatic and proteinaceous material.
• **HABITAT** This species lived in shallow to deep marine waters, attached to the sea bed by a small basal disc.
• **REMARK** Members of this family have been variously placed in the mollusks, in a new group related to the wormlike phoronids, or most commonly with the jellyfish, because of the supposed tentacles sometimes preserved. The tentacles may have been used to catch small marine animals, stinging in the same way as sea anemones.

PARACONULARIA DERWENTENSIS (Johnston); Early Permian; Australia.

tentacled end in the living animal

growth lines

broken base

Typical length 4 in (10 cm)

Range E. Permian	Distribution Australia	Occurrence

GRAPTOLITES

G RAPTOLITES ARE AN extinct group of colonial organisms that lived from the Cambrian to the Carboniferous. Their remains can be mistaken for fossil plants, as they sometimes resemble fossilized twigs. Each colony had one or more branches (stipes), originating from an individual (sicula). Each subsequent individual was housed within a tubular structure (theca). Geologists find graptolites especially useful in dating rocks.

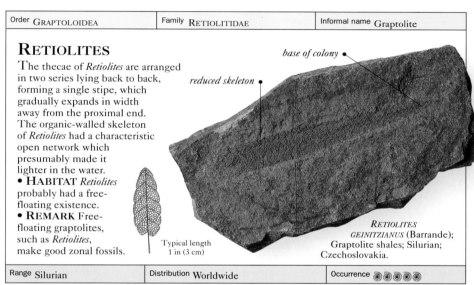

| Order GRAPTOLOIDEA | Family RETIOLITIDAE | Informal name Graptolite |

RETIOLITES

The thecae of *Retiolites* are arranged in two series lying back to back, forming a single stipe, which gradually expands in width away from the proximal end. The organic-walled skeleton of *Retiolites* had a characteristic open network which presumably made it lighter in the water.
• **HABITAT** *Retiolites* probably had a free-floating existence.
• **REMARK** Free-floating graptolites, such as *Retiolites*, make good zonal fossils.

base of colony

reduced skeleton

RETIOLITES GEINITZIANUS (Barrande); Graptolite shales; Silurian; Czechoslovakia.

Typical length 1 in (3 cm)

| Range Silurian | Distribution Worldwide | Occurrence ▨▨▨▨▨ |

| Order GRAPTOLOIDEA | Family DICHOGRAPTIDAE | Informal name Graptolite |

PHYLLOGRAPTUS

This colony comprised four series of thecae arranged back-to-back in a crosslike formation. Usually, due to compresssion, only a pair of thecae are clearly visible on shale specimens. The thecae are long and curved with small apertural lips. The generic name, *Phyllograptus*, refers to the leaflike appearance of these flattened colonies.
• **HABITAT** *Phyllograptus* floated freely in the open ocean.

PHYLLOGRAPTUS TYPUS Hall; Levis Shale; Early Ordovician; Canada.

Typical length 1⅜ in (3.5 cm)

shale matrix

| Range E.–M. Ordovician | Distribution Worldwide | Occurrence ▨▨▨▨▨ |

Order GRAPTOLOIDEA	Family DICHOGRAPTIDAE	Informal name Graptolite

EXPANSOGRAPTUS

These were small to large graptolites with approximately twenty to several hundred thecae. Two stipes diverge from the initial sicula, which is distinguished by its dorsally projecting nema (an extension of the initial sicula) at the point where the thecae of the two stipes diverge. The thecae are usually of relatively simple type, tubular or with a small apertural lip. The different species are distinguished by the number of thecae per centimeter, and by the width and shape of the stipes.
• **HABITAT** *Expansograptus* floated in open seas.

two extended stipes

EXPANSOGRAPTUS cf. *NITIDUS* (Hall); Mytton Formation; Early Ordovician; UK.

sicula

Typical length 2 in (5 cm)

Range E.–M. Ordovician	Distribution Worldwide	Occurrence ◉◉◉◉◉

Order GRAPTOLOIDEA	Family DICHOGRAPTIDAE	Informal name Graptolite

LOGANOGRAPTUS

These were large graptolites: the rapid initial dichotomies near the sicula produced a colony with sixteen stipes. These stipes were evenly separated in life, but frequently bent in fossils. The thecae are simple tubes – about 1 per millimeter.
• **HABITAT** This genus lived in the deeper parts of the Ordovician ocean.

missing distal parts of some stipes

LOGANOGRAPTUS LOGANI (Hall); Skiddaw Group; Early Ordovician; UK.

thecae slowly increase in size along stipes

Typical length 8 in (20 cm)

Range E. Ordovician	Distribution Worldwide	Occurrence ◉◉◉◉◉

| Order GRAPTOLOIDEA | Family DICHOGRAPTIDAE | Informal name Graptolite |

TETRAGRAPTUS

This graptolite had four stipes of variable form – they may have been reclined, or outstretched horizontally. Some species had a weblike structure connecting the four stipes. The thecae are usually of simple tubular form and may be inclined at high or low angles. Stipes vary in width from ⅟₂₅ to ⅔ in (1 to 10 mm).
• **HABITAT** *Tetragraptus* floated widely in Early Ordovician seas.

partially visible sicula

fissile shale

tubular thecae

TETRAGRAPTUS QUADRIBRACHIATUS Hall; Skiddaw Group; Early Ordovician; UK.

Typical length 4 in (10 cm)

| Range E. Ordovician | Distribution Worldwide | Occurrence ⊛⊛⊛⊛⊛ |

| Order GRAPTOLOIDEA | Family DIPLOGRAPIDAE | Informal name Graptolite |

ORTHOGRAPTUS

Orthograptus was a biserial graptolite, which means that it had two series of thecae lying back to back, producing a robust, double-edged colony. The proximal growth of the colony is a crucial identification feature. *Orthograptus* had a strongly developed spine. The thecal apertures were moderately straight. The variations in colony size, width, and thecal form, determine the species.
• **HABITAT** This graptolite is possibly epi-planktonic, and floated in very shallow seas.

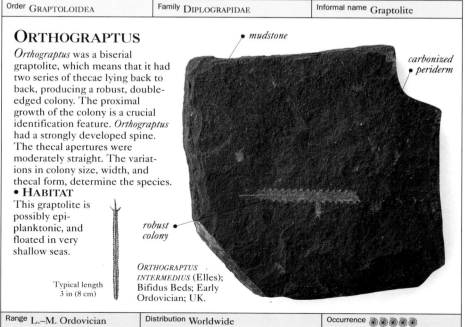

mudstone

carbonized periderm

robust colony

ORTHOGRAPTUS INTERMEDIUS (Elles); Bifidus Beds; Early Ordovician; UK.

Typical length 3 in (8 cm)

| Range L.–M. Ordovician | Distribution Worldwide | Occurrence ⊛⊛⊛⊛⊛ |

Order GRAPTOLOIDEA	Family MONOGRAPTIDAE	Informal name Graptolite

MONOGRAPTUS

Graptolites of this genus had a single stipe and a highly variable form; they could be completely straight, gently curved, or completely spiral. The form of the thecae is vital to identification. In this genus there was a tendency for thecae to become isolated from one another. Some evolved very rapidly, so species of this genus are easily recognizable and stratigraphically useful.
• **HABITAT** It floated in open seas.

• *isolated distal thecae*

triangulate • *thecae*

MONOGRAPTUS CONVOLUTUS Hisinger; Silurian Flags; Silurian; UK.

Typical diameter 8 in (20 cm)

Range Silurian–E. Devonian	Distribution Worldwide	Occurrence ◉◉◉◉◉

Order GRAPTOLOIDEA	Family DICHOGRAPTIDAE	Informal name Graptolite

DIDYMOGRAPTUS

These graptolites formed a shape similar to a tuning fork. The colonies were often robust, ranging in size from ⅜ in to 4 in (1 cm to 10 cm). The thecae are long with simple tubes. The stipes expand in width from the proximal end.
• **HABITAT** This genus floated in northern oceans.

siculae at pointed ends •

DIDYMOGRAPTUS MURCHISONI (Beck); Llanvirn Series; Early Ordovician; UK.

dark • *shale*

Typical length 4 in (10 cm)

• *mineralized periderm*

Range E.–M. Ordovician	Distribution Worldwide	Occurrence ◉◉◉◉◉

Order GRAPTOLOIDEA	Family RHABDINOPORIDAE	Informal name Graptolite

RHABDINOPORA

triangulate thecae •

The genus *Rhabdinopora*, originally known as *Dictyonema*, is characterized by its conical form and small thecae. It had numerous branches arising from the sicula. The branches are connected by dissepiments, giving a reticulate appearance (such dissepiments were lost on later graptoloids).
• **HABITAT** This fossil genus is commonly found in masses, and is believed to be the earliest planktonic graptolite.

Typical length
2½ in (6 cm)

• *fanlike colonies*

RHABDINOPORA SOCIALIS (Salter); Dictyonemaskiffern; Early Ordovician; Norway.

Range E. Ordovician	Distribution Worldwide, except Antarctica	Occurrence ⊛ ⊛ ⊛ ⊛ ⊛

Order GRAPTOLOIDEA	Family MONOGRAPTIDAE	Informal name Graptolite

RASTRITES

curved stipe •

RASTRITES MAGNUS (Mattock); Deep water shales; Silurian; UK.

The colony was thin and delicate, with comparatively few thecae. It had a single, elegantly curved stipe. The thecae were developed as long, isolated, narrow tubes with a restricted aperture. Such species could not survive turbulence.
• **HABITAT** *Rastrites* lived in open oceans. They are characteristic of black shales.

black shale •

Typical length
1½ in (4 cm)

long thecae •

Range Silurian	Distribution Worldwide	Occurrence ⊛ ⊛ ⊛ ⊛ ⊛

CORALS

ORALS ARE MARINE ANIMALS with a saclike body (polyp), mouth, tentacles, and skeleton. The polyp occupies a circular, polygonal, or elongate cavity (calice), which is generally surrounded by a wall. Calices are usually divided by starlike arrangements of plates (septa), which sometimes have a central structure. The calice wall, if present, forms horn- or tubelike features (corallites), often divided by simple transverse partitions (tabulae) or by series of plates (dissepiments), or both. Polyps may divide to form colonies, with corallites sometimes joined by inter-corallite structures (coenosteum). There are three main coral groups: two extinct (Rugosa, Tabulata), and one extant (Scleractinia).

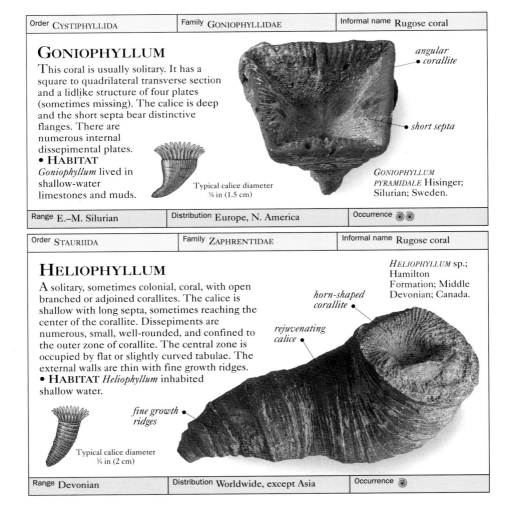

Order CYSTIPHYLLIDA	Family GONIOPHYLLIDAE	Informal name Rugose coral

GONIOPHYLLUM

This coral is usually solitary. It has a square to quadrilateral transverse section and a lidlike structure of four plates (sometimes missing). The calice is deep and the short septa bear distinctive flanges. There are numerous internal dissepimental plates.
• HABITAT *Goniophyllum* lived in shallow-water limestones and muds.

Typical calice diameter
⅗ in (1.5 cm)

angular corallite

short septa

GONIOPHYLLUM PYRAMIDALE Hisinger; Silurian; Sweden.

Range E.–M. Silurian	Distribution Europe, N. America	Occurrence ◉◉

Order STAURIIDA	Family ZAPHRENTIDAE	Informal name Rugose coral

HELIOPHYLLUM

A solitary, sometimes colonial, coral, with open branched or adjoined corallites. The calice is shallow with long septa, sometimes reaching the center of the corallite. Dissepiments are numerous, small, well-rounded, and confined to the outer zone of corallite. The central zone is occupied by flat or slightly curved tabulae. The external walls are thin with fine growth ridges.
• HABITAT *Heliophyllum* inhabited shallow water.

HELIOPHYLLUM sp.; Hamilton Formation; Middle Devonian; Canada.

horn-shaped corallite

rejuvenating calice

fine growth ridges

Typical calice diameter
¾ in (2 cm)

Range Devonian	Distribution Worldwide, except Asia	Occurrence ◉

Order STAURIIDA	Family LITHOSTROTIONIDAE	Informal name Rugose coral

SIPHONODENDRON

This colonial coral has branches separate from each other, with one corallite center to each branch. The colonies are bushy, with corallites radiating outward, often becoming more or less parallel. The axial structure is a distinctive flattened rod.
• **HABITAT** It is found in shallow-water limestones and muds.
• **REMARK** The name *Siphonodendron* is now used for forms previously called *Lithostrotion* that have branched colonies. *Lithostrotion* is still used for forms with closely adjoined corallites.

POLISHED SPECIMEN

SIPHONODENDRON JUNCEUM Fleming; Carboniferous Limestone; Early Carboniferous; UK.

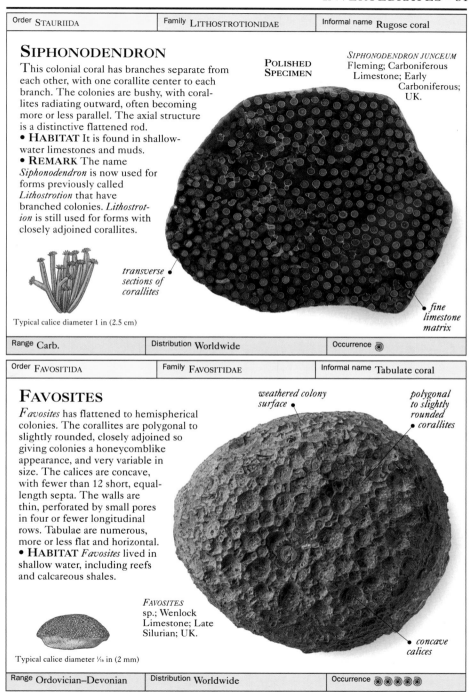

transverse sections of corallites

fine limestone matrix

Typical calice diameter 1 in (2.5 cm)

Range Carb.	Distribution Worldwide	Occurrence

Order FAVOSITIDA	Family FAVOSITIDAE	Informal name Tabulate coral

FAVOSITES

Favosites has flattened to hemispherical colonies. The corallites are polygonal to slightly rounded, closely adjoined so giving colonies a honeycomblike appearance, and very variable in size. The calices are concave, with fewer than 12 short, equal-length septa. The walls are thin, perforated by small pores in four or fewer longitudinal rows. Tabulae are numerous, more or less flat and horizontal.
• **HABITAT** *Favosites* lived in shallow water, including reefs and calcareous shales.

weathered colony surface

polygonal to slightly rounded corallites

FAVOSITES sp.; Wenlock Limestone; Late Silurian; UK.

concave calices

Typical calice diameter 1/16 in (2 mm)

Range Ordovician–Devonian	Distribution Worldwide	Occurrence

Order STAURIIDA	Family AXOPHYLLIDAE	Informal name Rugose coral

ACTINOCYATHUS

This colonial coral has flattened to rounded colonies of closely adjoined polygonal corallites of different sizes in a coarsely honeycomblike pattern. The calices are concave with a central boss. The septa are thin, often alternating long and short. The axial boss is complex, consisting of a steep sloping series of small blistery plates arranged in conical form around a small central plate and also intersected by septal plates. The dissepiments are in series, forming a wide outer zone within the corallites, distinctively very large and irregular. In transverse section, the septa appear to be largely absent from the dissepimental zone but actually form fine ridges running across upper surfaces of dissepiments. The tabulae are flat or concave. The corallites have thin external walls with fine growth ridges, but these are only visible in well-preserved specimens when broken along the corallite junctions.

• **HABITAT** *Actinocyathus* lived in shallow-water limestones and muds.

• **REMARK** The name *Actinocyathus* is now used for forms previously called *Lonsdaleia* with closely adjoined corallites. *Lonsdaleia* is still used for openly branched forms.

POLISHED CROSS-SECTION

variably sized polygonal calices

inner wall

concave calices

outer septal ridges

WEATHERED COLONY SURFACE

ACTINOCYATHUS CRASSICONUS (McCoy); Carboniferous Limestone; Early Carboniferous; UK.

inner septa

Typical calice diameter ¼ in (6 mm)

Range E. Carb.	Distribution Europe, Asia	Occurrence ⊛⊛⊛⊛⊛⊛

Order FAVOSITIDA	Family HALYSITIDAE	Informal name Chain coral

HALYSITES

This colonial coral has its corallites arranged in single series in "panpipe" formation, with a minute tube between each corallite. In transverse section they appear chainlike. The chains are straight to curved, dividing and rejoining each other, enclosing cell-like spaces between them. The individual corallites are rounded to elliptical. Septa are absent, or present as a few inconspicuous spines. The walls are thick and the tabulae numerous, mostly flat and horizontal.
• **HABITAT** *Halysites* inhabited warm, shallow waters, including reefs.

corallites

COLONY FROM ABOVE

HALYSITES CATENULARIUS (Linnaeus); Niagara Group; Silurian; USA.

Typical calice diameter ¹⁄₁₆ in (2 mm)

sediment in spaces between chains

Range M. Ordovician–L. Silurian	Distribution Worldwide	Occurrence ◉◉◉◉◉

Order SCLERACTINIA	Family ANDEMANTASTREIDAE	Informal name Compound coral

AMPAKABASTRAEA

This coral's colonies are usually flat to shallow domed. The individual corallites are closely adjacent. The calices are very shallow with weak walls. There are numerous septa between neighboring corallites. The sides of the septa bear fine ridges, and the upper edges bear small, sharp teeth. Within the corallites are numerous dissepiments and occasional small bars linking adjacent septa.
• **HABITAT** *Ampakabastraea* inhabited warm, shallow waters.

septa nearly continuous between calices

COLONY FROM ABOVE

AMPAKABASTRAEA EXSERTA (Gregory); Putchum Beds; Middle Jurassic; India.

Typical calice diameter ⅓ in (7 mm)

close, shallow calices

Range Jurassic	Distribution Worldwide	Occurrence ◉◉◉

Order SCLERACTINIA	Family MONLIVALTIIDAE	Informal name Colonial coral

THECOSMILIA

Thecosmilia is a colonial coral with branches separate from each other. It has one, occasionally two, large, corallite centers to each branch. The colonies are bushy with corallites radiating outward, often becoming more or less parallel. The calices are deeply concave. The septa are numerous, variable in size in transverse view, with successively shorter septa. The outsides of the branches bear toothed longitudinal ridges which are continuous with the septa.

• HABITAT *Thecosmilia* inhabited warm, shallow waters and reefs.

rejuvenating corallite •

sediment between • corallites

Typical calice diameter ½ in (1.2 cm)

THECOSMILIA TRICHOTOMA (Goldfuss); "Corallian"; Late Jurassic; Germany.

• septa arranged according to size

COLONY FROM ABOVE

Range Jurassic–Cretaceous	Distribution Worldwide	Occurrence ◉◉◉◉◉

Order SCLERACTINIA	Family FAVIIDAE	Informal name Brain coral

COLOPHYLLIA

This is a dome-shaped or flattened, colonial coral. The corallites are closely adjacent, with shared walls. In transverse view, they are very elongate and variable in length, with the longer corallites meandering. The calices are concave, valleylike, and quite deep, separated by acute, ridgelike walls. The septa slope down into "valleys." There are numerous blistery dissepiments within the corallites.

• HABITAT *Colopphyllia* lives in warm, shallow seas and reefs.

sharp, corallite walls •

COLONY SURFACE

COLOPHYLLIA STELLATA (Catullo); Castelgomberto Limestone; Late Oligocene; Italy.

Typical calice diameter ⅜ in (1 cm)

• meandering, calicinal "valleys"

Range Eocene–Recent	Distribution Europe, N. & S. America	Occurrence ◉◉◉◉

Order SCLERACTINIA	Family FAVIIDAE	Informal name Solitary coral

TRACHYPHYLLIA

Trachyphyllia is tapered to a sharp point; in transverse section, it is elliptical to elongate. The calices are gently concave to deep. There are numerous septa, variable in size; in transverse section, successively shorter septa are arranged in sets between those of the next longer size. The septal edges bear numerous fine teeth. The external wall is thin, sometimes discontinuous, covered with fine growth ridges. The internal wall is supported by arched dissepiments.

• **HABITAT**
Trachyphyllia lives unattached on the sea floor in sheltered areas of flat soft sand in and around reefs.

elongate calice •

• *external wall with fine growth ridges*

TRACHYPHYLLIA CHIPOLANA Vaughan; Chipola Formation; Miocene; USA.

Typical calice head
1½ in (4 cm)

Range Miocene–Recent	Distribution Worldwide	Occurrence ⊛

Order SCLERACTINIA	Family RHIZANGIIDAE	Informal name Horn coral

SEPTASTRAEA

This colonial coral has a highly variable morphology. The colonies form irregular nodular masses, sometimes also branched, with numerous corallites within each branch. The corallites are closely adjoining, usually with shared walls, giving them a honeycomb appearance. There are usually 12 septa, all reaching the corallite center. The interiors of the corallites have a few thin dissepiments.

• **HABITAT** This horn coral inhabited warm, shallow-water reefs.

• **REMARK** This coral is sometimes found encrusting marine snail shells, which were probably inhabited by hermit crabs. The coral continued growth outward from the shell, extending the space that could be occupied by the crab. There was probably a symbiotic association between the crab and the coral.

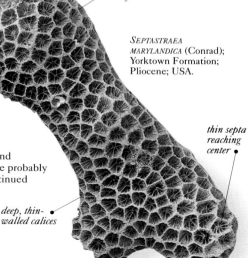
nodular branching • *colony*

SEPTASTRAEA MARYLANDICA (Conrad); Yorktown Formation; Pliocene; USA.

thin septa reaching center •

deep, thin-walled calices •

Typical calice diameter 1/16 in (4 mm)

Range Miocene–Pleistocene	Distribution N. America, Europe	Occurrence ⊛ ⊛ ⊛ ⊛

TRILOBITES

ALTHOUGH THEY ARE now extinct, these arthropods flourished in the sea, from the Cambrian through the Permian. They ranged in length from ¹⁄₂₅ in–39 in (one millimeter to one meter). The name, trilobite, derives from their division into three longitudinal lobes: a slightly raised central lobe (the axis), with two flatter pleural lobes on either side. They were also divided into a head shield (cephalon), a thorax of up to 30 segments, and a tail shield (pygidium). The axial region of the head shield (glabella) had cheeks on either side and often well-developed eyes. Each segment of the thorax had limbs, but these are rarely preserved. Trilobites could roll up (enroll) their external skeletons, probably for defense.

Order AGNOSTIDA	Family AGNOSTIDAE	Informal name Trilobite

ACADAGNOSTUS

This was a small, blind trilobite, with only two thoracic segments, but it was still able to roll up tightly. It has a furrow dividing the area in front of the glabella and a similar furrow behind the axis of the tail shield. The head and tail are the same size.
• **HABITAT** This genus lived in deep water.

cephalon •
• glabella
tail • shield

Typical length ¹⁄₃₀ in (8 mm)

ACADAGNOSTUS EXARATUS (Grönwall); Menevian Series; Middle Cambrian; UK.

Range M. Cambrian	Distribution N.E. America, Europe, Australia	Occurrence ⊛⊛⊛⊛⊛

Order REDLICHIIDA	Family OLENELLIDAE	Informal name Trilobite

OLENELLUS

This primitive trilobite has a small tail, large head, large eyes, and numerous spined thoracic segments, one of which is conspicuously wider than the rest. The thorax itself tapers gradually backward. Dorsal facial sutures – a feature of most other trilobites – had not yet developed in *Olenellus*. The head shield is surrounded by a narrow rim, which continues into the genal spines. The cuticle of the external skeleton is thin.
• **HABITAT** This not-very-active swimmer lived close to the sea bed.

long, crescent-shaped eyes
thin, needlelike • genal spines
long pleural • spine

Typical length 2½ in (6 cm)

OLENELLUS THOMSONI Hall; Olenellian Series; Early Cambrian; USA.

Range E. Cambrian	Distribution Scotland, N. America	Occurrence ⊛⊛⊛⊛

Order PTYCHOPARIIDA	Family OLENIDAE	Informal name Trilobite

TRIARTHRUS

The external skeleton of this trilobite is more than twice as long as it is wide. It has a large head shield and a small tail shield. There are no genal spines, but two pairs of deep furrows are visible on the glabella.

• **HABITAT** *Triarthrus* lived on or close to the sea bed.

• **REMARK** This specimen is one of the rare examples in which the limbs of the trilobite are preserved – the traces of the walking legs may be clearly seen. These were preserved because they were covered at an early stage of burial by a film of iron pyrites, which remains even after the soft tissue has decayed.

rounded cephalon

rectangular, truncate glabella

limbs

long thorax

TRIARTHRUS EATONI (Hall); Utica Shale; Ordovician; USA.

Typical length
1¼ in (3 cm)

Range Ordovician	Distribution Worldwide	Occurrence ⊚⊚⊚⊚⊚

Order REDLICHIIDA	Family PARADOXIDIDAE	Informal name Trilobite

PARADOXIDES

This trilobite was larger than any other Cambrian genus – the largest known individuals may have approached 39 inches (one meter) in length. It has a broad head, a small tail, and a long thorax that tapers gradually, and to which numerous segments were added as it grew. The eyes are well developed, the frontal lobe of the glabella inflated, and the tips of the lateral cheeks extended into long spines.

• **HABITAT** This trilobite lived in shelf muds.

wide, inflated glabella

genal spines

PARADOXIDES BOHEMICUS (Barrande); Skryje Beds; Middle Cambrian; Czechoslovakia.

Typical length 8 in (20 cm)

long thorax

small tail shield

Range M. Cambrian	Distribution Europe, USA, N. Africa	Occurrence ⊚⊚⊚⊚

Order REDLICHIIDA	Family XYSTRIDURIDAE	Informal name Trilobite

XYSTRIDURA

This trilobite is broadly oval in outline. Its head section is about twice as wide as it is long, with a well-furrowed glabella and large eyes. The genal angle has extended to form short genal spines. The thorax is divided into 13 segments, with the axis much narrower than the deeply furrowed pleural lobes. The tail shield is also furrowed, and spines are present around the posterior margin.

• HABITAT *Xystridura* lived on or near the sediment of the sea bed.

XYSTRIDURA SAINT-SMITHII (Chapman); Middle Cambrian; Australia.

large • eyes

thorax • with short spines

moderately • large tail shield

Typical length
2½ in (6 cm)

Range M. Cambrian	Distribution Australia	Occurrence 🌼🌼

Order ASAPHIDA	Family TRINUCLEIDAE	Informal name Trilobite

ONNIA

This trilobite is wide in relation to its length. The convex head section is surrounded by a pitted fringe, with the regular arrangement of the pits characteristic of the genus. The thorax is made up of six narrow segments, followed by an unfurrowed, triangular tail shield. The narrow axis reaches almost to the margin.

• HABITAT *Onnia* burrowed just below the surface of the sea bed.

pitted cephalic fringe •

large • cephalon

short • thorax

ONNIA SUPERBA (Bancroft); Caradoc Series; Ordovician; UK.

Typical length
1¼ in (3 cm)

Range M.–L. Ordovician	Distribution Europe, N. Africa	Occurrence 🌼🌼🌼

| Order PHACOPIDA | Family CHEIRURIDAE | Informal name Trilobite |

KTENOURA

This trilobite has an elongate external skeleton, with a thorax made up of 11 segments. Facial sutures are of the proparian type, cutting into the side margin of the head. The cheeks and pleurae are narrow, with the eyes situated anteriorly and close to the glabella. The glabella itself is convex, expanding gently forward in width. The complex boss-and-socket articulation between segments enabled it to roll up tightly. It has a moderate-size tail shield, with three pairs of long marginal spines which curve backward.

• **HABITAT** This trilobite was a typical inhabitant of shelf seas.

Typical length
2 in (5 cm)

small eyes

spinose
thorax

tail shield
with long spines

*KTENOURA
RETROSPINOSA*
Lane; Wenlock
Series; Silurian; UK.

| Range L. Ordovician–Silurian | Distribution Worldwide | Occurrence 🌐 |

| Order PHACOPIDA | Family CHEIRURIDAE | Informal name Trilobite |

SPHAEREXOCHUS

The external skeleton of this trilobite is convex and elongate, with a thick, calcite cuticle. Its raised central lobe is especially convex, and the inflated glabella occupies the bulk of the head width. The genal spines are reduced. Its thorax has 11 segments, with spiny pleural tips, curved downward. The short tail shield is also spiny.

• **HABITAT** *Sphaerexochus* probably lived in fairly shallow water, on and around coral reefs.

• **REMARK** This genus is usually found in Late Ordovician and Silurian limestones.

Typical length
1¼ in (3 cm)

glabella

swollen
glabellar
lobes

thorax

small tail
shield

*SPHAEREXOCHUS
MIRUS* Beyrich;
Wenlock
Limestone;
Silurian; UK.

| Range Ordovician–Silurian | Distribution Worldwide | Occurrence 🌐🌐🌐 |

| Order ODONTOPLEURIDA | Family ODONTOPLEURIDAE | Informal name Trilobite |

SELENOPELTIS

This trilobite has a wide external skeleton, with the head and tail sections short in relation to the thorax. The wide glabella has complex furrows and an inflated central lobe. The genal spines are very long, and the pleural tips of each thoracic segment are prolonged into great spines, which project backward. One similar pair of spines is found on the tail shield.
• HABITAT *Selenopeltis* is thought to have floated freely in ocean waters.

wide glabella

long spinose tips

SELENOPELTIS BUCHI Barrande; Sarká Formation; Ordovician; Czechoslovakia.

Typical length
1⅜ in (3.5 cm)

short pygidium with few segments

| Range E.–M. Ordovician | Distribution Europe, N. Africa | Occurrence |

| Order PHACOPIDA | Family PHACOPIDAE | Informal name Trilobite |

PHACOPS

This trilobite has a convex glabella that expands forward. The large eyes have fewer lenses than usual, which may have improved optics. The thorax has 12 segments, equipped with facets that facilitate enrollment. The deeply furrowed tail shield is smaller than its head. A sculpture of tubercles ornaments the thick cuticle.
• HABITAT *Phacops* inhabited shallow water in warm seas.

large eye

ENROLLED SPECIMEN

PHACOPS AFRICANUS Burton & Eldredge; Shelf limestones; Devonian; Western Sahara.

tail tucks beneath head when enrolled

tuberculate head

head and tail shield margins

Typical length
1¾ in (4.5 cm)

| Range Devonian | Distribution Worldwide | Occurrence |

Order PHACOPIDA	Family CALYMENIDAE	Informal name Trilobite

CALYMENE

Trilobites of this genus have a convex external skeleton, with pleural tips steeply down-turned, and a tail shield smaller than the head. The smallish eyes are placed close to the deeply furrowed glabella.
• **HABITAT** This trilobite was a sluggish swimmer, so it probably walked on the sea bed.
• **REMARK** In the 19th century, miners called it the "Dudley Locust."

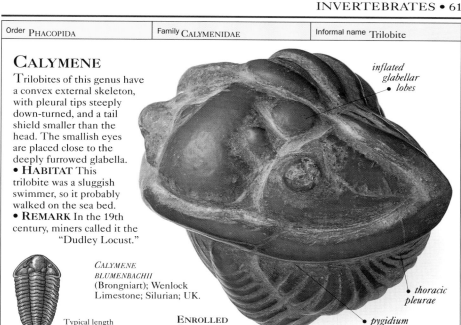

inflated
glabellar
lobes

thoracic
pleurae

pygidium
tucked in

*CALYMENE
BLUMENBACHII*
(Brongniart); Wenlock
Limestone; Silurian; UK.

Typical length
2¾ in (7 cm)

**ENROLLED
SPECIMEN**

Range L. Ordovician–Silurian	Distribution Worldwide	Occurrence ◉◉◉◉

Order ODONTOPLEURIDA	Family ODONTOPLEURIDAE	Informal name Trilobite

LEONASPIS

Leonaspis has a wide head, drawn out to the side and rear into exceptionally stout genal spines, and with small, slightly elevated eyes. The ten thoracic segments have wide pleurae, extending into robust spines, and straight pleural furrows. The tail shield is also very spiny.
• **HABITAT** A bottom-dweller, this genus used its spines for protection.
• **REMARK** This type of trilobite had a long stratigraphic range.

down-turned
head shield

very stout
pleural spines

paired tail-
shield spines

Typical length
⅝ in (1.5 cm)

LEONASPIS CORONATA
(Salter); Wenlock
Limestone; Silurian; UK.

Range Silurian–Devonian	Distribution Worldwide	Occurrence ◉◉◉

| Order PHACOPIDA | Family DALMANITIDAE | Informal name Trilobite |

HUNTONIA

The exoskeleton of *Huntonia* is two-thirds as wide as it is long. At the front of the cephalic shield is a short but robust "snout," typical of the genus, while at the back of the head there are exceptionally stout genal spines. The eyes are very large, strongly curved, and slightly elevated, with large lenses. The glabella extends forward and has three pairs of side furrows, the front pair of which slopes backward. The large segmented tail shield is triangular in outline, with numerous segments and a pointed tip.
• **HABITAT** This was an active, bottom-dwelling trilobite with a well-developed visual system. It may have had predatory habits.

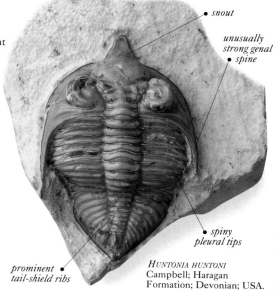

• snout

unusually strong genal spine

• *spiny pleural tips*

prominent • *tail-shield ribs*

HUNTONIA HUNTONI Campbell; Haragan Formation; Devonian; USA.

Typical length
1¼ in (3 cm)

| Range Devonian | Distribution N. America | Occurrence |

| Order PHACOPIDA | Family ENCRINURIDAE | Informal name Trilobite |

ENCRINURUS

Especially large tubercles ornament the head shield. The eyes are often stalked, and there are short genal spines. The relatively long tail shield has many more segments in the axis than on the pleural lobes.
• **HABITAT** This trilobite lived in shallow seas in the Silurian.
• **REMARK** *Encrinurus* is known as the "strawberry-headed trilobite" because of its distinctive tubercular head shield.

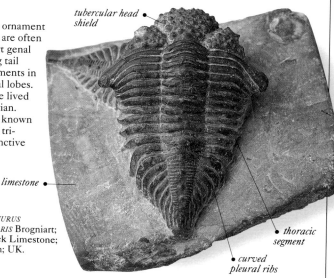

tubercular head • *shield*

limestone •

thoracic segment

curved pleural ribs

ENCRINURUS VARIOLARIS Brogniart; Wenlock Limestone; Silurian; UK.

Typical length
2½ in (6 cm)

| Range L. Ordovician–Silurian | Distribution Worldwide | Occurrence |

Order ODONTOPLEURIDA	Family ACIDASPIDAE	Informal name Trilobite

ACIDASPIS

Acidaspis has a wide exoskeleton, with exceptionally long genal spines. Glabellar furrows outline the swollen side lobes. The fairly small eyes are placed at the rear, and small tubercles appear on the head shield, with a fringe of spines around the margin. There are nine narrow thoracic segments, with tubular spines becoming longer toward the rear. The rear margin is also fringed with long spines.
• **HABITAT** This trilobite lived in open shelf seas and reefs.
• **REMARK** The extended spines may have been protective.

Typical length
⅜ in (1 cm)

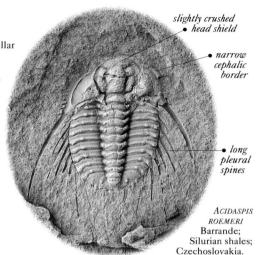

slightly crushed
head shield

narrow
cephalic
border

long
pleural
spines

ACIDASPIS
ROEMERI
Barrande;
Silurian shales;
Czechoslovakia.

Range Ordovician–Devonian	Distribution Worldwide	Occurrence ⊚⊚⊚

Order PHACOPIDA	Family PHACOPIDAE	Informal name Trilobite

TRIMEROCEPHALUS

Trilobites molted periodically as they grew, and trilobite molts of *Trimerocephalus* are often found preserved. A fossil can be recognized as a molt when all parts of the exoskeleton are present but separated. The head shield is also inverted in many examples. In this genus the head shield is relatively short. There are no eyes and no genal spines. The wide pleurae have down-turned tips.
• **HABITAT** This was a deep-water, bottom-dwelling trilobite.
• **REMARK** This genus is typically found in Devonian shales.

Typical length
1¼ in (3 cm)

TRIMEROCEPHALUS
LAEVIS Münster;
Devonian shales;
Devonian; UK.

cephalon reversed

eyes absent
from
cheeks

thoracic
pleurae

tail shield

Range Devonian	Distribution Europe	Occurrence ⊚⊚⊚

Order PTYCHOPARIIDA	Family PTYCHOPARIIDAE	Informal name Trilobite

ELRATHIA

Elrathia has a small head compared with its thorax, with a small, flowerpot-shaped glabella; small, centrally placed eyes; and short, triangular genal spines. There are 13 narrow segments in the thorax, with a narrow axis and wide pleurae ending in short, spiny tips. The tail is moderately sized, twice as wide as it is long, with a well-defined axis extending far back.
• **HABITAT** This genus of trilobite swarmed in outer shelf-sea bottoms.
• **REMARK** One of the few species to have been mined commercially, it is often offered for sale.

oval dorsal exoskeleton •

• *furrowed thoracic pleurae*

relatively small tail • *shield*

Typical length ¾ in (2 cm)

ELRATHIA KINGII (Meek); Wheeler Shale; Middle Cambrian; USA.

Range M. Cambrian	Distribution N. America	Occurrence ◉◉◉◉◉

Order CORYNEXOCHIDA	Family OGYGOPSIDAE	Informal name Trilobite

OGYGOPSIS

The exoskeleton of this genus is broadly oval and gently convex, with the axis tapering along its whole length. The near-rectangular glabella extends close to the head margin, with moderate-size eyes in a central position, and triangular cheeks. The thorax is made up of eight segments, with deep furrows in the pleurae. For a Cambrian trilobite the tail shield is exceptionally large – its length actually exceeds that of the head shield. The pleural fields in the tail are strongly furrowed.
• **HABITAT** *Ogygopsis* lived on the bottom of shelf seas.

short genal • *spines*

short, spiny • *pleural tips*

• *large tail shield with long axis*

axis close • *to margin*

Typical length 3⅛ in (8 cm)

OGYGOPSIS KLOTZI; Stephen Group; Middle Cambrian; Canada.

Range M. Cambrian	Distribution N. America, Siberia	Occurrence ◉

Order CORYNEXOCHIDA	Family SCUTELLUIDAE	Informal name Trilobite

PARALEJURUS

Paralejurus has a convex and nearly semicircular head shield. Subdued dorsal furrows mean that the glabella and the glabellar furrows may be faint or obscure. There are no genal spines, and the eyes are positioned at the rear. In the ten segments of the thorax, the axis is not clearly differentiated from the pleurae. The large and fanlike tail shield has a relatively short axis.
• **HABITAT** This was an inhabitant of warm shelf seas.
• **REMARK** This is a sporadically common genus in limestones that accumulated in shallow-water conditions.

• *eyes positioned at rear*

• *narrow thoracic pleurae*

• *fan-shaped tail shield*

PARTLY ENROLLED SPECIMEN

PARALEJURUS sp.;
Taburight;
Devonian;
Morocco.

Typical length
4 in (10 cm)

Range Devonian	Distribution Worldwide	Occurrence

Order PROETIDA	Family CUMMINGELLIDAE	Informal name Trilobite

EOCYPHINIUM

Much of the convex head shield of this trilobite is occupied by the glabella, in which only the first pair of glabellar furrows is clearly defined. The thorax has nine convex segments, and the tail shield is large, with many segments in the axis and pleurae.
• **HABITAT** This typical later trilobite inhabited shallow-water seas.

• *tuberculate glabella*

additional fragments on • *the same slab*

*EOCYPHINIUM
SEMINIFERUM*
(Phillips); Rotten
Stone; Early
Carboniferous; UK.

Typical length
1¼ in (3 cm)

• *large tail shield*

Range Carb.	Distribution Europe, N. America	Occurrence

CRUSTACEA

C RUSTACEA ARE mainly aquatic carnivorous arthropods whose body and legs are enclosed in a supporting chitinous shell. The body is divisible into head, thorax, and abdomen, but head and thorax may fuse together into a cephalothorax. The head has two pairs of tactile antennae and three pairs of limbs with food-handling abilities. The walking legs are divided in two and may have gills for breathing. The last abdominal appendage may become flattened, forming a tail fan with the end spine.

Order HYMENOSTRACA	Family HYMENOCARIDIDAE	Informal name Visored shrimp

HYMENOCARIS

The near-oval, smooth bivalve shell of *Hymenocaris* encloses, but does not coalesce with, the thorax. The thorax has eight segments (somites), each bearing a pair of flattened appendages. The abdomen comprises seven somites, and a tail spine (telson) with three pairs of spines – the middle being the longest, the outer very divergent.
• **HABITAT** *Hymenocaris* lived in shallow marine waters.

Typical length
2½ in (6 cm)

HYMENOCARIS VERMICAUDA Salter; Tremadoc Series; Late Cambrian; UK.

• *abdominal segments*

• *hingeless bivalve shell*

Range Cambrian–Ordovician	Distribution Europe, N. America, Australasia	Occurrence ◉

Order THORACICA	Family BALANIDAE	Informal name Acorn barnacle

BALANUS

This barnacle, shaped like a truncated cone, is made up of six calcareous plates on a solid base. The plates are hollow-walled, but the radii are solid. The operculum, which can be closed by four valves, is the opening through which six pairs of legs (cirri) pass to collect food suspended in water.
• **HABITAT** Barnacles live on rocky shores and floating objects worldwide.

operculum with • *four plates*

symmetrical compart- mental • *plates*

BALANUS CONCAVUS Bronn; Coralline Crag; Pliocene; UK.

Typical length
⅜ in (1 cm)

base cemented • *to substrate*

Range Eocene–Recent	Distribution Worldwide	Occurrence ◉◉◉◉

Order DECAPODA	Family CARPILIIDAE	Informal name Mud crab

PALEOCARPILIUS

The dorsal carapace of *Paleocarpilius* is egglike in outline, with a slightly extended front, strongly arched transversely, and more steeply rounded longitudinally. The front and side margins are spiny and the claws are robust, with the right one larger. The legs are long and stout. On the ventral surface, the front curves downward and backward to meet the head of the narrow plate in front of the mouth.
• **HABITAT** The genus was largely tropical, living near the shore.

• *strong right claw*

• *frontal margin with orbits*

• *smaller claw*

• *abdomen with base of legs*

PALEOCARPILIUS AQUILINUS Collins & Morris; Wadi Thamit Group; Middle Eocene; Libya.

Typical length 2½ in (6 cm)

Range Eocene–Miocene	Distribution Europe, Africa	Occurrence

Order THORACICA	Family STRAMENTIDAE	Informal name Goose barnacle

STRAMENTUM

Like most cirripedes, the stalked *Stramentum* remained attached as an adult. It is divided into a capitulum, which contains the body, the mouth parts, and thoracic appendages, and a peduncle or stalk, which contains the gonads. The capitulum is protected by ten calcareous plates. The peduncle is also protected by calcareous plates, but in eight regularly overlapping columns. Each column is surmounted by a plate in the capitulum.
• **HABITAT** These animals frequently lived attached to the empty shells of ammonites, bivalves, or gastropods lying on the sea floor.
• **REMARK** It was once believed that these fossils grew into geese.

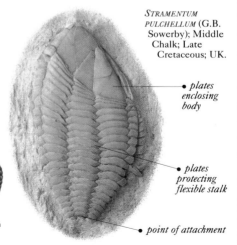

STRAMENTUM PULCHELLUM (G.B. Sowerby); Middle Chalk; Late Cretaceous; UK.

• *plates enclosing body*

• *plates protecting flexible stalk*

• *point of attachment*

Typical length ¾ in (2 cm)

Range Cretaceous	Distribution Europe, N. Africa, N. America	Occurrence

Order PODOCOPIDA	Family ILYOCYPRIDIDAE	Informal name Ostracod

CYAMOCYPRIS

The bivalve shell of this creature is thin and nearly oval, with an extended border. The top margin is nearly straight, while the underside is slightly sinuate, converging at the back with the upper margin. The left valve is larger than the right, overlapping on all margins. Each valve bears a marginal notch toward the front and, in typical specimens, a ventral projection known as a beak. The surface of the valves may be pitted, smooth, blistered, or grooved.
• **HABITAT** *Cyamocypris* lived in fresh water.

CYAMOCYPRIS VALDENSIS (Fitton); Weald Shales; Early Cretaceous; UK.

ROCK CONTAINING NUMEROUS SPECIMENS

Typical length
⅟₅₀ in (½ mm)

Cyamocypris •
shell

CLOSE-UP VIEW

Range E. Cretaceous	Distribution Europe	Occurrence ⊛⊛⊛⊛⊛

Order ISOPODA	Family Unclassified	Informal name Sea slater

CYCLOSPHAEROMA

This creature has a broad body, arched transversely, with a small trilobed head and large eyes near the side margin. Its thorax is composed of eight segments, each having a single-branched appendage. Five abdominal segments are fused as an enlarged triangular tail spine (pleotelson), longitudinally bisected by a median ridge. There are notches on each side of the pleotelson for the insertion of rear abdominal appendages (uropods).
• **HABITAT** An omnivorous scavenger and occasionally a predator, *Cyclosphaeroma* lived at intertidal to moderate depths.

EXTERNAL MOLD

• *thoracic segments*

triangular pleotelson •

INTERNAL MOLD

Typical length
³⁄₁₆ in (5 mm)

CYCLOSPHAEROMA WOODWARDI van Straelen; Purbeck Beds; Late Jurassic; UK.

Range Jurassic	Distribution Europe	Occurrence ⊛⊛

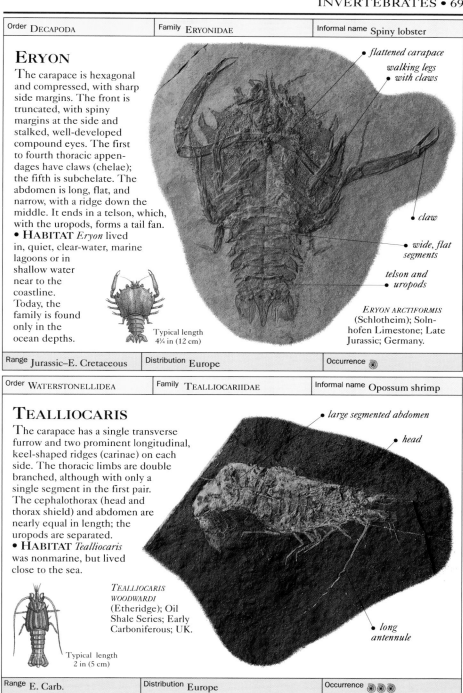

| Order DECAPODA | Family ERYONIDAE | Informal name Spiny lobster |

ERYON

The carapace is hexagonal and compressed, with sharp side margins. The front is truncated, with spiny margins at the side and stalked, well-developed compound eyes. The first to fourth thoracic appendages have claws (chelae); the fifth is subchelate. The abdomen is long, flat, and narrow, with a ridge down the middle. It ends in a telson, which, with the uropods, forms a tail fan.
• HABITAT *Eryon* lived in, quiet, clear-water, marine lagoons or in shallow water near to the coastline. Today, the family is found only in the ocean depths.

• *flattened carapace*
walking legs
• *with claws*

• *claw*

• *wide, flat segments*

telson and
• *uropods*

Typical length
4¾ in (12 cm)

ERYON ARCTIFORMIS (Schlotheim); Soln-hofen Limestone; Late Jurassic; Germany.

| Range Jurassic–E. Cretaceous | Distribution Europe | Occurrence |

| Order WATERSTONELLIDEA | Family TEALLIOCARIIDAE | Informal name Opossum shrimp |

TEALLIOCARIS

The carapace has a single transverse furrow and two prominent longitudinal, keel-shaped ridges (carinae) on each side. The thoracic limbs are double branched, although with only a single segment in the first pair. The cephalothorax (head and thorax shield) and abdomen are nearly equal in length; the uropods are separated.
• HABITAT *Tealliocaris* was nonmarine, but lived close to the sea.

• *large segmented abdomen*

• *head*

TEALLIOCARIS WOODWARDI (Etheridge); Oil Shale Series; Early Carboniferous; UK.

Typical length
2 in (5 cm)

• *long antennule*

| Range E. Carb. | Distribution Europe | Occurrence |

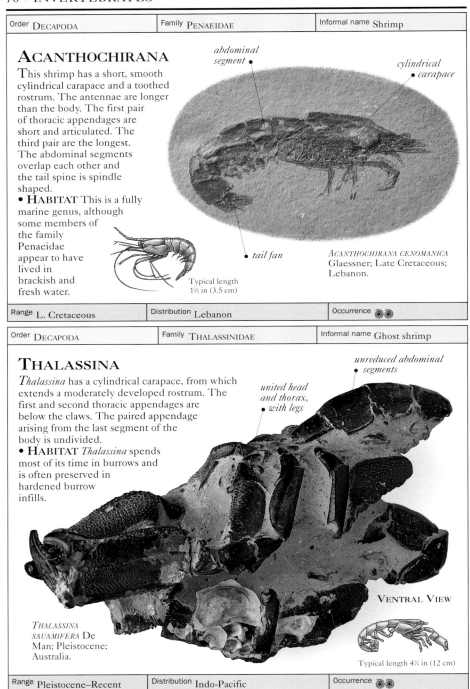

| Order DECAPODA | Family PENAEIDAE | Informal name Shrimp |

ACANTHOCHIRANA

This shrimp has a short, smooth cylindrical carapace and a toothed rostrum. The antennae are longer than the body. The first pair of thoracic appendages are short and articulated. The third pair are the longest. The abdominal segments overlap each other and the tail spine is spindle shaped.

• **HABITAT** This is a fully marine genus, although some members of the family Penaeidae appear to have lived in brackish and fresh water.

abdominal segment

cylindrical carapace

tail fan

Typical length
1⅜ in (3.5 cm)

ACANTHOCHIRANA CENOMANICA Glaessner; Late Cretaceous; Lebanon.

| Range L. Cretaceous | Distribution Lebanon | Occurrence |

| Order DECAPODA | Family THALASSINIDAE | Informal name Ghost shrimp |

THALASSINA

Thalassina has a cylindrical carapace, from which extends a moderately developed rostrum. The first and second thoracic appendages are below the claws. The paired appendage arising from the last segment of the body is undivided.

• **HABITAT** *Thalassina* spends most of its time in burrows and is often preserved in hardened burrow infills.

unreduced abdominal segments

united head and thorax, with legs

THALASSINA SAUAMIFERA De Man; Pleistocene; Australia.

VENTRAL VIEW

Typical length 4¼ in (12 cm)

| Range Pleistocene–Recent | Distribution Indo-Pacific | Occurrence |

Order DECAPODA	Family PALINURIDAE	Informal name Spiny lobster

LINUPARUS

Closely related to the langouste, *Linuparus* has a carapace compressed from top to bottom, without a rostrum, but with three longitudinal ridges. It has spines, also compressed, above the eye sockets and close to the midline. The base of the antenna is fused to the epistome and to the side margin. There are no claws on the first four legs, and the fifth leg has a claw only in the female. The uropods and the telson form a broad tail fan.
• **HABITAT** These fossils are found in shallow, marine seas.

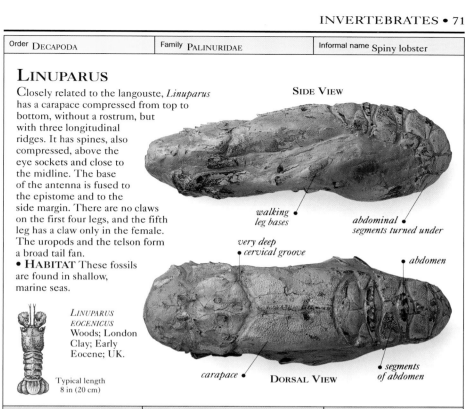

SIDE VIEW

walking leg bases

abdominal segments turned under

very deep cervical groove

abdomen

LINUPARUS EOCENICUS Woods; London Clay; Early Eocene; UK.

Typical length 8 in (20 cm)

carapace

DORSAL VIEW

segments of abdomen

Range E. Cretaceous–Recent	Distribution Worldwide	Occurrence

Order DECAPODA	Family PAGURIDAE	Informal name Hermit crab

PAGURUS

This hermit crab has a long, weakly calcified carapace, and a completely uncalcified abdomen, which consequently coils in the same direction as the host shell (usually a gastropod). The main claws commonly have a right pincer much larger than the left. When not used for walking or scavenging, the claws can be withdrawn to close the aperture of the host shell for protection.
• **HABITAT** It lives in shallow water in temperate seas.
• **REMARK** Complete specimens are rare due to the lack of calcification.

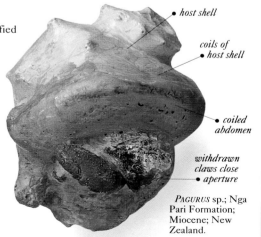

host shell

coils of host shell

coiled abdomen

withdrawn claws close aperture

PAGURUS sp.; Nga Pari Formation; Miocene; New Zealand.

Typical length 1¼ in (3 cm)

Range Jurassic–Recent	Distribution Worldwide	Occurrence

Order DECAPODA	Family PORTUNIDAE	Informal name Swimming crab

PORTUNITES

DORSAL VIEW

The hexagonal carapace is a little broader than it is long, with four teeth along the front, and four or five along the side, of which the most posterior is the longest. The walking legs are as long as the front claws, and the fifth leg is unflattened.
• **HABITAT** *Portunites* lived in shallow, warm seas.

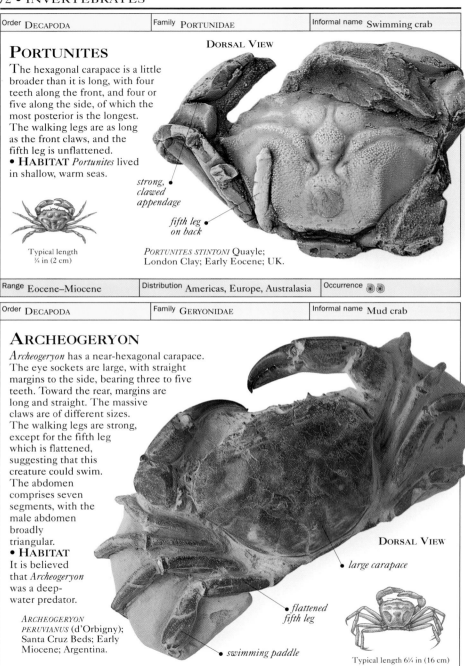

Typical length
¾ in (2 cm)

strong, clawed appendage

fifth leg on back

PORTUNITES STINTONI Quayle;
London Clay; Early Eocene; UK.

Range Eocene–Miocene	Distribution Americas, Europe, Australasia	Occurrence ◉◉

Order DECAPODA	Family GERYONIDAE	Informal name Mud crab

ARCHEOGERYON

Archeogeryon has a near-hexagonal carapace. The eye sockets are large, with straight margins to the side, bearing three to five teeth. Toward the rear, margins are long and straight. The massive claws are of different sizes. The walking legs are strong, except for the fifth leg which is flattened, suggesting that this creature could swim. The abdomen comprises seven segments, with the male abdomen broadly triangular.
• **HABITAT**
It is believed that *Archeogeryon* was a deep-water predator.

ARCHEOGERYON PERUVIANUS (d'Orbigny); Santa Cruz Beds; Early Miocene; Argentina.

DORSAL VIEW

large carapace

flattened fifth leg

swimming paddle

Typical length 6¼ in (16 cm)

Range Miocene	Distribution S. America	Occurrence ◉

CHELICERATA

T HE CHELICERATES include spiders, scorpions, and horse-shoe crabs. They have bodies divided into a head and thorax shield and an abdomen. Unlike other arthropods, they have no antennae. Of the six pairs of appendages, the first are claws for feeding (chelicerae), the second have various functions (pedipalps), and the third to sixth are designed for walking.

Order XIPHOSURIDA	Family EUPROOPIDAE	Informal name Sea scorpion

EUPROOPS

A shield-shaped carapace covers the front of this sea scorpion, the upper surface being divided into a middle and two side regions by prominent ridges near the simple eyes. The abdomen is composed of seven fused segments bearing marginal spines. The last segment ends in a long, articulating tail spine (telson).
• HABITAT
Euproops is generally be-lieved to be a nonmarine genus.

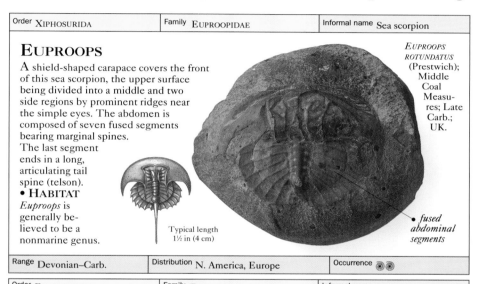

EUPROOPS ROTUNDATUS (Prestwich); Middle Coal Measures; Late Carb.; UK.

Typical length 1½ in (4 cm)

• *fused abdominal segments*

Range Devonian–Carb.	Distribution N. America, Europe	Occurrence ◉◉

Order EURYPTERIDA	Family EURYPTERIDAE	Informal name Sea scorpion

PARACARCINOSOMA

The body of this scorpionlike creature, including its squarish head shield and six pairs of appendages, is encased in a chitinous exoskeleton. Twelve other segments and a final pointed spine articulate with the head shield and with each other. Beneath the head shield are six pairs of appendages: the first with a claw, the second to fifth for walking, and the sixth paddle shaped.
• HABITAT
Originally marine, this genus later lived in brackish to fresh water.

abdomen •

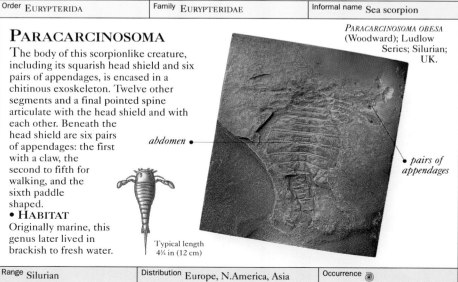

PARACARCINOSOMA OBESA (Woodward); Ludlow Series; Silurian; UK.

• *pairs of appendages*

Typical length 4¾ in (12 cm)

Range Silurian	Distribution Europe, N.America, Asia	Occurrence ◉

Order LIMULIDA	Family MESOLIMULIDAE	Informal name Horseshoe crab

MESOLIMULUS

This is the precursor of the living horseshoe crab, so called because the carapace is horseshoe shaped. The upper surface of the carapace is smooth, except for a central ridge and two longitudinal ridges. The eyes are small and widely spaced, lying just outside the longitudinal ridges. The abdomen is unsegmented, but six short spines are ranged around the margin. The abdomen articulates with the carapace and posteriorly with the long, sharp tail spine (telson).
• **HABITAT** Modern horseshoe crabs are common along the eastern seaboard of the USA, in the Indian Ocean, and in Southeast Asia. They are tolerant of changes in salinity and migrate to lay eggs in shallow intertidal mud flats. They are relatively omnivorous, living on seaweed, dead fish, and small crustaceans.

head-shield • with eyes

• fused abdomen with spine

Typical length
4¾ in (12 cm)

MESOLIMULUS WALCHII (Desmarest); Solnhofen Limestone; Late Jurassic; Germany.

Range Jurassic–Cretaceous	Distribution Europe, M. East	Occurrence ◉◉

Order SCORPIONIDA	Family PARAISOBUTHIDAE	Informal name Water scorpion

PARAISOBUTHUS

This aquatic scorpion has abdominal plates divided into two lobes. The first two pairs of coxae (the leg segments nearest to the body) are greatly enlarged into maxillary lobes for feeding. The carapace is squarish, with two well-developed cheeks, separated by a deep groove. The stinger is very similar in shape to those of Recent terrestrial scorpions.
• **HABITAT** These animals were largely aquatic and were able to leave water for only a short time. They are presumed to have been carnivorous, as are modern scorpions but the stinger may have been used for defense as well as attack.

• powerful claws

• walking legs

• body

• long tail

• stinger

PARAISOBUTHUS PRANTLI Kjellesvig-Waering; Radnice Group; Late Carboniferous; Czechoslovakia.

Typical length
2¾ in (7 cm)

Range L. Carb.	Distribution N. America, Europe	Occurrence ◉

Order PHRYNICHIDA	Family PHRYNICHIDAE	Informal name "Spider"

GRAEOPHONUS

This genus, which is close to true spiders, has an undivided carapace, with a distinct frontal projection. A single pair of round eyes sits on sharply defined, knoblike projections. To the front is a pair of slender tactile feeding claws (chelicerae), with a powerful first walking leg adapted to seize prey. The abdomen is composed of 12 segments, and the legs are segmented like those of modern spiders.
• **HABITAT**
Graeophonus lived in shallow-water swamps, deltas, or lagoons.

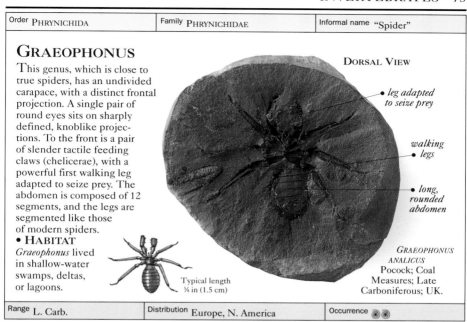

DORSAL VIEW

• *leg adapted to seize prey*

walking legs

• *long, rounded abdomen*

GRAEOPHONUS ANALICUS
Pocock; Coal Measures; Late Carboniferous; UK.

Typical length
⅝ in (1.5 cm)

Range L. Carb.	Distribution Europe, N. America	Occurrence

Order ARANEIDA	Family PISAURIDAE	Informal name Spider

DOLOMEDES

The cephalothorax of this true spider is slightly longer than it is broad and is high and convex near the eyes. Set in two rows, the eyes in the posterior row are larger. The legs are strongly developed and of almost equal length, except for the third pair which is shorter.
• **HABITAT** *Dolomedes* lives near freshwater, running on the surface to capture its insect prey.

SPECIMEN IN KAURI RESIN

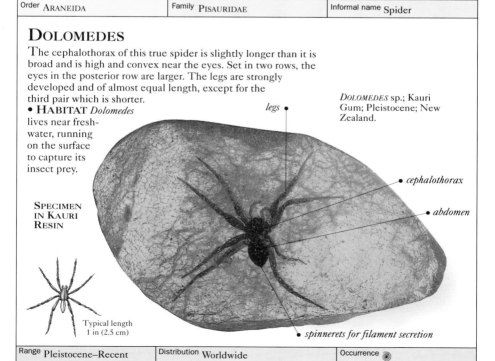

DOLOMEDES sp.; Kauri Gum; Pleistocene; New Zealand.

legs •

• *cephalothorax*

• *abdomen*

Typical length
1 in (2.5 cm)

• *spinnerets for filament secretion*

Range Pleistocene–Recent	Distribution Worldwide	Occurrence

INSECTS

I NSECTS ARE TERRESTRIAL and freshwater arthropods, with greater diversity of species than any other animal. Their bodies are divided into head, thorax, and abdomen, with three pairs of walking legs attached to the thorax. The earliest insects, found in the Early Devonian, are wingless. However, the majority are winged, and, by the Late Carboniferous, this group became the first animals to evolve powered flight. Most insects undergo a metamorphosis, with a pupa as a resting stage.

Order ODONATA	Family PETALURIDAE	Informal name Dragonfly

PETALURA

This dragonfly has four broad, richly veined wings. The body is long and slender.
• **HABITAT** The young (nymphs) live in fresh water, feeding on other aquatic animals, whilst the adults hunted flying insects near fresh water.
• **REMARK** The reconstructed species shown is a true dragonfly, but its relationship with the Recent *Petalura* is open to question.

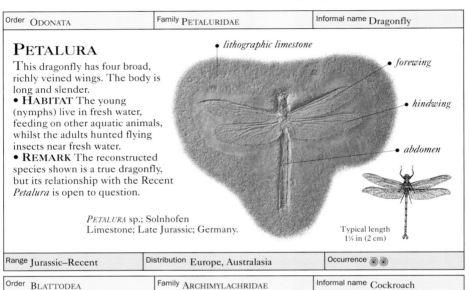

lithographic limestone

forewing

hindwing

abdomen

PETALURA sp.; Solnhofen Limestone; Late Jurassic; Germany.

Typical length 1¼ in (2 cm)

Range Jurassic–Recent	Distribution Europe, Australasia	Occurrence ◉◉

Order BLATTODEA	Family ARCHIMYLACHRIDAE	Informal name Cockroach

ARCHIMYLACRIS

Archimylacris was an early terrestrial cockroach, with folded wings, a large head shield (pronotum), and strengthened forewings (tegmina).
• **HABITAT** *Archimylacris* lived in warm, moist forests and was probably an omnivorous scavenger.
• **REMARK** In this specimen, the wings are well preserved. This quality of preservation enables paleontologists to determine that the specimen is an adult; immature stages do not have full wings.

Typical length 1¼ in (2 cm)

ironstone nodule

thorax

forewing

hindwing

ARCHIMYLACRIS EGGINTONI (Bolton); Coal Measures; Late Carboniferous; UK.

Range L. Carb.	Distribution Europe, N. America	Occurrence ◉◉◉

| Order PLECOPTERA | Family MESOLEUCTRIDAE | Informal name Stonefly |

MESOLEUCTRA

Mesoleuctra was a slender, aquatic nymph with a terrestrial adult, with folded wings. The nymph had two tails (cerci) and four wing pads.
• **HABITAT** Adults lived among stones and foliage, near the streams, rivers, and lakes in which the nymphs lived. The stonefly's diet was probably of small plants, such as lichens and small algae. Today, stonefly nymphs are an important source of food for freshwater fish.
• **REMARK** This specimen was probably buried very quickly in lake sediments, thus preserving the fragile legs. Fossil aquatic insects are relatively rare. More commonly insect-bearing rocks contain terrestrial species, blown into lake sediments.

Typical length
1¼ in (2 cm)

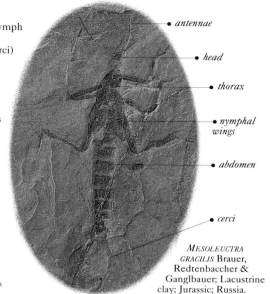

• *antennae*

• *head*

• *thorax*

• *nymphal wings*

• *abdomen*

• *cerci*

MESOLEUCTRA GRACILIS Brauer, Redtenbaccher & Ganglbauer; Lacustrine clay; Jurassic; Russia.

| Range E. Jurassic–Recent | Distribution Asia | Occurrence ◉◉◉ |

| Order COLEOPTERA | Family HYDROPHILIDAE | Informal name Water beetle |

HYDROPHILUS

The forewings of *Hydrophilus* are modified into hindwing cases (elytra) in the adult. These, along with the abdominal hairs, trap air, and act as air reservoirs under water.
• **HABITAT** Both young and adult live in fresh water, feeding on plant and animal matter. The larvae are carnivorous.
• **REMARK** This specimen was mired in asphalt, which had naturally seeped into a shallow lake in sandy wetland. Such "tar" pits preserved a wealth of Pleistocene animals in California, USA, including imperial mammoths and sabre-toothed cats.

Typical length
1¼ in (2 cm)

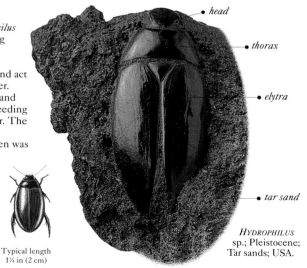

• *head*

• *thorax*

• *elytra*

• *tar sand*

HYDROPHILUS sp.; Pleistocene; Tar sands; USA.

| Range Pliocene–Recent | Distribution N. America, Europe | Occurrence ◉◉◉◉◉ |

Order COLEOPTERA	Family TENEBRIONIDAE	Informal name Beetle

BLAPSIUM

This beetle has folded wings with roughly sculptured elytra (compare *Hydrophilus, p.77*). The basal leg segments (coxae) of the hindlegs evidently do not divide the first ventral plate (sternite) of the abdomen. The coxae, which were attached to the thorax by muscles, have dropped out, leaving cavities.

• **HABITAT** *Blapsium* was an omnivorous scavenger which lived close to the sea. It is found fossilized alongside marine shells.

• **REMARK** The Stonesfield Slate is famous for its fossils, which are a mixture of marine dwellers, land animals, and plants washed out to sea.

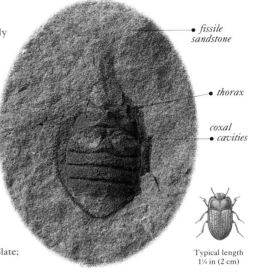

fissile sandstone

thorax

coxal cavities

BLAPSIUM EGERTONI
Westwood; Stonesfield Slate;
Middle Jurassic; UK.

Typical length
1¼ in (2 cm)

Range Jurassic	Distribution Europe	Occurrence ✸

Order DIPTERA	Family BIBIONIDAE	Informal name March fly

BIBIO

This insect has only one pair of wings (forewings), folded and developed internally, with the hindwings reduced to balance organs (halteres), characteristic of true flies. The forewings have reduced vein patterns and pigmentation.

• **HABITAT** March flies typically inhabit grassland, often appearing in spring (hence their name) and visiting flowers.

BIBIO MACULATUS
Heer; Miocene;
Croatia.

limestone

forewing

abdomen

leaf impression

Typical length
1¼ in (2 cm)

Range Pliocene–Recent	Distribution Europe	Occurrence ✸ ✸

BRACHIOPODS

A LTHOUGH LIVING SPECIES are now rare, brachiopods are common in marine fossiliferous rocks. Over 3,000 genera have been described, from Cambrian to Recent times, and they form the most abundant fauna in many Paleozoic rocks. The shell comprises two valves: the pedicle valve on the ventral side, and the usually smaller brachial valve on the dorsal side. A stalk (pedicle) usually emerges from the rear of the pedicle valve, attaching the brachiopod to the sea floor. The two main groups – the hinged Articulata and the hingeless Inarticulata – are further divided into 12 orders.

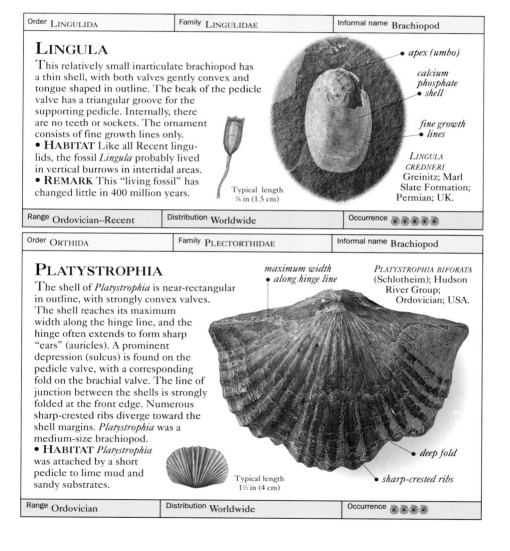

Order LINGULIDA	Family LINGULIDAE	Informal name Brachiopod

LINGULA

This relatively small inarticulate brachiopod has a thin shell, with both valves gently convex and tongue shaped in outline. The beak of the pedicle valve has a triangular groove for the supporting pedicle. Internally, there are no teeth or sockets. The ornament consists of fine growth lines only.
• **HABITAT** Like all Recent lingulids, the fossil *Lingula* probably lived in vertical burrows in intertidal areas.
• **REMARK** This "living fossil" has changed little in 400 million years.

Typical length
⅝ in (1.5 cm)

apex (umbo)

calcium phosphate shell

fine growth lines

LINGULA
CREDNERI
Greinitz; Marl Slate Formation; Permian; UK.

Range Ordovician–Recent	Distribution Worldwide	Occurrence ◉◉◉◉◉

Order ORTHIDA	Family PLECTORTHIDAE	Informal name Brachiopod

PLATYSTROPHIA

The shell of *Platystrophia* is near-rectangular in outline, with strongly convex valves. The shell reaches its maximum width along the hinge line, and the hinge often extends to form sharp "ears" (auricles). A prominent depression (sulcus) is found on the pedicle valve, with a corresponding fold on the brachial valve. The line of junction between the shells is strongly folded at the front edge. Numerous sharp-crested ribs diverge toward the shell margins. *Platystrophia* was a medium-size brachiopod.
• **HABITAT** *Platystrophia* was attached by a short pedicle to lime mud and sandy substrates.

maximum width along hinge line

PLATYSTROPHIA BIFORATA
(Schlotheim); Hudson River Group; Ordovician; USA.

deep fold

sharp-crested ribs

Typical length
1½ in (4 cm)

Range Ordovician	Distribution Worldwide	Occurrence ◉◉◉◉

Order ORTHIDA	Family DICOELOSIIDAE	Informal name Brachiopod

DICOELOSIA

The shell of this brachiopod has a characteristic bilobed, near-triangular outline, with a strongly convex pedicle valve and less convex brachial valve. Both valves have a pronounced sulcus, with a strongly incurved beak on the pedicle valve. The hinge line is of variable width but is generally short. The interarea (between the valves) is medium size, with an open groove for passage of the pedicle. Numerous fine ribs diverge near the front of the shell.

• **HABITAT** *Dicoelosia* was attached to bryozoans and shelly fragments in shallow to mid-depths.

twin-lobed pedicle valve

DICOELOSIA BILOBATA (Linnaeus); Wenlock Limestone; Silurian; UK.

Typical length ⅗ in (1.5 cm)

deep sulcus

ornament of fine ribs

Range Ordovician–Devonian	Distribution Worldwide	Occurrence ⊛⊛⊛⊛⊛

Order STROPHOMENIDA	Family LEPTANIDAE	Informal name Brachiopod

LEPTAENA

This articulate brachiopod has a shell with a semicircular outline, with prominent auricles and a straight hinge line. The pedicle valve is slightly convex and the brachial valve usually flat, except at the front margins, where both valves bend almost at right angles. The ornament consists of numerous very fine, clustered ribs, and strong, concentric wrinkles (rugae).

• **HABITAT** *Leptaena* lay on the sea floor with its pedicle valve downward. The upward-projecting front margin was kept clear of the sediment surface, allowing the brachial valve to be almost completely buried.

• **REMARK** It is thought that the concentric rugae stabilized the shell in soft substrates. *Leptaena* is usually found with both valves separated in fine-grained limestones shales.

hinge line

LEPTAENA sp.; Longhope Formation; Silurian; USA.

Typical length 1½ in (4 cm)

sharp bends at front margin

clustered ribs

strong rugae

Range Ordovician	Distribution Worldwide	Occurrence ⊛⊛⊛⊛⊛

Order STROPHOMENIDA	Family PRODUCTIDAE	Informal name Brachiopod

PRODUCTUS

The shell has a flat to concave brachial valve that is nearly circular in outline. The pedicle valve is thick and strongly convex, with a short hinge line and long trail (the extension of the valve beyond the mantle cavity). The ornament consists of numerous ribs and irregular wrinkles. Scattered spines can be found on the pedicle valve but are usually preserved only as spine bases. No spines are found on the brachial valve.
• **HABITAT** *Productus* lived in soft muddy sediments, its thicker pedicle valve partially buried.
• **REMARK** The spines stabilized the shell, preventing it from sinking too far into the sediment. The long trail probably projected vertically upward, keeping the valve margins clear of the substrate.

ribs

PRODUCTUS PRODUCTUS (Martin); Carboniferous Limestone; Early Carboniferous; UK.

rugae
pedicle valve
trail

Typical length
1¾ in (4.5 cm)

Range Carboniferous	Distribution Europe, Worldwide	Occurrence

Order STROPHOMENIDA	Family BUXTONIIDAE	Informal name Brachiopod

PARAJURESANIA

The shell of this medium-size brachiopod has a flat to slightly concave brachial valve and a pedicle valve that is strongly convex, with a short trail and shallow middle depressions. Both valves are strongly ornamented by concentrically arranged, overlapping rows of spines, with concentric ridges more prominent near the front.
• **HABITAT** *Parajuresania* lay in soft sediment.

nearly erect spines

PARAJURESANIA SYMMETRICA (McChesney); Finis Formation; Late Carboniferous; USA.

Typical length
1¾ in (3 cm)

prostrate spines
concentric wrinkles

Range L. Carb.	Distribution Worldwide	Occurrence

Order PENTAMERIDA	Family PENTAMERIDAE	Informal name Brachiopod

PENTAMERUS

In this relatively large brachiopod, both pedicle and brachial valves are convex and often tongue shaped in outline. The pedicle valve umbo (apex area) is stout and curved strongly backward, with a prominent middle partition (septum). Two prominent near-parallel septa are found on the brachial valve. The shell exterior is smooth, with fine growth lines.
• **HABITAT** *Pentamerus* is very common in shallow-water limestones, often forming shell banks. The pedicle was not functional in adults, so they lived umbones downward on silty and muddy substrates.

• *pedicle valve*

near-parallel
• *septa*

• *line of junction*

Typical length 1¾ in (4.5 cm)

*PENTAMERUS
OBLONGUS*
(J. de C. Sowerby);
Jupiter Formation;
Silurian; Canada.

• *smooth shell*

Range Silurian	Distribution Worldwide	Occurrence ⊛⊛⊛⊛⊛

Order RHYNCHONELLIDA	Family PUGNACIDAE	Informal name Brachiopod

PUGNAX

The shell of this small to large brachiopod has a distinctive four-sided outline. The brachial valve is globelike, with a pronounced fold at the front. In juvenile forms, the pedicle valve is convex, but in large individuals it becomes concave toward the shell margins, forming a deep and nearly rounded sulcus. Apart from a few faint ribs, there is almost no ornament on either the brachial or pedicle valve.
• **HABITAT** *Pugnax* was tethered by a functional pedicle to shelly fragments or other hard surfaces. It is commonly found in large clusters, especially in Carboniferous mud-mounds and shallow water reef-mounds.

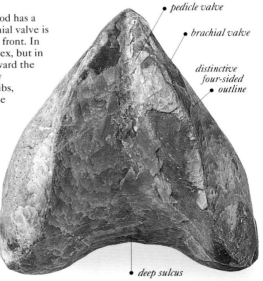

• *pedicle valve*

• *brachial valve*

*distinctive
four-sided*
• *outline*

Typical length
1¾ in (4.5 cm)

*PUGNAX
ACUMINATUS*
(J. Sowerby);
Carboniferous
Limestone; Early
Carboniferous; UK.

• *deep sulcus*

Range Devonian–L. Carb.	Distribution Europe	Occurrence ⊛⊛⊛⊛

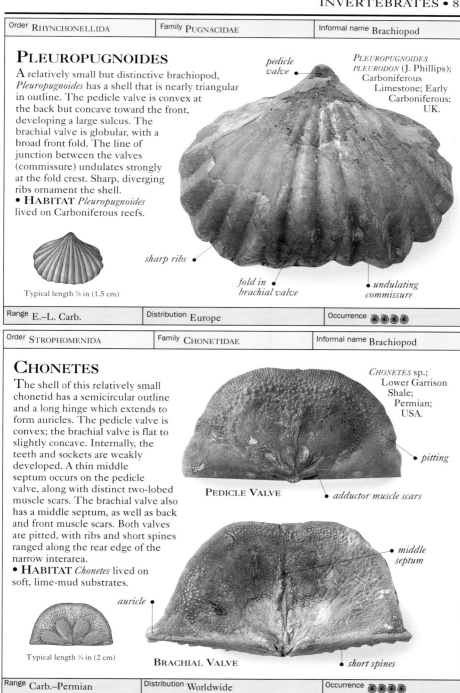

| Order RHYNCHONELLIDA | Family PUGNACIDAE | Informal name Brachiopod |

PLEUROPUGNOIDES

A relatively small but distinctive brachiopod, *Pleuropugnoides* has a shell that is nearly triangular in outline. The pedicle valve is convex at the back but concave toward the front, developing a large sulcus. The brachial valve is globular, with a broad front fold. The line of junction between the valves (commissure) undulates strongly at the fold crest. Sharp, diverging ribs ornament the shell.
• **HABITAT** *Pleuropugnoides* lived on Carboniferous reefs.

pedicle valve

PLEUROPUGNOIDES PLEURODON (J. Phillips); Carboniferous Limestone; Early Carboniferous; UK.

sharp ribs

fold in brachial valve

undulating commissure

Typical length ⅗ in (1.5 cm)

| Range E.–L. Carb. | Distribution Europe | Occurrence 🔘🔘🔘 |

| Order STROPHOMENIDA | Family CHONETIDAE | Informal name Brachiopod |

CHONETES

The shell of this relatively small chonetid has a semicircular outline and a long hinge which extends to form auricles. The pedicle valve is convex; the brachial valve is flat to slightly concave. Internally, the teeth and sockets are weakly developed. A thin middle septum occurs on the pedicle valve, along with distinct two-lobed muscle scars. The brachial valve also has a middle septum, as well as back and front muscle scars. Both valves are pitted, with ribs and short spines ranged along the rear edge of the narrow interarea.
• **HABITAT** *Chonetes* lived on soft, lime-mud substrates.

CHONETES sp.; Lower Garrison Shale; Permian; USA.

pitting

PEDICLE VALVE

adductor muscle scars

middle septum

auricle

short spines

Typical length ¾ in (2 cm)

BRACHIAL VALVE

| Range Carb.–Permian | Distribution Worldwide | Occurrence 🔘🔘🔘 |

| Order RHYNCHONELLIDA | Family RHYNCHONELLIDAE | Informal name Brachiopod |

CYCLOTHYRIS

The shell of this relatively large and conspicuous rhynchonellid is characterized by a wide, near-triangular outline. The beak is erect, and contains a large hole (foramen) for the pedicle. Both valves are convex, with a pronounced sulcus on the pedicle valve and a fold on the brachial valve. The commissure zigzags, and numerous small, sharp-crested ribs ornament both valves.

• HABITAT *Cyclothyris* is commonly found in sediments deposited in moderate- to high-energy environments.

CYCLOTHYRIS DIFFORMIS
(Valenciennes); Lower Chalk; Late Cretaceous; UK.

• foramen

brachial valve •

• sharp-crested ribs

• fold

Typical length
1¼ in (3 cm)

| Range Cretaceous | Distribution Europe, N. America | Occurrence 🐚🐚🐚 |

| Order ATRYPIDA | Family ATRYPIDAE | Informal name Brachiopod |

ATRYPA

The brachial valve of this genus is more convex than the pedicle valve and has a broad, shallow fold. The pedicle valve has a small depression and a slight, curved-in beak. The commissure is often slightly deflected toward the brachial valve. The ornament consists of numerous fine rounded ribs, and prominent, concenric growth lines commonly forming frills on both valves.

• HABITAT *Atrypa* lived in shallow water on soft substrates.

• pedicle valve

• fine ribs

• deflected commissure

ATRYPA sp.; Eke Beds; Silurian; Sweden.

Typical length
½ in (1.2 cm)

• growth-line frills

| Range Silurian | Distribution Europe, Asia, N. America | Occurrence 🐚🐚🐚🐚 |

Order SPIRIFERIDA	Family ATHYRIDIDAE	Informal name Brachiopod

ACTINOCONCHUS

The valves of this distinctive brachiopod are nearly equally convex, and the shell outline is near-circular. Specimens commonly lack a well-developed fold or depression. Broad, thin-layered expansions are developed at growth lines. These are traversed by a series of fine ribs that diverge toward the front margins of the shell.
• **HABITAT** *Actinoconchus* was attached by a short, functional pedicle to hard substrates. The shape of the brachial valve commonly conforms to that of the surface of the substrate.
• **REMARK** The thin-layered expansions on *Actinoconchus* served as camouflage and prevented the shell from sinking into muddy sediments.

brachial valve •   • ribs

• growth-line expansions

• line of junction

ACTINOCONCHUS PARADOXUS Mc-Coy; Carboniferous Limestone; Early Carboniferous; Republic of Ireland.

Typical length
1¼ in (4.5 cm)

Range E. Carb.	Distribution Europe	Occurrence ◉◉◉

Order SPIRIFERIDA	Family MERISTELLIDAE	Informal name Brachiopod

MERISTINA

The shells of these relatively large brachiopods are triangular to round in shape and are often longer than they are wide. The brachial valve has a broad, shallow fold, with a corresponding sulcus on the pedicle valve. The apex areas on both valves are strongly curved in, concealing the pedicle opening in large forms. Both valves are unornamented.
• **HABITAT** *Meristina* is found in small clusters in fine-grained muddy limestones. It probably lived in shallow water.

• fold in brachial valve

umbo •

• sulcus in pedicle valve

MERISTINA OBTUSA (J. de C. Sowerby); Wenlock Limestone; Silurian; UK.

Typical length
1¼ in (4.5 cm)

Range Silurian–Devonian	Distribution Worldwide	Occurrence ◉◉◉◉

Order SPIRIFERIDA	Family MUCROSPIRIFERIDA	Informal name Butterfly shell

MUCROSPIRIFER

The shell of this relatively large spiriferid reaches its maximum width along the hinge line, which is extended outward forming sharp points. The brachial valve has a pronounced fold, with a corresponding depression on the pedicle valve. The apex area (umbo) of the pedicle valve contains a small hole for the pedicle.
• **HABITAT** *Mucrospirifer* lived in soft, muddy substrates.

MUCROSPIRIFER MUCRONATA (Conrad); Hamilton Group; Devonian; Canada.

• *umbo of pedicle valve*

• *alate hinge line separating inhalant and exhalant currents*

• *regularly overlapping growth layers*

ribs •

Typical length 1 in (2.5 cm)

Range Devonian	Distribution Worldwide	Occurrence

Order ORTHIDA	Family ENTELETIDAE	Informal name Brachiopod

AULACOPHORIA

In outline, the shell of this medium-size orthid varies from nearly circular to nearly square. The brachial valve is more convex than the pedicle valve and has a broad front fold, corresponding to the depression on the pedicle valve. The pedicle itself is prominent and the inter-area relatively narrow. Both valves are ornamented by many fine ribs.
• **HABITAT** *Aulacophoria* lived in lime-mud sediments.

pedicle valve •

• *small interarea*

AULACOPHORIA KEYSERLINGIANA (de Koninck); Yoredales; Early Carboniferous; UK.

Typical length 1¼ in (3 cm)

• *fold in brachial valve*

Range E. Carb.	Distribution Europe	Occurrence

Order TEREBRATULIDA	Family TEREBRATULIDAE	Informal name Lamp shell

EPITHYRIS

The shell of this medium-size to large terebratulid has a near-circular outline. Its convex pedicle valve forms an incurved erect beak that contains a large pedicle opening (foramen) with a well-developed collar. The commissure undulates, with two folds on the brachial valve and a corresponding depression (sulcus) on the pedicle valve. The folds can be sharp crested or rounded. There is little surface ornament – only fine growth lines which can become incised and attenuated near the front edges of the shell.

• **HABITAT** It is likely that *Epithyris* lived in relatively quiet, lagoonal waters.

• **REMARK** These brachiopods formed communal "nests," sometimes extending for several yards.

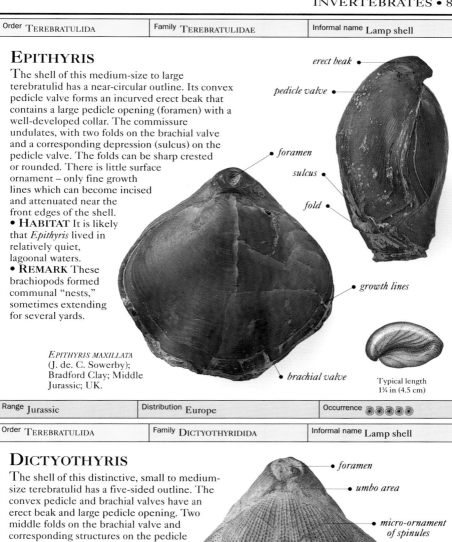

erect beak

pedicle valve

foramen

sulcus

fold

growth lines

brachial valve

EPITHYRIS MAXILLATA
(J. de. C. Sowerby);
Bradford Clay; Middle
Jurassic; UK.

Typical length
1¾ in (4.5 cm)

Range Jurassic	Distribution Europe	Occurrence ⊛⊛⊛⊛⊛

Order TEREBRATULIDA	Family DICTYOTHYRIDIDA	Informal name Lamp shell

DICTYOTHYRIS

The shell of this distinctive, small to medium-size terebratulid has a five-sided outline. The convex pedicle and brachial valves have an erect beak and large pedicle opening. Two middle folds on the brachial valve and corresponding structures on the pedicle valve produce a W-shaped junction at the front. The valves are ornamented with five longitudinal and transverse ribs, with spinules.

• **HABITAT** *Dictyothyris* lived attached to shelly fragments in soft muddy sediments.

foramen

umbo area

micro-ornament of spinules

Typical length
¾ in (2 cm)

DICTYOTHYRIS COARCTATA
(Parkinson);
Bradford Clay;
Middle Jurassic; UK.

Range Jurassic	Distribution Europe	Occurrence ⊛⊛⊛⊛⊛

Order STROPHOMENIDA	Family STROPHOMENIDAE	Informal name Brachiopod

STROPHOMENA

In this medium-size brachiopod, the brachial valve is convex and the pedicle valve concave, with the maximum width along the hinge line. Internally, the brachial valve has well-developed sockets and a prominent cardinal process (the projection from the hinge line to which the diductor muscles are attached). The hole for the pedicle is small and partially covered by a plate. Both valves are ornamented by fine ribs that diverge toward the front of the shell.

• HABITAT The small foramen indicates that *Strophomena* was probably free-lying, resting with its brachial valve downward on a variety of soft substrates.

well-developed sockets •

STROPHOMENA GRANDIS (J. de C. Sowerby); Cheney Longville Formation; Ordovician; UK.

commissure •

Typical length
1¼ in (3 cm)

fine ribs •

BRACHIAL VALVE INTERIOR

Range Ordovician	Distribution Worldwide	Occurrence ◉◉◉

Order SPIRIFERIDA	Family CYRTINIDAE	Informal name Brachiopod

CYRTINA

The shell of this small to medium-size spiriferid has a characteristic caplike shape and maximum width along the hinge line. On the pedicle valve there is a large triangular interarea, with a large hole for the pedicle near the apex and a prominent sulcus that widens toward the front. The brachial valve is weakly convex, with an unornamented fold and depression. Several distinct ribs on both valves produce an undulating commissure, and growth lines become prominent near the front margins.

• HABITAT *Cyrtina* lived in soft sediments.

sulcus on pedicle valve •

distinctive caplike shape

prominent growth lines •

CYRTINA HAMILTONENSIS Hall; Hamilton Group; Devonian; Canada.

• *aperture covered with plates*

• *lateral folds*

Typical length
1⅘ in (5 cm)

Range Devonian–Permian	Distribution Worldwide	Occurrence ◉◉◉◉

Order STROPHOMENIDA	Family ORTHOTETIDAE	Informal name Brachiopod

DERBYIA

The shell of this medium-size strophomenid is semicircular in outline, with convex valves. A shallow depression may appear in the pedicle valve, the depth of which may vary across the shell. The short, stubby apex area is sometimes offset. Numerous fine radiating ribs and prominent growth lines ornament the shell.
• **HABITAT** It is likely that *Derbyia* was free-living.

short umbo

DERBYIA GRANDIS (Waagen); Middle Productus Limestone; Early Permian; India.

ornament of fine ribs

growth lines

PEDICLE VALVE

Typical length 1⅜ in (3.5 cm)

Range E. Carb.–L. Permian	Distribution Worldwide	Occurrence ◉◉◉◉

Order SPIRIFERIDA	Family SPIRIFERINIDAE	Informal name Brachiopod

SPIRIFERINA

The shell of *Spiriferina* is triangular to near-pentagonal in outline, with convex valves. The umbones are strongly curved in, with a prominent pedicle and well-developed interarea. A deep fold is found on the brachial valve and a deep sulcus on the pedicle valve. The commissure undulates strongly, and both valves are ornamented by large, rounded ribs. Well-preserved specimens often display a microornament of fine spines.
• **HABITAT** *Spiriferina* lived with its umbones downward on soft muddy sediments.

PEDICLE VALVE

umbo

sulcus

undulating commissure

BRACHIAL VALVE

interarea

growth lines

ribs

fold

Typical length ⅝ in (1.5 cm)

SPIRIFERINA WALCOTTI (J. Sowerby); Lower Lias; Early Jurassic; UK.

Range Triassic–E. Jurassic	Distribution Worldwide	Occurrence ◉◉◉◉◉

Order RHYNCHONELLIDA	Family RHYNCHONELLIDAE	Informal name Brachiopod

GONIORHYNCHIA

The medium-size shell of this brachiopod has a near-triangular outline. The convex pedicle valve has a prominent beak and a well-developed sulcus, while the fold in the brachial valve is most prominent near the front of the shell. A strongly undulating commissure is highlighted by attenuated growth lines. Both valves are ornamented with numerous sharp-crested ribs.
• **HABITAT** This solitary brachiopod rested with its umbones downward on firm substrates. The functional pedicle acted as a tether.
• **REMARK** A typical thick-shelled rhynchonellid, *Goniorhynchia* can be very abundant in certain areas.

prominent beak on pedicle valve

brachial valve

GONIORHYNCHIA BOUETI (Davidson); Boueti Bed; Forest Marble; Middle Jurassic; UK.

Typical length ¾ in (2 cm)

fold

ornament of sharp-crested ribs

Range M. Jurassic	Distribution Europe	Occurrence

Order TEREBRATULIDA	Family ZEILLERIIDAE	Informal name Lamp shell

DIGONELLA

The shell of this relatively small to medium-size terebratulid is long and oval to sack shaped in outline. Both valves are convex, and the shell reaches its maximum width near the front. The apex area is flattened toward the back, and the pedicle is curved and short, with a large opening (foramen) for the stalk to pass through. The commissure is straight, and there is no ornament other than the very fine growth lines.
• **HABITAT** *Digonella* was attached by a short pedicle to shelly fragments, in sediments of soft mud or lime-mud, and is very abundant in fine-grained limestones in shallow waters.

foramen

pedicle valve

brachial valve

DIGONELLA DIGONA (J. Sowerby); Bradford Clay; Middle Jurassic; UK.

Typical length 1 in (2.5 cm)

straight commisure

Range M. Jurassic	Distribution Worldwide	Occurrence

Order TEREBRATULIDA	Family TEREBRATELLIDAE	Informal name Lamp shell

TEREBRIROSTRA

This genus is distinguished by a long, curving umbo, which extends behind the rear margin of the shell. The brachial valve is oval to near-triangular in outline. Along the front line of junction between the valves are many undulations and depressions. Both the brachial and pedicle valves are ornamented by radial ribs and fine, concentric growth lines.
• **HABITAT** *Terebrirostra* was probably a solitary brachiopod, attached to hard substrates by a short functional pedicle. The conspicuous curved umbo on the pedicle valve may have kept the shell clear of the substrate, preventing sediment from entering the mantle cavity. This genus is fairly common in shallow water sediments, particularly glauconite chalks.

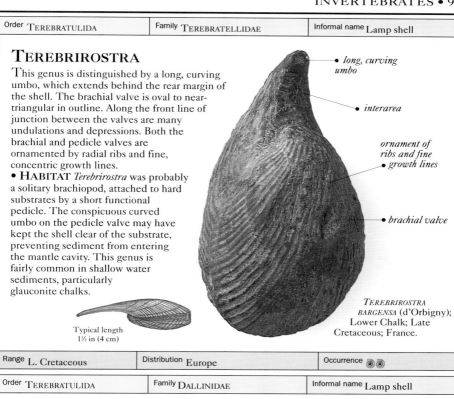

• long, curving umbo

• interarea

ornament of ribs and fine
• growth lines

• brachial valve

Typical length
1½ in (4 cm)

*TEREBRIROSTRA
BARGENSA* (d'Orbigny);
Lower Chalk; Late
Cretaceous; France.

Range L. Cretaceous	Distribution Europe	Occurrence 🌑🌑

Order TEREBRATULIDA	Family DALLINIDAE	Informal name Lamp shell

KINGENA

This medium-size terebratulid has a shell with convex valves. The shell is characterized by a rounded to near-pentagonal outline, with a broad, shallow fold in the brachial valve and faint depression on the pedicle valve. The pedicle itself is short and curves slightly backward. The brachial valve commonly exhibits a prominent middle partition (septum). Fine growth lines and minute granules ornament the shell.
• **HABITAT** *Kingena* was attached to hard substrates by a short, thick, fleshy pedicle. This is a common brachiopod on shallow-water limestones.

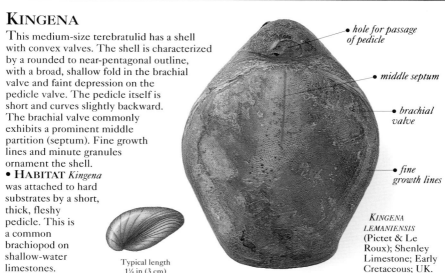

• hole for passage of pedicle

• middle septum

• brachial valve

• fine growth lines

*KINGENA
LEMANIENSIS*
(Pictet & Le
Roux); Shenley
Limestone; Early
Cretaceous; UK.

Typical length
1¼ in (3 cm)

Range Cretaceous	Distribution Worldwide	Occurrence 🌑🌑🌑🌑

| Order ACROTRETIDA | Family CRANIIDAE | Informal name Brachiopod |

ANCISTROCRANIA

The shell of this small brachiopod is almost circular in
outline, with a straight rear margin. The shape of the
pedicle valve conforms to the underlying
substrate. Both valves exhibit a well-
developed pair of circular muscle scars,
accompanied by smaller muscle
scars, and both thicken at their
front margins. Apart from
surface blisters (pustules), the
ornament consists of concentric
growth lines, and may have
provided some form of camouflage.
• **HABITAT** Most genera in the
family are cemented to hard
substrates by their pedicle valves.
• **REMARK** The family appeared in
the Early Mesozoic and is still alive in
today's oceans. They are unique in
lacking a pedicle.

*ANCISTROCRANIA
TUBERCULATA* (Nilsson);
Danian chalk;
Paleocene; Denmark.

Typical length
⅜ in (1 cm)

• *circular
muscle scars*

• *straight
rear margin*

*pustulose •
ornament*

| Range E. Paleocene | Distribution Worldwide | Occurrence 🔘🔘🔘🔘🔘 |

| Order ACROTRETIDA | Family DISCINIDAE | Informal name Brachiopod |

DISCINISCA

Discinisca is characterized by a gently conical brachial
valve, and a flat to slightly convex pedicle valve. The
often shiny shell is near-circular to spatulate in
outline, with a thin, slitlike pedicle opening
that is closed in adult forms and open at the
rear in juveniles. The ornament consists of
fine concentric growth lines, prominent
near the front margin of the shell.
• **HABITAT** This genus is attached
by a short, functional pedicle to a
variety of substrates. It is
commonly found in its life
position, attached to
other shells.
• **REMARK**
Some genera
from the
family Discinidae
are "living fossils."

*conical brachial
valve •*

*position of
• apical opening*

• *calcium
phosphate shell*

Typical length
⅓ in (8 mm)

• *accentuated
growth lines*

DISCINISCA LUGUBRIS
(Conrad); Choptank
Formation;
Miocene; USA.

| Range Permian–Recent | Distribution Worldwide | Occurrence 🔘🔘🔘🔘 |

Order TEREBRATULIDA	Family CANCELLOTHYRIDIDAE	Informal name Lamp shell

CANCELLOTHYRIS

This medium-size to relatively large brachiopod is characterized by an egg-shaped shell, with convex valves and a short but massive apex area that is truncated by a large pedicle opening. The largest specimens may display a slight fold in the brachial valve and a corresponding depression in the pedicle valve. The shell of *Cancellothyris* has an external ornament consists of growth lines and numerous fine ribs.

• **HABITAT** *Cancellothyris* was attached to hard surfaces by a stout pedicle. It is commonly found in clusters, especially in shallow-water, high-energy environments such as rocky shorelines. It also inhabited crevices and fissures.

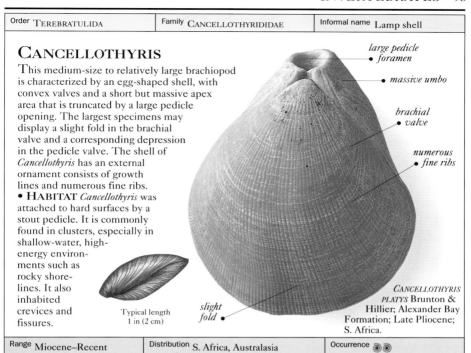

large pedicle foramen

massive umbo

brachial valve

numerous fine ribs

slight fold

Typical length 1 in (2 cm)

CANCELLOTHYRIS PLATYS Brunton & Hillier; Alexander Bay Formation; Late Pliocene; S. Africa.

Range Miocene–Recent	Distribution S. Africa, Australasia	Occurrence 🔘🔘

Order TEREBRATULIDA	Family TEREBRATULIDAE	Informal name Lamp shell

TEREBRATULA

The shell of this terebratulid is elongate to elliptical in outline, with convex valves. There is a short, massive, and slightly curved-in umbo, and a large pedicle opening with a well-developed pedicle collar. Internally, the teeth and sockets are prominent, with a short middle septum on the brachial valve. At the front, the commissure is straight, with no fold or depression. Both valves are ornamented by fine growth lines, that become prominent near the shell margins.

• **HABITAT** This large lamp shell had a thick, fleshy pedicle that branched into rootlets, attaching to shelly particles in unconsolidated sediments.

pedicle foramen

well-developed pedicle collar

commissure

growth lines

Typical length 2½ in (6 cm)

TEREBRATULA MAXIMA Charlesworth; Coralline Crag; Late Pliocene; UK.

Range Miocene–Pliocene	Distribution Europe	Occurrence 🔘🔘

BIVALVES

BIVALVES are mollusks in which the shells are made up of two valves connected by a ligament of organic material, rarely preserved in fossils. The valves are articulated by a hinge, usually with interlocking teeth. In most cases, the valves are closed by two main muscles, whose points of attachment to the shell are marked by distinct scars. Bivalves feed by filtering particles from the water through siphons. Although they possess a foot, they have limited mobility. Many burrow in sediment or bore into stone or wood. Others cement themselves to submerged objects, or attach themselves with a byssus of organic threads. Bivalves are classified by their hinges.

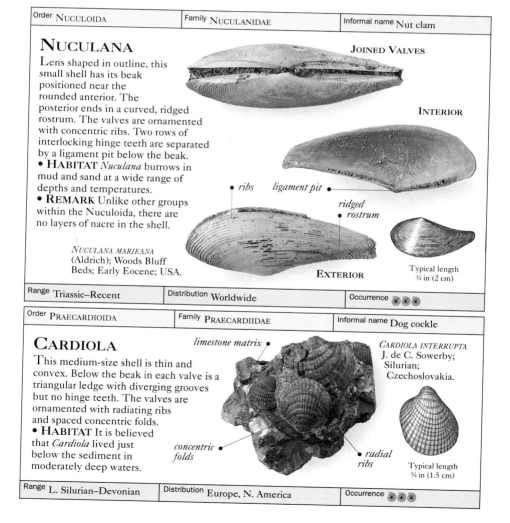

Order NUCULOIDA	Family NUCULANIDAE	Informal name Nut clam

NUCULANA

JOINED VALVES

Lens shaped in outline, this small shell has its beak positioned near the rounded anterior. The posterior ends in a curved, ridged rostrum. The valves are ornamented with concentric ribs. Two rows of interlocking hinge teeth are separated by a ligament pit below the beak.
• **HABITAT** *Nuculana* burrows in mud and sand at a wide range of depths and temperatures.
• **REMARK** Unlike other groups within the Nuculoida, there are no layers of nacre in the shell.

INTERIOR

• *ribs*   *ligament pit* •

ridged rostrum •

NUCULANA MARIEANA (Aldrich); Woods Bluff Beds; Early Eocene; USA.

EXTERIOR

Typical length ¼ in (2 cm)

Range Triassic–Recent	Distribution Worldwide	Occurrence

Order PRAECARDIOIDA	Family PRAECARDIIDAE	Informal name Dog cockle

CARDIOLA

limestone matrix •

CARDIOLA INTERRUPTA J. de C. Sowerby; Silurian; Czechoslovakia.

This medium-size shell is thin and convex. Below the beak in each valve is a triangular ledge with diverging grooves but no hinge teeth. The valves are ornamented with radiating ribs and spaced concentric folds.
• **HABITAT** It is believed that *Cardiola* lived just below the sediment in moderately deep waters.

concentric folds •

• *radial ribs*

Typical length ⅝ in (1.5 cm)

Range L. Silurian–Devonian	Distribution Europe, N. America	Occurrence

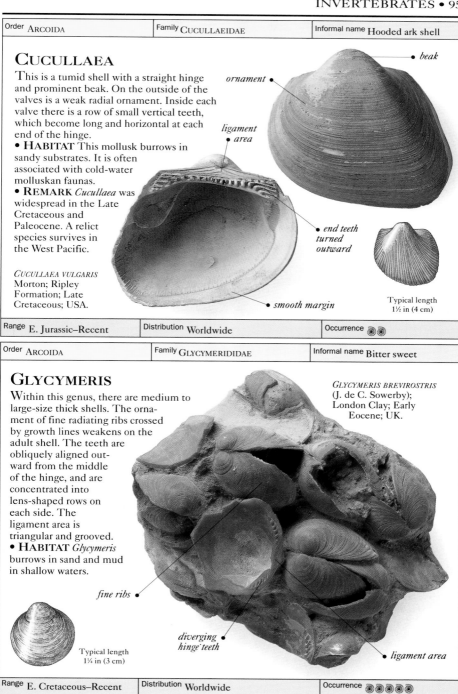

| Order ARCOIDA | Family CUCULLAEIDAE | Informal name Hooded ark shell |

CUCULLAEA

This is a tumid shell with a straight hinge and prominent beak. On the outside of the valves is a weak radial ornament. Inside each valve there is a row of small vertical teeth, which become long and horizontal at each end of the hinge.
• **HABITAT** This mollusk burrows in sandy substrates. It is often associated with cold-water molluskan faunas.
• **REMARK** *Cucullaea* was widespread in the Late Cretaceous and Paleocene. A relict species survives in the West Pacific.

CUCULLAEA VULGARIS Morton; Ripley Formation; Late Cretaceous; USA.

• *beak*

ornament •

ligament area

• *end teeth turned outward*

• *smooth margin*

Typical length 1½ in (4 cm)

| Range E. Jurassic–Recent | Distribution Worldwide | Occurrence ◉◉ |

| Order ARCOIDA | Family GLYCYMERIDIDAE | Informal name Bitter sweet |

GLYCYMERIS

Within this genus, there are medium to large-size thick shells. The ornament of fine radiating ribs crossed by growth lines weakens on the adult shell. The teeth are obliquely aligned outward from the middle of the hinge, and are concentrated into lens-shaped rows on each side. The ligament area is triangular and grooved.
• **HABITAT** *Glycymeris* burrows in sand and mud in shallow waters.

GLYCYMERIS BREVIROSTRIS (J. de C. Sowerby); London Clay; Early Eocene; UK.

fine ribs •

diverging hinge teeth •

• *ligament area*

Typical length 1¼ in (3 cm)

| Range E. Cretaceous–Recent | Distribution Worldwide | Occurrence ◉◉◉◉◉ |

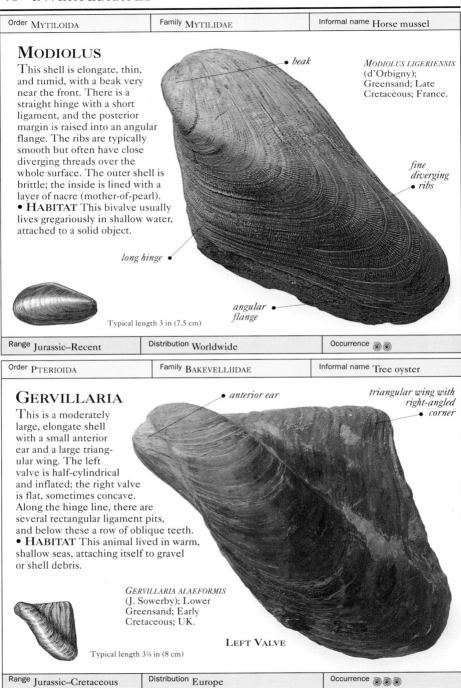

Order MYTILOIDA	Family MYTILIDAE	Informal name Horse mussel

MODIOLUS

This shell is elongate, thin, and tumid, with a beak very near the front. There is a straight hinge with a short ligament, and the posterior margin is raised into an angular flange. The ribs are typically smooth but often have close diverging threads over the whole surface. The outer shell is brittle; the inside is lined with a layer of nacre (mother-of-pearl).
• **HABITAT** This bivalve usually lives gregariously in shallow water, attached to a solid object.

beak

MODIOLUS LIGERIENSIS (d'Orbigny); Greensand; Late Cretaceous; France.

fine diverging ribs

long hinge

angular flange

Typical length 3 in (7.5 cm)

Range Jurassic–Recent	Distribution Worldwide	Occurrence

Order PTERIOIDA	Family BAKEVELLIIDAE	Informal name Tree oyster

GERVILLARIA

This is a moderately large, elongate shell with a small anterior ear and a large triangular wing. The left valve is half-cylindrical and inflated; the right valve is flat, sometimes concave. Along the hinge line, there are several rectangular ligament pits, and below these a row of oblique teeth.
• **HABITAT** This animal lived in warm, shallow seas, attaching itself to gravel or shell debris.

anterior ear

triangular wing with right-angled corner

GERVILLARIA ALAEFORMIS (J. Sowerby); Lower Greensand; Early Cretaceous; UK.

LEFT VALVE

Typical length 3⅛ in (8 cm)

Range Jurassic–Cretaceous	Distribution Europe	Occurrence

Order MYTILOIDA	Family PINNIDAE	Informal name Fan mussel

PINNA

This large wedge-shaped bivalve has weak radial ribs running the length of the shell. In the living creature, the brittle calcitic valves are joined by a narrow ligament that runs along the entire hinge margin. Inside each valve is a pearly area, divided into two lobes by a distinct furrow, which shows as a slight ridge on the outside.
• **HABITAT** *Pinna* lives in groups, with its pointed anterior end buried in the sediment.
• **REMARK** When sediment fills the space between a pair of valves, it may harden into a siltstone nodule, preserving the fossil shell.

• *expanded margin*

PINNA HARTMANNI Zieten; Lower Lias; Early Jurassic; UK.

longitudinal ribs •

MODERN *PINNA*

• *ridge*

long hinge for • *ligament*

anterior buried • *in mud in life*

• *iridescent area*

• *dark ligament*

terminal beak •

Typical length 8 in (20 cm)

Range E. Carb.–Recent	Distribution Worldwide	Occurrence

Order PTERIOIDA	Family INOCERAMIDAE	Informal name Inoceramid oyster

VOLVICERAMUS

This shell has an outer layer of calcite and an iridescent interior. Its straight hinge has narrow ligament pits. The left valve is large, thick, and spirally coiled, and the right valve sits within it. Concentric ridges are found on both valves, but they are stronger on the right valve.

• **HABITAT** The growth and habits of this oyster are believed to have been similar to those of the genus *Gryphaea* (*see p.101*).

• ligament pits on hinge   *• right valve*

Typical length
12 in (30 cm)

concentric •
ridges

VOLVICERAMUS
INVOLUTUS
(J. de C. Sowerby);
Upper Chalk; Late
Cretaceous; UK.

Range L. Cretaceous	Distribution Europe, N. America	Occurrence ⊛⊛⊛⊛⊛

Order PTERIOIDA	Family AVICULOPECTINIDAE	Informal name Scallop

AVICULOPECTEN

This is a small shell, obliquely fan shaped, with a short hinge. Both valves have the posterior ear enlarged into a pointed wing, while the anterior ear is set off by a byssal notch, much deeper in the right valve. The shell is ornamented with radial ribs. In one valve the ribs increase by bifurcation, and in the other by forming intermediary ribs.

• **HABITAT** *Aviculopecten* was anchored to objects by a byssal thread.

byssal notch •

AVICULOPECTEN
TENUICOLLIS Dana;
Carboniferous; West
Australia.

Typical length
1 in (2.5 cm)

• posterior wing

Range Carb.–Permian	Distribution Worldwide	Occurrence ⊛⊛⊛⊛

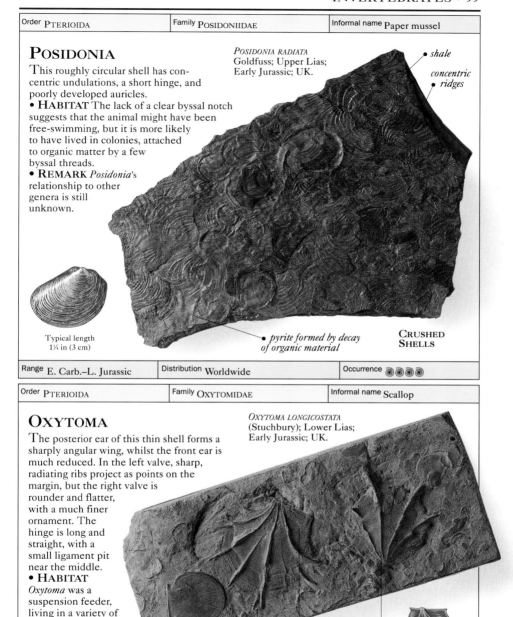

| Order PTERIOIDA | Family POSIDONIIDAE | Informal name Paper mussel |

POSIDONIA

This roughly circular shell has concentric undulations, a short hinge, and poorly developed auricles.
• **HABITAT** The lack of a clear byssal notch suggests that the animal might have been free-swimming, but it is more likely to have lived in colonies, attached to organic matter by a few byssal threads.
• **REMARK** *Posidonia*'s relationship to other genera is still unknown.

POSIDONIA RADIATA
Goldfuss; Upper Lias;
Early Jurassic; UK.

shale

concentric ridges

Typical length
1¼ in (3 cm)

pyrite formed by decay of organic material

CRUSHED SHELLS

| Range E. Carb.–L. Jurassic | Distribution Worldwide | Occurrence |

| Order PTERIOIDA | Family OXYTOMIDAE | Informal name Scallop |

OXYTOMA

The posterior ear of this thin shell forms a sharply angular wing, whilst the front ear is much reduced. In the left valve, sharp, radiating ribs project as points on the margin, but the right valve is rounder and flatter, with a much finer ornament. The hinge is long and straight, with a small ligament pit near the middle.
• **HABITAT** *Oxytoma* was a suspension feeder, living in a variety of marine habitats, and probably attached by a byssus to shell or gravel on the sea bed.

OXYTOMA LONGICOSTATA
(Stuchbury); Lower Lias;
Early Jurassic; UK.

sharp ribs on left valve

posterior ear

Typical length 1⅜ in (3.5 cm)

| Range L. Triassic–L. Cretaceous | Distribution Worldwide | Occurrence |

Order PTERIOIDA	Family PECTINIDAE	Informal name Scallop

PECTEN

CONVEX RIGHT VALVE

This large, circular shell has a convex right valve and a flattened left valve, both ornamented with broad, radiating ribs. The straight hinge has a central ligament pit, with diverging ridges on either side.
• HABITAT Scallops like *Pecten* prefer clean sand in moderately shallow waters, where they rest on the bed in self-made depressions. When necessary, they swim by opening and closing their valves.

PECTEN BEUDANTI
Basterot;
Miocene;
France.

ribs •

• ear

• hinge line

FLATTENED
LEFT VALVE

• ligament pit

• ridges

Typical length
3⅛ in (8 cm)

Range L. Eocene–Recent	Distribution Worldwide	Occurrence ◉◉◉◉◉

Order PTERIOIDA	Family PECTINIDAE	Informal name Scallop

NEITHEA

• main ribs

This is a narrow, oval shell. Its main ribs have weaker ribs between them. The right valve is convex, over-hanging the flattened left valve. There are denticles along the margin of the hinge.
• HABITAT *Neithea* lived in sand, but it may have had the ability to swim.

Typical length
1½ in (4 cm)

NEITHEA COQUANDI (Peron);
Late Cretaceous;
Tunisia.

RIGHT VALVE

beak •

LEFT VALVE

Range L. Cretaceous	Distribution Worldwide	Occurrence ◉◉◉◉

Order PTERIOIDA	Family GRYPHAEIDAE	Informal name Devil's Toenail

GRYPHAEA

This heavy shell is composed mostly of calcite. The concave right valve fits like a lid within the larger left valve, which has a narrow, inrolled beak. Internally, the single muscle scar is circular; the adult hinge has no teeth.
• **HABITAT** *Gryphaea* lived on muddy sea beds, originally cemented to a small particle of rock by its tip.
• **REMARK** The coiled shell, adapted for living in soft sediment, is popularly called the Devil's Toenail.

GRYPHAEA ARCUATA (Lamarck); Lower Lias; Early Jurassic; UK.

inrolled beak

Typical length 2¾ in (7 cm)

coarse growth ridges

TWO LEFT VALVES

Range L. Triassic–L. Jurassic	Distribution Worldwide	Occurrence

Order PTERIOIDA	Family GRYPHAEIDAE	Informal name Oyster

EXOGYRA

Both valves grow spirally. The left valve is inflated and rather weakly ribbed, with the beak coiled off to one side. The flattened right valve is ornamented by concentric frills. The left valve hinge has two groups of ridges below the beak.
• **HABITAT** *Exogyra* lived cemented to solid objects in warm seas.

EXOGYRA AFRICANA (Lamarck); Late Cretaceous; Algeria.

LEFT VALVE, TOP VIEW

concentric frills

LEFT VALVE, SIDE VIEW

beak

Typical length 2 in (5 cm)

RIGHT VALVE

Range L. Cretaceous	Distribution Worldwide	Occurrence

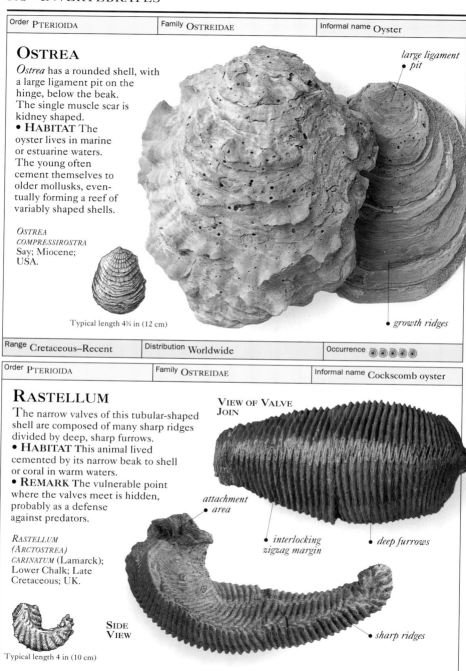

Order PTERIOIDA	Family OSTREIDAE	Informal name Oyster

OSTREA

Ostrea has a rounded shell, with a large ligament pit on the hinge, below the beak. The single muscle scar is kidney shaped.
• **HABITAT** The oyster lives in marine or estuarine waters. The young often cement themselves to older mollusks, eventually forming a reef of variably shaped shells.

OSTREA COMPRESSIROSTRA Say; Miocene; USA.

• large ligament pit

• growth ridges

Typical length 4¾ in (12 cm)

Range Cretaceous–Recent	Distribution Worldwide	Occurrence ◉◉◉◉◉

Order PTERIOIDA	Family OSTREIDAE	Informal name Cockscomb oyster

RASTELLUM

The narrow valves of this tubular-shaped shell are composed of many sharp ridges divided by deep, sharp furrows.
• **HABITAT** This animal lived cemented by its narrow beak to shell or coral in warm waters.
• **REMARK** The vulnerable point where the valves meet is hidden, probably as a defense against predators.

RASTELLUM (ARCTOSTREA) CARINATUM (Lamarck); Lower Chalk; Late Cretaceous; UK.

VIEW OF VALVE JOIN

attachment area

• *interlocking zigzag margin*

• *deep furrows*

SIDE VIEW

• *sharp ridges*

Typical length 4 in (10 cm)

Range M. Jurassic–L. Cretaceous	Distribution Worldwide	Occurrence ◉◉◉◉

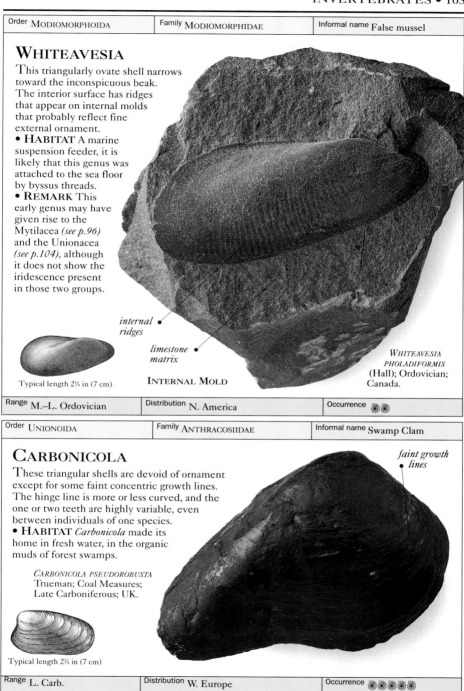

| Order MODIOMORPHOIDA | Family MODIOMORPHIDAE | Informal name False mussel |

WHITEAVESIA

This triangularly ovate shell narrows toward the inconspicuous beak. The interior surface has ridges that appear on internal molds that probably reflect fine external ornament.
• **HABITAT** A marine suspension feeder, it is likely that this genus was attached to the sea floor by byssus threads.
• **REMARK** This early genus may have given rise to the Mytilacea *(see p.96)* and the Unionacea *(see p.104)*, although it does not show the iridescence present in those two groups.

internal ridges

limestone matrix

Typical length 2¾ in (7 cm)

INTERNAL MOLD

WHITEAVESIA PHOLADIFORMIS (Hall); Ordovician; Canada.

| Range M.–L. Ordovician | Distribution N. America | Occurrence |

| Order UNIONOIDA | Family ANTHRACOSIIDAE | Informal name Swamp Clam |

CARBONICOLA

These triangular shells are devoid of ornament except for some faint concentric growth lines. The hinge line is more or less curved, and the one or two teeth are highly variable, even between individuals of one species.
• **HABITAT** *Carbonicola* made its home in fresh water, in the organic muds of forest swamps.

faint growth lines

CARBONICOLA PSEUDOROBUSTA Trueman; Coal Measures; Late Carboniferous; UK.

Typical length 2¾ in (7 cm)

| Range L. Carb. | Distribution W. Europe | Occurrence |

Order UNIONOIDA	Family UNIONIDAE	Informal name Freshwater mussel

UNIO

JOINED VALVES

This oblong to ovate shell is rather smooth with a bluish or purplish pearl interior. The middle shell layer is prismatic and covered with a thin organic layer. There are two hinge teeth situated in front of the beak, and two long teeth behind it.

• **HABITAT** This animal lives in an upright position, partly embedded in the sands, silts, and gravels of lakes and rivers. Its larvae burrow under the scales of fish, but drop off later, ensuring a wide dispersal.

• *ligament*

beak •

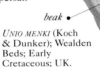

UNIO MENKI (Koch & Dunker); Wealden Beds; Early Cretaceous; UK.

Typical length 3¼ in (8 cm)

• *coarse growth lines*

Range Triassic–Recent	Distribution Worldwide	Occurrence 🌑🌑🌑🌑

Order TRIGONIOIDA	Family TRIGONIIDAE	Informal name Brooch clam

MYOPHORELLA

SHELLS IN SANDSTONE

The thick valves of *Myophorella* are semicircular, and each is divided into two parts: the main area, with obliquely concentric rows of tubercles, and the smaller posterior slope (the escutcheon), which is relatively smooth. Internally the shells are iridescent. Two corrugated and diverging teeth, suspended below the beak of the right valve, fit into sockets in the left valve.

• **HABITAT** This clam flourished in the deep seas of the Mesozoic Era.

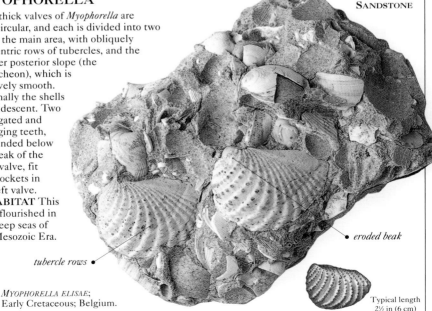

tubercle rows •

MYOPHORELLA ELISAE; Early Cretaceous; Belgium.

• *eroded beak*

Typical length 2½ in (6 cm)

Range E. Jurassic–E. Cretaceous	Distribution Worldwide	Occurrence 🌑🌑🌑🌑🌑

| Order VENEROIDA | Family FIMBRIIDAE | Informal name Basket shell |

FIMBRIA

This is a tumid, ovate shell. The ornament is netted, with stronger concentric ridges at first, but file-like radial ribs then thicken at both ends of the valve. The whole shell margin is crenulated on the inside by a row of denticles. There are two main teeth below the beak, and two lateral teeth in each valve.
• **HABITAT** This suspension feeder lives in shallow, warm seas.

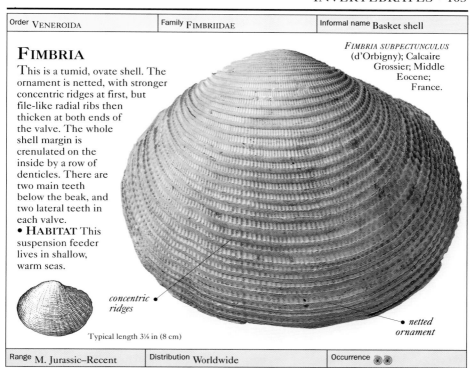

FIMBRIA SUBPECTUNCULUS (d'Orbigny); Calcaire Grossier; Middle Eocene; France.

concentric ridges •

• *netted ornament*

Typical length 3⅛ in (8 cm)

| Range M. Jurassic–Recent | Distribution Worldwide | Occurrence 🔘🔘 |

| Order VENEROIDA | Family CHAMIDAE | Informal name Jewel-box shell |

CHAMA

The left valve of this shell is thick and convex, cemented to the substrate by the spiral beak. The right valve may show a fine microsculpture. Both valves have concentric frills, bearing fragile grooved spines. The hinge is degenerate with one or two large crudely shaped teeth, which interlock.
• **HABITAT** *Chama* inhabits sandy areas in warm, shallow seas, attached to rocks, coral, or shells.
• **REMARK** The spines attract the growth of algae and other animals, which then act as a form of camouflage.

spiral beak •

CHAMA CALCARATA Lamarck; Calcaire Grossier; Middle Eocene; France.

Typical length 1⅜ in (3.5 cm)

• *wide frills*

• *grooved spine*

| Range Paleocene–Recent | Distribution Tropics, Europe, N. America | Occurrence 🔘🔘🔘 |

| Order VENEROIDA | Family CARDITIDAE | Informal name False cockle |

VENERICOR

This large, thick, oval to triangular shell has a prominent beak. When very young, it has narrow, radial ribs, which may be armed with small tubercles. These soon become smooth, flat ribbons separated by shallow grooves. In each valve, the wide, triangular hinge plate bears three massive teeth. The inner shell margin is marked by a row of flat denticles.
• **HABITAT** *Venericor* lived in warm, shallow waters, burrowing into the sand or silt.
• **REMARK** Paired valves in life position are found in large numbers in some strata.

denticles •

muscle scar •

• *hinge plate*

beak •

• *broad, flat ribs*

VENERICOR PLANICOSTA (Lamarck); Earnley Formation; Middle Eocene; UK.

Typical length
3 in (7.5 cm)

| Range Paleocene–Eocene | Distribution Europe, N. America | Occurrence ◉◉◉◉ |

| Order VENEROIDA | Family ASTARTIDAE | Informal name Astarte clam |

ASTARTE

This is a thick shell with regular concentric ridges. The hinge is thick, with three main teeth in the right valve and two in the left.
• **HABITAT** *Astarte* burrows into mud, sand, or gravel offshore, to considerable depths. It is most characteristic of the Boreal and Arctic regions.
• **REMARK** Geologists regard it as a good indicator of cold conditions.

concentric ridges •

ASTARTE SHELLS IN LIMESTONE

ASTARTE ELEGANS J. de C. Sowerby; Inferior Oolite; Middle Jurassic; UK.

Typical length
¾ in (2 cm)

| Range Jurassic–Recent | Distribution Worldwide | Occurrence ◉◉◉◉◉ |

Order VENEROIDA	Family CRASSATELLIDAE	Informal name Clam

CRASSATELLA

This is a solid rectangular shell, with two
V-shaped cardinal teeth in the left valve
and one in the right, flanked by elongate
lateral teeth. There are two muscle scars,
which are joined by a roundly curved
pallial line. The margins of the valves are
finely crenulated.
• HABITAT *Crassatella* was common in
warm, shallow seas and lived by
burrowing into soft substrates.
• REMARK Species of this genus evolved
relatively rapidly.

*hole made by
predator*

CRASSATELLA LAMELLOSA
Lamarck; Calcaire Grossier;
Middle Eocene; France.

muscle scars

lateral tooth

cardinal teeth

Typical length
¾ in (2 cm)

Range M. Cretaceous–Miocene	Distribution Europe, N. America	Occurrence ◉◉◉◉◉

Order VENEROIDA	Family CARDINIIDAE	Informal name Clam

CARDINIA

The valves of *Cardinia* are ornamented with irregular concentric
bands. There is a triangular
area, which is angled
inward in front of the
beak, deeply under-
cutting it. The lateral
hinge teeth are thick
and dominant.
• HABITAT This
appears to have
been a marine genus,
burrowing into sands,
silts, and muds in
warm, shallow waters.

beak

*irregular
concentric bands*

CARDINIA OVALIS
(Stuchbury); Lower Lias;
Early Jurassic; UK.

Typical length
⅝ in (1.7 cm)

Range L. Triassic–E. Jurassic	Distribution Worldwide	Occurrence ◉◉

Order VENEROIDA	Family CARDIIDAE	Informal name Cockle

ACROSTERIGMA

Smooth, radial ribs separated by grooves ornament this elliptical shell. The hinge plate is small and sharply curved. In the middle of the hinge of the left valve are two small diverging teeth, which meet one narrow tooth in the right valve. The front end of the hinge is extended to form one or two lateral teeth. On the other side is a raised plate (the nymph), where the ligament is attached. The inside edges of both valves are sharply furrowed.
• **HABITAT** This creature burrows into the sands, silts, and muds of shallow tropical seas.

A RANGE OF SHELL SIZES

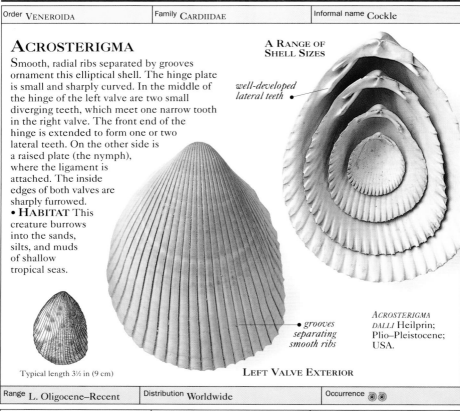

well-developed lateral teeth •

• *grooves separating smooth ribs*

ACROSTERIGMA DALLI Heilprin; Plio–Pleistocene; USA.

Typical length 3½ in (9 cm)

LEFT VALVE EXTERIOR

Range L. Oligocene–Recent	Distribution Worldwide	Occurrence

Order VENEROIDA	Family ARCTICIDAE	Informal name Iceland cockle

ARCTICA

This is a thick, smooth shell, ovate to heart shaped, with the beak turned toward the shorter anterior end. In each valve the hinge has three teeth below the beak, and a long lateral tooth behind. The hinge plate in front of the cardinal teeth is pitted and crenulated.
• **HABITAT** This cockle rests on both firm and muddy sand, from the intertidal zone down to considerable depths.
• **REMARK** The distribution of the genus indicates cold-water conditions. As fossils, they are regularly associated with other cold-water mollusks.

beak •

ARCTICA UMBONARIA (Lamarck); Pliocene; Italy.

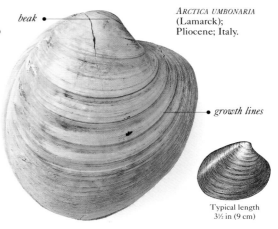

• *growth lines*

Typical length 3½ in (9 cm)

Range L. Cretaceous–Recent	Distribution Europe, N. America	Occurrence

| Order VENEROIDA | Family CORBICULIDAE | Informal name Marsh clam |

POLYMESODA

Polymesoda has an oval shell, with weak concentric growth ridges and wrinkles. There are three cardinal teeth below the beak and strong elongate lateral teeth. Some fossils still show radiating color bands.
• **HABITAT** This clam lives in tidal marshes and brackish lagoons in tropical and subtropical regions.
• **REMARK** European fossils differ from the American forms in details of the teeth and pallial line.

SLAB WITH SHELLS

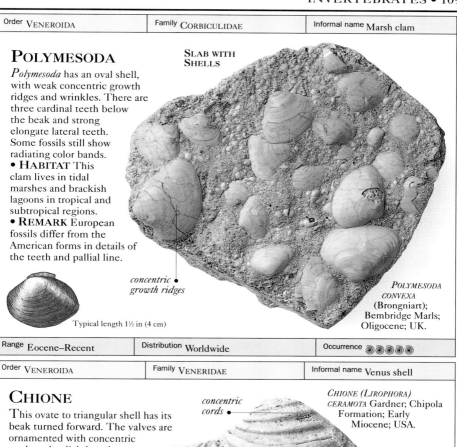

concentric
growth ridges

*POLYMESODA
CONVEXA*
(Brongniart);
Bembridge Marls;
Oligocene; UK.

Typical length 1½ in (4 cm)

| Range Eocene–Recent | Distribution Worldwide | Occurrence ◉◉◉◉◉ |

| Order VENEROIDA | Family VENERIDAE | Informal name Venus shell |

CHIONE

This ovate to triangular shell has its beak turned forward. The valves are ornamented with concentric cords and radial threads, and there are three diverging hinge teeth in each valve. Internally, the muscle scars are joined by the pallial line which has a short embayment in front of the rear scar.
• **HABITAT** This clam burrows below the sand in shallow seas.

concentric
cords

*CHIONE (LIROPHORA)
CERAMOTA* Gardner; Chipola
Formation; Early
Miocene; USA.

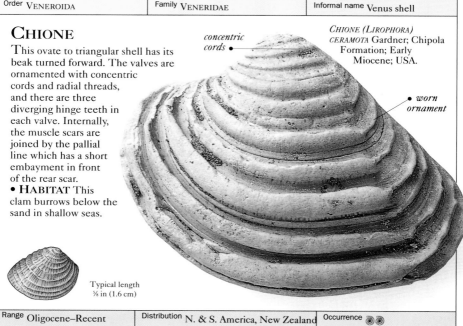

• *worn
ornament*

Typical length
⅝ in (1.6 cm)

| Range Oligocene–Recent | Distribution N. & S. America, New Zealand | Occurrence ◉◉ |

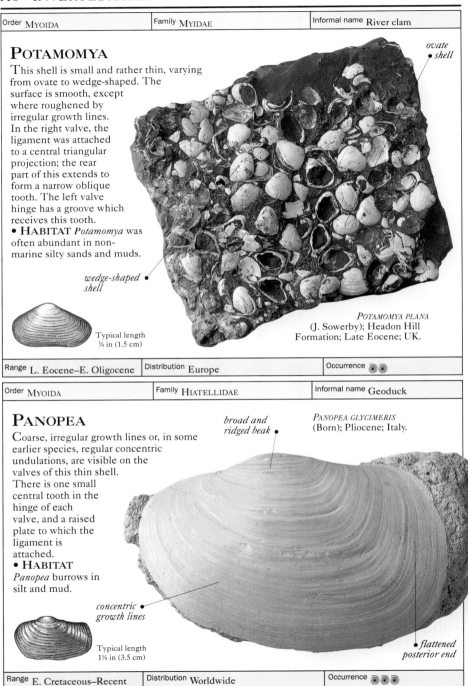

Order MYOIDA	Family MYIDAE	Informal name River clam

POTAMOMYA

This shell is small and rather thin, varying from ovate to wedge-shaped. The surface is smooth, except where roughened by irregular growth lines. In the right valve, the ligament was attached to a central triangular projection; the rear part of this extends to form a narrow oblique tooth. The left valve hinge has a groove which receives this tooth.

• **HABITAT** *Potamomya* was often abundant in non-marine silty sands and muds.

ovate • shell

wedge-shaped • shell

Typical length
⅗ in (1.5 cm)

POTAMOMYA PLANA
(J. Sowerby); Headon Hill
Formation; Late Eocene; UK.

Range L. Eocene–E. Oligocene	Distribution Europe	Occurrence 🔘🔘

Order MYOIDA	Family HIATELLIDAE	Informal name Geoduck

PANOPEA

Coarse, irregular growth lines or, in some earlier species, regular concentric undulations, are visible on the valves of this thin shell. There is one small central tooth in the hinge of each valve, and a raised plate to which the ligament is attached.

• **HABITAT** *Panopea* burrows in silt and mud.

broad and ridged beak •

PANOPEA GLYCIMERIS
(Born); Pliocene; Italy.

concentric • growth lines

• flattened posterior end

Typical length
1⅜ in (3.5 cm)

Range E. Cretaceous–Recent	Distribution Worldwide	Occurrence 🔘🔘🔘

| Order MYOIDA | Family PHOLADIDAE | Informal name Shipworm |

TEREDINA

Teredina was equipped with two small, inflated, triangular valves, cemented to a tube. When young, the two valves gaped widely both at front and rear, but later a callum was secreted to cover the anterior gape. As the animal grew, it enlarged its tube in stages.
• **HABITAT** With the use of its valves, this animal bored its way into wood submerged in fresh to brackish water.

CROSS-SECTION OF LOG

DETAIL

TEREDINA PERSONATA (Lamarck); London Clay Formation; Early Eocene; UK.

Overall length 2 in (5 cm)

• *animals bore toward the middle*

| Range L. Cretaceous–M. Miocene | Distribution Europe | Occurrence |

| Order MYOIDA | Family TEREDINIDAE | Informal name Shipworm |

TEREDO

The shipworm *Teredo* has serrated, convex, T-shaped valves. The hinge is a long, slender protuberance to which the muscle is attached.
• **HABITAT** It lives gregariously in floating and sunken timber.

A FOSSIL LOG IN CLAY

TEREDO cf. *ANTENAUTAE* J. Sowerby; London Clay Formation; Early Eocene; UK.

• *tubes deviate to avoid others*

pyrite crystals infill •

animals bore along grain of wood •

• *small outer end containing pallets*

Tube length 4 in (10 cm)

| Range Eocene–Recent | Distribution Worldwide | Occurrence |

Order HIPPURITOIDA	Family HIPPURITIDAE	Informal name Rudist

HIPPURITES

This genus belongs to an extraordinary group of complex bivalves known as rudists. One valve is conical in shape, enlarging rapidly from the base, where it is cemented to the substrate. The other valve is more or less flat, fitting like a small lid, with two long teeth descending from its inner surface and two bosses where the muscles were attached. The outside of the cone is corrugated by longitudinal ribs. Internally, the walls are folded, forming vertical pillars, a narrow tooth, and sockets to receive the teeth in the other valve. The structure of the shell allows water to pass through.
• HABITAT *Hippurites* lived near corals or on firm sand in warm seas. Although some species were solitary, others were gregarious and may have grouped together to form reefs.

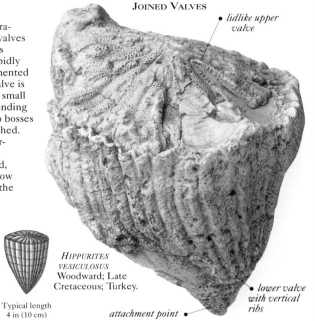

JOINED VALVES

• *lidlike upper valve*

HIPPURITES VESICULOSUS Woodward; Late Cretaceous; Turkey.

Typical length 4 in (10 cm)

attachment point •

• *lower valve with vertical ribs*

Range L. Cretaceous	Distribution Europe, N.E. Africa, USA, Asia	Occurrence ◉◉◉◉◉

Order PHOLADOMYOIDA	Family GRAMMYSIIDAE	Informal name False razor shell

SOLENOMORPHA

A fairly long, narrow shell, *Solenomorpha* is widest near the front, where the beak is situated, but then tapers gently behind. The paired valves, which have a slight gape at the posterior end, are smooth, and have concentric growth lines.
• HABITAT *Solenomorpha* burrowed in soft sediments.

• *tapering rear end*

SOLENOMORPHA MINOR (McCoy); Carboniferous Limestone; Early Carboniferous; UK.

INTERNAL MOLD

Typical length ¾ in (1.8 cm)

Range E. Devonian–L. Permian	Distribution Worldwide	Occurrence ◉◉◉

Order PHOLADOMYOIDA	Family PHOLADOMYIDAE	Informal name Paper clam

PHOLADOMYA

The surface of this shell is roughened by numerous minute pustules, and the radial ribs, crossed by weaker concentric ridges, are strongest in the mid-valve. The hinge is thin, without teeth. The outer shell generally dissolves away, leaving a pearly film around the shell's internal mold. The interior is iridescent.

• HABITAT *Pholadomya* inhabited shallow seas, buried in sand or mud, but surviving species live in deep water. Fossils can be found in life position, with the valves closed.

PHOLADOMYA AMBIGUA (J. Sowerby); Middle Lias; Early Jurassic; UK.

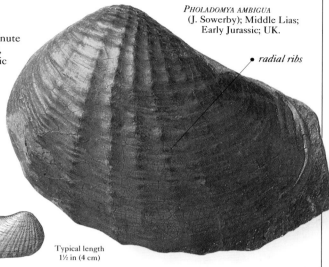

• *radial ribs*

Typical length 1½ in (4 cm)

Range L. Triassic–Recent	Distribution Worldwide	Occurrence ⬤⬤⬤⬤⬤

Order PHOLADOMYOIDA	Family PHOLADOMYIDAE	Informal name Clam

WILKINGIA

This is a thin shell, with an iridescent interior. The beaks are placed close to the front of the shell, which has a long, rounded posterior end. The valves have strong, concentric undulations, usually stronger in the middle. The ends of the valves, which are almost smooth in some species, show radial rows of very fine pustules. The hinge line is without teeth, but has a short ridge to hold the ligament.

• HABITAT It burrowed in the soft sediments of shallow seas.

• *muscle scar*

strongly ridged • *area*

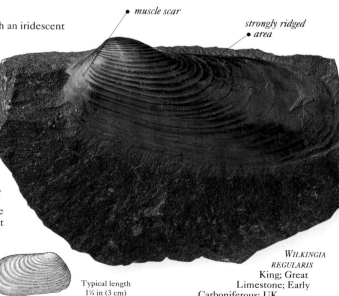

WILKINGIA REGULARIS King; Great Limestone; Early Carboniferous; UK.

Typical length 1¼ in (3 cm)

Range E. Carb.–Permian	Distribution Worldwide	Occurrence ⬤⬤⬤

SCAPHOPODS AND CHITONS

T HE SCAPHOPOD SHELL is a tapering tube, open at both ends, with concentric ornament or longitudinal ribs. The larger end contains the animal's head and foot and is buried in the sediment; the smaller end is often notched and is regularly discarded as the animal grows. Chitons have a powerful foot for gripping hard surfaces, covered by a shell of eight overlapping valves held in place by a scaly or spiny girdle. The valves contain secretory and sense organs, which reach the surface as small pores.

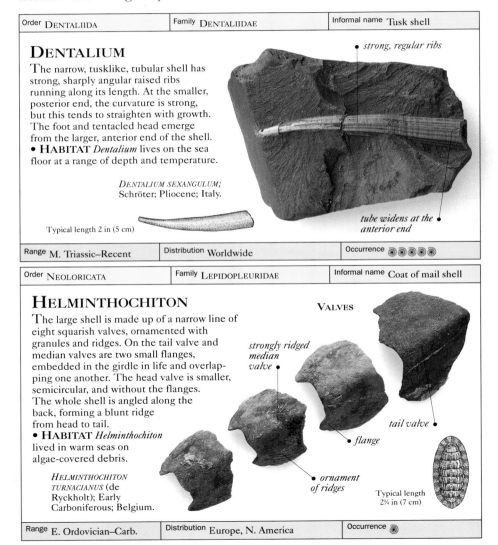

Order DENTALIIDA	Family DENTALIIDAE	Informal name Tusk shell

DENTALIUM

The narrow, tusklike, tubular shell has strong, sharply angular raised ribs running along its length. At the smaller, posterior end, the curvature is strong, but this tends to straighten with growth. The foot and tentacled head emerge from the larger, anterior end of the shell.
• HABITAT *Dentalium* lives on the sea floor at a range of depth and temperature.

strong, regular ribs

DENTALIUM SEXANGULUM;
Schröter; Pliocene; Italy.

tube widens at the anterior end

Typical length 2 in (5 cm)

Range M. Triassic–Recent	Distribution Worldwide	Occurrence ⚬⚬⚬⚬⚬

Order NEOLORICATA	Family LEPIDOPLEURIDAE	Informal name Coat of mail shell

HELMINTHOCHITON

The large shell is made up of a narrow line of eight squarish valves, ornamented with granules and ridges. On the tail valve and median valves are two small flanges, embedded in the girdle in life and overlapping one another. The head valve is smaller, semicircular, and without the flanges. The whole shell is angled along the back, forming a blunt ridge from head to tail.
• HABITAT *Helminthochiton* lived in warm seas on algae-covered debris.

HELMINTHOCHITON TURNACIANUS (de Ryckholt); Early Carboniferous; Belgium.

VALVES

strongly ridged median valve

tail valve

flange

ornament of ridges

Typical length 2¾ in (7 cm)

Range E. Ordovician–Carb.	Distribution Europe, N. America	Occurrence ⚬

GASTROPODS

GASTROPODS ARE the largest, most successful, class of mollusks; They have been able to exploit a wide variety of marine, freshwater, and land habitats. They have a head with eyes and a mouth, a flattened foot for crawling, and viscera that are generally coiled and carried in a spiral shell. A few groups cease the coiling at some stage, and some have abandoned the shell altogether. Shells are composed of calcium carbonate, usually in the form of aragonite, but sometimes in layers of calcite. An inner nacreous layer is characteristic of some more primitive forms, but the organic outer coat of many living gastropods is usually lost in fossils. Some families have an inhalant siphon, emerging through a channel in the aperture.

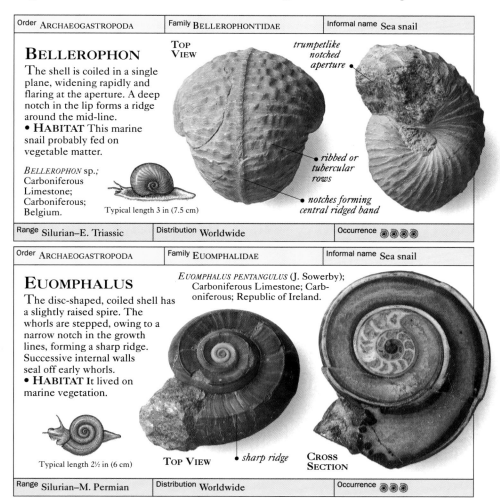

Order ARCHAEOGASTROPODA	Family BELLEROPHONTIDAE	Informal name Sea snail

BELLEROPHON

The shell is coiled in a single plane, widening rapidly and flaring at the aperture. A deep notch in the lip forms a ridge around the mid-line.
• **HABITAT** This marine snail probably fed on vegetable matter.

BELLEROPHON sp.;
Carboniferous
Limestone;
Carboniferous;
Belgium.

TOP VIEW

trumpetlike notched aperture

ribbed or tubercular rows

notches forming central ridged band

Typical length 3 in (7.5 cm)

Range Silurian–E. Triassic	Distribution Worldwide	Occurrence

Order ARCHAEOGASTROPODA	Family EUOMPHALIDAE	Informal name Sea snail

EUOMPHALUS

The disc-shaped, coiled shell has a slightly raised spire. The whorls are stepped, owing to a narrow notch in the growth lines, forming a sharp ridge. Successive internal walls seal off early whorls.
• **HABITAT** It lived on marine vegetation.

EUOMPHALUS PENTANGULUS (J. Sowerby);
Carboniferous Limestone; Carboniferous; Republic of Ireland.

Typical length 2½ in (6 cm)

TOP VIEW

sharp ridge

CROSS SECTION

Range Silurian–M. Permian	Distribution Worldwide	Occurrence

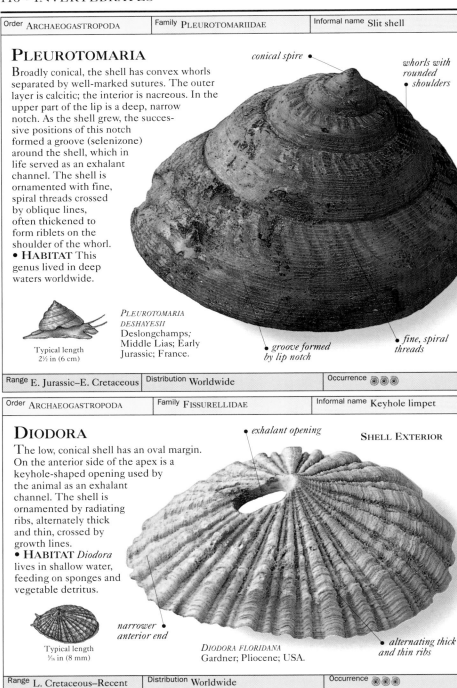

Order ARCHAEOGASTROPODA	Family PLEUROTOMARIIDAE	Informal name Slit shell

PLEUROTOMARIA

Broadly conical, the shell has convex whorls separated by well-marked sutures. The outer layer is calcitic; the interior is nacreous. In the upper part of the lip is a deep, narrow notch. As the shell grew, the successive positions of this notch formed a groove (selenizone) around the shell, which in life served as an exhalant channel. The shell is ornamented with fine, spiral threads crossed by oblique lines, often thickened to form riblets on the shoulder of the whorl.
• **HABITAT** This genus lived in deep waters worldwide.

conical spire

whorls with rounded shoulders

PLEUROTOMARIA DESHAYESII Deslongchamps; Middle Lias; Early Jurassic; France.

Typical length
2½ in (6 cm)

groove formed by lip notch

fine, spiral threads

Range E. Jurassic–E. Cretaceous	Distribution Worldwide	Occurrence

Order ARCHAEOGASTROPODA	Family FISSURELLIDAE	Informal name Keyhole limpet

DIODORA

The low, conical shell has an oval margin. On the anterior side of the apex is a keyhole-shaped opening used by the animal as an exhalant channel. The shell is ornamented by radiating ribs, alternately thick and thin, crossed by growth lines.
• **HABITAT** *Diodora* lives in shallow water, feeding on sponges and vegetable detritus.

exhalant opening

SHELL EXTERIOR

narrower anterior end

Typical length
5/16 in (8 mm)

DIODORA FLORIDANA Gardner; Pliocene; USA.

alternating thick and thin ribs

Range L. Cretaceous–Recent	Distribution Worldwide	Occurrence

| Order ARCHAEOGASTROPODA | Family SYMMETROCAPULIDAE | Informal name Cap shell |

SYMMETROCAPULUS

This limpet had a large, cap-shaped shell with an oval margin, ornamented with numerous narrow, radiating ribs, interrupted by irregular, concentric folds. The first two small whorls are smooth, turned forward, and dextrally coiled, a little to the left of the shell's highest point.
• HABITAT
This marine limpet was adapted for grazing on rock surfaces.

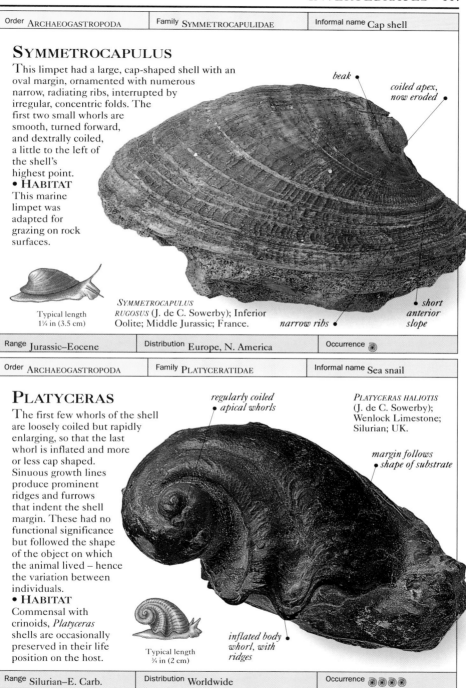

beak •

coiled apex, now eroded •

• *short anterior slope*

narrow ribs •

SYMMETROCAPULUS RUGOSUS (J. de C. Sowerby); Inferior Oolite; Middle Jurassic; France.

Typical length
1¼ in (3.5 cm)

| Range Jurassic–Eocene | Distribution Europe, N. America | Occurrence |

| Order ARCHAEOGASTROPODA | Family PLATYCERATIDAE | Informal name Sea snail |

PLATYCERAS

The first few whorls of the shell are loosely coiled but rapidly enlarging, so that the last whorl is inflated and more or less cap shaped. Sinuous growth lines produce prominent ridges and furrows that indent the shell margin. These had no functional significance but followed the shape of the object on which the animal lived – hence the variation between individuals.
• HABITAT
Commensal with crinoids, *Platyceras* shells are occasionally preserved in their life position on the host.

regularly coiled apical whorls •

PLATYCERAS HALIOTIS (J. de C. Sowerby); Wenlock Limestone; Silurian; UK.

margin follows shape of substrate •

inflated body whorl, with ridges

Typical length
¾ in (2 cm)

| Range Silurian–E. Carb. | Distribution Worldwide | Occurrence |

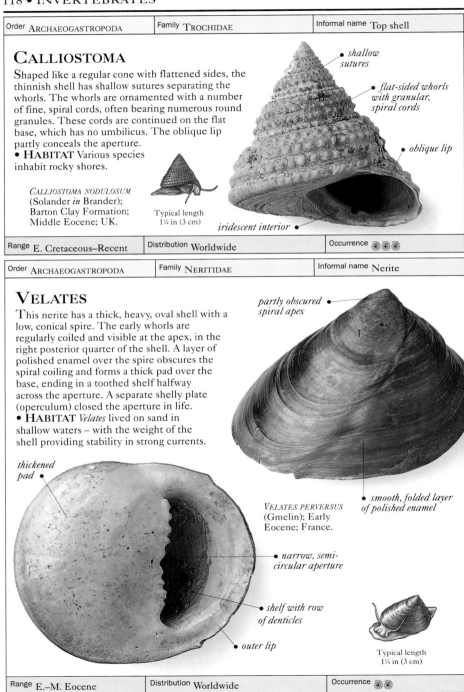

Order ARCHAEOGASTROPODA	Family TROCHIDAE	Informal name Top shell

CALLIOSTOMA

Shaped like a regular cone with flattened sides, the thinnish shell has shallow sutures separating the whorls. The whorls are ornamented with a number of fine, spiral cords, often bearing numerous round granules. These cords are continued on the flat base, which has no umbilicus. The oblique lip partly conceals the aperture.
• **HABITAT** Various species inhabit rocky shores.

shallow sutures

flat-sided whorls with granular, spiral cords

oblique lip

CALLIOSTOMA NODULOSUM (Solander *in* Brander); Barton Clay Formation; Middle Eocene; UK.

Typical length 1¼ in (3 cm)

iridescent interior

Range E. Cretaceous–Recent	Distribution Worldwide	Occurrence

Order ARCHAEOGASTROPODA	Family NERITIDAE	Informal name Nerite

VELATES

This nerite has a thick, heavy, oval shell with a low, conical spire. The early whorls are regularly coiled and visible at the apex, in the right posterior quarter of the shell. A layer of polished enamel over the spire obscures the spiral coiling and forms a thick pad over the base, ending in a toothed shelf halfway across the aperture. A separate shelly plate (operculum) closed the aperture in life.
• **HABITAT** *Velates* lived on sand in shallow waters – with the weight of the shell providing stability in strong currents.

partly obscured spiral apex

thickened pad

smooth, folded layer of polished enamel

VELATES PERVERSUS (Gmelin); Early Eocene; France.

narrow, semi-circular aperture

shelf with row of denticles

outer lip

Typical length 1¼ in (3 cm)

Range E.–M. Eocene	Distribution Worldwide	Occurrence

Order MESOGASTROPODA	Family VIVIPARIDAE	Informal name Pond snail

VIVIPARUS

The small to medium-size, thin, brittle shell has evenly rounded whorls, which are generally convex and smooth, crossed by faint growth lines. The lip is vertical in profile and the aperture oval with a continuous margin, slightly narrowed at the top. This margin almost hides the narrow umbilicus. In life, the aperture is closed by a flexible, horny plate.
• **HABITAT** *Viviparus* lives in freshwater lakes, swamps, and slow rivers.
• **REMARK** Because they can tolerate only the slightest degree of salinity, shells of *Viviparus* are an excellent indicator of nonmarine conditions in the fossil record.

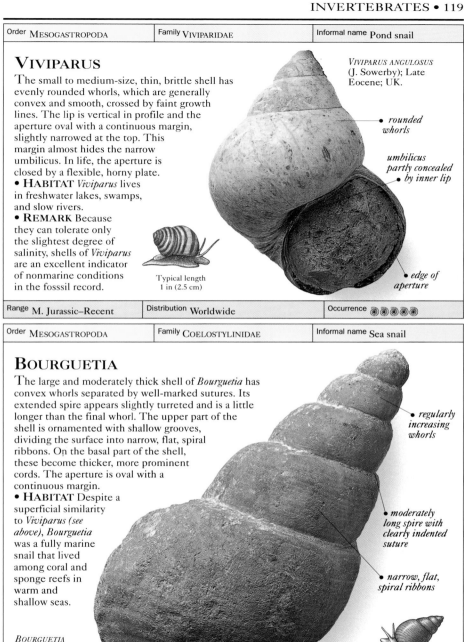

VIVIPARUS ANGULOSUS (J. Sowerby); Late Eocene; UK.

• *rounded whorls*

umbilicus partly concealed
• *by inner lip*

• *edge of aperture*

Typical length
1 in (2.5 cm)

Range M. Jurassic–Recent	Distribution Worldwide	Occurrence 🔴🔴🔴🔴🔴

Order MESOGASTROPODA	Family COELOSTYLINIDAE	Informal name Sea snail

BOURGUETIA

The large and moderately thick shell of *Bourguetia* has convex whorls separated by well-marked sutures. Its extended spire appears slightly turreted and is a little longer than the final whorl. The upper part of the shell is ornamented with shallow grooves, dividing the surface into narrow, flat, spiral ribbons. On the basal part of the shell, these become thicker, more prominent cords. The aperture is oval with a continuous margin.
• **HABITAT** Despite a superficial similarity to *Viviparus (see above)*, *Bourguetia* was a fully marine snail that lived among coral and sponge reefs in warm and shallow seas.

BOURGUETIA SAEMANNI (Oppel); Osmington Oolite; Middle Jurassic; UK.

• *regularly increasing whorls*

• *moderately long spire with clearly indented suture*

• *narrow, flat, spiral ribbons*

• *more prominent cords on base*

Typical length
4½ in (11 cm)

Range M. Triassic–L. Jurassic	Distribution Europe, New Zealand	Occurrence 🔴🔴

| Order MESOGASTROPODA | Family POTAMIDIDAE | Informal name Marsh creeper |

BROTIA

shelly plug in apex •

Brotia has a narrow, elongate, and turreted shell. When no longer in use, juvenile whorls are sealed off with a plug and then discarded or eroded away. The variable ornament usually consists of a few sharp, spiral cords broken up by the low, oblique ribs. The uppermost cord has the most prominent denticles and sets off the smooth concave shoulder. There is a broad, V-shaped embayment high on the lip and a weak channel at the base of the aperture.
• **HABITAT** *Brotia* feeds on detritus in the mud of warm, brackish lagoons.

• *sharp, oblique ribs*

• *denticulate shoulder cord*

BROTIA MELANOIDES (J. de C. Sowerby); Woolwich Beds; Paleocene; UK.

• *V-shaped growth lines showing former positions of lip*

broad, shallow • *channel*

Typical length 1½ in (4 cm)

| Range Paleocene–Recent | Distribution Europe, Asia | Occurrence ◉◉◉ |

| Order MESOGASTROPODA | Family TURRITELLIDAE | Informal name Turritella |

ARCHIMEDIELLA

plugged apex •

The shell of *Archimediella* is a narrow, elongate cone with flattened sides. Whorls increase in size slowly, each one slightly overhanging the next. The tip of the spire is often sealed off and discarded, as in *Brotia*. The few distinct spiral cords on the early whorls increase in number as the shell grows. The aperture is nearly square, with a thin lip, often showing signs of breakage.
• **HABITAT** *Archimediella* is a suspension feeder, usually abundant in shallow off-shore waters.

• *whorls overhang the suture*

ARCHIMEDIELLA PONTONI (Mansfield); Pliocene; USA.

• *thin lip*

• *square aperture with no channel at base*

Typical length 2½ in (6 cm)

| Range L. Eocene–Recent | Distribution Worldwide | Occurrence ◉◉◉◉◉ |

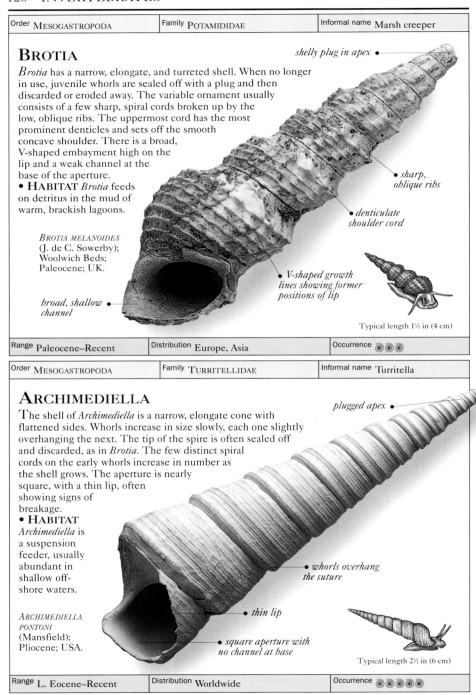

Order MESOGASTROPODA	Family CAMPANILIDAE	Informal name Giant cerith

CAMPANILE

A giant among gastropods, the shell of *Campanile* can reach a length of 24 in (60 cm), and if this could be uncoiled, it would make a tube more than 10 ft (3 m) long. There may be more than 30 whorls constructed in the animal's lifetime, but the earlier ones are backfilled with shell once they have been evacuated and are periodically lost by abrasion, leaving the apex sealed. Early whorls are turreted by an upper row of tubercles, with finer cords below. On the last few whorls, the ornament deteriorates, leaving a single row of blunt knobs. The large, flared aperture is developed only on fully adult shells. The central pillar (columella) is strengthened by two encircling ridges that are obsolete at the aperture but can be seen clearly when the shell is broken. A calcified outer layer is covered with rows of small pits.

• **HABITAT** *Campanile* feeds on algae on sandy bottoms in very shallow, warm seas. The tip of the heavy shell trails behind it as it crawls, eventually wearing flat on one side.

• **REMARK** Only a single species survives today, in the shallow coastal waters off Australia.

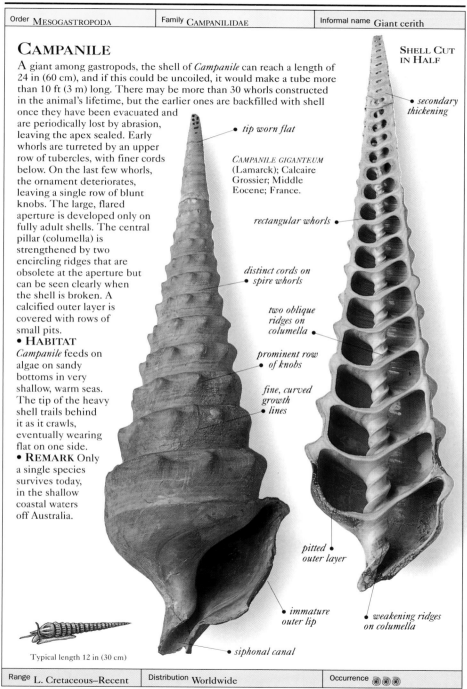

SHELL CUT IN HALF

• *secondary thickening*

• *tip worn flat*

CAMPANILE GIGANTEUM (Lamarck); Calcaire Grossier; Middle Eocene; France.

rectangular whorls •

distinct cords on • *spire whorls*

two oblique ridges on columella •

prominent row • *of knobs*

fine, curved growth • *lines*

pitted • *outer layer*

immature outer lip

weakening ridges on columella

Typical length 12 in (30 cm)

• *siphonal canal*

Range L. Cretaceous–Recent	Distribution Worldwide	Occurrence ◉ ◉ ◉

Order MESOGASTROPODA	Family APORRHAIDAE	Informal name Pelican's foot

TESSAROLAX

The small, biconical, ridged shell of *Tessarolax* was much enlarged by having the extremities drawn out into four slender, and delicate, curved spines. The bases of these are connected by an outgrowth of the lip, like the web of a duck's foot.
• **HABITAT** This creature was probably a detritus feeder, living on muddy sand in moderately deep water.
• **REMARK** The spines may have helped prevent the shell sinking into the substrate.

spine joined to spire

curved basal spine

lip enlarged with two labial spines

TESSAROLAX FITTONI (Forbes); Lower Greensand; Early Cretaceous; UK.

Typical length 2½ in (6 cm)

Range Cretaceous	Distribution Worldwide	Occurrence

Order MESOGASTROPODA	Family STRUTHIOLARIIDAE	Informal name Ostrich foot

STRUTHIOLARIA

This sturdy, medium-size mollusk has a proportionately large body whorl and a turreted spire. Distinct sinuous lines mark the positions of the lip during growth. When adult, both the lip and the inner margins of the aperture are thickened with enamel, spreading to form a pad. Spiral cords often ornament the whole shell, with a series of ribs or nodes on the whorl shoulder. Some species, however, are smooth and polished.
• **HABITAT** This genus feeds on algal detritus in shallow waters.

stepped spire whorls with deep sutures

growth lines following lip profile

aperture enameled and thickened into a pad

Typical length 1½ in (4 cm)

STRUTHIOLARIA (*STRUTHIOLARIELLA*) *AMEHINOI* Ihering; Santa Cruz Formation; Eocene/ Oligocene; Argentina.

Range Paleocene–Recent	Distribution Australasia, S. America	Occurrence

| Order MESOGASTROPODA | Family STROMBIDAE | Informal name Beak shell |

RIMELLA

The elongate shell of *Rimella* had gently convex whorls, ornamented with numerous sharp ribs. The spiral sculpture consists of close cords, largely obsolete in some species. The aperture is narrow and lens shaped, and the last whorl tapers down to a narrow rostrum, separated from the lip by a distinct notch. When adult, a long, narrow channel was secreted from the upper corner of the aperture to the apical area, where it was usually bent round. As this channel was too narrow to accommodate the syphon, its function is unclear.
• HABITAT *Rimella* was probably a herbivorous snail that lived in the muds and sands of warm, shallow seas.

RIMELLA FISSURELLA
(Linnaeus); Calcaire
Grossier; Middle
Eocene; France.

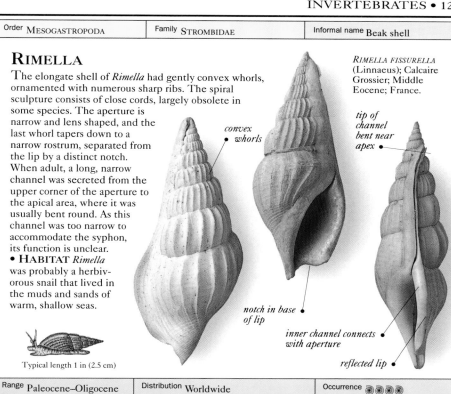

convex whorls

tip of channel bent near apex

notch in base of lip

inner channel connects with aperture

reflected lip

Typical length 1 in (2.5 cm)

| Range Paleocene–Oligocene | Distribution Worldwide | Occurrence ⊛⊛⊛⊛ |

| Order MESOGASTROPODA | Family HIPPONICIDAE | Informal name Hoof shell |

HIPPONIX

The small to medium-size caplike shell tends to be rather variable in shape. The juvenile shell is smooth and coiled slightly to the right of the apex but is soon worn away, leaving a blunt point. The adult shell expands rapidly to form a low cone with an extended beak often overhanging the rear shell margin. It is ornamented with close, fine, radiating ridges.
• HABITAT *Hipponix* lives on other shells and corals in warm, shallow seas, feeding on particles in suspension.

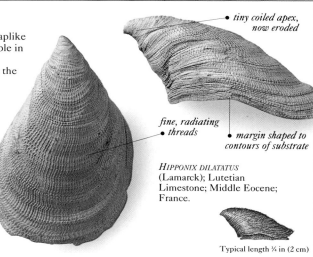

tiny coiled apex, now eroded

fine, radiating threads

margin shaped to contours of substrate

HIPPONIX DILATATUS
(Lamarck); Lutetian
Limestone; Middle Eocene;
France.

Typical length ¾ in (2 cm)

| Range L. Cretaceous–Recent | Distribution Worldwide | Occurrence ⊛⊛⊛ |

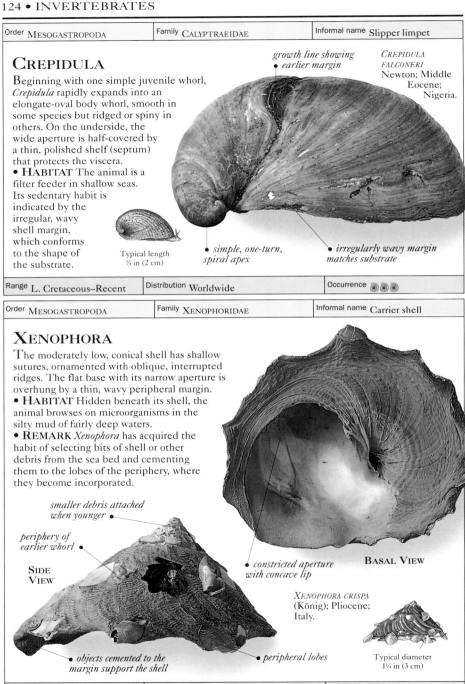

Order MESOGASTROPODA	Family CALYPTRAEIDAE	Informal name Slipper limpet

CREPIDULA

Beginning with one simple juvenile whorl, *Crepidula* rapidly expands into an elongate-oval body whorl, smooth in some species but ridged or spiny in others. On the underside, the wide aperture is half-covered by a thin, polished shelf (septum) that protects the viscera.
• HABITAT The animal is a filter feeder in shallow seas. Its sedentary habit is indicated by the irregular, wavy shell margin, which conforms to the shape of the substrate.

growth line showing
• *earlier margin*

CREPIDULA FALCONERI Newton; Middle Eocene; Nigeria.

Typical length ¾ in (2 cm)

• *simple, one-turn, spiral apex*

• *irregularly wavy margin matches substrate*

Range L. Cretaceous–Recent	Distribution Worldwide	Occurrence

Order MESOGASTROPODA	Family XENOPHORIDAE	Informal name Carrier shell

XENOPHORA

The moderately low, conical shell has shallow sutures, ornamented with oblique, interrupted ridges. The flat base with its narrow aperture is overhung by a thin, wavy peripheral margin.
• HABITAT Hidden beneath its shell, the animal browses on microorganisms in the silty mud of fairly deep waters.
• REMARK *Xenophora* has acquired the habit of selecting bits of shell or other debris from the sea bed and cementing them to the lobes of the periphery, where they become incorporated.

smaller debris attached when younger •

periphery of earlier whorl •

SIDE VIEW

• *constricted aperture with concave lip*

BASAL VIEW

XENOPHORA CRISPA (König); Pliocene; Italy.

• *objects cemented to the margin support the shell*

• *peripheral lobes*

Typical diameter 1¼ in (3 cm)

Range L. Cretaceous–Recent	Distribution Worldwide	Occurrence

Order MESOGASTROPODA	Family CYPRAEIDAE	Informal name Egg cowrie

UMBILIA

This cowrie has a large, globular shell with a flattened underside, narrowed at each end. The spire is a flat coil obscured by a shiny enamel coating that covers the rest of the shell. When adult, the lip is inflated and wholly curled inward narrowing the long aperture. This curves toward the top and is guarded by a line of strong, ridgelike teeth on the body whorl and by a row of finer denticles on the lip.

• **HABITAT** Most cowries feed on detritus but the habits of *Umbilia* are not well known.

outer lip curled inward •

apical spout, bent • sideways

flat spire, partly • covered

aperture •

small tubercles •

• *globular body whorl, glazed with layer of enamel*

lips lined with • different-sized teeth

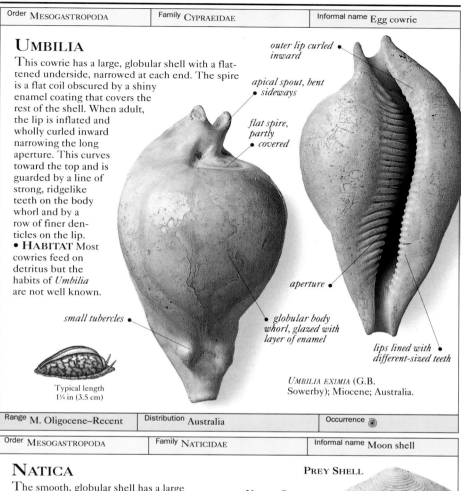

Typical length
1¼ in (3.5 cm)

UMBILIA EXIMIA (G.B. Sowerby); Miocene; Australia.

Range M. Oligocene–Recent	Distribution Australia	Occurrence ⊚

Order MESOGASTROPODA	Family NATICIDAE	Informal name Moon shell

NATICA

The smooth, globular shell has a large body whorl with a much smaller spire and an umbilicus with a central ridge. The outer lip is thin, and the aperture is closed in life by a tight-fitting operculum.

• **HABITAT** This gastropod lives at various depths in marine to slightly brackish waters. It is carnivorous, drilling bevel-edged holes in other mollusk shells and sucking out the contents.

PREY SHELL

NATICA SHELL, APICAL VIEW

• *feeding hole drilled in bivalve*

Typical length
1¼ in (3 cm)

NATICA MILLEPUNCTATA Lamark; Pliocene; Italy.

Range Paleocene–Recent	Distribution Worldwide	Occurrence ⊚⊚⊚⊚⊚

| Order MESOGASTROPODA | Family CASSIDAE | Informal name Helmet shell |

CASSIS

Cassis has a strong, medium to large shell, with an inflated body whorl ornamented with both spiral and transverse threads, and two to four spiral rows of tubercles. The uppermost of these is situated on the angulated shoulder of the whorl, giving rise to a low, flat-sided, conical spire. The reflected and thickened lip is corrugated inside, and a roughly ridged layer of enamel is spread around the aperture on to the body whorl. At the bottom of the aperture, and bent away from it, is the tubular siphonal canal.
• **HABITAT** *Cassis* is an active predator, living on coral rubble or sand in warm waters.

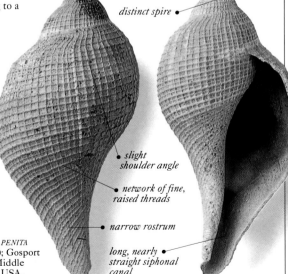

reflected lip •

flat-sided • spire

• row of shoulder nodes

• tubular siphonal canal

Typical length
4 in (10 cm)

CASSIS CANCELLATA
Lamarck; Calcaire
Grossier; Middle
Eocene; France.

| Range Paleocene–Recent | Distribution Worldwide | Occurrence |

| Order MESOGASTROPODA | Family FICIDAE | Informal name Fig shell |

FICOPSIS

Ficopsis had a thinnish shell tapering to a narrow rostrum. The raised spire, which is much shorter than the body whorl, has gently convex whorls, a narrow apex, and well-defined sutures. A latticework of fine, regular threads covers the whole shell. The body whorl is convex and varies from being evenly rounded to having a polygonal profile, caused by the accentuation of the slight shoulder and spiral ridges. The aperture is thin lipped and ovate, narrowing into a long siphonal canal.
• **HABITAT** This animal lived on sandy substrates in warm regions.

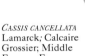

• narrow apex

distinct spire •

• slight shoulder angle

network of fine, • raised threads

• narrow rostrum

long, nearly • straight siphonal canal

Typical length
2½ in (6 cm)

FICOPSIS PENITA
(Conrad); Gosport
Sands; Middle
Eocene; USA.

| Range Eocene | Distribution N. America, Europe | Occurrence |

Order MESOGASTROPODA	Family EPITONIIDAE	Informal name Wentletrap

CIRSOTREMA

Cirsotrema has an elongate calcitic shell, with convex whorls separated by deep sutures, and an ornament of numerous raised and frilled ribs, each made up of a number of compressed laminae. In some species they connect up from one whorl to the next. The last rib frames the small, circular aperture. A few weak spirals are visible between, and sometimes cross, the ribs, while the base of the shell is surrounded by a strong cord.
• **HABITAT** This marine-dwelling animal is carnivorous, using its long proboscis to feed on sedentary creatures.

ribs made up of laminae

deep sutures

CIRSOTREMA LAMELLOSUM (Brocchi); Pliocene; Italy.

less prominent spiral ornament

basal cord

circular aperture, with no siphonal canal

Typical length 1¼ in (3 cm)

Range Paleocene–Recent	Distribution Worldwide	Occurrence

Order NEOGASTROPODA	Family MURICIDAE	Informal name Comb shell

MUREXSUL

Murexsul has a medium-size shell with sharp ribs and a long rostrum. The whorls are sharply shouldered and the sutures deep, giving rise to a turreted spire ornamented with closely packed spiral cords. These rise at intervals to form a rib, composed of a wall of fluted spines. The last rib surrounds the smooth, enameled aperture, slightly detached from the rest of the shell. The base of the aperture is suddenly narrowed into a siphonal canal, which is virtually closed to form a tube, and this rostrum is armed with a few more spines.
• **HABITAT** *Murexsul* is a carnivore, inhabiting moderately deep waters.

turreted spire with deep sutures

thick, rounded, spiral ridges

rib made of row of tubular spines

spiny rostrum

MUREXSUL OCTOGONUS (Quoy & Gaimard); Late Pliocene; New Zealand.

Typical length 3½ in (9 cm)

Range Miocene–Recent	Distribution Australasia, W. Pacific	Occurrence

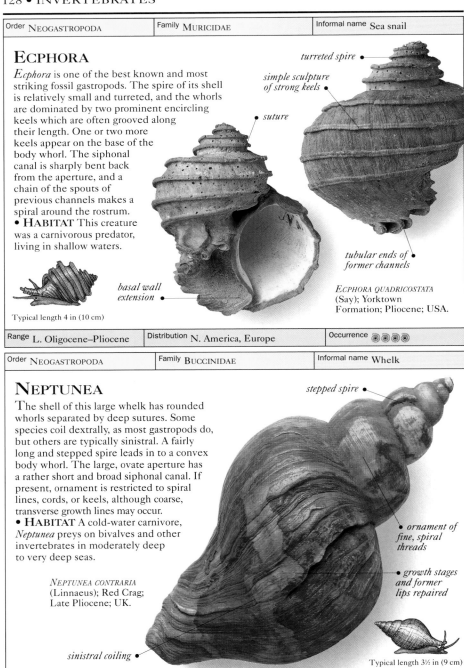

| Order NEOGASTROPODA | Family MURICIDAE | Informal name Sea snail |

ECPHORA

Ecphora is one of the best known and most striking fossil gastropods. The spire of its shell is relatively small and turreted, and the whorls are dominated by two prominent encircling keels which are often grooved along their length. One or two more keels appear on the base of the body whorl. The siphonal canal is sharply bent back from the aperture, and a chain of the spouts of previous channels makes a spiral around the rostrum.
• **HABITAT** This creature was a carnivorous predator, living in shallow waters.

turreted spire •

simple sculpture of strong keels •

• *suture*

tubular ends of former channels •

basal wall extension •

Typical length 4 in (10 cm)

ECPHORA QUADRICOSTATA (Say); Yorktown Formation; Pliocene; USA.

| Range L. Oligocene–Pliocene | Distribution N. America, Europe | Occurrence |

| Order NEOGASTROPODA | Family BUCCINIDAE | Informal name Whelk |

NEPTUNEA

The shell of this large whelk has rounded whorls separated by deep sutures. Some species coil dextrally, as most gastropods do, but others are typically sinistral. A fairly long and stepped spire leads in to a convex body whorl. The large, ovate aperture has a rather short and broad siphonal canal. If present, ornament is restricted to spiral lines, cords, or keels, although coarse, transverse growth lines may occur.
• **HABITAT** A cold-water carnivore, *Neptunea* preys on bivalves and other invertebrates in moderately deep to very deep seas.

stepped spire •

NEPTUNEA CONTRARIA (Linnaeus); Red Crag; Late Pliocene; UK.

• *ornament of fine, spiral threads*

• *growth stages and former lips repaired*

sinistral coiling •

Typical length 3½ in (9 cm)

| Range L. Eocene–Recent | Distribution Worldwide | Occurrence |

Order NEOGASTROPODA	Family FASCIOLARIIDAE	Informal name Sea snail

CLAVILITHES

Clavilithes had a medium to large, fusiform shell. The young shell begins as a smooth column of equal-sized whorls, developing low ribs crossed by spiral threads. The sculpture soon dies away, leaving only a few spiral lines, and the whorls become flat-sided. A sharp shelf at the top of the whorl gives the spire a stepped shape. The last whorl is usually cup-shaped and the aperture oval.

• **HABITAT** Probably carnivorous, this gastropod was an inhabitant of sand, silt, and mud in moderately deep, warm waters.

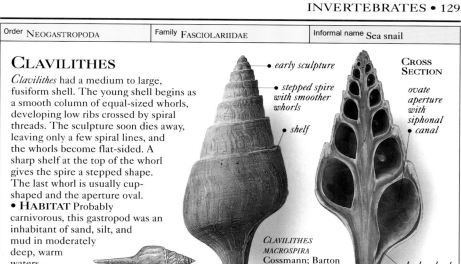

• *early sculpture*

• *stepped spire with smoother whorls*

• *shelf*

CROSS SECTION

ovate aperture with siphonal • *canal*

CLAVILITHES MACROSPIRA Cossmann; Barton Clay Formation; Middle Eocene; UK.

• *body whorl narrows abruptly*

Typical length 4¾ in (12 cm)

Range Paleocene–Pliocene	Distribution Worldwide	Occurrence ⊛⊛⊛⊛

Order NEOGASTROPODA	Family VOLUTIDAE	Informal name Volute

VOLUTOSPINA

The medium to large biconic shell has an acutely pointed apex. Despite the shallow sutures the spire has a turreted appearance, resulting from the short ribs that end in sharp spines on the shoulder. The body whorl is ornamented with weak, flat, spiral ribbons, crossed by numerous inconspicuous vertical growth lines. The rather narrow aperture tapers down to an open siphonal canal and the outer lip is not thickened. There are several ridges on the columella, the lowest one being the strongest, and a layer of enamel spreads from the interior onto the body whorl.

• **HABITAT** This creature inhabited sandy or muddy sea beds in warm waters.

• **REMARK** Like other volutes, *Volutospina* was a fast-moving predator.

VOLUTOSPINA LUCTATOR (Solander *in* Brander); Barton Clay Formation; Middle Eocene; UK.

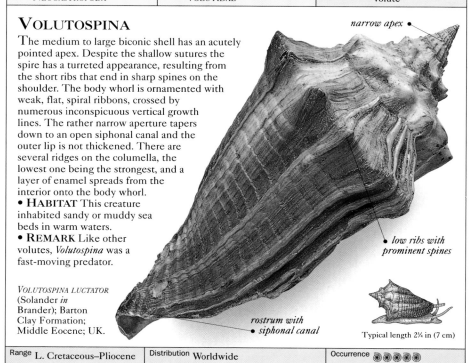

narrow apex •

• *low ribs with prominent spines*

rostrum with • *siphonal canal*

Typical length 2¾ in (7 cm)

Range L. Cretaceous–Pliocene	Distribution Worldwide	Occurrence ⊛⊛⊛⊛⊛

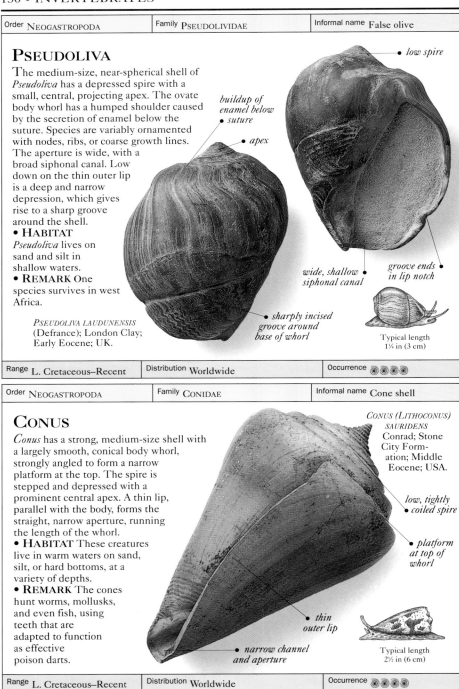

Order NEOGASTROPODA	Family PSEUDOLIVIDAE	Informal name False olive

PSEUDOLIVA

The medium-size, near-spherical shell of
Pseudoliva has a depressed spire with a
small, central, projecting apex. The ovate
body whorl has a humped shoulder caused
by the secretion of enamel below the
suture. Species are variably ornamented
with nodes, ribs, or coarse growth lines.
The aperture is wide, with a
broad siphonal canal. Low
down on the thin outer lip
is a deep and narrow
depression, which gives
rise to a sharp groove
around the shell.
• **HABITAT**
Pseudoliva lives on
sand and silt in
shallow waters.
• **REMARK** One
species survives in west
Africa.

PSEUDOLIVA LAUDUNENSIS
(Defrance); London Clay;
Early Eocene; UK.

low spire

buildup of enamel below suture

apex

wide, shallow siphonal canal

groove ends in lip notch

sharply incised groove around base of whorl

Typical length
1¼ in (3 cm)

Range L. Cretaceous–Recent	Distribution Worldwide	Occurrence

Order NEOGASTROPODA	Family CONIDAE	Informal name Cone shell

CONUS

Conus has a strong, medium-size shell with
a largely smooth, conical body whorl,
strongly angled to form a narrow
platform at the top. The spire is
stepped and depressed with a
prominent central apex. A thin lip,
parallel with the body, forms the
straight, narrow aperture, running
the length of the whorl.
• **HABITAT** These creatures
live in warm waters on sand,
silt, or hard bottoms, at a
variety of depths.
• **REMARK** The cones
hunt worms, mollusks,
and even fish, using
teeth that are
adapted to function
as effective
poison darts.

*CONUS (LITHOCONUS)
SAURIDENS*
Conrad; Stone
City Form-
ation; Middle
Eocene; USA.

low, tightly coiled spire

platform at top of whorl

thin outer lip

narrow channel and aperture

Typical length
2½ in (6 cm)

Range L. Cretaceous–Recent	Distribution Worldwide	Occurrence

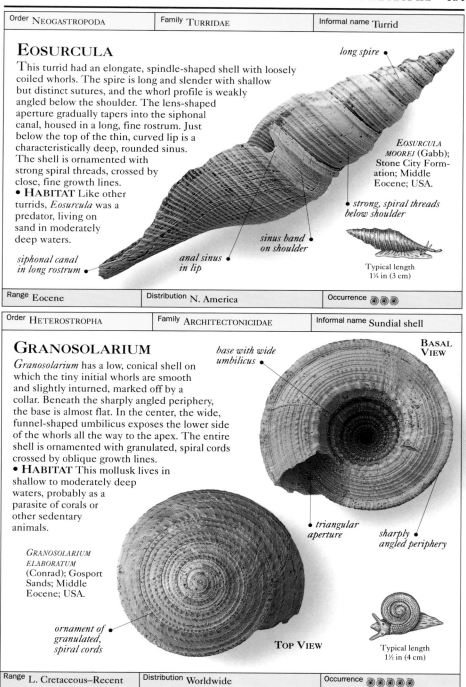

Order NEOGASTROPODA	Family TURRIDAE	Informal name Turrid

EOSURCULA

long spire •

This turrid had an elongate, spindle-shaped shell with loosely coiled whorls. The spire is long and slender with shallow but distinct sutures, and the whorl profile is weakly angled below the shoulder. The lens-shaped aperture gradually tapers into the siphonal canal, housed in a long, fine rostrum. Just below the top of the thin, curved lip is a characteristically deep, rounded sinus. The shell is ornamented with strong spiral threads, crossed by close, fine growth lines.
• HABITAT Like other turrids, *Eosurcula* was a predator, living on sand in moderately deep waters.

EOSURCULA MOOREI (Gabb); Stone City Formation; Middle Eocene; USA.

• *strong, spiral threads below shoulder*

siphonal canal in long rostrum •

anal sinus in lip •

sinus band on shoulder •

Typical length 1¼ in (3 cm)

Range Eocene	Distribution N. America	Occurrence ◉◉◉

Order HETEROSTROPHA	Family ARCHITECTONICIDAE	Informal name Sundial shell

GRANOSOLARIUM

base with wide umbilicus •

BASAL VIEW

Granosolarium has a low, conical shell on which the tiny initial whorls are smooth and slightly inturned, marked off by a collar. Beneath the sharply angled periphery, the base is almost flat. In the center, the wide, funnel-shaped umbilicus exposes the lower side of the whorls all the way to the apex. The entire shell is ornamented with granulated, spiral cords crossed by oblique growth lines.
• HABITAT This mollusk lives in shallow to moderately deep waters, probably as a parasite of corals or other sedentary animals.

GRANOSOLARIUM ELABORATUM (Conrad); Gosport Sands; Middle Eocene; USA.

• *triangular aperture*

sharply angled periphery •

ornament of granulated, spiral cords •

TOP VIEW

Typical length 1½ in (4 cm)

Range L. Cretaceous–Recent	Distribution Worldwide	Occurrence ◉◉◉◉◉

Order CEPHALASPIDEA	Family BULLIDAE	Informal name Bubble shell

BULLA

apical umbilicus •

Bulla has a rather thin, almost spherical shell, only one whorl of which is visible. The few tiny initial whorls coil sinistrally, but the shell then resumes dextral coiling. Each whorl wholly encloses the previous one, so that there is no apparent spire. The aperture is at least as long as the shell, and an enamel layer strengthens the columella wall.

• **HABITAT** Unlike some of its nearest relatives, this herbivorous animal lives on sandy or muddy bottoms in shallow, warm waters.

• **REMARK** An unusual feature of this gastropod is that its body is twice the size of the shell and is unable to withdraw into it.

BULLA AMPULLA
Linnaeus; Reef limestone; Pleistocene; Red Sea.

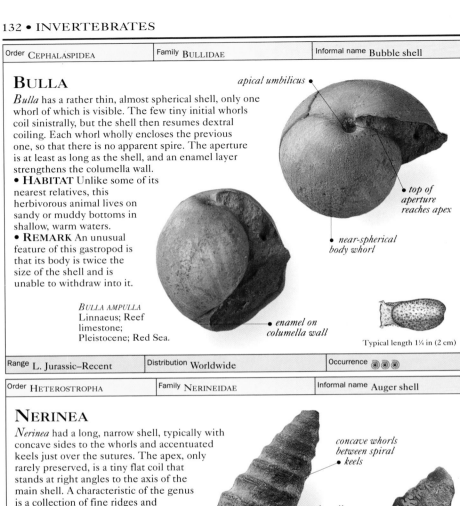

• *top of aperture reaches apex*

• *near-spherical body whorl*

• *enamel on columella wall*

Typical length 1¼ in (2 cm)

Range L. Jurassic–Recent	Distribution Worldwide	Occurrence ⊛⊛⊛

Order HETEROSTROPHA	Family NERINEIDAE	Informal name Auger shell

NERINEA

Nerinea had a long, narrow shell, typically with concave sides to the whorls and accentuated keels just over the sutures. The apex, only rarely preserved, is a tiny flat coil that stands at right angles to the axis of the main shell. A characteristic of the genus is a collection of fine ridges and processes on the walls of the small aperture; there may be up to seven of these, best seen in cross section.

• **HABITAT** *Nerinea* is often associated with coral reef deposits.

NERINEA sp.;
Cretaceous; Israel.

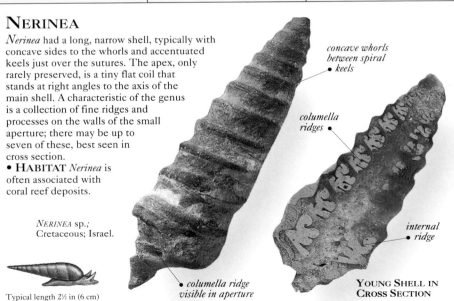

concave whorls between spiral
• *keels*

columella ridges •

• *columella ridge visible in aperture*

internal • *ridge*

YOUNG SHELL IN CROSS SECTION

Typical length 2½ in (6 cm)

Range E. Jurassic–L. Cretaceous	Distribution Worldwide	Occurrence ⊛⊛⊛⊛

Order BASOMMATOPHORA	Family PLANORBIDAE	Informal name Ramshorn snail

AUSTRALORBIS

Rather thin and disc shaped, the shells of this family are in fact sinistrally coiled, although they appear to be dextral. The inverted spire takes the form of a deep and widely open umbilicus containing close, convex whorls. Bluntly angled at the periphery, the base is flat and ornamented with occasional weak, spiral lines. Oblique growth lines cover the whole shell. The aperture is small and triangular-oval.

• HABITAT Today, the family Planorbidae is known to live exclusively in fresh water, and the genus *Australorbis* feeds on vegetable matter in lakes, marshes, and rivers. It is fairly certain that this was always the case, so this fossil is a useful indicator of non-marine conditions of the past.

flat base with faint ornament

BASAL VIEW

TOP VIEW

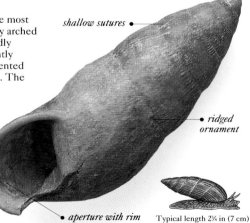

• *sinistral shell that appears to be built upside down*

AUSTRALORBIS EUOMPHALUS (J. Sowerby); Headon Hill Formation; Late Eocene; UK.

small, oval aperture •

• *deeply sunk whorls*

Typical length 1¼ in (3 cm)

Range L. Cretaceous–Recent	Distribution Europe, Asia, N. & S. America	Occurrence ◉◉◉◉

Order STYLOMMATOPHORA	Family CLAUSILIIDAE	Informal name Land snail

RILLYAREX

The large shell is sinistrally coiled, unlike most gastropods. The elongate spire is narrowly arched in profile, with gently rounded sides, hardly indented by the shallow sutures and slightly convex whorls. The whole shell is ornamented with numerous oblique, transverse ridges. The ovate aperture has a continuous, slightly flared rim, except at its upper junction.

• HABITAT Although larger than its living relatives, *Rillyarex* had all the characteristics of an air-breathing terrestrial snail and was probably washed into the freshwater deposits in which it is found.

shallow sutures •

• *ridged ornament*

RILLYAREX PREECEI Nordsieck; Bembridge Limestone; Late Eocene; UK.

• *aperture with rim*

Typical length 2¾ in (7 cm)

Range M. Eocene–Oligocene	Distribution Europe	Occurrence ◉◉

NAUTILOIDS

NAUTILOIDS ARE PRIMITIVE, marine cephalopods that possess a shell. They were most abundant during the Paleozoic Era – 400 million years ago; today, only a single genus survives – the pearly nautilus of the south west Pacific Ocean. The shell is divided into a body chamber and many smaller chambers. The chambered part of the shell is known as the phragmocone. Nautiloids have heads with well-developed eyes, as well as grasping tentacles. They swim by squirting water out of the body cavity.

Order ORTHOCERATIDA	Family ORTHOCERATIDAE	Informal name Nautiloid

ORTHOCERAS

The shell of *Orthoceras* is shaped like a slowly tapering cylindrical cone and is made up of closely spaced concavo-convex chambers, joined together by a centrally placed tube called the siphuncle.
• **HABITAT** *Orthoceras* was an active swimmer, with the shell positioned horizontally in the water. It scavenged and preyed on small animals.

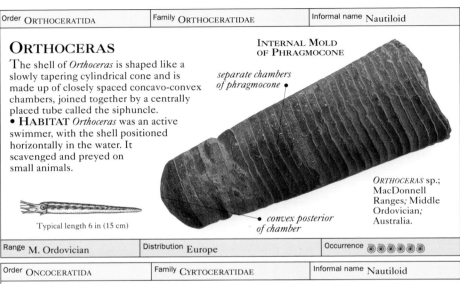

INTERNAL MOLD
OF PHRAGMOCONE

separate chambers of phragmocone •

Typical length 6 in (15 cm)

ORTHOCERAS sp.; MacDonnell Ranges; Middle Ordovician; Australia.

• *convex posterior of chamber*

Range M. Ordovician	Distribution Europe	Occurrence ◉◉◉◉◉◉

Order ONCOCERATIDA	Family CYRTOCERATIDAE	Informal name Nautiloid

CYRTOCERAS

The shell is strongly curved in an open hook shape and nearly circular in cross section. The posterior part is made up of numerous closely spaced chambers, while the long-living chamber makes up the anterior part of the shell.
• **HABITAT** Experiments suggest that the animal lived head-down in the water, probably near the bottom of the sea. It was able to swim and adjust its buoyancy.
• **REMARK** The specimen featured is an internal mold, from which the original shell has been completely lost.

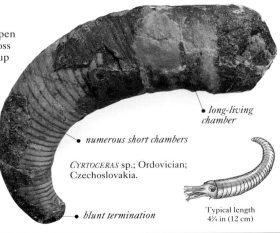

• *long-living chamber*

• *numerous short chambers*

CYRTOCERAS sp.; Ordovician; Czechoslovakia.

• *blunt termination*

Typical length 4¾ in (12 cm)

Range Ordovician	Distribution Worldwide	Occurrence ◉◉

Order ACTINOCERATIDA	Family HURONIIDAE	Informal name Nautiloid

HURONIA

Shells of this genus have a large, straight siphuncle, with long segments separated by strong constrictions. Complex canals are present. The central canal is very narrow.
• **HABITAT** This genus lived in shallow seas as a scavenger or predator. It was able to swim and adjust its position in the water column by moving liquid along the siphuncle from chamber to chamber.
• **REMARK** Only the robust siphuncle of this species is preserved in the specimen. The chambers and outer wall are missing.

HURONIA VERTEBRALIS
Stokes; Ordovician; Canada.

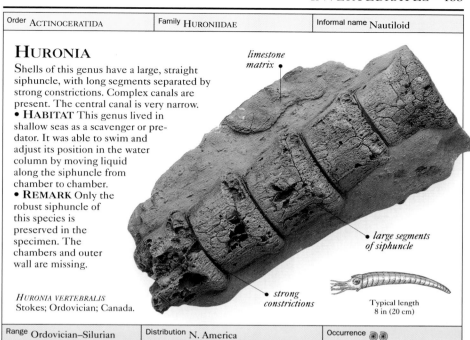

limestone matrix

large segments of siphuncle

strong constrictions

Typical length
8 in (20 cm)

Range Ordovician–Silurian	Distribution N. America	Occurrence

Order TARPHYCERATIDA	Family ESTONIOCERATIDAE	Informal name Nautiloid

ESTONIOCERAS

The spiral shell of this nautiloid is loosely coiled, with a final whorl growing away from the preceding part of the shell. It has a broad, shallow umbilicus. Growth lines are present on the flanks of the shell. Most unusually for nautiloids, the siphuncle is near the outside of the whorl (ventral).
• **HABITAT** This genus adapted to a swimming existence *(see life position)* by having a loosely coiled shell. It lived in fairly deep water and probably used its tentacles to grasp food.
• **REMARK** This is a well-preserved specimen of a rare species, preserved as an internal mold.

uncoiled final whorl

rounded venter

umbilicus

ESTONIOCERAS PERFORATUM
Schröder;
Early
Ordovician;
Estonia.

Typical diameter
4 in (10 cm)

Range E. Ordovician	Distribution Europe	Occurrence

| Order NAUTILIDA | Family TRIGONOCERATIDAE | Informal name Nautiloid |

DISCITOCERAS

This nautiloid had an evolute shell with a widely open umbilicus and a rounded venter. A spiral ornament of fine, closely spaced ribs is present on the shell's exterior.

• **HABITAT** *Discitoceras* lived around deep-water algal reefs in the Early Carboniferous seas and probably swam poorly, like the living pearly nautilus.

• **REMARK** An external mold of another specimen is present on the outside of the living chamber.

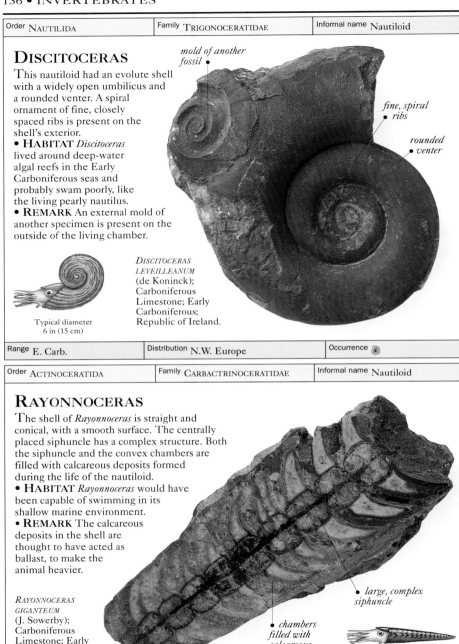

mold of another fossil

fine, spiral ribs

rounded venter

DISCITOCERAS LEVEILLEANUM (de Koninck); Carboniferous Limestone; Early Carboniferous; Republic of Ireland.

Typical diameter 6 in (15 cm)

| Range E. Carb. | Distribution N.W. Europe | Occurrence |

| Order ACTINOCERATIDA | Family CARBACTRINOCERATIDAE | Informal name Nautiloid |

RAYONNOCERAS

The shell of *Rayonnoceras* is straight and conical, with a smooth surface. The centrally placed siphuncle has a complex structure. Both the siphuncle and the convex chambers are filled with calcareous deposits formed during the life of the nautiloid.

• **HABITAT** *Rayonnoceras* would have been capable of swimming in its shallow marine environment.

• **REMARK** The calcareous deposits in the shell are thought to have acted as ballast, to make the animal heavier.

RAYONNOCERAS GIGANTEUM (J. Sowerby); Carboniferous Limestone; Early Carboniferous; Republic of Ireland.

large, complex siphuncle

chambers filled with calcareous deposits

Typical diameter 8 in (20 cm)

| Range E. Carb. | Distribution Europe, N. America | Occurrence |

Order NAUTILIDA	Family TRIGONOCERATIDAE	Informal name Nautiloid

VESTINAUTILUS

The shell is notable for its extremely evolute form. It has an open umbilicus and a distinctive mid-flank ridge, running along each side, on which the sutures form a forwardly directed V-shaped fold. There are numerous small chambers.

• **HABITAT** *Vestinautilus* was a poor swimmer, living on the bottom of shelf seas.

• **REMARK** The specimen is preserved as an internal mold in limestone; the body chamber has broken away. The sutures are well displayed.

VESTINAUTILUS CARINIFEROUS (J. de C. Sowerby); Carboniferous; Locality Unknown.

open umbilicus

folded suture

Typical diameter 2½ in (6 cm)

Range E. Carb.	Distribution Europe, USA, S. America	Occurrence ◉◉

Order NAUTILIDA	Family NAUTILIDAE	Informal name Nautilus

UNDETERMINED NAUTILUS

As in all nautiloids, the phragmocone is made up of numerous compartments, which are concave posteriorly and convex anteriorly. They are separated by thin walls made of shell, joined by a tube – the siphuncle. Nautiloids were able to change buoyancy by altering the levels of gas and liquid in their chambers.

• **HABITAT** Like the living nautilus, it probably inhabited deeper waters by day, moving into the shallows at night to feed on small marine prey.

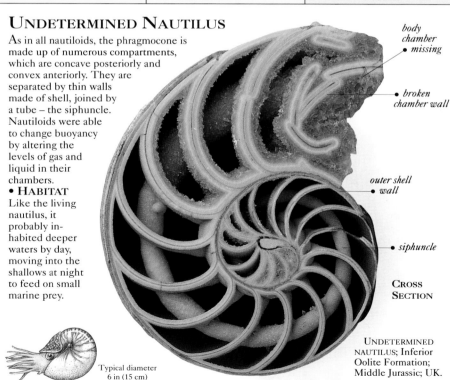

body chamber missing

broken chamber wall

outer shell wall

siphuncle

CROSS SECTION

UNDETERMINED NAUTILUS; Inferior Oolite Formation; Middle Jurassic; UK.

Typical diameter 6 in (15 cm)

Range L. Triassic–M. Jurassic	Distribution Worldwide	Occurrence ◉◉◉◉

| Order NAUTILIDA | Family NAUTILIDAE | Informal name Nautilus |

CENOCERAS

The shell form is involute, the umbilicus narrow. The whorl height increases rapidly. The venter is broad and rounded. The suture lines are closely spaced and gently curved, lacking any complex folds. The living chamber occupies about half a whorl. Internally, the numerous chambers have a concavo-convex form in cross section and a large siphuncle positioned near the dorsal margin.

• **HABITAT** This marine-dwelling animal fed on small, bottom-dwelling animals.

• **REMARK** Many of the chambers of this specimen are filled with red lime-mud, hardened into limestone. Some are filled with calcite crystals, and many of the walls are broken – probably from the implosion resulting from the shell sinking in deeper water, after the animal died.

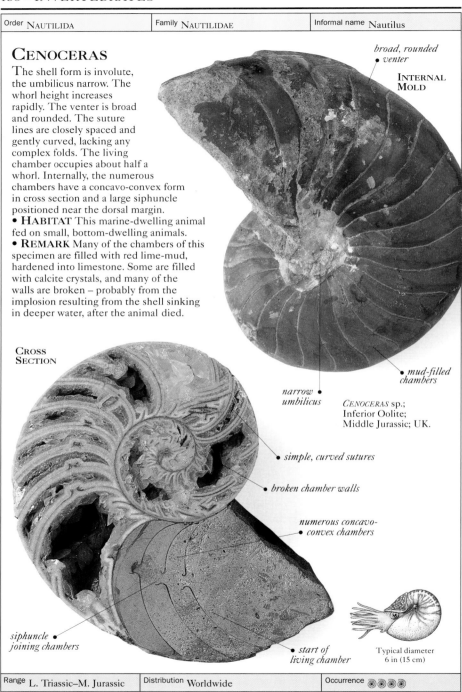

broad, rounded venter

INTERNAL MOLD

mud-filled chambers

CENOCERAS sp.;
Inferior Oolite;
Middle Jurassic; UK.

CROSS SECTION

narrow umbilicus

simple, curved sutures

broken chamber walls

numerous concavo-convex chambers

siphuncle joining chambers

start of living chamber

Typical diameter
6 in (15 cm)

| Range L. Triassic–M. Jurassic | Distribution Worldwide | Occurrence ◉◉◉◉ |

Order NAUTILIDA	Family NAUTILIDAE	Informal name Nautilus

CENOCERAS

Cenoceras has a very tightly coiled shell with a rapidly increasing whorl height. The outside of the shell has an ornament of fine growth lines, irregular folds parallel to the aperture, and fine, closely spaced, radial ribs.
• **HABITAT** This species of *Cenoceras* probably lived in seas 164–350 ft (50 to 100 m) deep. Its form suggests it was a slow swimmer.

• *growth lines*

• *narrow umbilicus*

• *irregular folds*

fine, radial ribs •

CENOCERAS SIMILLIUM (Foord & Crick); Lower Lias; Early Jurassic; UK.

Typical diameter 6 in (15 cm)

Range L. Triassic–Recent	Distribution Worldwide	Occurrence ◉◉

Order NAUTILIDA	Family NAUTILIDAE	Informal name Nautilus

EUTREPHOCERAS

The coiling of the shell is very involute, the umbilicus extremely narrow. The outline of the shell is nearly globular, the venter is very broadly rounded. The individual chambers of the phragmocone are fewer than in the genus *Cenoceras (see above)*.
• **HABITAT** *Eutrephoceras* probably lived as a slow-moving predator in the rather shallow waters of the Western Interior Seaway, which occupied the midwestern USA during much of the Late Cretaceous period.
• **REMARK** This particular specimen is preserved as an internal mold in dark mudstone; patches of the original shell adhere to the surface. These patches of shell have the "mother-of-pearl" colors characteristic of all cephalopod shells.

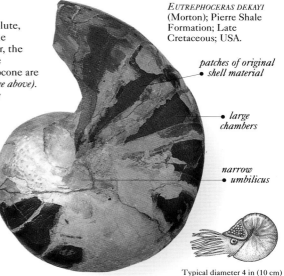

EUTREPHOCERAS DEKAYI (Morton); Pierre Shale Formation; Late Cretaceous; USA.

patches of original shell material •

• *large chambers*

narrow umbilicus •

Typical diameter 4 in (10 cm)

Range L. Cretaceous	Distribution USA	Occurrence ◉◉

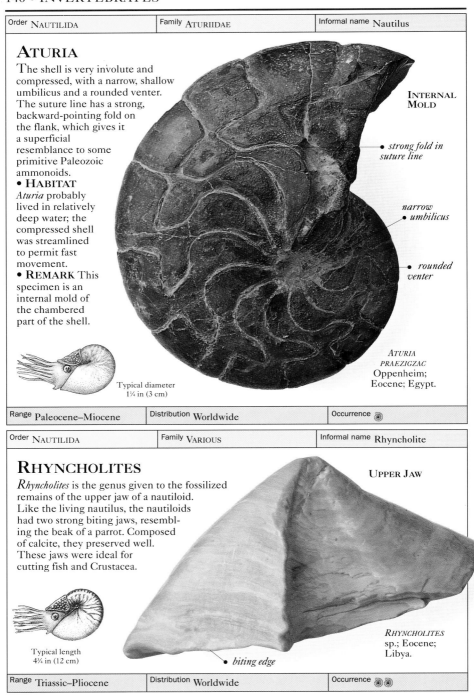

| Order NAUTILIDA | Family ATURIIDAE | Informal name Nautilus |

ATURIA

The shell is very involute and compressed, with a narrow, shallow umbilicus and a rounded venter. The suture line has a strong, backward-pointing fold on the flank, which gives it a superficial resemblance to some primitive Paleozoic ammonoids.
• **HABITAT** *Aturia* probably lived in relatively deep water; the compressed shell was streamlined to permit fast movement.
• **REMARK** This specimen is an internal mold of the chambered part of the shell.

INTERNAL MOLD

• *strong fold in suture line*

*narrow
• umbilicus*

• *rounded venter*

ATURIA PRAEZIGZAC
Oppenheim;
Eocene; Egypt.

Typical diameter
1¼ in (3 cm)

| Range Paleocene–Miocene | Distribution Worldwide | Occurrence |

| Order NAUTILIDA | Family VARIOUS | Informal name Rhyncholite |

RHYNCHOLITES

Rhyncholites is the genus given to the fossilized remains of the upper jaw of a nautiloid. Like the living nautilus, the nautiloids had two strong biting jaws, resembling the beak of a parrot. Composed of calcite, they preserved well. These jaws were ideal for cutting fish and Crustacea.

UPPER JAW

RHYNCHOLITES
sp.; Eocene;
Libya.

Typical length
4¾ in (12 cm)

• *biting edge*

| Range Triassic–Pliocene | Distribution Worldwide | Occurrence |

AMMONOIDEA

A MMONOIDS EVOLVED from nautiloids in the early Devonian
period, about 400 million years ago.
They were abundant in world seas for
the next 370 million years, after which
they vanished suddenly at the end of
the Cretaceous period. The rapid
evolution of ammonoids and their
widespread distribution make them of
great value in the subdivision of Late
Paleozoic and Mesozoic time. As a
group, they are characterized by the
position of the siphuncle (the tube
connecting the chambers of the shell),
which is near the outside of the shell
(ventral). Ammonoidea sutures can be
simple, as found in Paleozoic species,
or complex, as found in Mesozoic
species. Because they are extinct, we
know very little about the soft parts
and life habits of the ammonoids. It is
rare to find the biting jaws, the tonguelike rasping radula, or the ink sacs
preserved in living chambers.

Order CLYMENIIDA	Family CLYMENIIDAE	Informal name Clymeniid

CLYMENIA

The evolute shell has a wide, open umbilicus.
It is either nearly smooth or it carries weak,
gently curved growth lines. The
whorl section is compressed,
and the venter is
rounded. The
suture is very
simple.
• **HABITAT**
This genus lived
a predatory
existence on or
near the floor of
Devonian seas.
• **REMARK** One
of the more primitive
ammonoids, *Clymenia*
was locally common in
Late Devonian rocks,
but not well preserved.

CLYMENIA LAEVIGATA
(Münster); Late
Devonian; Germany.

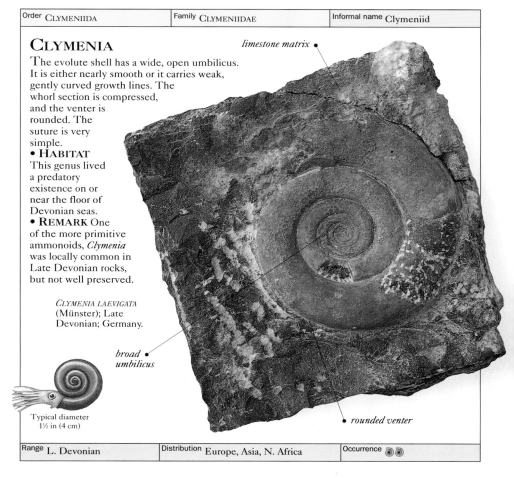

limestone matrix •

broad •
umbilicus

Typical diameter
1½ in (4 cm)

• *rounded venter*

Range L. Devonian	Distribution Europe, Asia, N. Africa	Occurrence

Order CLYMENIIDA	Family HEXACLYMENIIDAE	Informal name Clymeniid

SOLICLYMENIA

This is an unusually shaped ammonoid, with a very evolute shell that shows distinctive triangular coiling. It has a broad umbilicus and a rounded venter. The simple ribs are closely spaced; the suture is very simple.
• **HABITAT** It lived in moderately deep water. Although it could swim, its shell shape suggests it spent some time on the sea bed.

simple, close ribs

evolute shell form

triangular coiling

SOLICLYMENIA PARADOXA (Münster); Late Devonian; Germany.

Typical length ¾ in (2 cm)

Range L. Devonian	Distribution Eurasia, N. Africa, N. America	Occurrence 🌑🌑

Order PROLECANITIDA	Family PROLECANITIDAE	Informal name Goniatite

MEROCANITES

The shell of *Merocanites* is evolute and has a broad, open umbilicus; the profile is compressed, the sides parallel. The gently rounded flanks show a suture with several blade-shaped folds (a fairly complex form for Paleozoic ammonoids). The venter is rounded.
• **HABITAT** *Merocanites* lived in moderately deep water in the Early Carboniferous seas.
• **REMARK** The specimen is preserved in dark limestone as an iron-oxide-coated internal mold. The living chamber is not preserved.

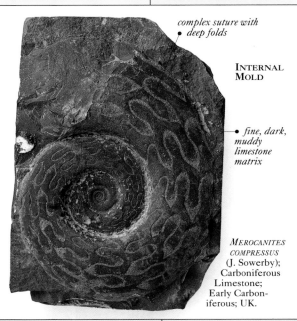

complex suture with deep folds

INTERNAL MOLD

fine, dark, muddy limestone matrix

MEROCANITES COMPRESSUS (J. Sowerby); Carboniferous Limestone; Early Carboniferous; UK.

Typical diameter 2 in (5 cm)

Range E. Carb.	Distribution Europe, Asia, N. America	Occurrence 🌑

Order GONIATITIDA	Family GASTRIOCOCERATIDAE	Informal name Goniatite

GASTRIOCERAS

The shell is moderately involute with a wide, deep umbilicus. The whorl section is strongly compressed, with a broad, gently rounded venter. The ornament consists of tubercles on its flanks, which give rise to ribs passing over the venter. The suture has a few strong folds, which are rounded anteriorly and pointed posteriorly.

• HABITAT *Gastrioceras* was widespread in the seas that surrounded the Carboniferous coal swamps in the northern hemisphere. It was a poor swimmer.

GASTRIOCERAS CORONATUM (Foord & Crick); Coal Measures; Late Carboniferous; UK.

wide, deep umbilicus

calcite-infilled chambers

suture with a few large folds

Typical length 2¾ in (7 cm)

Range E.–L. Carb.	Distribution Worldwide	Occurrence ◉◉◉

Order GONIATITIDA	Family GONIATITIDAE	Informal name Goniatite

GONIATITES

The shell is strongly involute, with a small, narrow umbilicus. The suture includes both pointed and rounded elements in the form of a zigzag. The thin shell has an ornament of fine, closely spaced growth lines.

• HABITAT *Goniatites* lived in Carboniferous shelf seas, occurring locally in swarms over reef structures. The shape of its shell suggests that *Goniatites* was a poor swimmer.

GONIATITES CRENISTRIA Bisat; Bowland Shales; Early Carboniferous; UK.

goniatitic suture line

narrow, deep umbilicus

broad, rounded venter

Typical diameter 2½ in (6 cm)

Range E. Carb.	Distribution Worldwide	Occurrence ◉◉◉

| Order CERATITIDA | Family CERATITIDAE | Informal name Ceratite |

CERATITES

The shell is moderately evolute with a broad umbilicus and a flat venter. The sides bear strong, simple, widely spaced ribs, which end on the ventral margin in a tubercle. The closely spaced suture lines have a highly distinctive form, with shallow, smoothly rounded folds facing anteriorly, and toothed folds facing posteriorly.
• HABITAT *Ceratites* lived in the shallow waters of the Triassic seas.

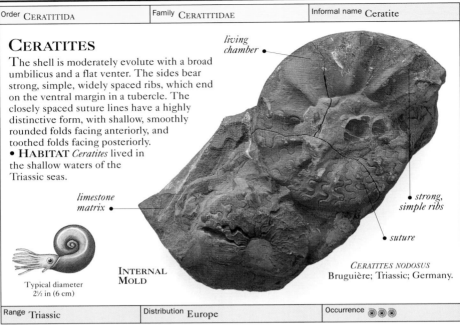

living chamber

limestone matrix

INTERNAL MOLD

Typical diameter 2½ in (6 cm)

strong, simple ribs

suture

CERATITES NODOSUS Bruguière; Triassic; Germany.

| Range Triassic | Distribution Europe | Occurrence |

| Order CERATIIDA | Family XENODISCIDAE | Informal name Ceratite |

XENODISCUS

The shell is very evolute with a wide, open umbilicus. It is slightly compressed, with parallel sides and a gently rounded venter. The ornament consists of faint, irregular ribs on the early whorls only. The distinctive, closely spaced suture lines have a deep, rounded anterior fold, and a weakly toothed posterior fold. The living chamber is long.
• HABITAT *Xenodiscus* was a slow-swimming genus which trapped prey in its tentacles.

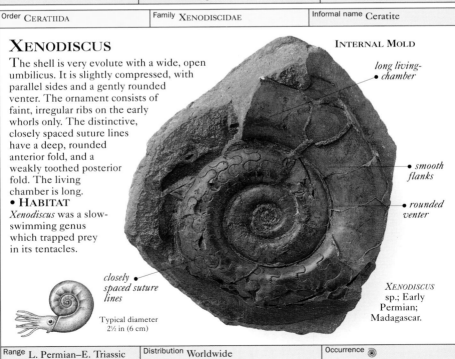

INTERNAL MOLD

long living-chamber

smooth flanks

rounded venter

closely spaced suture lines

Typical diameter 2½ in (6 cm)

XENODISCUS sp.; Early Permian; Madagascar.

| Range L. Permian–E. Triassic | Distribution Worldwide | Occurrence |

AMMONITES

A MMONITES ARE A FORM of ammonoid distinguished by their complex suture lines. They were abundant and diverse in the seas of the Mesozoic Era, and they evolved very rapidly to produce numerous species and genera. After a decline in diversity during the Late Cretaceous period, ammonites became extinct at the same time as other marine groups, such as belemnites, and terrestrial groups, such as dinosaurs. As both ammonites and all their close relatives are extinct, scientists know very little about their mode of life. What is known about them has been worked out mostly from experiments with model shells in water tanks.

Order PHYLLOCERATIDA	Family PHYLLOCERATIDAE	Informal name Phylloceratid

PHYLLOCERAS

A compressed, involute shell form and a distinctive frilly suture characterize the shells of these small-to medium-size ammonites. They are either simply ornamented with growth lines or nearly smooth. The aperture is gently curved.
• HABITAT The fairly streamlined profile of the shell, and the rounded venter, allowed this genus to swim at moderate speeds by jet propulsion.

Typical diameter
4 in (10 cm)

• *complex, frilled suture line*

POLISHED
INTERNAL MOLD

PHYLLOCERAS sp.;
Early Jurassic;
Mexico.

Range E. Jurassic–L. Cretaceous	Distribution Worldwide	Occurrence 🐚🐚🐚🐚

Order LYTOCERATIDA	Family LYTOCERATIDAE	Informal name Lytoceratid

LYTOCERAS

The shell of *Lytoceras* is evolute, with a wide umbilicus. The whorl section is evenly rounded. The shell is ornamented with fine, closely spaced ribs and less frequent flanges, which pass uninterrupted over the venter. The suture is complex.
• HABITAT The shell is ill-adapted for fast swimming, and it may have lived near the bottom of the sea.
• REMARK Like *Phylloceras* (*see above*), *Lytoceras* is most abundant in low-latitude, deep-water deposits of the ancient Tethys Ocean.

LYTOCERAS FIMBRIATUS
(J. de C. Sowerby);
Middle Lias; Early
Jurassic; UK.

• *fine ribs*

Typical diameter
4 in (10 cm)

Range E. Jurassic	Distribution Worldwide	Occurrence 🐚🐚

| Order AMMONITIDA | Family PSILOCERATIDAE | Informal name Ammonite |

PSILOCERAS

In many localities around the world, this small, rather smooth genus is taken as the marker of earliest Jurassic time. The Psiloceratidae probably evolved from the *Phylloceras* group *(see p.145)* and retain rather simple sutures. The preservation of original deep pink, pearly shell, crushed flat in shale, is typical of fossil shells found in north Somerset, UK.
• **HABITAT** *Psiloceras* was a moderately capable swimmer.
• **REMARK** This genus was abundant locally in the Early Jurassic period.

gray shale matrix

small individuals preserved as nacre shell

crushed shells

Typical diameter
2¾ in (7 cm)

PSILOCERAS PLANORBIS (J. de C. Sowerby); Lower Lias; Early Jurassic; UK.

| Range E. Jurassic | Distribution Worldwide | Occurrence |

| Order AMMONITIDA | Family AMALTHEIDAE | Informal name Ammonite |

AMALTHEUS

Amaltheus is characterized by its very compressed, involute shell and by the narrow keel which has an ornament resembling a piece of rope. The ornament of the flanks is weak and consists of sickle-shaped ribs or, more rarely, fine, spiral ribs.
• **HABITAT** The streamlined whorl profile and narrow keel suggest that it was quite a good swimmer.
• **REMARK** The genus may have evolved from *Phylloceras (see p.145).*

simple S-shaped ribs

BROWN SANDSTONE MOLD

Typical diameter
2¼ in (7 cm)

compressed shell with corded keel

AMALTHEUS STOKESI (J. Sowerby); Middle Lias; Early Jurassic; UK.

| Range E. Jurassic | Distribution Worldwide | Occurrence |

Order AMMONITIDA	Family OXYNOTICERATIDAE	Informal name Ammonite

OXYNOTICERAS

living chamber broken away •

INTERNAL
MOLD IN
PYRITES

This distinctive ammonite is characterized by its strongly compressed, involute shell and knife-sharp keel. The suture line is complex and frilled. The lower specimen has been cut in half to show the septa (pyrite) and the cameral chambers, now filled with yellow calcite. The siphuncle is just visible next to the venter – its characteristic position.

• HABITAT The sharp keel would have offered minimum resistance to the water through which *Oxynoticeras* swam, and it is interpreted as one of the fastest-swimming ammonites of all.

• REMARK The specimens are internal molds in bronzy iron pyrites – a common ammonite mode of preservation in clays.

involute shell with small umbilicus •

OXYNOTICERAS OXYNOTUM
(Quenstedt); Lower Lias;
Early Jurassic; UK.

cross section of individual, nearly straight septa •

siphuncle just visible on ventral margin of shell •

chamber full of yellow calcite •

sharp keel on margin of compressed shell •

PYRITIZED
AMMONITE
CUT IN HALF

Typical diameter
4 in (10 cm)

Range E. Jurassic	Distribution Worldwide	Occurrence ◉ ◉ ◉

Order AMMONITIDA	Family KOSMOCERATIDAE	Informal name Ammonite

KOSMOCERAS

This is a compressed, moderately evolute ammonite. It is very typical of Middle Jurassic deposits. The shell has a complex ornament of bunched ribs and rows of tubercles. The venter is narrow and flat.
• **HABITAT** *Kosmoceras* lived in deep water and was probably a moderately good swimmer.
• **REMARK** The specimen is preserved in original shell material, crushed in shales.

KOSMOCERAS DUNCANI (J. de C. Sowerby); Oxford Clay; Middle Jurassic; UK.

crushed nacre shell

Typical diameter
2½ in (6 cm)

Range M. Jurassic	Distribution Worldwide	Occurrence ◉◉◉◉◉

Order AMMONITIDA	Family PERISPHINCTIDAE	Informal name Ammonite

PAVLOVIA

This was a typical member of the abundant and widespread Late Jurassic family, Perisphinctidae. Members of the family are characterized by open, evolute shell forms, rounded whorl sections, and ornamentation of branching ribs. A long-living chamber occupies nearly a whole whorl of the shell. The suture is complex.
• **HABITAT** This genus lived in the extensive Late Jurassic seas.

branching ribs

evolute shell form

umbilicus

PAVLOVIA PRAECOX Spath; Upper Glauconite Series; Late Jurassic; Greenland.

Typical diameter
1½ in (4 cm)

Range L. Jurassic	Distribution Greenland, northern Europe	Occurrence ◉◉◉

| Order AMMONITIDA | Family DACTYLIOCERATIDAE | Informal name Ammonite |

DACTYLIOCERAS

The shell form is evolute, with many whorls visible, and a wide, shallow umbilicus. The fine, branching ribs are closely spaced and pass over a rounded venter.
• **HABITAT** Experiments have shown *Dactylioceras* to be a slow swimmer.
• **REMARK** In medieval times, ammonites were thought to be petrified snakes and were provided with carved heads for sale to pilgrims.

aperture •
• carved "head"
open-coiled, • evolute form

DACTYLIOCERAS COMMUNE (J. de C. Sowerby); Upper Lias; Early Jurassic; UK.

fine, branching ribs
rounded venter •

Typical diameter 2¾ in (7 cm)

| Range E. Jurassic | Distribution Worldwide | Occurrence |

| Order AMMONITIDA | Family HILDOCERATIDAE | Informal name Ammonite |

HARPOCERAS

This is a common Early Jurassic ammonite, characterized by a compressed, moderately involute shell that bore a sharp ventral keel, and flanks with distinctive sickle-shaped ribs. The aperture was drawn into a short rostrum on the ventral margin.
• **HABITAT** This genus was probably a good swimmer that fed by preying on small animals.
• **REMARK** The specimen is preserved as claystone coated with a thin layer of iron pyrites.

• short rostrum on aperture
• curved aperture
• sharp keel

HARPOCERAS FALCIFERUM (J. Sowerby); Upper Lias; Early Jurassic; UK.

Typical diameter 4¾ in (12 cm)

• sickle-shaped ribs

| Range E. Jurassic | Distribution Worldwide | Occurrence |

| Order AMMONITIDA | Family HILDOCERATIDAE | Informal name Ammonite |

HILDOCERAS

Hildoceras had an evolute, laterally compressed shell. The coarse, widely spaced, sickle-shaped ribbing on the sides is interrupted by a groove. The suture line is very complex. It has a very distinctive rectangular whorl section, which on the venter carries three low keels separated by two grooves.
• **HABITAT** *Hildoceras* was a moderate swimmer in the Early Jurassic shelf seas.
• **REMARK** This specimen is well preserved in a claystone nodule.

HILDOCERAS BIFRONS (Bruguière); Upper Lias; Early Jurassic; UK.

• *sickle-shaped ribs interrupted by groove*

• *wide umbilicus*

Typical diameter
2¾ in (7 cm)

• *triple-keeled venter*

| Range E. Jurassic | Distribution Europe, Asia Minor, Japan | Occurrence ◉◉◉ |

| Order AMMONITIDA | Family EODEROCERATIDAE | Informal name Ammonite |

BIFERICERAS

In common with many ammonites, the larger shell (macroconch) of *Bifericeras* is the female. The smaller (micro-conch) is the male. Females required a larger body size for egg production and possible brooding habit.
• **HABITAT** *Bifericeras* lived in open seas of moderate depth, and either preyed on or scavenged small marine invertebrates.

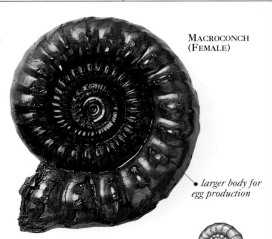

MACROCONCH
(FEMALE)

• *larger body for egg production*

MICROCONCH
(MALE)

BIFERICERAS BIFER (Quenstedt); Lower Lias; Early Jurassic; UK.

Typical diameter
1¼ in (3 cm)

| Range E. Jurassic | Distribution Europe | Occurrence ◉◉ |

| Order AMMONITIDA | Family PACHYDISCIDAE | Informal name Ammonite |

PACHYDISCUS

The family Pachydiscidae includes the giants of the ammonite group, and specimens up to 6½ ft (2 m) in diameter have been found in Late Cretaceous rocks. The shell is moderately involute and compressed and carries short, gently curved ribs. The venter is rounded.
• **HABITAT** A competent swimmer, *Pachydiscus* lived in open seas.
• **REMARK** The specimen is preserved in limestone but retains patches of the original shell.

PACHYDISCUS sp.; Late Cretaceous; Canada.

limestone-infilled living chamber

involute shell form

rounded venter

original shell material

Typical diameter 2½ in (6 cm)

| Range L. Cretaceous | Distribution Worldwide | Occurrence |

| Order AMMONITIDA | Family ANCYLOCERATIDAE | Informal name Ammonite |

CRIOCERATITES

The shell of *Crioceratites* is so loosely coiled that the whorls are not in contact. The whorl size increases rapidly. Stronger ribs carrying tubercles are separated by two to three weaker, finer ribs with no tubercles. The venter is rounded.
• **HABITAT** This genus was adapted to a predatory swimming habit in moderately deep shelf seas.
• **REMARK** The loosely coiled morphology evolved many times in the ammonoids and nautiloids.

open-coiled whorls

ribs with tubercles

fine ribs

CRIOCERATITES sp.; Early Cretaceous; South Africa.

Typical diameter 4 in (10 cm)

| Range E. Cretaceous | Distribution Worldwide | Occurrence |

| Order AMMONITIDA | Family DOUVILLEICERATIDAE | Informal name Ammonite |

DOUVILLEICERAS

The shell is involute and compressed in profile. Strong, simple ribs pass over the rounded venter, each divided into numerous, even-sized tubercles, which would originally have carried long spines.
• **HABITAT** This genus was certainly a poor swimmer – the broad profile of the whorl offered considerable resistance to the water. *Douvilleiceras* may well have spent much time scavenging or hunting on the sea bed.
• **REMARK** This well-preserved internal mold is composed of dark calcium phosphate set in a greenish, glauconitic sand of a younger age.

DOUVILLEICERAS MAMMILLATUM (Schlotheim); Gault Clay; Early Cretaceous; UK.

broad, rounded venter

tubercles

simple ribs

umbilicus

VIEW OF VENTER

SIDE VIEW

glauconitic sand

Typical diameter 4 in (10 cm)

| Range E. Cretaceous | Distribution Worldwide | Occurrence ✹✹✹✹ |

| Order AMMONITIDA | Family ANCYLOCERATIDAE | Informal name Ammonite |

AUSTRALICERAS

The simply coiled shell of this genus expanded rapidly as it grew. It carries an ornament of fine, closely spaced ribs that extend over the rounded venter. Many closely related forms in this family are uncoiled, so that the body chamber forms a hook.
• **HABITAT** *Australiceras* was probably a slow swimmer in the shallow shelf seas of the Early Cretaceous.
• **REMARK** Like many ammonites, *Australiceras* is most commonly found as whorl fragments rather than as complete specimens.

AUSTRALICERAS JACKI (Etheridge); Early Cretaceous; Australia.

fine, closely spaced ribs

rounded venter

rapid increase in whorl size

Typical diameter 4¾ in (12 cm)

| Range E. Cretaceous | Distribution Worldwide | Occurrence ✹✹✹ |

| Order AMMONITIDA | Family PLACENTICERATIDAE | Informal name Ammonite |

PLACENTICERAS

This Late Cretaceous genus grew to a considerable size (up to 9 in (20 cm)). The specimen shown here lacks the living chamber of the ammonite, which, in life, would have comprised almost another whorl. The highly compressed, very involute shell has a very narrow venter and a thick nacre shell.

• **HABITAT** Experiments in tanks with models of ammonite shells indicate that *Placenticeras*, with its large size and streamlined profile, was perhaps the fastest swimmer of all known ammonites, jetting through the water in pursuit of prey, or fleeing from predators such as reptiles and large fish.

• **REMARK** Several specimens recovered from the western interior of the USA display bite marks from the repeated attacks of a giant marine lizard.

tabulate venter •

WHORL PROFILE

compressed profile •

living chamber broken away

broken end of convoluted septum

PLACENTICERAS MEEKEI Boehm; Late Cretaceous; USA.

former position of aperture •

umbilicus •

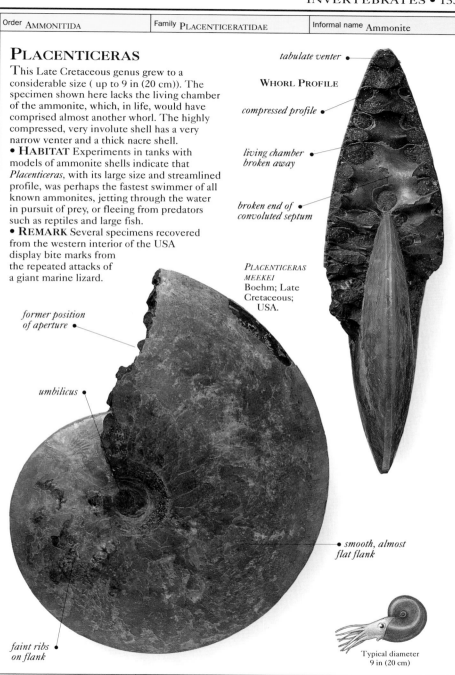

• *smooth, almost flat flank*

• *faint ribs on flank*

Typical diameter 9 in (20 cm)

| Range L. Cretaceous | Distribution Worldwide | Occurrence |

Order AMMONITIDA	Family EODEROCERATIDAE	Informal name Ammonite

PROMICROCERAS

This limestone (known as Marston Marble) is composed largely of closely packed, small, but complete, shells of the ammonite genus *Promicroceras*. A fragment of a larger genus, *Asteroceras*, is present on the corner of the block. *Promicroceras*'s shell is evolute and is ornamented by coarse, simple, straight ribs that form a forward-directed flange over the venter.

• **HABITAT** Marston Marble was formed by the mass mortality of *Promicroceras*, resulting either from a major storm, or perhaps poisoning by an algal bloom.

• **REMARK** The ammonite shells were rapidly buried in lime-mud, which hardened into limestone.

Asteroceras shell

small, perfectly preserved shells of Promicroceras

original shell

Typical diameter ¾ in (2 cm)

MARSTON MARBLE; Lower Lias; Early Jurassic; UK.

Range E. Jurassic	Distribution Worldwide	Occurrence ◉◉

Order AMMONITIDA	Family AREITITIDAE	Informal name Ammonite

ASTEROCERAS

Large, rather simply ornamented ammonites of this family are common in Early Jurassic sediments on a worldwide scale. The rather evolute shell carries curved ribs, and a keel is present on the venter.

• **HABITAT** *Asteroceras* lived at moderate depths in shelf seas, and was probably a slow swimmer, living by predation on small marine animals.

• **REMARK** The chambered part of this well-preserved shell has infilled with translucent brown calcite, and the living chamber with gray lime-mud. The shell has mostly broken away.

Typical diameter 8¾ in (22 cm)

ASTEROCERAS OBTUSUM (J. Sowerby); Lower Lias; Early Jurassic; UK.

simple ammonite sutures

chamber that housed the soft parts

Range E. Jurassic	Distribution Worldwide	Occurrence ◉◉◉

Order AMMONITIDA	Family ECHIOCERATIDAE	Informal name Ammonite

ECHIOCERAS

The shell is extremely evolute, with numerous visible whorls and a shallow umbilicus. Short, straight ribs are present on the flanks, but do not pass on to the low-keeled venter.
• **HABITAT** This ammonite inhabited the shelf seas of the Early Jurassic. From the very evolute shell shape, it is possible to infer that *Echioceras* was not adapted for fast swimming. It probably scavenged or caught slow-moving prey.

venter carries low keel

short, straight ribs on evolute shell

ECHIOCERAS FASTIGIATUM Trueman & Williams; Lower Lias; Early Jurassic; UK.

Typical diameter
2½ in (6 cm)

Range E. Jurassic	Distribution Worldwide	Occurrence

Order AMMONITIDA	Family KOSSMATICERATIDAE	Informal name Ammonite

GUNNARITES

The distinctive shell of *Gunnarites* is moderately evolute with a rounded venter. It is ornamented with strong, regular, crenulated ribs, arising from tubercles in the umbilicus.
• **HABITAT** *Gunnarites* lived in the shelf seas of the Late Cretaceous, and was probably a slow swimmer.
• **REMARK** This specimen is preserved as an internal mold, along with some of the original shell (yellow-brown).

GRAY SANDSTONE INTERNAL MOLD

strong, crenulated ribs arise from tubercles

original shell

GUNNARITES sp.; Marambio Group; Late Cretaceous; Antarctica.

Typical diameter
6¼ in (16 cm)

Range L. Cretaceous	Distribution Antarctica, India, Australasia	Occurrence

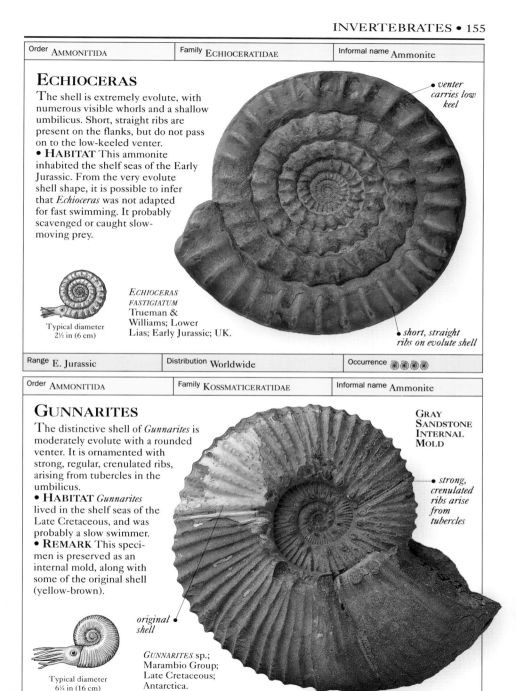

Order AMMONITIDA	Family ACANTHOCERATIDAE	Informal name Ammonite

MANTELLICERAS

The shell is involute, with a fairly small umbilicus. The whorl section is rectangular, the venter flat. Alternately long and short ribs are present on the flanks.
• HABITAT *Mantelliceras* and its relatives were probably poor swimmers, as they were not streamlined. They display strong sexual dimorphism in size, with the females (macroconchs) much larger.
• REMARK This genus is characteristic of the beginning of the Late Cretaceous in the northern hemisphere.

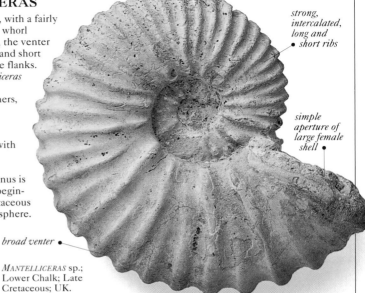

strong, intercalated, long and short ribs

simple aperture of large female shell

broad venter

Typical diameter 1¾ in (4.5 cm)

MANTELLICERAS sp.; Lower Chalk; Late Cretaceous; UK.

Range Cretaceous	Distribution Europe	Occurrence

Order AMMONITIDA	Family HOPLITIDAE	Informal name Ammonite

EUHOPLITES

The shell is moderately involute and it is inflated in profile. The flanks bear tubercles, from which arise bunched ribs. The venter has a narrow groove.
• HABITAT The numerous ribs and tubercles, together with the rectangular profile of the whorl, would have offered much resistance to water, and prevented *Euhoplites* from swimming fast.
• REMARK In life the shell would have been three times the size of this fragment, which has missing whorls.

living chamber broken away

strong ornament of ribs and tubercles

EUHOPLITES OPALINUS Spath; Gault Clay; Early Cretaceous; UK.

Typical diameter 1⅜ in (3.5 cm)

pyrite preservation

original nacre shell preserved

Range E. Cretaceous	Distribution Europe	Occurrence

Order AMMONITIDA	Family SCHLOENBACHIIDAE	Informal name Ammonite

SCHLOENBACHIA

Schloenbachia was one of the most typical Late Cretaceous ammonites of Europe. It displays considerable variation in the development of ornament – some specimens are nearly smooth and very flat; others are fat, with tubercles. The strongly developed ventral keel is characteristic of the genus. Individuals can grow up to 10 in (25 cm) across.
• HABITAT Ammonites of this genus are thought to have been fairly good swimmers.
• REMARK This specimen is preserved as a phosphatic internal cast.

ventral keel •

strong, rounded tubercles •

WHORL PROFILE

• *broken end of septum*

SCHLOENBACHIA VARIANS (J. de C. Sowerby); Lower Chalk; Late Cretaceous; UK.

Typical diameter 2 in (5 cm)

rows of well-developed tubercles on flanks •

Range L. Cretaceous	Distribution Europe, Greenland	Occurrence 🌑🌑🌑🌑🌑🌑

Order AMMONITIDA	Family BRANCOCERATIDAE	Informal name Ammonite

MORTONICERAS

The genus *Mortoniceras* is a very widespread form in Early Cretaceous sediments, and may grow to 20 in (50 cm). The highly characteristic shell form includes a strong keel on the venter and a squarish whorl section.
• HABITAT The genus was probably a poor swimmer and would have swum slowly through the water.
• REMARK The specimen has been crushed into an elliptical shape in the rock.

MORTONICERAS POTTERNENSE Spath; Early Cretaceous; UK.

• *irregular tubercles set on ribs*

• *evolute, open-coiling style*

Typical diameter 3¼ in (8 cm)

• *strong ventral keel*

Range E. Cretaceous	Distribution Europe, Africa, USA	Occurrence 🌑🌑

| Order AMMONITIDA | Family DESHAYESITIDAE | Informal name Ammonite |

DESHAYESITES

Deshayesites was an evolute, compressed ammonite, whose shell carries a rather simple ornament of sinuous ribs. The ribs pass over the narrow, rounded venter. The genus was common in and absolutely diagnostic of Aptian times.
• **HABITAT** The streamlined profile and weak ornament suggest that this genus was capable of fast movement through the water.
• **REMARK** The specimen is preserved as an internal mold with traces of original shell.

sinuous ribs

broken end of living chamber

rounded edge of venter

Typical diameter
1¾ in (4.5 cm)

DESHAYESITES FORBESI Casey; Early Cretaceous; Russia.

| Range E. Cretaceous | Distribution Worldwide | Occurrence ◉ ◉ ◉ |

| Order AMMONITIDA | Family NOSTOCERATIDAE | Informal name Ammonite |

NIPPONITES

Of all the Late Cretaceous ammonites that coiled in an irregular fashion, *Nipponites* was the most bizarre, appearing to be an irregular tangle of whorls. On closer inspection, however, it proves to be a three-dimensional network of Us. It possesses a typical complex ammonite suture and a simple ornament of ribs, and probably evolved from a helically coiled form *(see p.159)*.
• **HABITAT** *Nipponites* probably lived as a planktonic form, drifting through the mid-level or upper waters of the warm Late Cretaceous seas, and feeding on small animals, which it caught with its tentacles.

BROWN SANDSTONE INTERNAL MOLD

simple ribs of varying size

apparently irregular coiling pattern

NIPPONITES MIRABILIS Yabe; Late Cretaceous; Japan.

Typical diameter
2½ in (6 cm)

| Range L. Cretaceous | Distribution Japan, USA | Occurrence ◉ |

Order AMMONITIDA	Family NOSTOCERATIDAE	Informal name Ammonite

BOSTRYCHOCERAS

In this genus, and in the closely related family Turrilitidae, the coiling of the shell has become helical (like that of a snail or gastropod), in contrast to the planispiral flat coiling of most ammonites. Although superficially similar to gastropods, such fossils are readily identifiable as ammonites from the characteristic suture lines. In *Bostrychoceras*, the coiling is loose, so that successive whorls are not in contact. The simple ornament of fine, closely spaced ribs is interrupted on the living chamber by the development of tubercles. The living chamber is U shaped, and the aperture was directed forward in life, so that the protruding tentacles would not have been in contact with the sea bed below.

• **HABITAT** Paleontologists believe that this genus was probably planktonic, floating in the open ocean, and feeding on small animals in the water column. The very widespread distribution accords with this theory, since ocean-going species are commonly of global occurrence.

• **REMARK** *Bostrychoceras* is most often found as small pieces of broken whorls, the ornamentation of which allows identification.

YELLOW LIMESTONE MOLD

Typical height
5½ in (14 cm)

BOSTRYCHOCERAS sp.; Late Cretaceous; Germany.

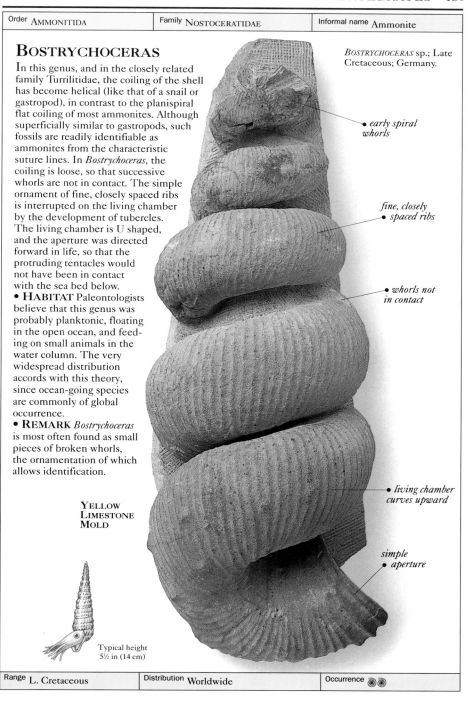

• *early spiral whorls*

• *fine, closely spaced ribs*

• *whorls not in contact*

• *living chamber curves upward*

• *simple aperture*

Range L. Cretaceous	Distribution Worldwide	Occurrence

| Order AMMONITIDA | Family BACULITIDAE | Informal name Ammonite |

BACULITES

In this Late Cretaceous genus, only the very earliest part of the shell remained coiled; the latter part grew into a straight shaft. *Baculites* can occur in vast numbers at some localities, often to the virtual exclusion of other species, and could grow to over 39 in (1 meter) in length.

• **HABITAT** The mode of life of these straight ammonites is controversial: some paleontologists believe that they lived upright in the water, with the tentacles on the sea bed foraging for food; others that they had horizontal orientation and lived nearer the surface of the sea.

fragment of chambered shell

complex suture

BACULITES sp.; Calcaire a Baculites; Late Cretaceous; France.

traces of suture

living chamber

tapering early part of shell

Typical length 4 in (10 cm)

| Range L. Cretaceous | Distribution Worldwide | Occurrence |

| Order AMMONITIDA | Family SCAPHITIDAE | Informal name Ammonite |

SCAPHITES

The family Scaphitidae represents a different design of Late Cretaceous uncoiled ammonite. The chambered early whorls are tightly coiled in the usual fashion, but the living chamber, comprising a short, straight shaft and a terminal hook, is shaped like a shepherd's crook.

• **HABITAT** The shell form of *Scaphites* suggests it was unable to swim actively but could use gas and liquid in its chambered shell to alter its buoyancy, and thus the position in the water column, in common with other ammonite genera.

• **REMARK** This specimen is preserved as an internal mold in calcium phosphate-cemented glauco-nitic chalk.

PHOSPHATIZED INTERNAL MOLD

tightly coiled early whorls

living chamber

Typical diameter 3 in (8 cm)

SCAPHITES EQUALIS (J. de C. Sowerby); Late Cretaceous; France.

| Range L. Cretaceous | Distribution Worldwide | Occurrence |

BELEMNITES AND SQUIDS

BELEMNITES AND SQUIDS belong to a diverse group of cephalopods, which include the living squid, cuttlefish, and octopus. The group is characterized by an internal, chambered shell enclosed entirely by soft, muscular tissues. Many forms have a hard internal support structure, made of calcium carbonate or protein, known as the pen or guard. Belemnites possessed strong, usually cylindrical, calcite guards that preserved well and occur abundantly in Mesozoic marine rocks. Squids possess an internal support called a pen, which is made of proteinaceous chitin. This is only rarely preserved. However, in a few instances, the soft tissue has been preserved, and an entire squid, complete with tentacles, is recognizable.

Order BELEMNITIDA	Family ACROTEUTHIDAE	Informal name Belemnite

ACROTEUTHIS

• *blunt termination*

The large stout guard tapers to a blunt posterior end. The cylindrical cavity (alveolus) is deep. Grooves are present on the sides.
• **HABITAT** This marine creature was probably a slow swimmer.
• **REMARK** The surface of the guard is often worn by erosion to show clearly the concentric "onion skin" layers of calcite that make it up.

worn surface
• *of guard*

ACROTEUTHIS LATERALIS (Phillips); Speeton Clay; Early Cretaceous; UK.

• *deep alveolus*

Typical length 20 in (50 cm)

• *grooves*

Range E. Cretaceous	Distribution Europe	Occurrence

Order BELEMNITIDA	Family HIBOLITHIDAE	Informal name Belemnite

HIBOLITHES

The guard is long, slender, and delicately constructed, with a slightly bulbous posterior end. A strong, narrow groove is present near the anterior margin on the ventral side. This is fragile and often broken in the fossil state.
• **HABITAT** This slender belemnite swam in the Early Cretaceous seas.

clay matrix •

part of guard • *housing alveolus*

HIBOLITHES JACULOIDES Swinnerton; Speeton Clay; Early Cretaceous; UK.

• *bulbous posterior*

Typical length 12 in (30 cm)

Range M. Jurrasic–L. Cretaceous	Distribution Northern hemisphere	Occurrence

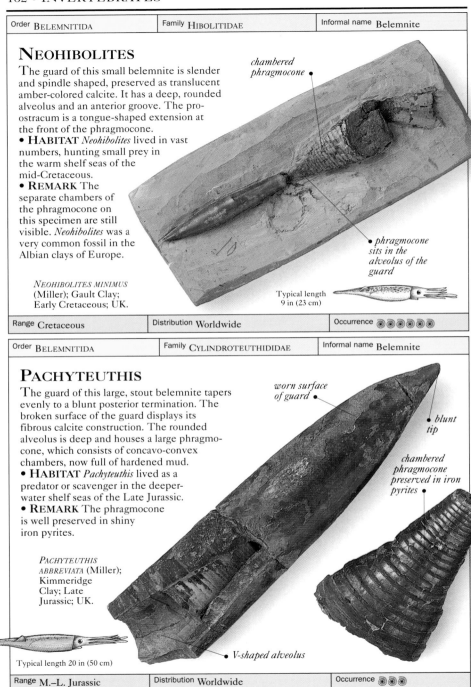

| Order BELEMNITIDA | Family HIBOLITIDAE | Informal name Belemnite |

NEOHIBOLITES

The guard of this small belemnite is slender and spindle shaped, preserved as translucent amber-colored calcite. It has a deep, rounded alveolus and an anterior groove. The pro-ostracum is a tongue-shaped extension at the front of the phragmocone.
• **HABITAT** *Neohibolites* lived in vast numbers, hunting small prey in the warm shelf seas of the mid-Cretaceous.
• **REMARK** The separate chambers of the phragmocone on this specimen are still visible. *Neohibolites* was a very common fossil in the Albian clays of Europe.

chambered phragmocone

phragmocone sits in the alveolus of the guard

NEOHIBOLITES MINIMUS (Miller); Gault Clay; Early Cretaceous; UK.

Typical length 9 in (23 cm)

| Range Cretaceous | Distribution Worldwide | Occurrence ⬡⬡⬡⬡⬡⬡ |

| Order BELEMNITIDA | Family CYLINDROTEUTHIDIDAE | Informal name Belemnite |

PACHYTEUTHIS

The guard of this large, stout belemnite tapers evenly to a blunt posterior termination. The broken surface of the guard displays its fibrous calcite construction. The rounded alveolus is deep and houses a large phragmo-cone, which consists of concavo-convex chambers, now full of hardened mud.
• **HABITAT** *Pachyteuthis* lived as a predator or scavenger in the deeper-water shelf seas of the Late Jurassic.
• **REMARK** The phragmocone is well preserved in shiny iron pyrites.

worn surface of guard

blunt tip

chambered phragmocone preserved in iron pyrites

PACHYTEUTHIS ABBREVIATA (Miller); Kimmeridge Clay; Late Jurassic; UK.

Typical length 20 in (50 cm)

V-shaped alveolus

| Range M.–L. Jurassic | Distribution Worldwide | Occurrence ⬡⬡⬡ |

Order BELEMNITIDA	Family BELEMNITELLIDAE	Informal name Belemnite

BELEMNITELLA

The guard of *Belemnitella* tapers only gently, and is terminated posteriorly by a tip called a mucron. The anterior part of the guard is paper-thin and houses a deep alveolus. The surface of the guard carries a network of intricately branching, shallow grooves, which are probably impressions created by the blood vessels in the soft tissues of the living belemnite.
• **HABITAT** *Belemnitella* swam in the shallower waters of the Late Cretaceous Chalk sea, and used its hooked tentacles to catch small prey.
• **REMARK** This is one of the belemnites that survived nearly to the end of the Cretaceous. It occurs in huge numbers at some localities in so-called "belemnite graveyards."

BELEMNITELLA MUCRONATA (Schlotheim); Maastrichtian; Late Cretaceous; Holland.

deep alveolus

impression of veins on surface of guard

point on tip of guard

Typical length 16 in (40 cm)

Range L. Cretaceous	Distribution Northern hemisphere	Occurrence ⬤⬤⬤⬤⬤

Order BELEMNITIDA	Family CYLINDROTEUTHIDIDAE	Informal name Belemnite

CYLINDROTEUTHIS

The guard is long and cylindrical, and tapers gradually to a posterior point. The chambered phragmocone expands anteriorly.
• **HABITAT** This genus lived as a predator in the deeper parts of shelf seas.
• **REMARK** This is one of the largest species of belemnite, growing up to 10 in (25 cm) in length.

CYLINDROTEUTHIS PUZOSIANA (d'Orbigny); Oxford Clay; Late Jurassic; UK.

apex of guard

alveolus of guard

long, cylindrical guard

Typical length 10 in (25 cm)

Range M.–L. Jurassic	Distribution Europe, N. America	Occurrence ⬤⬤⬤⬤

Order Not applicable	Family Not applicable	Informal name Belemnite limestone

BELEMNITE LIMESTONE

alveolus •   • *concentric growth rings*

This cut and polished piece of marine shelly limestone shows several belemnites in different cross sections. These illustrate well the massive construction of the belemnite guard, composed of the mineral calcite (calcium carbonate). The belemnites show fine, radially arranged, calcite crystals, and display strong, concentric growth lines. The V-shaped space at the anterior end of the guard is called the alveolus, and housed the chambered phragmocone, used for buoyancy control by the belemnite in life.

• **HABITAT** These various belemnites would have had differing life-styles, although all would have been marine dwellers.

• **REMARK** The term "marble" is loosely applied to any polished limestone.

BELEMNITE LIMESTONE; Jurassic; Germany.

calcite of belemnite guards •   • *shell fragments in limestone*

Range Cretaceous–Triassic	Distribution Worldwide	Occurrence ▧ ▧ ▧ ▧ ▧

Order VAMPYROMORPHA	Family TRACHYTEUTHIDIDAE	Informal name Belemnite

TRACHYTEUTHIS

• *growth lines on surface*

Only the guard of this genus has ever been found preserved as a fossil. The outline is an elongated oval, and a lobe is present on each side. Growth lines are visible on the dorsal surface .

• **HABITAT** This animal probably resembled a cuttlefish in its life habits, living on the sea bed and preying on crustaceans.

• **REMARK** It is open to debate whether this genus is closer to the squid or cuttlefish in affinity.

TRACHYTEUTHIS sp.; Solnhofen Limestone; Late Jurassic; Germany.

flattened guard • *resembling cuttlebone*

Typical length 10 in (25 cm)

• *limestone*

Range L. Jurassic	Distribution Europe	Occurrence ▧

Order BELEMNITIDA	Family BELEMNOTHEUTIDIDAE	Informal name Belemnite

BELEMNOTHEUTIS

The head region carries ten arms, on which hooks are present. The anterior part of the body is called the mantle, and has two fins – very much like a living squid. The hindmost part of the animal is the chambered phragmocone, which tapers posteriorly. At the end, a thin guard is sometimes preserved.

• **HABITAT** *Belemnotheutis* lived in the open sea at a moderate depth and swam by jet propulsion (water expulsion from the mantle) in exactly the same way that modern squid do. It used its hooked and suckered arms to catch prey.

• **REMARK** This specimen displays a very rare phenomenon in the fossil record – the preservation of soft parts, which normally would decay and be completely lost. This type of preservation is caused by rapid burial of the animal in stagnant oxygen-free water, where scavengers and most bacteria cannot live. The belemnite's soft parts are replaced by calcium phosphate.

arms with
• *small hooks*

• *head region*

chambered •
phragmocone

• *mantle*
with two
fins

BELEMNOTHEUTIS
ANTIQUA Pearce;
Oxford Clay;
Late Jurassic; UK.

Typical length 5 in (12 cm)

Range L. Jurassic	Distribution Europe	Occurrence

CRINOIDS

CRINOIDS, POPULARLY known as sea lilies and feather stars, possess a massive calcite skeleton. They were so abundant in the Paleozoic seas that their remains formed vast thicknesses of limestone. Most crinoids are attached to the sea bed by a flexible stem, circular or pentagonal in section, and made up of numerous disclike plates called columnals. At the top of the stem is a swollen cup or calyx, to which the arms are attached. The arms are used to filter food from the water. Soon after the animal's death, the entire skeleton normally falls apart into the small, separate plates called ossicles. By contrast, well-preserved crinoids are rare and beautiful fossils.

Order MONOBATHRIDA	Family DIMEROCRINITIDAE	Informal name Sea lily

DIMEROCRINITES

The stem of this crinoid is cylindrical, with a low, conical cup made up of many small swollen plates. The 20 short arms form a compact crown.
• **HABITAT** *Dimerocrinites* lived in shallow, warm waters, attached to the sea bed by a root.
• **REMARK** In life, the arms formed a fan-like array, to strain food from the water.

Typical cup diameter
1 in (2.5 cm)

cylindrical stem made of many small columnals

broken base of stem

DIMEROCRINITES ICOSIDACTYLUS Phillips; Wenlock Limestone; Middle Silurian; UK.

Range Silurian–Devonian	Distribution Europe, N. America	Occurrence

Order CLADIDA	Family EUSPIROCRINIDAE	Informal name Sea lily

PARISANGULOCRINUS

The long and narrow stem of *Parisangulo-crinus* is circular in cross section. A few large plates make up the small cup, and the arms are long, branching many times. Waste material was disposed of by a long tube, made of numerous small plates situated between the arms. The wide fanlike crown has many branches.
• **HABITAT** This genus lived in deep water.
• **REMARK** In life, the arms of this crinoid were held permanently in a wide fan, to trap particles of food.

Typical cup diameter
⅝ in (1.5 cm)

wide, fan-like crown

long, narrow stem made of circular columnals

PARISANGULO-CRINUS ZEAFORMIS (Schultze); Hunsruck-schiefer; Devonian; Germany.

Range Silurian–Carb.	Distribution Europe, N. America	Occurrence

Order CLADIDA	Family CUPRESSOCRINITIDAE	Informal name Sea lily

CUPRESSOCRINITES

This robust crinoid has a cylindrical stem and a large conical cup made up of ten large plates in two alternating circles. The short arms, five in number, are unbranched and triangular in shape. They fit together closely to form a short, pointed crown.
• **HABITAT** The very strong form of this species is perhaps related to the rough current-swept environment in which it lived, in which fragile forms would not have survived.
• **REMARK** The ancestry and relationships of *Cupressocrinites* are not well understood.

compact crown

cup made up of ten large plates

cylindrical stem

CUPRESSOCRINITES CRASSUS
Goldfuss; Crinoiden Schichten; Middle Devonian; Germany.

Typical cup diameter
1 in (2.5 cm)

Range Devonian	Distribution W. Europe	Occurrence ◉

Order CLADIDA	Family CYATHOCRINITIDAE	Informal name Sea lily

CYATHOCRINITES

Cyathocrinites has a cylindrical stem made up of numerous disc-shaped columnals. The bowl-shaped cup includes a few smoothly rounded plates, and the narrow arms branch regularly to form a large complex crown composed of many small units.
• **HABITAT** This genus lived in calm, shallow water, which provided an abundant supply of food.

CYATHOCRINITES ACTINOTUBUS
Angelin; Wenlock Limestone; Middle Silurian; UK.

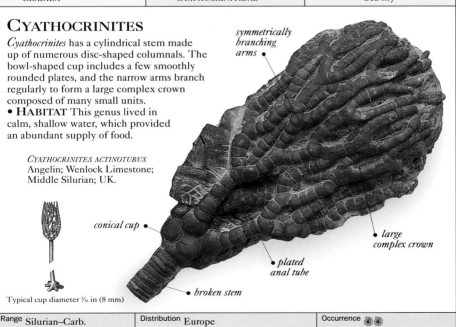

symmetrically branching arms

conical cup

large complex crown

plated anal tube

broken stem

Typical cup diameter ⁵⁄₁₆ in (8 mm)

Range Silurian–Carb.	Distribution Europe	Occurrence ◉◉

Order SAGENOCRINIDA	Family SAGENOCRINIDAE	Informal name Sea lily

SAGENOCRINITES

The stem of *Sagenocrinites* is cylindrical and composed of numerous very thin columnals. Its crown is very broad and oval in shape. The polygonal plates of the lower arms display clear growth lines and form part of the cup. The free parts of the arms are short and are made up of many small plates.
• HABITAT The very compact form of this species suggests that it had adapted to relatively turbulent sea bed conditions.

SAGENOCRINITES EXPANSUS Phillips; Wenlock Limestone; Middle Silurian; UK.

stem of very thin columnals •

• *short, free arms*

• *broad crown*

• *arm bases forming part of cup*

Typical cup diameter
1 in (2.5 cm)

Range M. Silurian	Distribution Europe, N. America	Occurrence

Order Unclassified	Family Unclassified	Informal name Crinoidal limestone

CLIFTON BLACK ROCK

This striking black limestone contains a length of crinoid stem and many small crinoid ossicles in the background. The structure of the stem is well shown: it is made up of short columnals of even height and has a large central cavity running along its length, now full of the limestone.
• HABITAT Crinoidal limestone forms from the detritus washed from a reef.
• REMARK The black color is due to bitumen.

crinoid stem •

CLIFTON BLACK ROCK; Carboniferous Limestone; Carboniferous; UK.

large central cavity •

Typical cup diameter
1½ in (4 cm)

Range Carb.	Distribution UK	Occurrence

Order MONOBATHRIDA	Family ACTINOCRINITIDAE	Informal name Sea lily

ACTINOCRINITES

This well-preserved cup is typical of many crinoids of the subclass Camerata. The large rigid globular cup is made up of many polygonal plates, clearly outlined on this specimen. These plates are arranged into several rings at the base, above the point of attachment to the stem. Above this point, the plates of the lower arms form a more irregular mosaic pattern, passing out to the five projecting stumps of the arms. The domed upper surface of the cup consists of fairly large plates. The stem is circular and includes many very short columnals. In the Early Carboniferous sea, current action could cause such large drifts of crinoidal debris that they became a major constituent of the limestone. A separate artificial classification has been developed for isolated stem segments.

• **HABITAT**
Actinocrinites lived on reefs in deep water, anchored to the sea bed by a rootlike structure. Its short, simple arms trapped small food particles.

base of free arm

domed top of cup

SIDE VIEW

ACTINOCRINITES PARKINSONI Wright; Carboniferous Limestone; Early Carboniferous; UK.

TOP VIEW

curved surface between arms

polygonal plates

CRINOIDAL LIMESTONE

stem segments

Typical cup diameter 1½ in (4 cm)

Range Carb.	Distribution Worldwide	Occurrence

Order ROVEACRINIDA	Family SACCOCOMIDAE	Informal name Feather star

SACCOCOMA

This is a delicately constructed stemless crinoid with a small, globular cup. The arms branch once, to give a total of ten. The lower parts of the arms have small winglike extensions; the upper parts have long narrow side branches.
• **HABITAT** *Saccocoma* was free-living, and probably able to tolerate variations in salinity.
• **REMARK** This species is one of the most common fossils in the Solnhofen Limestone.

globular cup

branched arms

SACCOCOMA TENELLUM (Goldfuss); Solnhofen Limestone; Late Jurassic; Germany.

Typical cup diameter ¾ in (2 cm)

Range L. Jurassic	Distribution Worldwide	Occurrence ⊚⊚⊚⊚⊚

Order CYRTOCRINIDA	Family HEMICRINIDAE	Informal name Sea lily

HEMICRINUS

This curiously shaped crinoid has arms set at right angles to its cup, which is shaped like a spoon. The stemlike extension is actually formed from elongated cup plates, attached directly to a holdfast.
• **HABITAT** *Hemicrinus* lived attached to pebbles by a holdfast and inhabited shallow turbulent waters.
• **REMARK** The cyrtocrinids are squat compact crinoids, locally common in Cretaceous rocks.

end of cup

arm attachment point

point of attachment to root

elongated base of cup

HEMICRINUS CANON (Seeley); Hunstanton Red Rock; Early Cretaceous; UK.

Typical cup diameter ⁵⁄₁₆ in (8 mm)

Range L. Jurassic–E. Cretaceous	Distribution Europe	Occurrence ⊚⊚

Order COMATULIDA	Family PTEROCOMIDAE	Informal name Feather star

PTEROCOMA

This comatulid or feather star has a small cup that bears ten long, featherlike arms of equal length. Each of these has a row of little branches (pinnules) on either side. It possessed a stem only in the earliest stages of development.
• **HABITAT** *Pterocoma* was a free-swimming crinoid, advancing with graceful movements of the arms, like its living relatives.
• **REMARK** Comatulids are rarely found as entire specimens.

long featherlike • arms

PTEROCOMA PENNATA (Schlotheim); Solnhofen Limestone; Late Jurassic; Germany.

small, • centrally placed cup

Typical cup diameter
⅗ in (1.5 cm)

Range L. Jurassic–L. Cretaceous	Distribution Europe, Asia	Occurrence

Order CLADIDA	Family ENCRINIDAE	Informal name Sea lily

ENCRINUS

The long cylindrical stem of this crinoid includes regularly spaced swollen columnals. The crown is squat and compact; the plates are large and swollen. Each arm branches once at the base to give a total of ten short, sturdy arms.
• **HABITAT** *Encrinus* lived in shallow seas.
• **REMARK** This creature could splay its arms to form a feeding fan. Plankton, entrapped in the fan, were conveyed to the mouth along the grooves lying inside the arms. When threatened, the arms closed tightly together in a defensive movement.

crown, with ten tightly closed arms •

Typical cup diameter
1 in (2.5 cm)

ENCRINUS LILIIFORMIS (Lamarck); Muschelkalk; Middle Triassic; Germany.

• long round stem

Range M. Triassic	Distribution Europe	Occurrence

Order ISOCRINIDA	Family PENTACRITINIDAE	Informal name Sea lily

PENTACRINITES

This distinctive crinoid has a long pentagonal stem, with no root structure at the base. Regularly spaced whorls of fine branches (cirri) arise from the stem. The cup is small and inconspicuous, and the fan-shaped crown is made up of multi-branched arms and many small pinnules (branches).

• **HABITAT** Masses of *Pentacrinites* are commonly found preserved under large pieces of fossil wood, leading to the belief that it was pseudopelagic (living in the open sea), in colonies attached to the underside of floating logs. The dispersed debris is locally abundant around logs and formed thin sheets of limestone.

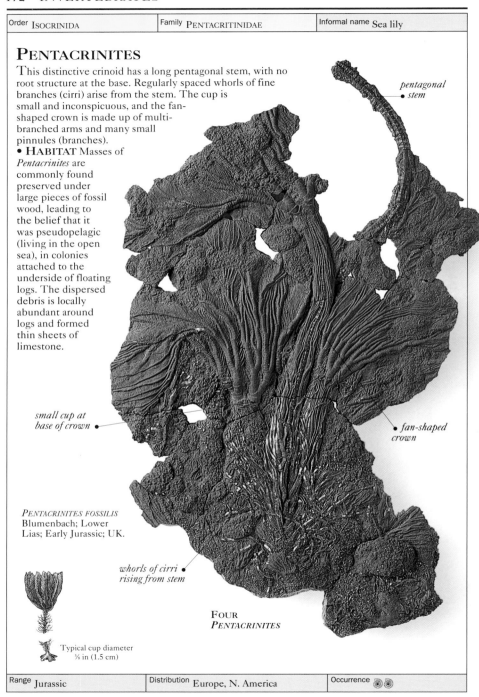

pentagonal stem

small cup at base of crown

fan-shaped crown

PENTACRINITES FOSSILIS
Blumenbach; Lower Lias; Early Jurassic; UK.

whorls of cirri rising from stem

FOUR
PENTACRINITES

Typical cup diameter
⅝ in (1.5 cm)

Range Jurassic	Distribution Europe, N. America	Occurrence

Order MILLERICRINIDA	Family APIOCRINITIDAE	Informal name Sea lily

APIOCRINITES

This stoutly constructed crinoid has a narrow, cylindrical, tapering stem with a conical, irregularly shaped root cemented at the base. The bulbous cup is made up of enlarged columnals, two cycles of cup plates, and the bases of the arms. The arms branch once, symmetrically, to give an elegant fan-shaped crown with a total of ten arms.
• **HABITAT** *Apiocrinites* lived attached to hard, current-swept pavements on the Jurassic sea floor. It filtered food from the water with its arms.
• **REMARK** Remains of this species are found most commonly as separate discoidal cup plates or columnals. The surface of the stem and the holdfast are often colonized by bryozoa and serpulid worms.

broken bases
of arms •

large, bulbous
cup made of
separate plates •

cycle of radial •
plates

cycle of •
basal plates

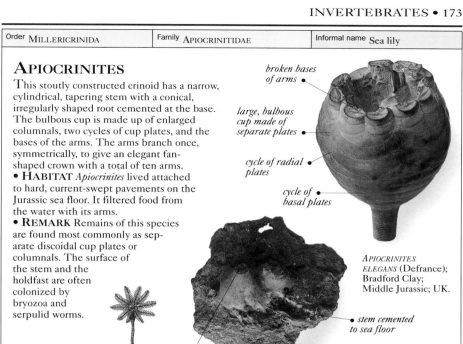

*APIOCRINITES
ELEGANS* (Defrance);
Bradford Clay;
Middle Jurassic; UK.

• *stem cemented
to sea floor*

Typical cup diameter
1¼ in (3 cm)

column •
base attachment

• *conical root*

Range Jurassic–Cretaceous	Distribution Europe, Africa, N. America	Occurrence ◉◉◉◉

Order UINTACRINIDA	Family MARSUPITIDAE	Informal name Sea lily

MARSUPITES

The cup is large and globular and is made up of 11 large, thin, polygonal plates that have a radially arranged ornament. There is no stem, but in its place sits a large pentagonal plate. The arms are long and very narrow and branch to give a total of ten.
• **HABITAT** The adult *Marsupites* nestled in chalky mud on the sea floor and strained food using its arms. The larval form was planktonic.
• **REMARK** The large separate cup plates are distinctive fossils and are used as zonal markers in western Europe.

*MARSUPITES
TESTUDINARIUS*
(Schlotheim);
Upper Chalk; Late
Cretaceous; UK.

• *branching arms*

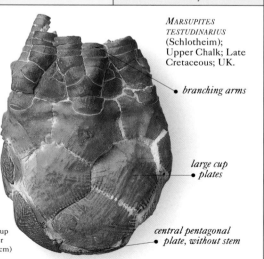

large cup •
plates

Typical cup
diameter
1⅜ in (3.5 cm)

central pentagonal •
plate, without stem

Range L. Cretaceous	Distribution Worldwide	Occurrence ◉◉◉◉

Order UINTACRINIDA	Family UINTACRINIDAE	Informal name Sea lily

UINTACRINUS

This crinoid has no stem but has a very large and globular cup, composed of many small polygonal plates. The bases of the arms are incorporated in the cup, and the arms themselves are very narrow and greatly elongated, reaching up to 50 in (1.25 m).

UINTACRINUS SOCIALIS Grinnell; Niobrara Chalk; Late Cretaceous; USA.

• **HABITAT** Crinoids of this genus lived in soft muddy areas of the sea floor, using their very long arms to catch plankton.

• **REMARK** Fossilized remains of *Uintacrinus* are usually found in the form of separate plates.

large • globular cup

base of long • narrow arms

• fragments of arms

Typical cup diameter 1¾ in (4.5 cm)

Range L. Cretaceous	Distribution Worldwide	Occurrence

Order MILLERICRINIDA	Family MILLERICRINIDAE	Informal name Feather star

AILSACRINUS

This was a very short-stemmed crinoid, with a small central cup, and ten long very narrow arms. The arms carry feathery pinnules on either side.

AILSACRINUS ABBREVIATUS Taylor; Sharps Hill Formation; Middle Jurassic; UK.

• **HABITAT** *Ailsacrinus* was probably a poor swimmer, living in dense colonies on the sea bed in relatively shallow water.

• **REMARK** This genus represents a Jurassic evolutionary experiment in unattached living, a mode of life also achieved in other groups such as the comatulids. It is rare to find an entire fossilized crinoid calyx. Usually only frag- mentary remains, such as the ones seen in this speci- men, are preserved.

portions of feathery • arms

• bases of long arms

• small central cup

Typical cup diameter ⅗ in (1.5 cm)

Range M. Jurassic	Distribution UK	Occurrence

ECHINOIDS

T HE ECHINOIDS possess a rigid globular skeleton (test) made up of columns of thin, calcite plates (ambulacrals and interambulacrals). The plates known as ambulacrals have small pores for tube feet. All plates have swollen tubercles for the ball- and-socket articulation of spines, which are used for defense and some- times for walking. Regular echinoids, which forage on the sea bed, show radial symmetry; irregular echinoids, which usually burrow in soft sea beds, show bilateral symmetry.

Order ECHINOCYSTITOIDA	Family PALECHINIDAE	Informal name Sea urchin

MELONECHINUS

The large, nearly spherical test is formed of many thick, polygonal plates. Both ambulacrals and interambulacrals are made up of numerous plate columns. The midline of the ambulacrals forms a distinct ridge.
• HABITAT
Melonechinus lived in areas between reefs in the Carbon- iferous sea.

Typical diameter 3 in (8 cm)

*numerous columns
• of polygonal plates*

UPPER
SURFACE
OF TEST

*• ridged
ambulacral
columns*

*MELONECHINUS
MULTIPORA*
(Norwood &
Owens); Early
Carboniferous;
USA.

Range E. Carb.	Distribution Worldwide	Occurrence 🞙🞙

Order CIDAROIDA	Family CIDARIDAE	Informal name Sea urchin

PLEGIOCIDARIS

The circular, slightly flattened test comprises five paired, narrow ambulacral plate columns and five paired, broad interambulacra, made up of large plates with prominent tubercles. The hole on the top is the apical disc.
• HABITAT *Plegiocidaris* lived on rocky sea floors, grazing on algae.
• REMARK Large spines were attached to the tubercles in life.

Typical diameter
1½ in (4 cm)

*large
interambulacral
• tubercles*

*narrow
• ambulacra*

*• position of
apical disc*

*PLEGIOCIDARIS
CORONATA*
(Schlotheim); Weisser
Jura; Jurassic; Germany.

Range Jurassic	Distribution Europe	Occurrence 🞙🞙🞙

Order ARCHAEOCIDAROIDA	Family ARCHAEOCIDARIDAE	Informal name Sea urchin

ARCHAEOCIDARIS

The large test, which retains many spines on its surface, is crushed flat. The paired ambulacral columns are narrow, and the broad interambulacra are made up of four columns of plates, each of which carries a single, centrally placed tubercle. A long, narrow spine articulates with each large tubercle. Short spines form a felt-like covering over much of the test. The teeth and jaws are present on the underside but are dissociated.

ARCHAEOCIDARIS WHATLEYENSIS Lewis & Ensom; Carboniferous Limestone; Early Carboniferous; UK.

• **HABITAT** The genus was probably an omnivorous browser, living on the open sea floor, protected by its long spines.

scattered elements of jaw system

long, narrow spine

large tubercle

LOWER SURFACE OF TEST

small, fine spines

position of mouth

UPPER SURFACE OF TEST

ambulacral column

smooth spines

feltlike covering of fine spines

position of apical disc

Typical diameter 3 in (8 cm)

Range E. Carb.–Permian	Distribution Worldwide	Occurrence ◉ ◉

Order CIDAROIDA	Family PSYCHOCIDARIDAE	Informal name Sea urchin

TYLOCIDARIS

The small test is circular in outline and slightly flattened. The ten columns of large interambulacral tubercles carry massive club-shaped defensive spines. The central aperture on the base housed the jaw mechanism (known as Aristotle's Lantern) in life.
• **HABITAT** *Tylocidaris* lived as an omnivorous grazer on shells and sponges on the Chalk sea floor.
• **REMARK** Isolated spines and fragments of the test are quite common Chalk fossils.

large, club-shaped spines

underside

Typical diameter 1¼ in (3 cm)

large interambulacral tubercles

position of mouth opening

TYLOCIDARIS CLAVIGERA (König); Upper Chalk; Late Cretaceous; UK.

Range L. Cretaceous–Eocene	Distribution Europe, N. America	Occurrence 🌑🌑🌑🌑

Order CIDAROIDA	Family CIDARIDAE	Informal name Sea urchin

TEMNOCIDARIS

The nearly spherical test is made up of five paired columns of large interambulacral plates, each having a large conspicuous tubercle. The five paired ambulacral columns are narrow and sinuous. The large, spindle-shaped spines attached to the large interambulacral tubercles had a rough, thorny surface in life.
• **HABITAT** *Temnocidaris* lived on the Chalk sea floor. It was an omnivorous scavenger, using its sharp teeth to rasp food.
• **REMARK** *Temnocidaris* is very rarely preserved in its entirety. The apical disc is missing in this specimen.

TEMNOCIDARIS SCEPTRIFERA (Mantell); Upper Chalk; Late Cretaceous; UK.

narrow ambulacrum

large interambulacral tubercle

position of apical disc

large primary spine

Typical diameter 1¾ in (4.5 cm)

Range L. Cretaceous	Distribution Europe	Occurrence 🌑🌑🌑

Order CALYCINA	Family SALENIIDAE	Informal name Sea urchin

TRISALENIA

The circular flattened test of *Trisalenia* is capped by a very large flat apical disc made up of two rings of plates plus a single central plate and a hole in which the anus was situated in life. The large genital plates carry pores through which eggs and sperm were released. The large interambulacral tubercles carried smooth, pointed spines.
• **HABITAT** *Trisalenia* lived among large granite boulders on the rocky shoreline that fringed part of southern Sweden during the Late Cretaceous.
• **REMARK** The family Saleniidae occurs commonly in marine Cretaceous sediments.

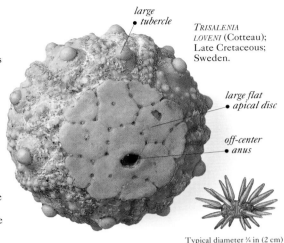

TRISALENIA LOVENI (Cotteau); Late Cretaceous; Sweden.

large tubercle

large flat apical disc

off-center anus

Typical diameter ¾ in (2 cm)

Range L. Cretaceous	Distribution Sweden	Occurrence 🔘🔘

Order HEMICIDAROIDA	Family HEMICIDARIDAE	Informal name Sea urchin

HEMICIDARIS

The test of *Hemicidaris* has a rounded outline from above and a rather small apical disc. The ten columns of interambulacral plates each carry a very prominent tubercle bearing long smooth, tapering spines. The ambulacra are narrow.
• **HABITAT** *Hemicidaris* lived among rocky outcrops on the sea bed, held by the sticky tube feet on its underside. It grazed hard surfaces using its five sharp teeth.
• **REMARK** This well-preserved specimen was buried rapidly by sediment.

long, tapering, smooth spines

large tubercles

apical disc

smaller short spines

HEMICIDARIS INTERMEDIA (Fleming); Coralline limestone; Late Jurassic; UK.

Typical diameter 1¼ in (3 cm)

Range M. Jurassic–E. Cretaceous	Distribution Worldwide	Occurrence 🔘🔘

| Order PHYMOSOMATOIDA | Family PHYMOSOMATIDAE | Informal name Sea urchin |

PHYMOSOMA

The test is circular and flattened. The areas occupied by both the apical disc and the membrane around the mouth are very broad. The ambulacral and interambulacral tubercles are about the same size; in life they bore tapering, smooth, cylindrical or flattened spines. Isolated spines are common Chalk fossils.

• **HABITAT** *Phymosoma* lived on the Chalk sea floor, grazing on hard surfaces to obtain algae, sponge, and other soft organisms.

chalk matrix •

• numerous smooth spines

• *test with many tubercles*

PHYMOSOMA KOENIGI (Mantell); Upper Chalk; Late Cretaceous; UK.

Typical diameter 1¼ in (3 cm)

| Range L. Jurassic–Eocene | Distribution Worldwide | Occurrence 🌑🌑🌑 |

| Order PHYMOSOMATOIDEA | Family ARBACIOIDAE | Informal name Sea urchin |

COLEOPLEURUS

The small test has a pentagonal outline and is hemispherical in profile. The ambulacrals are broad and swollen and carry large tubercles. The interambulacrals are smooth and devoid of tubercles on the upper part of the test. The apical disc has five large genital pores and a central opening in which the anus was enclosed.

• **HABITAT** This genus lived on hard rocky substrates in shallow water.

• **REMARK** The large, basally situated ambulacral tubercles imply that *Coleopleurus* had stout spines in life. It is probable that these spines were used for stability, rather than for protection.

apical disc •

genital • pores

large tubercles on ambulacra •

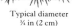

Typical diameter ¾ in (2 cm)

smooth interambulacra •

COLEOPLEURUS PAUCITUBERCULATUS (Gregory); Morgan Limestone; Miocene; South Australia.

| Range Miocene | Distribution Australia | Occurrence 🌑🌑 |

Order HOLECTYPOIDA	Family CONULIDAE	Informal name Sea urchin

CONULUS

The test is rounded or slightly pentagonal when viewed from above and conical in its side aspect. The base is flattened or concave. The mouth was positioned centrally on the base, the anus on the edge of the base. The surface of the test bears very small tubercles, which in life carried a feltlike covering of small spines.
• HABITAT *Conulus* ploughed through the soft mud of the sea floor. In certain thin stratigraphic levels tests are very common.

CONULUS ALBOGALERUS Leske; Upper Chalk; Late Cretaceous; UK.

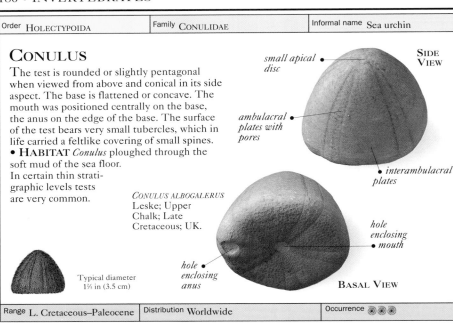

small apical disc

SIDE VIEW

ambulacral plates with pores

interambulacral plates

hole enclosing mouth

hole enclosing anus

BASAL VIEW

Typical diameter 1⅜ in (3.5 cm)

Range L. Cretaceous–Paleocene	Distribution Worldwide	Occurrence

Order CLYPEASTEROIDA	Family CLYPEASTERIDAE	Informal name Sand dollar

CLYPEASTER

The large, thick test of *Clypeaster* has a rounded pentagonal outline and a low conical profile. On the upper surface the ambulacra are expanded to form distinctive petals that carry many elongated pores. The small, circular mouth is surrounded by jaws, and lies at the center of the depressed base. The anus also lies on the lower surface near the posterior. The surface of the test is covered with small tubercles that, in life, bear short spines.
• HABITAT *Clypeaster* is a typical sand dweller, living partly or completely submerged in sand in shallow water, feeding on sediment. It is a "living fossil," and is found today in shallow, tropical seas.

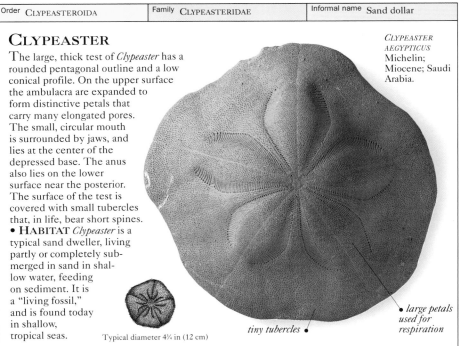

CLYPEASTER AEGYPTICUS Michelin; Miocene; Saudi Arabia.

large petals used for respiration

tiny tubercles

Typical diameter 4¾ in (12 cm)

Range L. Eocene–Recent	Distribution Worldwide	Occurrence

Order CLYPEASTEROIDA	Family MELLITIDAE	Informal name Sand dollar

ENCOPE

The sand dollar, *Encope*, is very flat and thin in profile. The five petals are well developed but smaller than in *Clypeaster (see opposite)*. Each of the five ambulacra is perforated by an oval hole (a lunule) near the margin, which passes right through the test. A single, larger sixth hole is present in the posterior ambulacrum.
• HABITAT *Encope* lives buried in sand in shallow tropical water, often in large numbers. The lunules aid the animal in feeding on fine sediment.

UPPER SURFACE OF TEST

ENCOPE MICROPORA Agassiz; Recent; Peru.

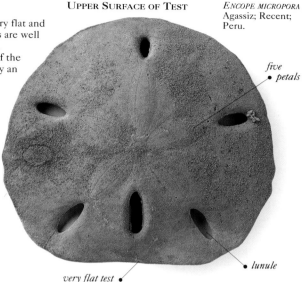

five • *petals*

lunule

very flat test •

Typical diameter 3½ in (9 cm)

Range Miocene–Recent	Distribution N. & S. America	Occurrence ⊛ ⊛ ⊛

Order CASSIDULOIDA	Family ECHINOLAMPADIDAE	Informal name Sea urchin

PLESIOLAMPAS

The test has a rounded pentagonal outline; in profile it is low and conical. The oval mouth is deeply set in the center of the underside; the anus is situated on the posterior margin. The five petals are elongated and have elongated pores. A fine even cover of tubercles is present on the upper surface of the test.
• HABITAT *Plesiolampas* buried itself in sandy sediment, on which it fed.
• REMARK This species is locally abundant.

even covering of • *fine tubercles*

elongated • *petals*

UPPER SURFACE OF TEST

Typical diameter 2¾ in (7 cm)

PLESIOLAMPAS SAHARAE (Bather); Calcareous Group; Eocene; Nigeria.

Range Paleocene–Eocene	Distribution Worldwide	Occurrence ⊛ ⊛

Order CASSIDULOIDA	Family FAUJASIIDAE	Informal name Sea urchin

HARDOUINIA

The large test of *Hardouinia* is conical in profile with a flat base. The petals, which in life bore tube feet specialized for respiration, are short and broad and very conspicuous. The interambulacral plates are low and broad. The mouth lies centrally on the lower surface and has five prominent projections, giving it a stellate outline. The anus is inset on the posterior side of the upper test. The surface originally carried short fine spines.

• **HABITAT** This genus lived partially buried in sandy sediment, into which it burrowed with the aid of the short spines. It swallowed the sand that it lived in to obtain nourishment.

• **REMARK** *Hardouinia* is common in sandy limestone faces, in the eastern USA. Juvenile specimens are much less conical in shape.

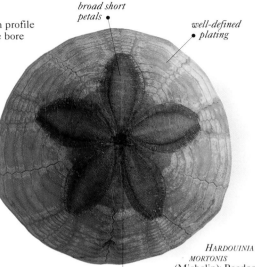

broad short petals

well-defined plating

position of anus

Typical diameter
1⅜ in (3.5 cm)

HARDOUINIA
MORTONIS
(Michelin); Peedee
Formation; Late
Cretaceous; USA.

Range L. Cretaceous	Distribution N. America	Occurrence ⬤⬤⬤

Order HOLASTEROIDA	Family HOLASTERIDAE	Informal name Sea urchin

ECHINOCORYS

The elongated test is large and conical in profile, often with a flattened top. It has a covering of small tubercles. The base is flat, and the oval mouth is positioned near the anterior border. In life, the spine cover was fine and short. It has a large, elongated apical disc and long petals.

• **HABITAT** This genus lived partially buried in mud or sand. It ploughed through this to find nutritious particles of sediment.

• **REMARK** *Echinocorys* is one of the most common of the Late Cretaceous Chalk echinoids. The top of the test is often broken. This is probably due to the attack of predators, such as fish.

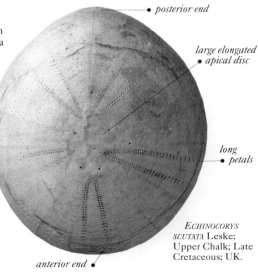

posterior end

large elongated apical disc

long petals

ECHINOCORYS
SCUTATA Leske;
Upper Chalk; Late
Cretaceous; UK.

Typical diameter
2¾ in (7 cm)

anterior end

Range L. Cretaceous–Paleocene	Distribution Worldwide	Occurrence ⬤⬤⬤⬤⬤

Order SPATANGOIDA	Family HEMIASTERIDAE	Informal name Heart urchin

HEMIASTER

Heart-shaped in outline and oval in profile, the test is covered in small, fine tubercles. The mouth is positioned on the flat base near the anterior margin and the anus is positioned on the posterior. The well-developed petals are set in grooves. The anterior margin is notched.
• **HABITAT** *Hemiaster* lives buried deep in muddy sediment, feeding on mud, which it channels to its mouth via the anterior notch.
• **REMARK** *Hemiaster* was abundant in muddy sediments of the Cretaceous.

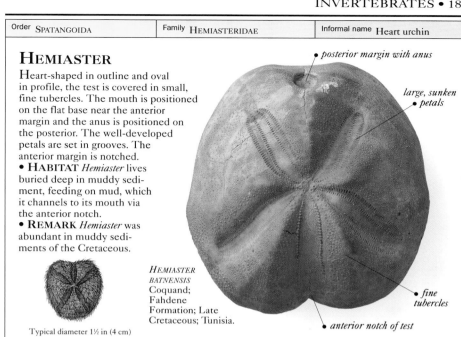

posterior margin with anus

large, sunken petals

fine tubercles

anterior notch of test

HEMIASTER BATNENSIS Coquand; Fahdene Formation; Late Cretaceous; Tunisia.

Typical diameter 1½ in (4 cm)

Range Cretaceous–Recent	Distribution Worldwide	Occurrence

Order SPATANGOIDA	Family SCHIZASTERIDAE	Informal name Heart urchin

LINTHIA

Linthia was a rather small, compact heart urchin with a very strong, deep notch on the anterior margin and conspicuous petals with large pores. Four large genital pores on the apical disc were used to discharge eggs and sperm.
• **HABITAT** This genus lived as a burrower in soft sediments.
• **REMARK** Weathering of the test surface of this particular specimen has revealed the boundaries between plates in places.

etched plate boundaries

pores of petals

genital pores in disc

strong anterior notch

LINTHIA SUDANENSIS Bather; Kalanbaina; Early Paleocene; Niger Republic.

Typical diameter 2¾ in (7 cm)

Range Paleocene	Distribution Northern Africa	Occurrence

Order SPATANGOIDA	Family SCHIZASTERIDAE	Informal name Heart urchin

SCHIZASTER

The anterior petal in the heart urchin, *Schizaster*, is deeply inset and enlarged. The pores, which in life bear respiratory tube feet, are very conspicuous on the petals.

• **HABITAT** *Schizaster* lives deeply buried in muds. It uses its long tube feet as a funnel-like connection to the sea bed. *Schizaster* feeds on fine particles of sediment.

• **REMARK** This group of entire and broken individuals probably represents a storm-swept residue – the result of waves scouring deeply buried urchins from their burrows. Most specimens are preserved as internal molds, as the shell usually breaks away.

BLOCK WITH COMPLETE AND BROKEN HEART URCHINS

well-developed petals

clay matrix

pores for respiratory tube feet

SCHIZASTER BRANDERIANUS Forbes; Barton Beds; Middle Eocene; UK.

large anterior petal

Typical diameter 1 in (2.5 cm)

Range Eocene–Recent	Distribution Worldwide	Occurrence

Order SPATANGOIDA	Family MICRASTERIDAE	Informal name Heart urchin

MICRASTER

The Chalk heart urchin, *Micraster*, is pointed posteriorly and has a strong anterior notch. The five petals are narrow and fairly short.

- **HABITAT** This genus lived buried in the soft mud of the Chalk sea floor, and channeled a stream of mud into its mouth through the strong anterior notch.
- **REMARK** This species is one of the more advanced forms, occurring in the higher beds of the Chalk.

MICRASTER CORANGUINUM (Leske); Upper Chalk; Late Cretaceous; UK.

Typical diameter 2 in (5 cm)

even, fine tubercles

strong anterior notch

narrow depressed petals

Range L. Cretaceous–Paleocene	Distribution Worldwide	Occurrence ◉◉◉◉

Order SPATANGOIDA	Family LOVENIIDAE	Informal name Heart urchin

LOVENIA

This heart urchin has an elongated, flattened test with a flat base. The petals are shallow and taper toward the margin of the test. In addition to the fine covering of tubercles, large deeply inset tubercles are present on both sides of the test. These carry long curved protective spines.

- **HABITAT** *Lovenia* is a shallow burrower in sand, usually occurring in inshore marine deposits.
- **REMARK** The few large tubercles on the upper surface of this heart urchin make it very distinctive.

posterior

UPPER SURFACE

anus

flat base

LOWER SURFACE

large tubercles

anterior notch

crescent-shaped mouth

LOVENIA FORBESI (Woods); Morgan Limestone; Miocene; South Australia.

anterior

Typical diameter 1 in (2.5 cm)

Range L. Eocene–Recent	Distribution Worldwide	Occurrence ◉◉◉

ASTEROIDS

T HE ASTEROIDS, which include many of the species popularly called starfish, are common marine animals. Their long history extends back into the Ordovician. Most have five arms, although some species have more. The mouth is centrally placed on the underside, and five ambulacral grooves, floored by ambulacral and adambulacral ossicles, run along the midline of each arm. The grooves house the soft, muscular tube feet, which are used for walking, burrowing, and manipulating prey. Asteroids are rarely preserved as complete specimens.

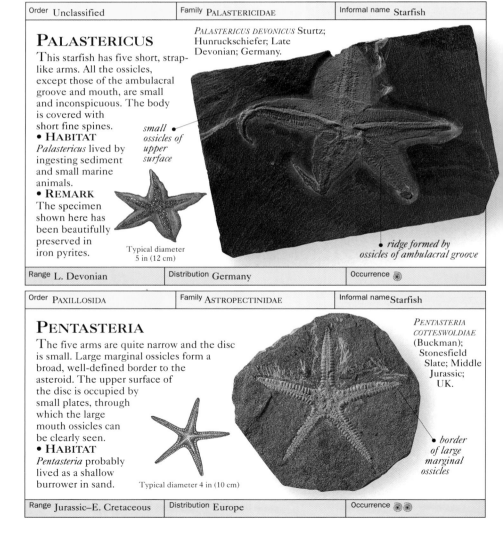

| Order Unclassified | Family PALASTERICIDAE | Informal name Starfish |

PALASTERICUS

This starfish has five short, straplike arms. All the ossicles, except those of the ambulacral groove and mouth, are small and inconspicuous. The body is covered with short fine spines.

• **HABITAT**
Palastericus lived by ingesting sediment and small marine animals.

• **REMARK**
The specimen shown here has been beautifully preserved in iron pyrites.

PALASTERICUS DEVONICUS Sturtz; Hunruckschiefer; Late Devonian; Germany.

small ossicles of upper surface

Typical diameter 5 in (12 cm)

• *ridge formed by ossicles of ambulacral groove*

| Range L. Devonian | Distribution Germany | Occurrence ⊛ |

| Order PAXILLOSIDA | Family ASTROPECTINIDAE | Informal name Starfish |

PENTASTERIA

The five arms are quite narrow and the disc is small. Large marginal ossicles form a broad, well-defined border to the asteroid. The upper surface of the disc is occupied by small plates, through which the large mouth ossicles can be clearly seen.

• **HABITAT**
Pentasteria probably lived as a shallow burrower in sand.

PENTASTERIA COTTESWOLDIAE (Buckman); Stonesfield Slate; Middle Jurassic; UK.

• *border of large marginal ossicles*

Typical diameter 4 in (10 cm)

| Range Jurassic–E. Cretaceous | Distribution Europe | Occurrence ⊛⊛ |

Order Unclassified	Family STENASTERIDAE	Informal name Starfish

STENASTER

This small and enigmatic form has been variously classified as an ophiuroid and as an asteroid. The five arms are short, the disc rather broad in form. The broad ambulacral ossicles extend across the width of the arm.
• **HABITAT** This was a marine-dwelling animal.
• **REMARK** The Starfish Bed at Girvan in Scotland, UK, formerly yielded a large number of beautifully preserved starfish and other fossils. These starfish were present as natural molds, where the calcite skeletons had dissolved. A storm was probably responsible for the rapid deposition of sand that smothered the animals. *Stenaster* is a starfish with poorly understood relationships to other asteroids.

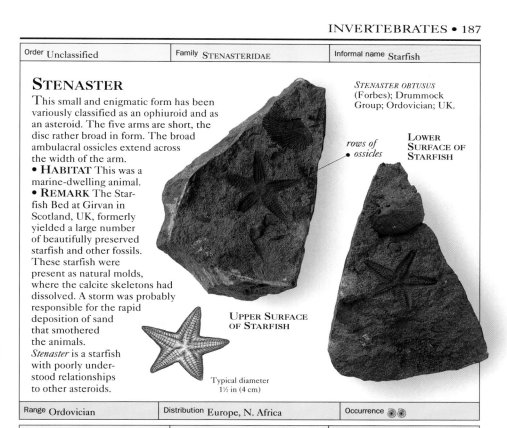

STENASTER OBTUSUS (Forbes); Drummock Group; Ordovician; UK.

rows of ossicles

LOWER SURFACE OF STARFISH

UPPER SURFACE OF STARFISH

Typical diameter 1½ in (4 cm)

Range Ordovician	Distribution Europe, N. Africa	Occurrence

Order FORCIPULIDA	Family TROPIDASTERIDAE	Informal name Starfish

TROPIDASTER

This small form has five blunt, petal-shaped arms and very large, conspicuous mouth plates. The ambulacral groove is widely open, and broad ambulacral ossicles make up the underside of the arm. In life, these each bore a row of prominent spines.
• **HABITAT** This starfish dwelled in shallow marine water.
• **REMARK** The photograph shows two specimens, a juvenile and a fully grown adult, both displaying the underside.

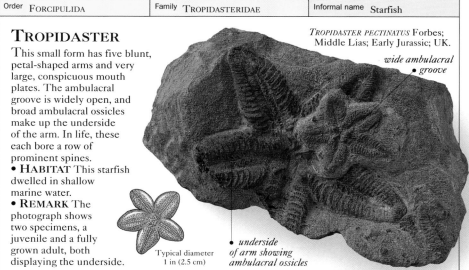

TROPIDASTER PECTINATUS Forbes; Middle Lias; Early Jurassic; UK.

wide ambulacral groove

underside of arm showing ambulacral ossicles

Typical diameter 1 in (2.5 cm)

Range E. Jurassic	Distribution UK	Occurrence

| Order VALVATIDA | Family GONIASTERIDAE | Informal name Starfish |

METOPASTER

The arms are very short and the disc is large (the body resembles a pentagonal wafer). The marginal ossicles are large, few in number, and conspicuous; in life they bore small, granular spines. The marginals, which form the tips of the arms, are elongated and triangular. The disc was covered with small polygonal ossicles.

• **HABITAT** Like its living relatives, *Metopaster* probably lived as a sediment feeder or scavenger on the Chalk sea floor.

• **REMARK** Marginal ossicles of this genus are common fossils.

small ossicles

pentagonal form

large marginal ossicles form broad border

Typical diameter 2 in (5 cm)

METOPASTER PARKINSONI (Forbes); Upper Chalk; Late Cretaceous; UK.

| Range L. Cretaceous | Distribution Europe | Occurrence ◉◉◉ |

| Order Unclassified | Family STAURANDERASTERIDAE | Informal name Starfish |

STAURANDERASTER

This starfish has long, narrow arms and a medium-size disc, which was originally dome shaped, but has collapsed in this specimen. This disc is made up of fairly large rounded ossicles. The large marginal ossicles of the arms overlap, permitting greater flexibility.

• **HABITAT** This genus was probably a surface dweller on the Chalk sea floor, and either fed on sediment or scavenged dead material.

STAURANDERASTER CORONATUS (Forbes); Lower Chalk; Late Cretaceous; UK.

long narrow arms

soft chalk matrix

Typical diameter 4 in (10 cm)

marginals overlap to increase flexibility

disc made of large ossicles

| Range L. Cretaceous | Distribution Europe | Occurrence ◉ |

OPHIUROIDEA

T HE OPHIUROIDS ARE commonly called starfish or brittle stars. Closely related to echinoids, they possess five long, often fragile, arms which radiate from a flat, nearly circular disc. These arms are very flexible and very different in structure from those of asteroids. They consist of a central column of vertebrae, covered by four rows of plates. The ambulacral groove is covered in ophiuroids. Today, ophiuroids occur in vast masses on the sea floor; similar quantities are found in the fossil state.

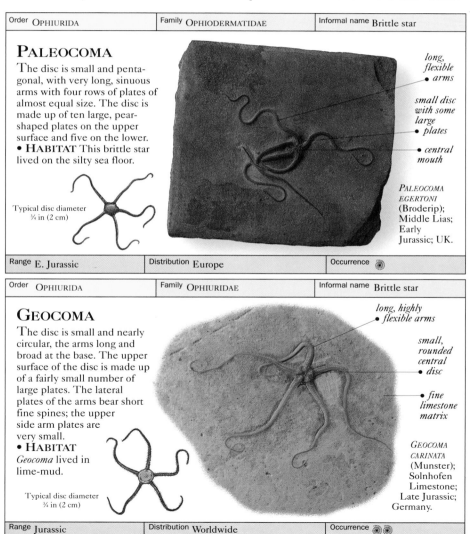

Order OPHIURIDA	Family OPHIODERMATIDAE	Informal name Brittle star

PALEOCOMA

The disc is small and penta-gonal, with very long, sinuous arms with four rows of plates of almost equal size. The disc is made up of ten large, pear-shaped plates on the upper surface and five on the lower.
• HABITAT This brittle star lived on the silty sea floor.

Typical disc diameter
¾ in (2 cm)

long, flexible arms

small disc with some large plates

central mouth

PALEOCOMA EGERTONI (Broderip); Middle Lias; Early Jurassic; UK.

Range E. Jurassic	Distribution Europe	Occurrence ⬤

Order OPHIURIDA	Family OPHIURIDAE	Informal name Brittle star

GEOCOMA

The disc is small and nearly circular, the arms long and broad at the base. The upper surface of the disc is made up of a fairly small number of large plates. The lateral plates of the arms bear short fine spines; the upper side arm plates are very small.
• HABITAT *Geocoma* lived in lime-mud.

Typical disc diameter
¾ in (2 cm)

long, highly flexible arms

small, rounded central disc

fine limestone matrix

GEOCOMA CARINATA (Munster); Solnhofen Limestone; Late Jurassic; Germany.

Range Jurassic	Distribution Worldwide	Occurrence ⬤⬤

BLASTOIDS

T HE BLASTOIDS ARE a small well-defined group of echinoderms, that in life were attached to the substrate by a thin stem, and in which the compact theca is shaped like a rosebud. The theca is made up of three circles of five plates, known as basals, radials, and deltoids. The five columns of ambulacral plates are V-shaped, bearing short brachioles used for filtering food from the water. These fossils are locally common from the Silurian to the Permian, in marine shales and limestones.

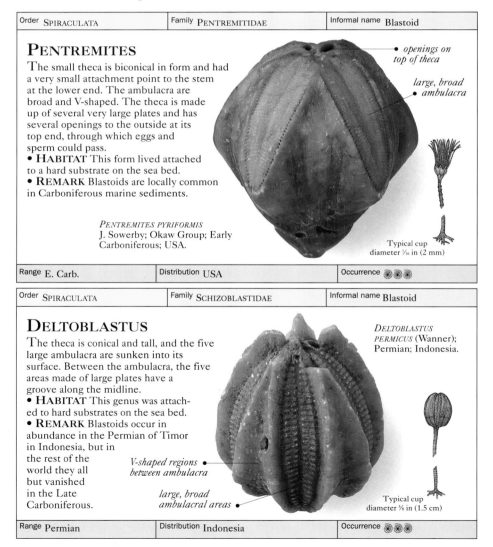

Order SPIRACULATA	Family PENTREMITIDAE	Informal name Blastoid

PENTREMITES

The small theca is biconical in form and had a very small attachment point to the stem at the lower end. The ambulacra are broad and V-shaped. The theca is made up of several very large plates and has several openings to the outside at its top end, through which eggs and sperm could pass.
• HABITAT This form lived attached to a hard substrate on the sea bed.
• REMARK Blastoids are locally common in Carboniferous marine sediments.

openings on top of theca

large, broad ambulacra

PENTREMITES PYRIFORMIS J. Sowerby; Okaw Group; Early Carboniferous; USA.

Typical cup diameter ⅟₁₆ in (2 mm)

Range E. Carb.	Distribution USA	Occurrence 🔘🔘 🔘🔘

Order SPIRACULATA	Family SCHIZOBLASTIDAE	Informal name Blastoid

DELTOBLASTUS

The theca is conical and tall, and the five large ambulacra are sunken into its surface. Between the ambulacra, the five areas made of large plates have a groove along the midline.
• HABITAT This genus was attach-ed to hard substrates on the sea bed.
• REMARK Blastoids occur in abundance in the Permian of Timor in Indonesia, but in the rest of the world they all but vanished in the Late Carboniferous.

DELTOBLASTUS PERMICUS (Wanner); Permian; Indonesia.

V-shaped regions between ambulacra

large, broad ambulacral areas

Typical cup diameter ⅜ in (1.5 cm)

Range Permian	Distribution Indonesia	Occurrence 🔘🔘 🔘🔘

CYSTOIDS

C YSTOIDS SUPERFICIALLY resembled crinoids in that they were attached to the substrate by a stem and possessed a swollen theca made up of a variable number of plates. Cystoids, however, did not have true arms. Instead, they filtered food from the water by means of short unbranched limbs called brachioles. In addition, they had special pore structures on the plates, which were used for respiration. Cystoids are only found very occasionally, in Ordovician to Devonian rocks.

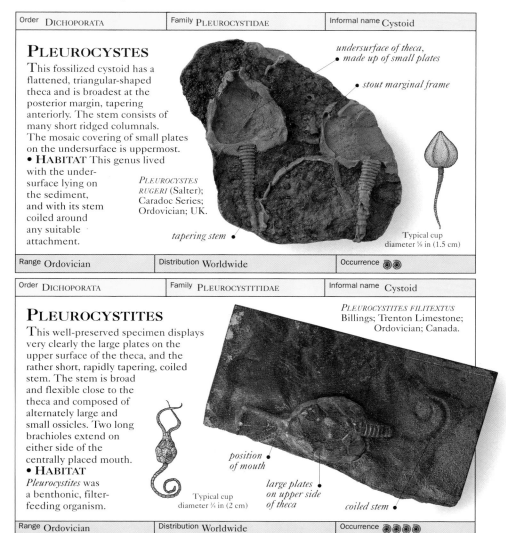

Order DICHOPORATA	Family PLEUROCYSTIDAE	Informal name Cystoid

PLEUROCYSTES

This fossilized cystoid has a flattened, triangular-shaped theca and is broadest at the posterior margin, tapering anteriorly. The stem consists of many short ridged columnals. The mosaic covering of small plates on the undersurface is uppermost.
• **HABITAT** This genus lived with the under-surface lying on the sediment, and with its stem coiled around any suitable attachment.

PLEUROCYSTES RUGERI (Salter); Caradoc Series; Ordovician; UK.

undersurface of theca, • made up of small plates

• stout marginal frame

tapering stem •

Typical cup diameter ⅝ in (1.5 cm)

Range Ordovician	Distribution Worldwide	Occurrence 🐚🐚

Order DICHOPORATA	Family PLEUROCYSTITIDAE	Informal name Cystoid

PLEUROCYSTITES

This well-preserved specimen displays very clearly the large plates on the upper surface of the theca, and the rather short, rapidly tapering, coiled stem. The stem is broad and flexible close to the theca and composed of alternately large and small ossicles. Two long brachioles extend on either side of the centrally placed mouth.
• **HABITAT** *Pleurocystites* was a benthonic, filter-feeding organism.

PLEUROCYSTITES FILITEXTUS Billings; Trenton Limestone; Ordovician; Canada.

position • of mouth

Typical cup diameter ¾ in (2 cm)

large plates • on upper side of theca

coiled stem •

Range Ordovician	Distribution Worldwide	Occurrence 🐚🐚🐚🐚

Order GLYPTOCYSTITIDA	Family CALLOCYSTIDAE	Informal name Cystoid

LEPADOCRINITES

Lepadocrinites had an elliptically shaped theca which is made up of a few rather large plates, with very large, rhomb-shaped respiratory pores. The five ambulacra are long and in life bore numerous brachioles. The stem is elongated and tapering, and made up of ridged columnals, which are short near the theca but are longer on the stem.
• **HABITAT** In life, *Lepadocrinites* was attached to hard substrates on the sea floor by a root.

theca with five
• *ambulacra*

originally attached by root •

• *long, tapering stem*

Typical cup diameter
1 in (2.5 cm)

LEPADOCRINITES QUADRIFASCIATUS
Pearce; Wenlock Limestone; Silurian; UK.

Range Silurian	Distribution UK	Occurrence ◉ ◉

Order GLYPTOCYSTITIDA	Family CALLOCYSTIDAE	Informal name Cystoid

PSEUDOCRINITES

The theca is strongly flattened and circular in outline, and has two narrow ambulacra that run around the margins and carry short, stout brachioles. The theca is made up of a few very large plates. It has one or two very large, rhomb-shaped respiratory pores. The short, tapering stem culminates in a club-shaped root.
• **HABITAT** This genus lived as a filter feeder, attached to a hard surface such as a shell or pebble, on the sea floor.

flattened theca
• *carrying brachioles*

• *rhombic respiratory pore*

short, tapering
• *stem*

PSEUDOCRINITES BIFASCIATUS
(Pearce); Wenlock Limestone; Silurian; UK.

Typical cup diameter
1 in (2.5 cm)

Range L. Silurian–E. Devonian	Distribution Europe, N. America	Occurrence ◉ ◉

CARPOIDS

T HE CARPOIDS WERE a small but diverse group of Cambrian to Devonian animals. They possessed a skeleton with the distinctive fine calcite structure of echinoderms, but without a trace of their fivefold symmetry *(see pp.175–185)*. They are probably ancestral to both the echinoderms and the chordates. Carpoids were free living, being able to move on the sea bed, and had a large head and a short, flexible tail. Gill slits (like those in fish) are conspicuous in some carpoid forms.

Order CORNUTA	Family COTHURNOCYSTIDAE	Informal name Cornute

COTHURNOCYSTIS

The head is boot shaped and has three pointed projections. A frame of marginal plates forms the border of the head, and the central area is made up of small plates; a single row of large gill slits is also present. The tail is quite short and flexible.

• **HABITAT** *Cothurnocystis* lived on the sea floor and was probably able to pull itself along with its tail.

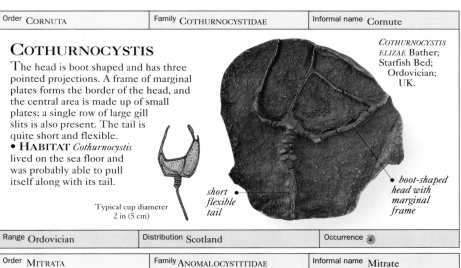

COTHURNOCYSTIS ELIZAE Bather; Starfish Bed; Ordovician; UK.

Typical cup diameter 2 in (5 cm)

short flexible tail

boot-shaped head with marginal frame

Range Ordovician	Distribution Scotland	Occurrence 🐚

Order MITRATA	Family ANOMALOCYSTITIDAE	Informal name Mitrate

PLACOCYSTITES

The head of this mitrate is flattened and rectangular in shape. It is made up of large thin calcite plates, which bear fine, wavy ridges. The anterior end has two rodlike appendages which are, in fact, spines. The mouth is placed centrally.

• **HABITAT** *Placocystites* lived on the surface of the sea bed and used its flexible tail as a lever to haul itself about.

• **REMARK** The tail is missing in this specimen.

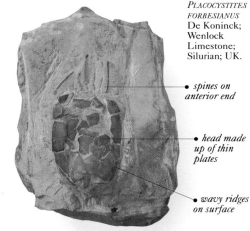

PLACOCYSTITES FORBESIANUS De Koninck; Wenlock Limestone; Silurian; UK.

spines on anterior end

head made up of thin plates

wavy ridges on surface

Typical cup diameter ¾ in (2 cm)

Range L. Silurian	Distribution Sweden, UK	Occurrence 🐚

VERTEBRATES

AGNATHANS

T HESE PRIMITIVE, jawless fishes have an ancient lineage, represented today by the lampreys and hagfishes. Living forms have funnel-like, suctional mouths with rasping, horny teeth, used for scraping flesh. Unlike jawed vertebrates, agnathan gills face inward from the gill arches.

They have no paired fins. Most of the extinct forms were tadpole shaped, swam by undulating their tails, and had thick plates and scales for armor. They first appeared in marine waters and then spread to fresh and brackish waters, dominating the Silurian and Devonian periods.

Order HETEROSTRACI	Family PTERASPIDAE	Informal name Pteraspid

PTERASPIS

The flattened head region of *Pteraspis* was enclosed by massive, bony plates, which may have been formed by scales fusing together. It had one middle dorsal plate, one rostral plate, and one ventral plate, plus a smaller lateral series. The plates were punctuated by sensory canals. The mouth, situated on the underside, was flanked by small plates which may have assisted suctional bottom feeding. The eyes were small and placed along the sides. The tail, with its larger lower lobe, caused upward driving of the head when rising from the bottom. A massive bony carapace may have acted as a phosphate store during times of shortage.

• **HABITAT** Fossil remains of *Pteraspis* are often found in marine and freshwater deposits.

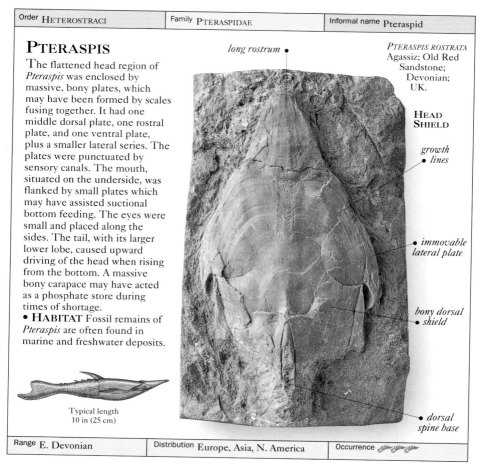

long rostrum

PTERASPIS ROSTRATA
Agassiz; Old Red Sandstone; Devonian; UK.

HEAD SHIELD

growth lines

immovable lateral plate

bony dorsal shield

dorsal spine base

Typical length
10 in (25 cm)

Range E. Devonian	Distribution Europe, Asia, N. America	Occurrence

Order OSTEOSTRACI	Family CEPHALASPIDAE	Informal name Cephalaspid

CEPHALASPIS

The small freshwater fish, *Cephalaspis*, had a bony dorsal head shield, with overlapping scales covering the rest of its body. The eyes were sited on top, close to the midline, with the mouth on the underside. A middle dorsal and two lateral areas of polygonal plates are thought to represent sensory areas.
• HABITAT *Cephalaspis* inhabited freshwater pools or streams.

CEPHALASPIS WHITEI Stensio; Old Red Sandstone; Devonian; UK.

• *sensory plate area*

• *eye socket*

• *cornua directed toward the back*

• *notch*

Typical length
8¾ in (22 cm)

HEAD SHIELD

Range E. Devonian	Distribution Europe	Occurrence

Order ANASPIDA	Family BIRKENIIDAE	Informal name Anaspid

BIRKENIA

The spindle-shaped body of this small fish is armored by deep, overlapping, articulated scales arranged in rows. A row of ridge scales runs along the top. The terminal mouth forms a vertical slit, surrounded by the smaller, less organized cranial scales.
• HABITAT *Birkenia* was a freshwater genus.

BIRKENIA ELEGANS Traquair; Slot Burn Formation; Middle Silurian; UK.

long, spindle-
• *shaped body*

• *dorsal scales*

tail •
scales

• *head*

• *terminal mouth*

Typical length 2½ in (6 cm)   • *deep body scales*

Range M. Silurian	Distribution Europe	Occurrence

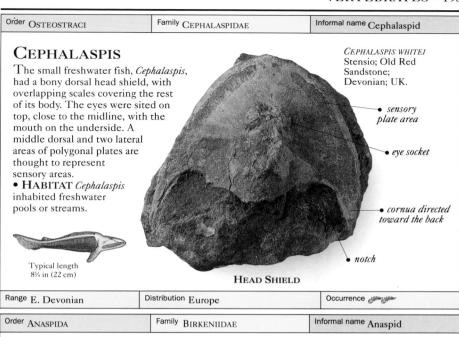

PLACODERMS

T HE PLACODERMS FORMED a diverse group of now-extinct fishes that had primitive jaws armed with slicing plates. Typically, these fish lived on the sea bed. They had a heavily armored head shield connected to a trunk shield which covered the anterior part of the body. The rest of the body and tail was covered by small scales. The moderate to large eyes were protected by a circlet of bony plates. Placoderms lived in marine and fresh water, from the Late Silurian to the Early Carboniferous. Most were moderately sized, but some grew to 20 ft (6 m) in length.

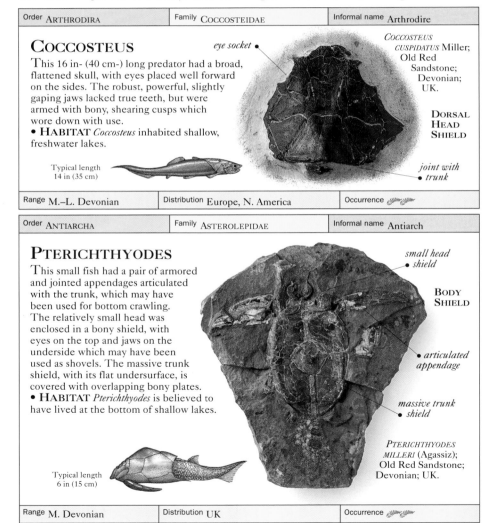

Order ARTHRODIRA	Family COCCOSTEIDAE	Informal name Arthrodire

COCCOSTEUS

eye socket •

This 16 in- (40 cm-) long predator had a broad, flattened skull, with eyes placed well forward on the sides. The robust, powerful, slightly gaping jaws lacked true teeth, but were armed with bony, shearing cusps which wore down with use.
• HABITAT *Coccosteus* inhabited shallow, freshwater lakes.

COCCOSTEUS CUSPIDATUS Miller; Old Red Sandstone; Devonian; UK.

DORSAL HEAD SHIELD

Typical length
14 in (35 cm)

joint with
• *trunk*

Range M.–L. Devonian	Distribution Europe, N. America	Occurrence

Order ANTIARCHA	Family ASTEROLEPIDAE	Informal name Antiarch

PTERICHTHYODES

This small fish had a pair of armored and jointed appendages articulated with the trunk, which may have been used for bottom crawling. The relatively small head was enclosed in a bony shield, with eyes on the top and jaws on the underside which may have been used as shovels. The massive trunk shield, with its flat undersurface, is covered with overlapping bony plates.
• HABITAT *Pterichthyodes* is believed to have lived at the bottom of shallow lakes.

small head
• *shield*

BODY SHIELD

• *articulated appendage*

massive trunk
• *shield*

PTERICHTHYODES MILLERI (Agassiz); Old Red Sandstone; Devonian; UK.

Typical length
6 in (15 cm)

Range M. Devonian	Distribution UK	Occurrence

Order PTYCTODONTIDA	Family PTYCTODONTIDAE	Informal name Ptyctodont

RHAMPHODOPSIS

The head and trunk armor of this genus was more restricted than in other placoderms; only a few plates covered the upper head and cheek region, while a short trunk girdle bearing just three spines was located just behind it. The unarmored rear of the trunk ended in a whiplash tail. Paired plates of teeth were carried on both jaws.

• HABITAT
This genus
lived in fresh
water.

*RHAMPHODOPSIS
THREIPLANDI*
Watson; Old
Red Sand-
stone; Middle
Devonian; UK.

*short dorsal
• spine*

Typical length
6 in (15 cm)

• long body

• unarmored flank

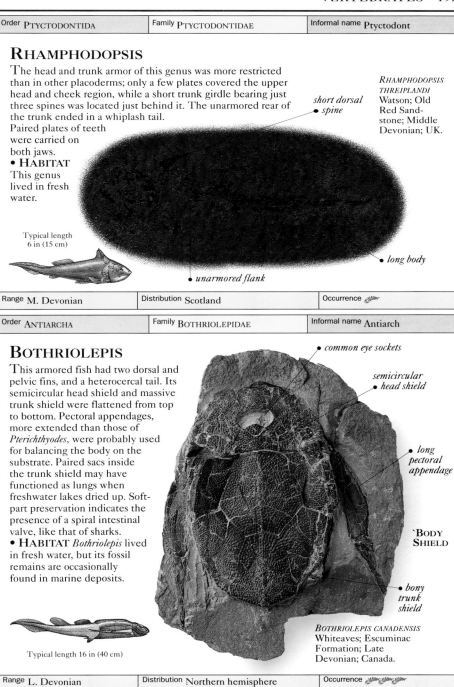

Range M. Devonian	Distribution Scotland	Occurrence

Order ANTIARCHA	Family BOTHRIOLEPIDAE	Informal name Antiarch

BOTHRIOLEPIS

This armored fish had two dorsal and pelvic fins, and a heterocercal tail. Its semicircular head shield and massive trunk shield were flattened from top to bottom. Pectoral appendages, more extended than those of *Pterichthyodes*, were probably used for balancing the body on the substrate. Paired sacs inside the trunk shield may have functioned as lungs when freshwater lakes dried up. Soft-part preservation indicates the presence of a spiral intestinal valve, like that of sharks.

• HABITAT *Bothriolepis* lived in fresh water, but its fossil remains are occasionally found in marine deposits.

• common eye sockets

*semicircular
• head shield*

*• long
pectoral
appendage*

`BODY
SHIELD

*• bony
trunk
shield*

BOTHRIOLEPIS CANADENSIS
Whiteaves; Escuminac
Formation; Late
Devonian; Canada.

Typical length 16 in (40 cm)

Range L. Devonian	Distribution Northern hemisphere	Occurrence

CHONDRICHTHYANS

C REATURES OF THIS CLASS are characterized by a cartilaginous skeleton made up of tiny calcified prisms. Living examples include the sharks, skates, rays, and ratfishes. Cartilage is not usually preserved, so common fossils tend to be teeth, scales, and dorsal-fin spines. Sharks'

teeth are continuously replaced from behind, being shed from the jaw margin or lost during feeding. Trace fossils (see p.42) ascribed to the group include spirally coiled fecal remains and intestines. Chondrichthyans diversified from Devonian origins to become very common in today's seas.

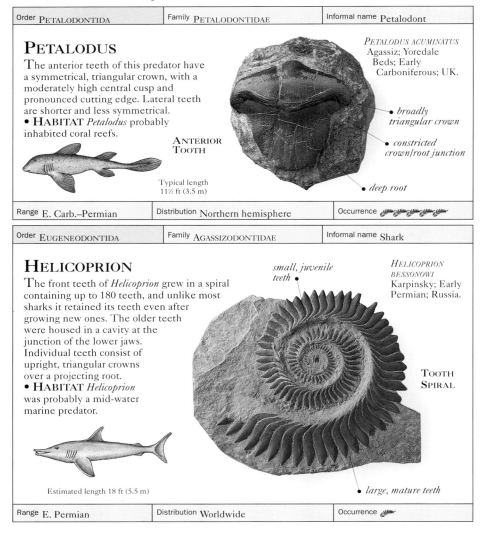

Order PETALODONTIDA	Family PETALODONTIDAE	Informal name Petalodont

PETALODUS

The anterior teeth of this predator have a symmetrical, triangular crown, with a moderately high central cusp and pronounced cutting edge. Lateral teeth are shorter and less symmetrical.
• HABITAT *Petalodus* probably inhabited coral reefs.

ANTERIOR TOOTH

Typical length
11½ ft (3.5 m)

PETALODUS ACUMINATUS
Agassiz; Yoredale Beds; Early Carboniferous; UK.

• *broadly triangular crown*

• *constricted crown/root junction*

• *deep root*

Range E. Carb.–Permian	Distribution Northern hemisphere	Occurrence

Order EUGENEODONTIDA	Family AGASSIZODONTIDAE	Informal name Shark

HELICOPRION

The front teeth of *Helicoprion* grew in a spiral containing up to 180 teeth, and unlike most sharks it retained its teeth even after growing new ones. The older teeth were housed in a cavity at the junction of the lower jaws. Individual teeth consist of upright, triangular crowns over a projecting root.
• HABITAT *Helicoprion* was probably a mid-water marine predator.

small, juvenile teeth •

HELICOPRION BESSONOWI
Karpinsky; Early Permian; Russia.

TOOTH SPIRAL

Estimated length 18 ft (5.5 m)

• *large, mature teeth*

Range E. Permian	Distribution Worldwide	Occurrence

Order HYBODONTIFORMES	Family ACRODONTIDAE	Informal name Hybodont shark

ACRODUS

The dorsal fin of this hybodont shark was supported by an extended spine, with coarse longitudinal ridges (costae) on the side walls and a trailing edge covered with small, toothlike projections. A long basal part, inserted into the soft tissues of the back, was supported by a fin cartilage. The fin itself cut through the water and prevented rolling during swimming. The underslung mouth was armed with a battery of robust teeth for crushing its food. Coarse ridges of each individual tooth radiate from the crown center, providing additional abrasion. Anterior and posterior teeth are small; lateral teeth have greatly expanded crowns supported on robust roots.
• **HABITAT** *Acrodus* was a slow-swimming marine shark, living close to the sea bottom on a diet of mollusks and crustaceans.

ACRODUS NOBILIS Agassiz; Lower Lias; Early Jurassic; UK.

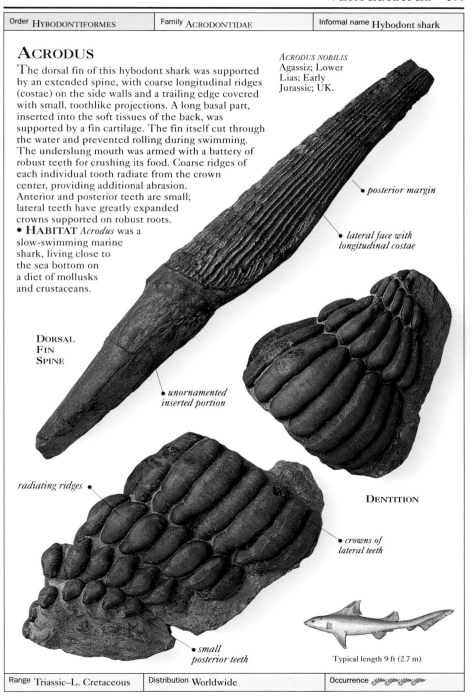

• *posterior margin*

• *lateral face with longitudinal costae*

DORSAL FIN SPINE

• *unornamented inserted portion*

radiating ridges •

DENTITION

• *crowns of lateral teeth*

• *small posterior teeth*

Typical length 9 ft (2.7 m)

Range Triassic–L. Cretaceous	Distribution Worldwide	Occurrence

| Order HYBODONTIFORMES | Family PTYCHODONTIDAE | Informal name Hybodont shark |

PTYCHODUS

This moderately large shark is known only from fossils of its shell-crushing teeth, and possibly from calcified vertebrae. The teeth were arranged in a tightly packed battery, with massive rectangular crowns traversed by sharp, coarse ridges, giving way to round projections at the tooth margin. The square root, directly underneath the crown, was perforated by tiny, closely packed blood vessels.
• HABITAT *Ptychodus* lived in shallow marine conditions, preying on thick-shelled invertebrates.

massive, rectangular, enameled crown •

PTYCHODUS LATISSIMUS Agassiz; Upper Chalk; Late Cretaceous; UK.

SINGLE TOOTH

Typical length
10 ft (3 m)

convex biting surface •   • *coarse ridges*

| Range L. Cretaceous | Distribution Worldwide | Occurrence |

| Order LAMNIFORMES | Family ANACORACIDAE | Informal name Anacoracid shark |

SQUALICORAX

Like the modern tiger shark, *Squalicorax* had triangular, flattened teeth with finely serrated crowns. In anterior files the teeth are upright, but become increasingly inclined toward the back. The simple flat root lacks a nutritive groove.
• HABITAT This shark usually inhabited shallow marine waters.

enamel crown •

finely serrated • *cutting edge*

SQUALICORAX PRISTODONTUS (Agassiz); Tuffeau de Maastricht; Late Cretaceous; Holland.

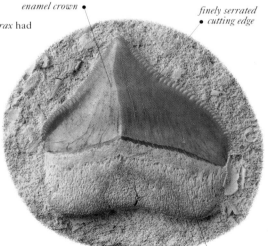

Typical length
8 ft (2.5 m)

SINGLE TOOTH   • *root*

| Range L. Cretaceous | Distribution Worldwide | Occurrence |

Order HEXANCHIFORMES	Family PALAEOSPINACIDAE	Informal name Palaeospinacid shark

SYNECHODUS

This was a small, probably slow-swimming shark, similar in shape to a dogfish. It had a weakly calcified braincase, with a short snout, and underslung mouth containing multi-pointed teeth. These were ornamented by vertical ridges, with crowns displaced in relation to the tongue. The high, central cusp was flanked by up to four pairs of lower, lateral cusplets. Teeth at the front were upright and symmetrical, whereas toward the back symmetry decreased, cusplets became shorter, and central cusps became more inclined. The side walls of the short, dorsal-fin spine were smooth and enameled, with round enamel projections at the base. Vertebrae were calcified and spool shaped, with a central perforation for the skeletal rod (notochord). Scales were simple and nongrowing.

• **HABITAT** *Synechodus* lived in shallow marine environments, feeding on small fish and thin-shelled, bottom-dwelling invertebrates.

SYNECHODUS
ENNISKILLENI Duffin
& Ward; Lower Lias;
Early Jurassic; UK.

meeting-point of lower jaws

teeth of lower jaw

skeleton of gill arch

vertebral column

dorsal-fin spine

displaced vertebral centra

PARTIAL SKELETON

Typical length
8 ft (2.5 m)

Range E. Triassic–Palaeocene	Distribution Worldwide	Occurrence

Order LAMNIFORMES	Family ODONTASPIDAE	Informal name Sand shark

STRIATOLAMIA

This extinct shark is known from fossils of its teeth and calcified vertebrae. In the front teeth, the crown is narrow and tapering, becoming triangular in side and back teeth. The labial surface (facing the lips) is ornamented with fine raised grooves (striae), and on either side of the crown is a single cusp – conical or broad and flat. A distinct nutritive groove divides the root.

• **HABITAT** *Striatolamia* is closely related to the modern sand shark and could tolerate low salinities.

• **REMARK** This and similar sand shark teeth are common in many Paleocene and Eocene deposits.

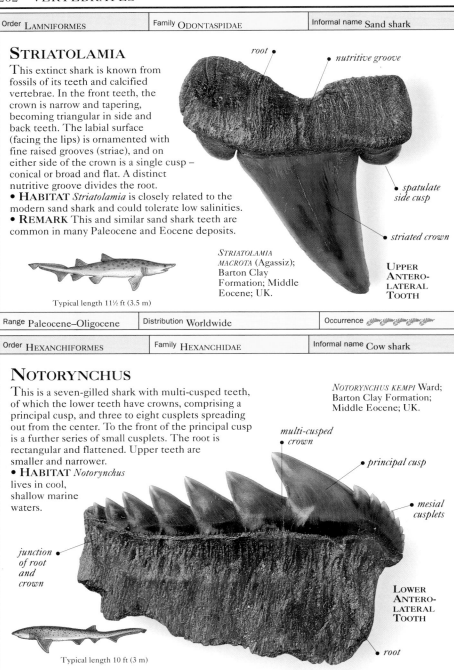

root

nutritive groove

spatulate side cusp

striated crown

STRIATOLAMIA MACROTA (Agassiz); Barton Clay Formation; Middle Eocene; UK.

UPPER ANTERO-LATERAL TOOTH

Typical length 11½ ft (3.5 m)

Range Paleocene–Oligocene	Distribution Worldwide	Occurrence

Order HEXANCHIFORMES	Family HEXANCHIDAE	Informal name Cow shark

NOTORYNCHUS

This is a seven-gilled shark with multi-cusped teeth, of which the lower teeth have crowns, comprising a principal cusp, and three to eight cusplets spreading out from the center. To the front of the principal cusp is a further series of small cusplets. The root is rectangular and flattened. Upper teeth are smaller and narrower.

• **HABITAT** *Notorynchus* lives in cool, shallow marine waters.

NOTORYNCHUS KEMPI Ward; Barton Clay Formation; Middle Eocene; UK.

multi-cusped crown

principal cusp

mesial cusplets

junction of root and crown

LOWER ANTERO-LATERAL TOOTH

root

Typical length 10 ft (3 m)

Range Eocene–Recent	Distribution Worldwide	Occurrence

Order LAMNIFORMES	Family OTODONTIDAE	Informal name Mackerel shark

CARCHAROCLES

The genus *Carcharocles* is an extinct lineage of sharks characterized by massively constructed teeth with serrated cutting edges. An estimated 42½ ft (13 m) long, it was one of the planet's largest predators. The crowns of its razor-sharp teeth are triangular, with or without cusplets at the side, and the roots massive, without a nutritive groove. There were approximately 24 teeth in the upper jaw and 20 in the lower. The species *Carcharocles megalodon* was the youngest and largest of the lineage, and had no side cusplets.

• **HABITAT** *Carcharocles* lived in warm seas, and its teeth are most abundant in deposits rich in marine mammals, its probable prey.

• **REMARK** This genus is often confused with the modern white shark, *Carcharodon*, because of their apparent, but in fact only superficial, similarities in lifestyle and prey; the two are only distantly related. Serrated teeth, similar to those of *Carcharocles*, often appear in large carnivores.

CARCHAROCLES MEGALODON (Agassiz); Yorktown Formation; Early Pliocene; USA.

FIRST OR SECOND UPPER RIGHT TOOTH

• *shrinkage crack in root*

• *crown*

almost • *symmetrical shape*

• *serrated cutting edge*

EIGHTH LOWER LEFT TOOTH

no side • *cusplets*

• *mesial cutting edge*

enamel •

distal cutting • *edge*

crown inclined away from the center •

• *massively constructed root*

TENTH LOWER RIGHT TOOTH

Typical length
42½ ft (13 m)

Range E. Eocene–Pliocene	Distribution Worldwide	Occurrence

Order CARCHARINIFORMES	Family CARCHARINIDAE	Informal name Tiger shark

GALEOCERDO

The tooth of this shark consists of a crown with a finely serrated cusp and more coarsely serrated blade. The root bears a shallow groove and several vascular openings (foraminae).
• **HABITAT** This genus inhabits coastal waters.

GALEOCERDO CUVIER
(Peron & LeSueur);
Yorktown Formation;
Early Pliocene; USA.

principal cusp •

• *blade*

serrated cutting edge •

Typical length 16½ ft (5 m)

LOWER ANTERO-LATERAL TOOTH

Range Eocene–Recent	Distribution Worldwide	Occurrence

Order CARCHARINIFORMES	Family HEMIGALEIDAE	Informal name Snaggletooth shark

HEMIPRISTIS

The upper teeth of this shark are triangular with serrated cutting edges. The symphyseal tooth (closest to the lower jaw junction) is almost symmetrical, while side teeth become increasingly inclined away from the center. Lower teeth are slimmer, with V-shaped roots. The symphyseal tooth has few serrations, but lateral teeth become progressively serrated and broad.
• **HABITAT** *Hemipristis* lived in warm coastal waters.
• **REMARK** Many fossil sharks, like *Hemipristis*, have differing upper and lower teeth.

HEMIPRISTIS SERRA
Agassiz; Pungo River Formation; Middle Miocene; USA.

RECONSTRUCTED DENTITION

• *posterior tooth*

UPPER TEETH

• *two antero-lateral teeth*

symphyseal tooth •

LOWER TEETH

Typical length 16½ ft (5 m)

• *posterior tooth*

• *three antero-lateral teeth*   *symphyseal tooth* •

Range Eocene–Recent	Distribution Worldwide	Occurrence

| Order RAJIFORMES | Family SCLERORHYNCHIDAE | Informal name Saw shark |

ISCHYRHIZA

Now extinct, *Ischyrhiza* was a genus of saw shark with small oral teeth and large teeth on the rostrum (snout). The cap (crown) of the rostral teeth is extended, flattened, and pointed, with cutting edges front and back. At the base of the posterior cutting edge is a small bulge. The root has a folded upper and lower surface and a divided base.
• **HABITAT** An inhabitant of inshore waters, this genus could tolerate a range of salinities.
• **REMARK** *Ischyrhiza* used its toothed rostrum to comb food – probably worms and crustaceans – from the sediment, and perhaps for defense.

ISCHYRHIZA NIGERIENSIS (Tabaste); Dukamaje Formation; Late Cretaceous; Niger.

• *cap*

surface polished • by wear

• *anterior cutting edge*

folded • root

• *posterior cutting edge*

• *bulge at cap base*

Typical length 7¼ ft (2.2 m)

VENTRAL VIEW   **POSTERIOR VIEW**

| Range L. Cretaceous | Distribution Americas, Africa, Europe | Occurrence |

| Order MYLIOBATIFORMES | Family MYLIOBATIDAE | Informal name Eagle ray |

MYLIOBATIS

The teeth of the eagle ray, *Myliobatis*, are arranged in an upper and lower plate, each with seven files. The middle file is wide and hexagonal, with a smooth, slightly convex oral surface, and crinkled surfaces on the lips and tongues. The three side files are narrow, and either hexagonal, pentagonal, or triangular.
• **HABITAT** *Myliobatis* inhabits warm, shallow marine environments, living on crustaceans, mollusks, and small fish.
• **REMARK** After death, the plates usually disintegrate.

LOWER TOOTH PLATE

MYLIOBATIS TOLIAPICUS Agassiz; London Clay; Early Eocene; UK.

small side file •

Typical length, incl. tail 5 ft (1.5 m)

• *large middle file*

| Range Paleocene–Recent | Distribution Worldwide | Occurrence |

Order MYLIOBATIFORMES	Family DASYATIDAE	Informal name Stingray

HELIOBATIS

Heliobatis was a stingray with a rounded disc, pointed snout, and long, barbed tail. A series of hooked dermal denticles ran along the dorsal midline. The whip-like tail was armed with up to three barbed spines. The 90 pectoral-fin rays almost meet in front of the skull, with the 16 pelvic-fin rays completing the circle behind. The teeth were small and tetrahedral, with a relatively flat occlusal surface. Males had a pair of pelvic claspers. The tail consisted of between 170 and 190 fully calcified vertebrae.

• **HABITAT** Living in freshwater streams and lakes, this stingray probably fed on crayfish, prawns, and other invertebrates.

• **REMARK** When not feeding, *Heliobatis* would lie partially buried in soft sediment. The poisonous tail spines could inflict serious injury to any potential predator.

HELIOBATIS RADIANS
Marsh; Green River Formation; Early Eocene; USA.

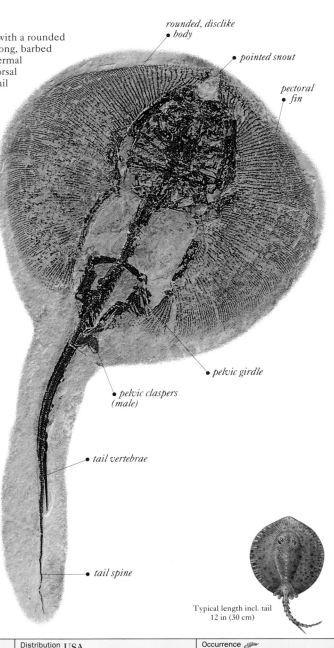

rounded, disclike
• *body*

• *pointed snout*

pectoral
• *fin*

• *pelvic girdle*

• *pelvic claspers (male)*

• *tail vertebrae*

• *tail spine*

Typical length incl. tail
12 in (30 cm)

Range E. Eocene	Distribution USA	Occurrence

Order CHIMAERIFORMES	Family COCHLIODONTIDAE	Informal name Ratfish

SANDALODUS

Although known only from isolated tooth plates, this fish is believed to have reached up to 6½ ft (2 m) in length. The lower teeth are curved strongly inward; the upper teeth are extended triangles in outline, with pointed anterior ends, and broad, rounded posterior ends. The biting surface is traversed by longitudinal ridges, giving the upper surface of the plate an undulating cross-section. Vertical pillars of hard dentine rise from the tooth plate surface.
• HABITAT *Sandalodus* used its teeth to crush thick-shelled invertebrates – and perhaps corals – in warm, shallow, shelf seas.

SANDALODUS MORRISII Davis; Carboniferous Limestone; Early Carboniferous; UK.

UPPER TOOTH PLATE

• grinding surface

• posterior

Estimated length 6½ ft (2 m)

Range Carb.	Distribution Europe	Occurrence

Order CHIMAERIFORMES	Family EDAPHODONTIDAE	Informal name Ratfish

EDAPHODON

This fossil ratfish is known only from isolated tooth plates. Its dentition consisted of one pair of lower tooth plates and two pairs of upper tooth plates. The crushing surface of each bony plate is made up of localized areas of specialized dentine (tritors), consisting of hard dentine pillars positioned normally to the tooth plate surface. These were effective in dealing with thick-shelled marine invertebrates.
• HABITAT Modern ratfish inhabit shallow to deep, cool marine waters.

anterior tip •

LOWER TOOTH PLATE

EDAPHODON BUCKLANDI Agassiz; Bracklesham Beds; Middle Eocene; UK.

• midline of jaw

central specialized • crushing area

Typical length 3½ ft (1.1 m)

Range Cretaceous–Pliocene	Distribution Worldwide	Occurrence

ACANTHODIANS

T HESE FISHES WERE among the earliest known gnathostomes, and flourished in the Devonian. They varied in size from 4 in (10 cm) to over 6½ ft (2 m), and were active swimmers with long, tapered bodies protected by scales. A strongly heterocercal tail provided considerable thrust when swimming, and all paired and median fins (except the tail) had strong, immovable spines on their leading edges. The gills were covered by a large scale (operculum), and the teeth often developed in whorls.

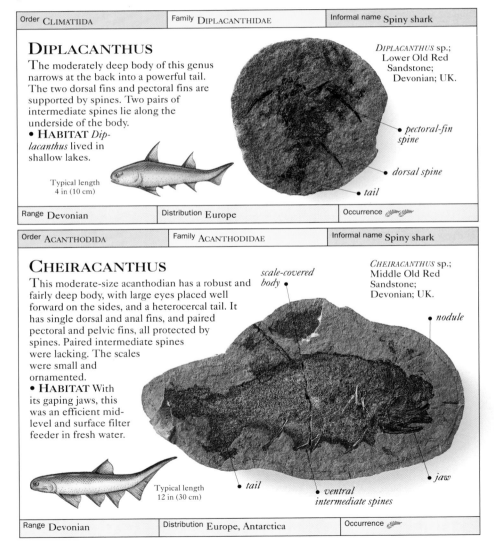

Order CLIMATIIDA	Family DIPLACANTHIDAE	Informal name Spiny shark

DIPLACANTHUS
The moderately deep body of this genus narrows at the back into a powerful tail. The two dorsal fins and pectoral fins are supported by spines. Two pairs of intermediate spines lie along the underside of the body.
• **HABITAT** *Diplacanthus* lived in shallow lakes.

Typical length
4 in (10 cm)

DIPLACANTHUS sp.;
Lower Old Red
Sandstone;
Devonian; UK.

• *pectoral-fin spine*

• *dorsal spine*

• *tail*

Range Devonian	Distribution Europe	Occurrence

Order ACANTHODIDA	Family ACANTHODIDAE	Informal name Spiny shark

CHEIRACANTHUS
This moderate-size acanthodian has a robust and fairly deep body, with large eyes placed well forward on the sides, and a heterocercal tail. It has single dorsal and anal fins, and paired pectoral and pelvic fins, all protected by spines. Paired intermediate spines were lacking. The scales were small and ornamented.
• **HABITAT** With its gaping jaws, this was an efficient mid-level and surface filter feeder in fresh water.

scale-covered body •

CHEIRACANTHUS sp.;
Middle Old Red
Sandstone;
Devonian; UK.

• *nodule*

• *jaw*

Typical length
12 in (30 cm)

• *tail*

• *ventral intermediate spines*

Range Devonian	Distribution Europe, Antarctica	Occurrence

OSTEICHTHYANS

FISH BELONGING TO this class are characterized by a bony internal skeleton. Two subgroups can be identified by their fin structure: the actinopterygians had fins supported by bony rods (radials), while the sarcopterygians had fleshy fins, which were supported by a single bone at the base. Actinopterygians (Devonian to Recent) are very diverse, and include the majority of present-day marine and freshwater fishes. The sarcopterygians dominated during the Devonian and include the lungfish and coelacanths.

Order CERATODONTIFORMES	Family CERATODONTIDAE	Informal name Lungfish

CERATODUS

A fossil relative of the extant Australian lungfish, *Ceratodus* had two upper and two lower tooth plates, anchored to the jaws. Up to six prominent, diagonal ridges with deep, intervening troughs cross the plates, from the inner posterior angle to the outer margin.
• HABITAT *Ceratodus* lived in fresh water, feeding on the bottom.

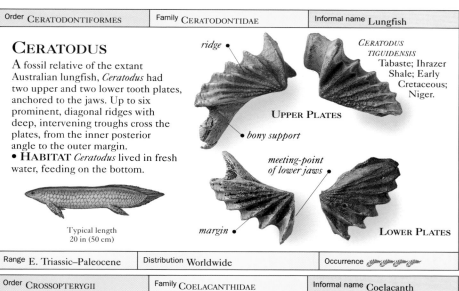

ridge

CERATODUS TIGUIDENSIS
Tabaste; Ihrazer Shale; Early Cretaceous; Niger.

UPPER PLATES

• *bony support*

meeting-point of lower jaws

margin

LOWER PLATES

Typical length 20 in (50 cm)

Range E. Triassic–Paleocene	Distribution Worldwide	Occurrence ~~~~~

Order CROSSOPTERYGII	Family COELACANTHIDAE	Informal name Coelacanth

MACROPOMA

This fossil coelacanth has a robust skull, large eyes positioned on the side, a relatively short body covered by scales, and reduced dentition. There are two dorsal fins and a tail divided into three – a central tuft as an extended axis, flanked by webs top and bottom. In life, it used its calcified swim bladder to remain buoyant in water.
• HABITAT *Macropoma* inhabited shallow, coastal waters.

MACROPOMA MANTELLI
Agassiz; Lower Chalk; Late Cretaceous; UK.

• *large eye*

calcified swim bladder

Typical length 16 in (40 cm)

Range Cretaceous	Distribution Europe	Occurrence ~~~

Order PALAEONISCIFORMES	Family CHEIROLEPIDAE	Informal name Palaeoniscid

CHEIROLEPIS

This early fish has a spindle-shaped body, large eyes, a short but distinct rostrum, and scales covered with thick layers of enamel. The paired fins are broad based and roughly triangular. They posessed fleshy, scaled lobes at the base supported by fin rays.
• HABITAT *Cheirolepis* was a freshwater predator, living in shallow lakes and streams.

CHEIROLEPIS TRAILLI Agassiz; Old Red Sandstone; Devonian; UK.

ridge scales on tail •

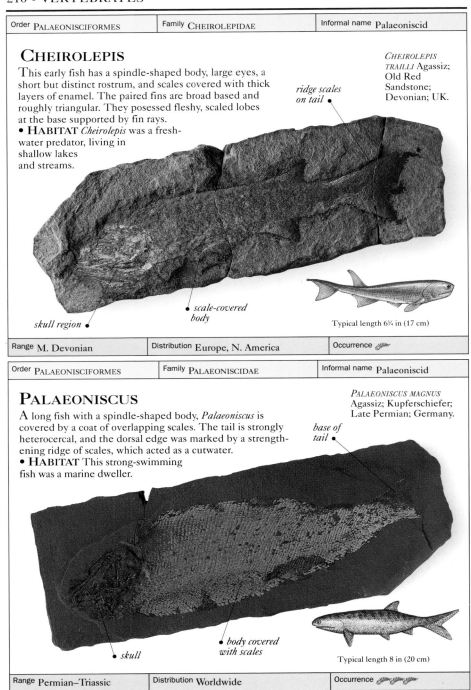

skull region •

scale-covered body •

Typical length 6¾ in (17 cm)

Range M. Devonian	Distribution Europe, N. America	Occurrence

Order PALAEONISCIFORMES	Family PALAEONISCIDAE	Informal name Palaeoniscid

PALAEONISCUS

A long fish with a spindle-shaped body, *Palaeoniscus* is covered by a coat of overlapping scales. The tail is strongly heterocercal, and the dorsal edge was marked by a strengthening ridge of scales, which acted as a cutwater.
• HABITAT This strong-swimming fish was a marine dweller.

PALAEONISCUS MAGNUS Agassiz; Kupferschiefer; Late Permian; Germany.

base of tail •

• *skull*

body covered with scales •

Typical length 8 in (20 cm)

Range Permian–Triassic	Distribution Worldwide	Occurrence

Order PALAEONISCIFORMES	Family BIRGERIIDAE	Informal name Palaeoniscid

BIRGERIA

Both jaws of this fish carried a row of large, predatory fangs flanked by smaller teeth. All were upright and conical, with a translucent enamel cap, folded root wall, and striated base.

• **HABITAT** *Birgeria* was a formidable marine predator.

outer surface covered by round projections

BIRGERIA ACUMINATA (Agassiz); Late Triassic; UK.

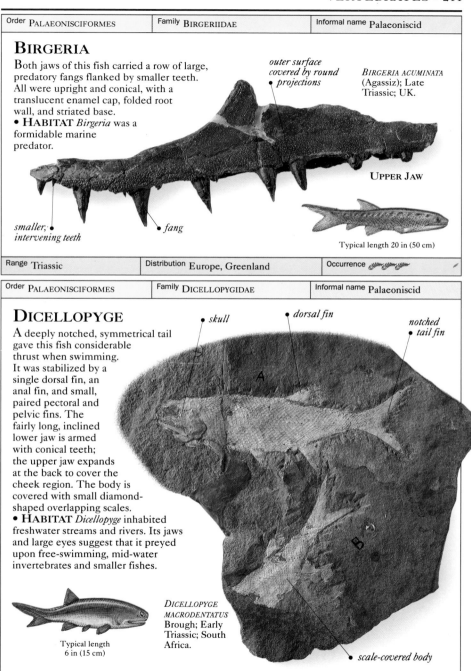

UPPER JAW

smaller, intervening teeth

fang

Typical length 20 in (50 cm)

Range Triassic	Distribution Europe, Greenland	Occurrence

Order PALAEONISCIFORMES	Family DICELLOPYGIDAE	Informal name Palaeoniscid

DICELLOPYGE

skull *dorsal fin* *notched tail fin*

A deeply notched, symmetrical tail gave this fish considerable thrust when swimming. It was stabilized by a single dorsal fin, an anal fin, and small, paired pectoral and pelvic fins. The fairly long, inclined lower jaw is armed with conical teeth; the upper jaw expands at the back to cover the cheek region. The body is covered with small diamond-shaped overlapping scales.

• **HABITAT** *Dicellopyge* inhabited freshwater streams and rivers. Its jaws and large eyes suggest that it preyed upon free-swimming, mid-water invertebrates and smaller fishes.

DICELLOPYGE MACRODENTATUS Brough; Early Triassic; South Africa.

Typical length 6 in (15 cm)

scale-covered body

Range E. Triassic	Distribution S. Africa	Occurrence

Order PYCNODONTIFORMES	Family PYCNODONTIDAE	Informal name Pycnodont

GYRODUS

This was a very deep-bodied fish with an almost circular outline. It had symmetrically placed dorsal and anal fins, a deeply notched, symmetrical tail fin, and reduced pelvic fins placed well forward. A delicate network of fine bones supported the body internally, and deep, rectangular scales covered the body surface.
• **HABITAT** *Gyrodus*'s dense pavement of rounded teeth suggests it may have browsed on a diet of coral or other hard-bodied prey.

LOWER JAW

densely packed teeth

longitudinal tooth rows

outer margin •

GYRODUS CUVIERI Agassiz; Kimmeridge Clay; Late Jurassic; UK.

Typical length 12 in (30 cm)

Range L. Jurassic–E. Cretaceous	Distribution Worldwide	Occurrence

Order SEMIONOTIFORMES	Family SEMIONOTIDAE	Informal name Neopterygian

DAPEDIUM

This deep-bodied fish was oval in outline and laterally compressed. Its body had larger dorsal, anal, and pelvic fins than *Gyrodus*, and a fan-shaped tail. The skull bones are distinctively ornamented with round projections, and the eyes were surrounded by a ring of plates. At the front of the mouth are nipping, upright teeth, which give way to a pavement of circular crushing teeth at the back.
• **HABITAT** Fishes of this genus probably fed on a variety of invertebrates, such as crustaceans, in warm, shallow seas.

DAPEDIUM POLITUM Agassiz; Lower Lias; Early Jurassic; UK.

skull roof •

eye socket

deep, rectangular body scales

PARTIAL SKULL

cheek region

• *operculum over gills*

Typical length 16 in (40 cm)

Range L. Triassic–Jurassic	Distribution Europe, Asia	Occurrence

Order PERLEIDIFORMES	Family CLEITHROLEPIDAE	Informal name Neopterygian

CLEITHROLEPIS

This small, deep-bodied fish has a notched, homocercal tail, and dorsal and anal fins lying opposite each other. The weak lower jaw is obliquely situated, with teeth at the tip only.
• HABITAT *Cleithrolepis* is believed to have been capable of strong, suctional feeding on small, mid-water prey.

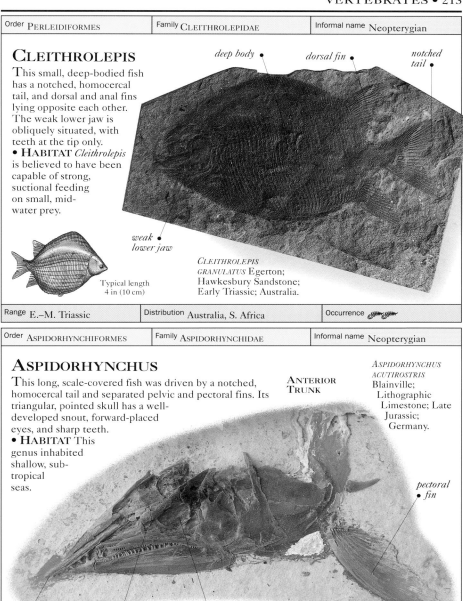

deep body • *dorsal fin* • *notched tail* •

weak lower jaw •

Typical length 4 in (10 cm)

CLEITHROLEPIS GRANULATUS Egerton; Hawkesbury Sandstone; Early Triassic; Australia.

Range E.–M. Triassic	Distribution Australia, S. Africa	Occurrence

Order ASPIDORHYNCHIFORMES	Family ASPIDORHYNCHIDAE	Informal name Neopterygian

ASPIDORHYNCHUS

This long, scale-covered fish was driven by a notched, homocercal tail and separated pelvic and pectoral fins. Its triangular, pointed skull has a well-developed snout, forward-placed eyes, and sharp teeth.
• HABITAT This genus inhabited shallow, sub-tropical seas.

ANTERIOR TRUNK

ASPIDORHYNCHUS ACUTIROSTRIS Blainville; Lithographic Limestone; Late Jurassic; Germany.

pectoral fin •

• *rostrum*

• *pointed skull*   • *eye socket*

Typical length 20 in (50 cm)

Range L. Jurassic–E. Cretaceous	Distribution Europe	Occurrence

Order PACHYCORMIFORMES	Family PACHYCORMIDAE	Informal name Neopterygian

PACHYCORMUS

This large fish had a powerfully built body and deeply notched, homocercal tail. The pelvic fins were much reduced, while the scythe-like pectoral fins were greatly elongated.
• **HABITAT** This fast, open-water predator inhabited shallow marine waters.
• **REMARK** This specimen is preserved three dimensionally in a calcareous nodule.

PACHYCORMUS MACROPTERUS (Blainville); Early Jurassic; France.

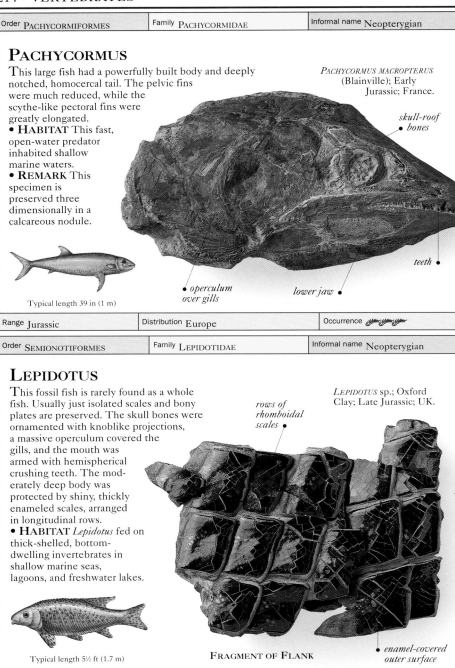

• *skull-roof bones*

• *teeth*

• *operculum over gills*

lower jaw •

Typical length 39 in (1 m)

Range Jurassic	Distribution Europe	Occurrence

Order SEMIONOTIFORMES	Family LEPIDOTIDAE	Informal name Neopterygian

LEPIDOTUS

This fossil fish is rarely found as a whole fish. Usually just isolated scales and bony plates are preserved. The skull bones were ornamented with knoblike projections, a massive operculum covered the gills, and the mouth was armed with hemispherical crushing teeth. The moderately deep body was protected by shiny, thickly enameled scales, arranged in longitudinal rows.
• **HABITAT** *Lepidotus* fed on thick-shelled, bottom-dwelling invertebrates in shallow marine seas, lagoons, and freshwater lakes.

rows of rhomboidal scales •

LEPIDOTUS sp.; Oxford Clay; Late Jurassic; UK.

Typical length 5½ ft (1.7 m)

FRAGMENT OF FLANK

• *enamel-covered outer surface*

Range Triassic–Cretaceous	Distribution Worldwide	Occurrence

Order ELOPIFORMES	Family PHYLLODONTIDAE	Informal name Elopiform

PHYLLODUS

This fish is known primarily from its convex tooth plates. The oval central teeth are the largest, and are organized into a rough, longitudinal row in the middle. These are flanked by long, slightly smaller crowns, giving way at the sides to almost concentric rows of smaller, near-circular teeth, and occasional ovoid teeth.
• **HABITAT** *Phyllodus* probably fed on thick-shelled, bottom-dwelling marine invertebrates, such as mollusks. As the fossil fish is also found in lagoonal and brackish deposits, it is believed that it may have been able to tolerate salinity.
• **REMARK** The affinities of the genus to other genera are uncertain.

UPPER
PHARYNGEAL
TOOTH PLATE

• *small marginal teeth*

• *laterally expanded central teeth*

PHYLLODUS TOLIAPICUS Agassiz; Blackheath Beds; Early Eocene; UK.

Estimated length 16 in (40 cm)

Range Eocene	Distribution N. America, Europe	Occurrence

Order ELOPIFORMES	Family MEGALOPIDAE	Informal name Tarpan

PACHYTHRISSOPS

Pachythrissops was a spindle-shaped fish, with a short skull and a prominent symmetrical, forked tail. The single dorsal and anal fins were much larger than the paired pectoral and pelvic fins. Thin, rounded scales protected the body.
• **HABITAT** *Pachythrissops* used its small, conical teeth to feed on small marine mollusks, arthropods, and small fish.

PACHYTHRISSOPS FURCATUS (Eastman); Solnhofen Limestone; Late Jurassic; Germany.

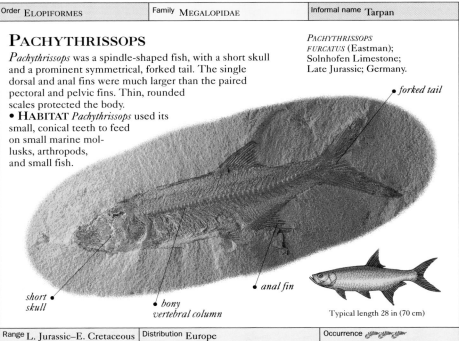

• *forked tail*

short skull •

• *bony vertebral column*

• *anal fin*

Typical length 28 in (70 cm)

Range L. Jurassic–E. Cretaceous	Distribution Europe	Occurrence

Order ELOPIFORMES	Family PACHYRHIZODONTIDAE	Informal name Elopiform

RHACOLEPIS

The body is spindle-shaped, covered with small rhomboidal scales. The skull is pointed. The lower jaw is long and upwardly inclined with a single row of small teeth.
• HABITAT *Rhacolepis* lived in shallow marine conditions. It is commonly found in calcareous (limestone) nodules, preserved in three dimensions.

RHACOLEPIS BUCCALIS Agassiz; Santana Formation; Early Cretaceous; Brazil.

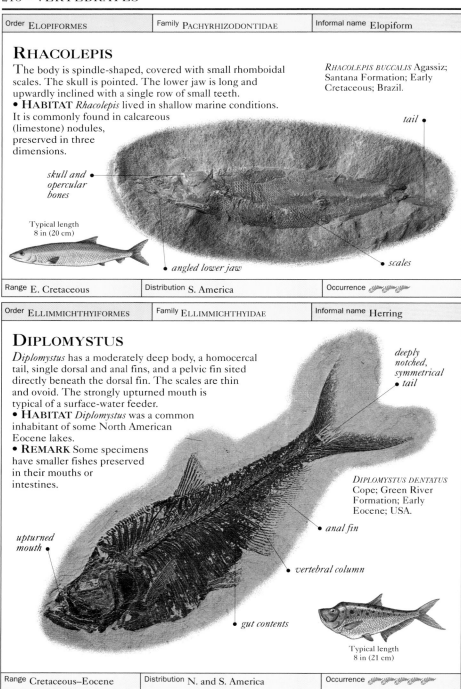

tail

skull and opercular bones

Typical length 8 in (20 cm)

angled lower jaw

scales

Range E. Cretaceous	Distribution S. America	Occurrence

Order ELLIMMICHTHYIFORMES	Family ELLIMMICHTHYIDAE	Informal name Herring

DIPLOMYSTUS

Diplomystus has a moderately deep body, a homocercal tail, single dorsal and anal fins, and a pelvic fin sited directly beneath the dorsal fin. The scales are thin and ovoid. The strongly upturned mouth is typical of a surface-water feeder.
• HABITAT *Diplomystus* was a common inhabitant of some North American Eocene lakes.
• REMARK Some specimens have smaller fishes preserved in their mouths or intestines.

deeply notched, symmetrical tail

DIPLOMYSTUS DENTATUS Cope; Green River Formation; Early Eocene; USA.

anal fin

upturned mouth

vertebral column

gut contents

Typical length 8 in (21 cm)

Range Cretaceous–Eocene	Distribution N. and S. America	Occurrence

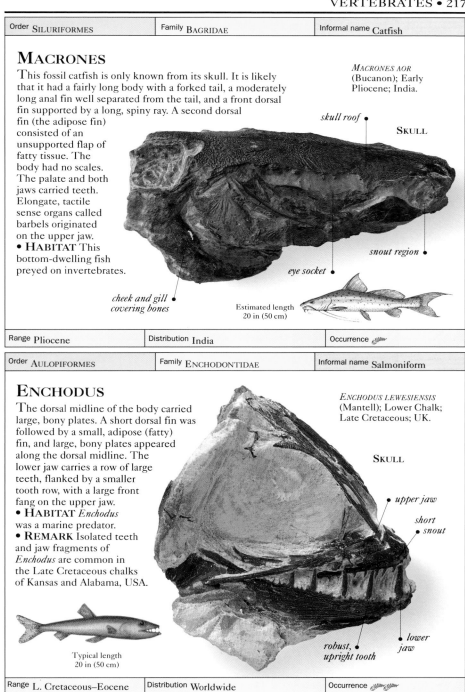

| Order SILURIFORMES | Family BAGRIDAE | Informal name Catfish |

MACRONES

This fossil catfish is only known from its skull. It is likely that it had a fairly long body with a forked tail, a moderately long anal fin well separated from the tail, and a front dorsal fin supported by a long, spiny ray. A second dorsal fin (the adipose fin) consisted of an unsupported flap of fatty tissue. The body had no scales. The palate and both jaws carried teeth. Elongate, tactile sense organs called barbels originated on the upper jaw.
• HABITAT This bottom-dwelling fish preyed on invertebrates.

MACRONES AOR (Bucanon); Early Pliocene; India.

skull roof

SKULL

snout region

eye socket

cheek and gill covering bones

Estimated length 20 in (50 cm)

| Range Pliocene | Distribution India | Occurrence |

| Order AULOPIFORMES | Family ENCHODONTIDAE | Informal name Salmoniform |

ENCHODUS

The dorsal midline of the body carried large, bony plates. A short dorsal fin was followed by a small, adipose (fatty) fin, and large, bony plates appeared along the dorsal midline. The lower jaw carries a row of large teeth, flanked by a smaller tooth row, with a large front fang on the upper jaw.
• HABITAT *Enchodus* was a marine predator.
• REMARK Isolated teeth and jaw fragments of *Enchodus* are common in the Late Cretaceous chalks of Kansas and Alabama, USA.

ENCHODUS LEWESIENSIS (Mantell); Lower Chalk; Late Cretaceous; UK.

SKULL

upper jaw

short snout

lower jaw

robust, upright tooth

Typical length 20 in (50 cm)

| Range L. Cretaceous–Eocene | Distribution Worldwide | Occurrence |

| Order CYPRINIFORMES | Family CYPRINIDAE | Informal name Dace |

LEUCISCUS

This dace has a small, but extended, body, small fins, relatively large scales, and a forked tail. It is a specialized herbivore with toothless jaws. The front vertebrae and ribs (known as the Weberian ossicles) are movable and, by transmitting vibrations from the swim bladder to the inner ear, improve sensitivity to high frequency sound. When injured, modern species of *Leuciscus* release a chemical from epidermal alarm cells, eliciting a fright reaction in related fish, causing them to scatter and swim to the bottom.
• HABITAT *Leuciscus* inhabit freshwater streams and lakes.
• REMARK This specimen shows a mass mortality, with subsequent irregular alignment of the bodies by the action of currents.

LEUCISCUS PACHECOI
Gomez; Miocene; Spain.

small but extended body

forked tail

fine-grained freshwater marl

head

fine vertebral column

Typical length
3½ in (9 cm)

| Range Oligocene–Recent | Distribution N. America, Asia, Africa | Occurrence |

Order BERYCIFORMES	Family BERYCIDAE	Informal name Alfonsino

CENTROBERYX

Some fossil fish, like this one, may be identified by their otoliths, which are concentrically laminated, aragonitic structures located in the inner ear. Otoliths are embedded in ciliated sense organs. They detect changes in body position. Of the three pairs, the sacculith (shown) is the largest.
• HABITAT *Centroberyx* lived in shoals in moderately deep oceans.

• *dorsal rim*

• *sulcus*

OTOLITH

CENTROBERYX EOCENICUS (Frost); London Clay; Early Eocene; UK.

• *typical orange color*

Typical length 24 in (60 cm)

Range L. Cretaceous–Oligocene	Distribution Worldwide	Occurrence

Order BERYCIFORMES	Family TRACHICHTHYIDAE	Informal name Slimehead

HOPLOPTERYX

Hoplopteryx has a dorsal fin supported by nine unjointed, bony fin rays, a deeply forked, homocercal tail, a moderately developed anal fin, and a pelvic fin located well forward. The snout is quite short, the eyes fairly large, and both jaws of the upturned mouth hold small teeth.
• HABITAT This was a marine fish, living in shallow chalk seas.

HOPLOPTERYX LEWESIENSIS (Mantell); Lower Chalk; Late Cretaceous; UK.

• *fin rays*

• *vertebral column*

eye socket •

bones covering gills •

small pectoral fin •

Typical length 10½ in (27 cm)

Range L. Cretaceous	Distribution Northern hemisphere	Occurrence

Order PERCIFORMES	Family POMACENTRIDAE	Informal name Perch

PRISCACARA

This fossil perch has a deep, oval body protected by dorsal and anal spines, and a fan-shaped tail. It has a slightly upturned, protruding lower jaw. The two jaws, as well as the enlarged bones in the mouth, are covered with fine teeth.

• **HABITAT** *Priscacara* lived in freshwater streams and lakes, feeding on snails and crustaceans.

PRISCACARA LIOPS Cope; Green River Formation; Middle Eocene; USA.

stout dorsal • spines

• vertebrae

• eye socket

unforked tail fin •

• lower jaw

Typical length 6 in (15 cm)

stout dorsal • spines

Range Eocene	Distribution N. America	Occurrence

Order PERCIFORMES	Family SCOMBRIDAE	Informal name Mackerel

WETHERELLUS

Although known from the cranial skeleton only, this fossil fish is thought to have been around 10 in (25 cm) long. Its moderately large eye, containing sclerotic plates, is centrally placed in the shallow skull. The jaws are armed with a row of upright, pointed teeth, flanked by a smaller, marginal series.

• **HABITAT** *Wetherellus* lived in moderately deep oceans.

• **REMARK** This skull is preserved in a phosphatic nodule.

WETHERELLUS CRISTATUS Casier; London Clay; Early Eocene; UK.

eye socket •

• sclerotic ring

upper • jaw

Estimated length 10 in (25 cm)

• operculum over gill

gaping • lower jaw

Range E. Eocene	Distribution Europe	Occurrence

AMPHIBIANS

A MPHIBIANS WERE THE first vertebrates to colonize the land, more than 400 million years ago. Although they were able to live on land, their eggs were laid in water, hence they were only semiterrestrial. From the Late Carboniferous period onward the evolution of fossil amphibians followed two major pathways. One led to modern groups – frogs, salamanders, and caecilians. The second pathway gave rise to reptiles, which developed a waterproof egg, allowing them to breed on land and so become completely terrestrial, unlike today's semiterrestrial amphibians.

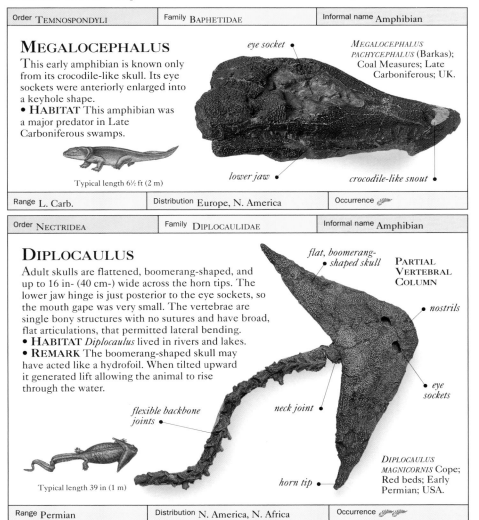

Order TEMNOSPONDYLI	Family BAPHETIDAE	Informal name Amphibian

MEGALOCEPHALUS

This early amphibian is known only from its crocodile-like skull. Its eye sockets were anteriorly enlarged into a keyhole shape.
• **HABITAT** This amphibian was a major predator in Late Carboniferous swamps.

Typical length 6½ ft (2 m)

eye socket •

lower jaw •

crocodile-like snout •

MEGALOCEPHALUS PACHYCEPHALUS (Barkas); Coal Measures; Late Carboniferous; UK.

Range L. Carb.	Distribution Europe, N. America	Occurrence

Order NECTRIDEA	Family DIPLOCAULIDAE	Informal name Amphibian

DIPLOCAULUS

Adult skulls are flattened, boomerang-shaped, and up to 16 in- (40 cm-) wide across the horn tips. The lower jaw hinge is just posterior to the eye sockets, so the mouth gape was very small. The vertebrae are single bony structures with no sutures and have broad, flat articulations, that permitted lateral bending.
• **HABITAT** *Diplocaulus* lived in rivers and lakes.
• **REMARK** The boomerang-shaped skull may have acted like a hydrofoil. When tilted upward it generated lift allowing the animal to rise through the water.

flat, boomerang-
• shaped skull

PARTIAL
VERTEBRAL
COLUMN

• nostrils

• eye
sockets

neck joint •

flexible backbone
joints •

horn tip •

DIPLOCAULUS MAGNICORNIS Cope; Red beds; Early Permian; USA.

Typical length 39 in (1 m)

Range Permian	Distribution N. America, N. Africa	Occurrence

Order TEMNOSPONDYLI	Family BRANCHIOSAURIDAE	Informal name Amphibian

APATEON

This small, neotenous amphibian resembles a salamander. Its skull usually measures between ⁵⁄₁₆–1 in (8–24 mm) in length. The posterior region of the skull behind the eyes is very short. There were three pairs of long, feathery external gills. The ribs were very reduced, and the bones of the wrists and ankles are unossified. The hand had four fingers. The tail bore a long, deep fin.
• HABITAT *Apateon* was a totally aquatic amphibian, inhabiting semipermanent lakes and ponds.
• REMARK Fluctuations in seasonal conditions caused mass deaths of thousands of individuals. These are now preserved in fine-grained, freshwater limestones.

APATEON PEDESTRIS Meyer; Freshwater limestone; Early Permian; Germany.

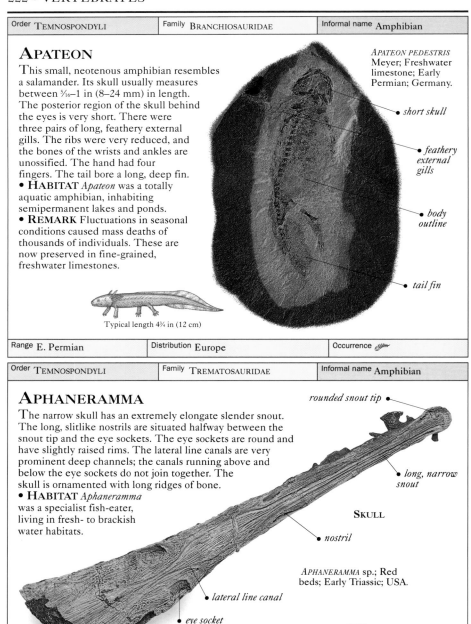

• *short skull*

• *feathery external gills*

• *body outline*

• *tail fin*

Typical length 4¾ in (12 cm)

Range E. Permian	Distribution Europe	Occurrence

Order TEMNOSPONDYLI	Family TREMATOSAURIDAE	Informal name Amphibian

APHANERAMMA

The narrow skull has an extremely elongate slender snout. The long, slitlike nostrils are situated halfway between the snout tip and the eye sockets. The eye sockets are round and have slightly raised rims. The lateral line canals are very prominent deep channels; the canals running above and below the eye sockets do not join together. The skull is ornamented with long ridges of bone.
• HABITAT *Aphaneramma* was a specialist fish-eater, living in fresh- to brackish water habitats.

rounded snout tip •

• *long, narrow snout*

SKULL

• *nostril*

APHANERAMMA sp.; Red beds; Early Triassic; USA.

• *lateral line canal*

• *eye socket*

• *striated bone ornament*

Typical length 6½ ft (2 m)

Range E. Triassic	Distribution Worldwide	Occurrence

Order TEMNOSPONDYLI	Family BRACHYOPIDAE	Informal name Amphibian

BATRACHOSUCHUS

The broad triangular short-faced skull of *Batrachosuchus* has nostrils set close together. The eye sockets are widely separate; the upper jaw bone forming part of the outer rim.
• HABITAT *Batrachosuchus* was a neotenous surface swimmer which probably fed on small prey by suction gulping.

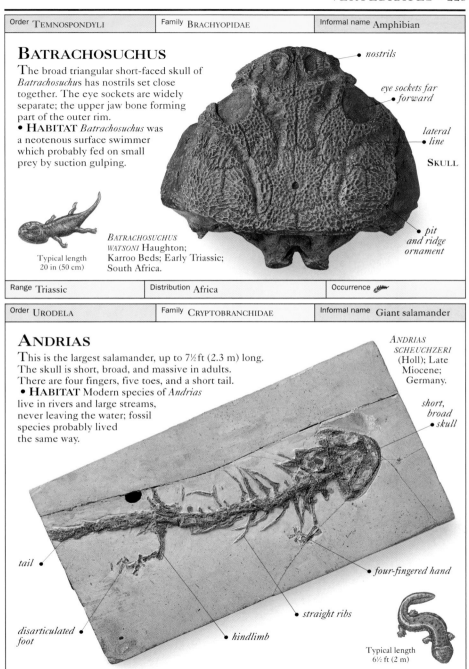

• *nostrils*

eye sockets far • *forward*

lateral • *line*

SKULL

• *pit and ridge ornament*

BATRACHOSUCHUS WATSONI Haughton; Karroo Beds; Early Triassic; South Africa.

Typical length 20 in (50 cm)

Range Triassic	Distribution Africa	Occurrence

Order URODELA	Family CRYPTOBRANCHIDAE	Informal name Giant salamander

ANDRIAS

This is the largest salamander, up to 7½ ft (2.3 m) long. The skull is short, broad, and massive in adults. There are four fingers, five toes, and a short tail.
• HABITAT Modern species of *Andrias* live in rivers and large streams, never leaving the water; fossil species probably lived the same way.

ANDRIAS SCHEUCHZERI (Holl); Late Miocene; Germany.

short, broad • *skull*

tail •

• *four-fingered hand*

• *straight ribs*

disarticulated • *foot*

• *hindlimb*

Typical length 6½ ft (2 m)

Range Miocene–Recent	Distribution Europe, Japan, N. America	Occurrence

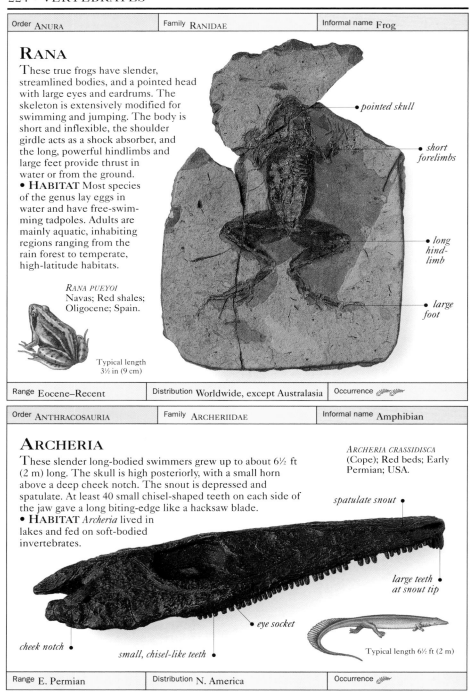

| Order ANURA | Family RANIDAE | Informal name Frog |

RANA

These true frogs have slender, streamlined bodies, and a pointed head with large eyes and eardrums. The skeleton is extensively modified for swimming and jumping. The body is short and inflexible, the shoulder girdle acts as a shock absorber, and the long, powerful hindlimbs and large feet provide thrust in water or from the ground.
• **HABITAT** Most species of the genus lay eggs in water and have free-swimming tadpoles. Adults are mainly aquatic, inhabiting regions ranging from the rain forest to temperate, high-latitude habitats.

RANA PUEYOI
Navas; Red shales; Oligocene; Spain.

• *pointed skull*

• *short forelimbs*

• *long hindlimb*

• *large foot*

Typical length
3½ in (9 cm)

| Range Eocene–Recent | Distribution Worldwide, except Australasia | Occurrence |

| Order ANTHRACOSAURIA | Family ARCHERIIDAE | Informal name Amphibian |

ARCHERIA

These slender long-bodied swimmers grew up to about 6½ ft (2 m) long. The skull is high posteriorly, with a small horn above a deep cheek notch. The snout is depressed and spatulate. At least 40 small chisel-shaped teeth on each side of the jaw gave a long biting-edge like a hacksaw blade.
• **HABITAT** *Archeria* lived in lakes and fed on soft-bodied invertebrates.

ARCHERIA CRASSIDISCA
(Cope); Red beds; Early Permian; USA.

spatulate snout •

large teeth at snout tip •

eye socket •

cheek notch •

small, chisel-like teeth •

Typical length 6½ ft (2 m)

| Range E. Permian | Distribution N. America | Occurrence |

ANAPSID REPTILES

T HE CLASS REPTILIA is divided into three subclasses (the Anapsida, Diapsida, and Synapsida), according to the number of openings in the skull roof and the configuration of the associated skull bones behind the eye sockets. In the Anapsida there are no such openings, indicating that they were among the first reptiles. The early forms, which first appeared about 300 million years ago, were usually small, lizardlike creatures. However, they are significant because they gave rise to the reptiles that produced birds and mammals, as well as the dinosaurs that ruled the world in the Mesozoic Era. Turtles are traditionally placed within the Anapsida subclass, despite appearing some 30 million years after the other anapsids became extinct.

Order CAPTORHINIDA	Family PROCOLOPHONIDAE	Informal name Procolophonid

PROCOLOPHON

Evolving from the early members of the anapsid line, the lizardlike, triangular-headed procolo-phonids retained many primitive features in their skeletons. For example, the skull has an obvious "third eye," which is more in keeping with the anapsids' amphibian ancestors, while the jaws and palate have numerous rows of simple teeth. The heavy limbs and relatively massive fore- and hind-limb girdles indicate slow move-ment and a sprawling gait.
• **HABITAT** All appear to have been land-living vegetarians.
• **REMARK** The family first appeared in the Early Triassic, but failed to survive beyond it.

PROCOLOPHON TRIGONICEPS
Owen; Karoo Formation;
Early Triassic; South Africa.

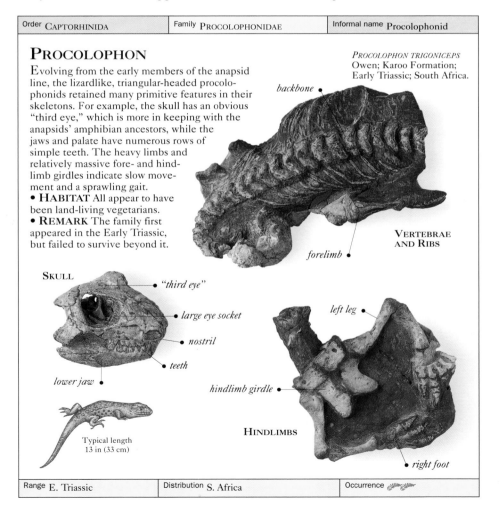

backbone

**VERTEBRAE
AND RIBS**

forelimb

SKULL

"third eye"

large eye socket

nostril

teeth

lower jaw

left leg

hindlimb girdle

Typical length
13 in (33 cm)

HINDLIMBS

right foot

Range E. Triassic	Distribution S. Africa	Occurrence

Order CAPTORHINIDA	Family PAREIASAURIDAE	Informal name Pareiasaurid

ELGINIA

This small example of the pareiasaur family is distinguished by the elaborate bony processes produced from the triangular-shaped skull, which probably acted either as a form of defense against would-be predators or as a display mechanism while courting.

• **HABITAT** The four-footed *Elginia* lived on land plants. It became extinct during the Late Permian.

ELGINIA MIRABILIS Newton; Elgin Sandstone; Late Permian; UK.

Typical length
5 ft (1.5 m)

Range L. Permian	Distribution Europe	Occurrence

Order MESOSAURIA	Family MESOSAURIDAE	Informal name Mesosaurid

STEREOSTERNUM

The aquatic preference of this anapsid is evident in the long needlelike teeth, the elongated head and body, which contain ten neck vertebrae, and the short limbs and flattened tail.

• **HABITAT** It has been suggested that the long fine teeth of this small carnivore combined to act as a sieve, enabling it to filter out the small swimming crustaceans abundant in its marine environment.

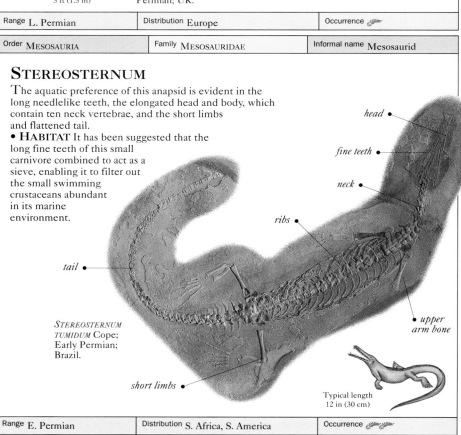

STEREOSTERNUM TUMIDUM Cope; Early Permian; Brazil.

Typical length
12 in (30 cm)

Range E. Permian	Distribution S. Africa, S. America	Occurrence

Order CHELONIA	Family PROGANOCHELYDAE	Informal name Primitive turtle

PROGANOCHELYS

Turtles and tortoises are recognizable by their large eye sockets, toothless jaws with horny coverings forming a beak, and bony shells. *Proganochelys* displays its primitiveness in retaining toothlike denticles on the palate, as well as nasal bones. It has an extra series of peripheral plates in the carapace.
• HABITAT This semiaquatic form fed on plants.

large eye socket

complete skull roof

toothless jaws

Typical length 39 in (1 m)

PROGANOCHELYS QUENSTEDTI Baur; Upper Stuben-sandstein (Keuper); Late Triassic; Germany.

Range L. Triassic	Distribution Europe, S. Asia	Occurrence

Order CHELONIA	Family PELOMEDUSIDAE	Informal name Side-necked turtle

PELUSIOS

The ability to withdraw the head sideways into the shell, the possession of a mesoplastral element not restricted to the lower shell's outer margin, and the firm attachment of the rear girdle to the lower shell are all features of the pelomedusid family. The first side-necked turtle appeared in the Early Cretaceous of Africa, but by the Tertiary they had a nearly worldwide distribution.
• HABITAT All pelomedusids appear to have been semi-aquatic omnivores. Living species are now restricted to the southern continents of Africa and South America.

anterior

mesoplastral element

entoplastron

hinge

INTERNAL VIEW

rear girdle scars

PELUSIOS SINUATUS (Smith); Olduvai Beds; Early Pleistocene; Tanzania.

EXTERNAL VIEW

Typical length 20 in (50 cm)

Range E. Pleistocene–Recent	Distribution Africa	Occurrence

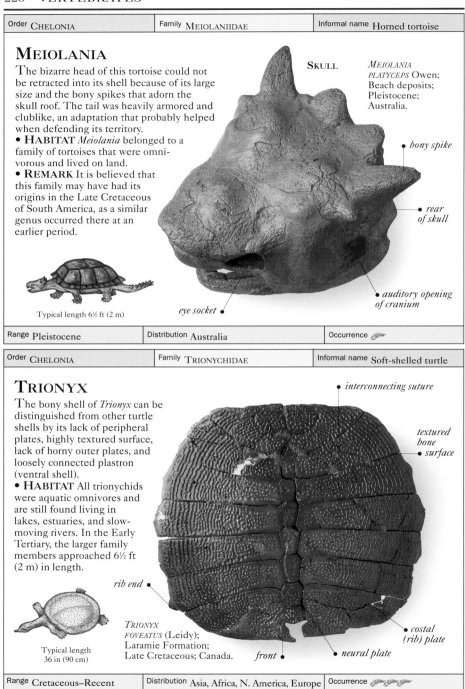

| Order CHELONIA | Family MEIOLANIIDAE | Informal name Horned tortoise |

MEIOLANIA

The bizarre head of this tortoise could not be retracted into its shell because of its large size and the bony spikes that adorn the skull roof. The tail was heavily armored and clublike, an adaptation that probably helped when defending its territory.
• **HABITAT** *Meiolania* belonged to a family of tortoises that were omnivorous and lived on land.
• **REMARK** It is believed that this family may have had its origins in the Late Cretaceous of South America, as a similar genus occurred there at an earlier period.

SKULL

MEIOLANIA PLATYCEPS Owen; Beach deposits; Pleistocene; Australia.

bony spike

rear of skull

auditory opening of cranium

Typical length 6½ ft (2 m)

eye socket

| Range Pleistocene | Distribution Australia | Occurrence |

| Order CHELONIA | Family TRIONYCHIDAE | Informal name Soft-shelled turtle |

TRIONYX

The bony shell of *Trionyx* can be distinguished from other turtle shells by its lack of peripheral plates, highly textured surface, lack of horny outer plates, and loosely connected plastron (ventral shell).
• **HABITAT** All trionychids were aquatic omnivores and are still found living in lakes, estuaries, and slow-moving rivers. In the Early Tertiary, the larger family members approached 6½ ft (2 m) in length.

interconnecting suture

textured bone surface

rib end

TRIONYX FOVEATUS (Leidy); Laramie Formation; Late Cretaceous; Canada.

front

costal (rib) plate

neural plate

Typical length 36 in (90 cm)

| Range Cretaceous–Recent | Distribution Asia, Africa, N. America, Europe | Occurrence |

Order CHELONIA	Family CHELONIIDAE	Informal name Marine turtle

PUPPIGERUS

This genus has characteristic adaptations for an aquatic existence: large eye sockets, with a secondary skull roof behind them and a fully formed secondary palate. The latter was especially important, as it prevented an unwanted intake of water while feeding below the surface. In adults, the shell is fully ossified, with an outer margin of peripheral plates, while the plastron (ventral shell) comprises four paired elements and one centrally placed, all of which are loosely connected by fingerlike projections in the midline. The forelimbs developed into flippers.

• **HABITAT** *Puppigerus* was a marine turtle and, like its modern counterparts, fed on sea grasses. Its hindlimbs were less flipperlike, a condition that possibly indicates a greater mobility on land.

• **REMARK** Like modern sea turtles, females would have buried their eggs on sandy beaches.

large orbit • SKULL

secondary roof •

PUPPIGERUS CRASSICOSTATA
(Owen); London Clay;
Early Eocene; UK.

single entoplastron •

hypoplastron •

• *epiplastron*

PLASTRON

PUPPIGERUS CAMPERI
(Gray); London Clay;
Early Eocene; UK.

hyoplastron •

xiphiplastron •

Typical length
36 in (90 cm)

Range Eocene	Distribution Europe	Occurrence

Order CHELONIA	Family CHELONIIDAE	Informal name Marine turtle

CIMOCHELYS

The low-profiled carapace of this small turtle is not completely ossified. This feature is clearly seen between the ends of each expanded rib and the marginal plates and is characteristic of some species of marine turtles. The central row of plates (neurals) are distinctly keeled in this genus.
• **HABITAT** *Cimochelys* was a marine vegetarian.
• **REMARK** Being very agile in water, marine turtles are less vulnerable to attack. So in many forms the bony armor of the shell has become reduced.

expanded rib •

CIMOCHELYS BENSTEDI (Owen); Chalk; Late Cretaceous; UK.

• *keeled neural*

reduced carapace •

Typical length 12 in (30 cm)

Range L. Cretaceous	Distribution Europe	Occurrence

Order CHELONIA	Family TESTUDINIDAE	Informal name Tortoise

GEOCHELONE

A common characteristic of tortoises like *Geochelone* is a high-arched, fully ossified, bumpy shell, embellished with concentric markings. Other characteristic features of this land-dwelling group include a skull that lacks a secondary bone covering behind the eye sockets and the ability to withdraw the head vertically and backward.
• **HABITAT** Like many tortoises, this genus lives in arid areas, feeding on a variety of plant matter.

• *high-arched shell*

GEOCHELONE PARDALIS (Bell); Laetolil Beds; Pliocene; Tanzania.

• *marginal plates*

lower shell •

Typical length 14 in (35 cm)

Range Eocene–Recent	Distribution Europe, Asia, Africa	Occurrence

DIAPSID REPTILES

T HE SECOND MAJOR DIVISION of the reptiles, the Diapsida evolved during the Carboniferous, shortly after the evolution of the anapsid reptiles from the amphibians. Diapsid reptiles are characterized by the possession of two skull openings behind the eye sockets, but this condition is often obscured by modifications evolved to accommodate the various life-styles of different species. Within the Diapsida are all modern forms, except turtles, and the majority of extinct species. The group reached maximum diversity during the Mesozoic era, when its members – dinosaurs, various marine reptiles, and pterosaurs – ruled land, sea, and air.

Order SPHENODONTA	Family SPHENODONTIDAE	Informal name Sphenodontid

HOMEOSAURUS

A small, lizardlike reptile, *Homeosaurus* resembles the last surviving member of its order – the tuatara of New Zealand – in many details. The group to which it belongs differs from the lizards by having skulls with a rigid articulation bone (quadrate). Also characteristic is the attachment of the few marginal teeth, which are firmly fused to the edge of the jaws. These were not replaced when worn but were added at the rear as growth continued. Additional teeth are present in the palate, and the snout is turned down to produce a chisel-like cutting edge.
• HABITAT *Homeosaurus* was probably a land dweller, living on plants and insects.
• REMARK First appearing during the Triassic, the order became widespread during the early part of the Mesozoic, before declining to the single species still alive today.

skull

upper leg bone

HOMEOSAURUS MAXIMILIANI Meyer; Solnhofen Limestone; Late Jurassic; Germany.

tail

foot

Typical length 8 in (20 cm)

Range L. Jurassic	Distribution Europe	Occurrence

Order SQUAMATA	Family KUEHNEOSAURIDAE	Informal name Flying lizard

KUEHNEOSUCHUS

This primitive gliding lizardlike diapsid had very long, fixed ribs, giving a "wingspan" of about 12 in (30 cm). It is thought that these ribs were attached to each other by tissue, thus forming a continuous membrane, that would have acted as a gliding surface, reminiscent of the present-day "flying lizards" such as *Draco*.
• HABITAT *Kuehneosuchus* is thought to have been insectivorous. It lived in open woodland.

• three vertebrae

KUEHNEOSUCHUS LATISSIMUS Robinson; Fissure fill; Late Triassic; UK.

long, hollow • rib

rib •

upper thigh • bone

fragments •

Typical "wingspan" 12 in (30 cm)

Range L. Triassic	Distribution Europe	Occurrence

Order SQUAMATA	Family AMPHISBAENIDAE	Informal name Worm lizard

LYSTROMYCTER

This wormlike lizard had a characteristically robust, wedge-shaped skull with simple, peglike teeth, and with one tooth centrally positioned in the front of the upper jaw. Living species of this family of burrowers have weak eyesight and legless bodies.
• HABITAT Living species of *Lystromycter* have a preference for burrowing into loose soil while ctively hunting worms and insects.

SIDE VIEW OF SKULL

• eye socket

• shovel-like snout

tooth row •

• palate

LYSTROMYCTER LEAKEYI Charig & Gans; Rusinga Beds; Early Miocene; Kenya.

• median tooth

UNDERSIDE OF SKULL

Typical length 12 in (30 cm)

Range E. Miocene	Distribution E. Africa	Occurrence

| Order SQUAMATA | Family VARANIDAE | Informal name Giant goanna |

MEGALANIA

This monitor lizard attained a length twice that of the Recent Komodo Dragon. It had a mandible hinged in the middle, and the widely spaced recurved teeth were attached to the inner sides of the jaws, with replacements arising between worn teeth. The long neck was made up of nine out of the 29 presacral vertebrae, which have strongly socketed front, and bulbous rear, articulations.
• HABITAT *Megalania* was a ferocious carnivore, living in Australia during the Pleistocene Epoch.
• REMARK The hunting technique of this lizard probably included ambushing around waterholes and then disabling its prey by severing its hamstrings.

• *neural spine*

MEGALANIA PRISCA Owen; River deposits; Pleistocene; Australia.

• *rear articulation facet*

VERTEBRA

Typical length 20 ft (6 m)

rear articulation boss

front articulation socket

| Range Pleistocene | Distribution Australia | Occurrence |

| Order SQUAMATA | Family MOSASAURIDAE | Informal name Mosasaur |

LEIODON

Leiodon was a medium-size example of the mosasaur family, the largest members of which grew to more than 33 ft (10 m) in length. Like other mosasaurs, its teeth have an almost smooth, recurved crown, slightly triangular in cross section, and set on a bulbous root. Individual teeth are located in separate sockets, but are not attached to the side of the jaw as in other lizards.
• HABITAT Mosasaurs were fast-moving marine carnivores, feeding on fish and other marine animals.

LEIODON sp.; Upper Chalk; Late Cretaceous; Holland.

recurved tooth
• *crown*

smooth enamel •

• *bulbous root of tooth*

JAW FRAGMENT WITH TEETH

replacement tooth

Typical length 16½ ft (5 m)

| Range L. Cretaceous | Distribution Europe | Occurrence |

Order SQUAMATA	Family MOSASAURIDAE	Informal name Mosasaur

TYLOSAURUS

The mosasaurs had large, lightly built skulls, armed with recurved teeth set in sockets and a lower jaw hinged in the middle. Their necks were short, with seven vertebrae, while the remainder of their bodies was elongate. Individual vertebrae had ball-and-socket articulations, allowing considerable sideways movement. The limbs were reduced and paddlelike, used for steering not propulsion.

• **HABITAT** The mosasaurs evolved from land forms that later returned to an aquatic environment. The group appears to be related to the varanid lizards living today. They actively hunted an assortment of marine organisms in shallow seas.

• **REMARK** Although a short-lived group that appeared and became extinct during the Late Cretaceous, the mosasaurs were the most important and widespread of the marine carnivores living at that time. Their remains have been recovered from around the world.

neural spine •

VERTEBRA

• socket articulation

• bulbous articulation

TYLOSAURUS NEPAEOLICUS (Cope); Kansas Chalk; Late Cretaceous; USA.

QUADRATE BONE

ulna •

radius •

finger bones •

• wrist bones

FORELIMB BONES

Typical length 20 ft (6 m)

Range L. Cretaceous	Distribution N. America	Occurrence

Order SQUAMATA	Family DINILYSIIDAE	Informal name Land snake

DINILYSIA

Common features of land snakes are a low, flat braincase, with high mobility of the palate, jaw elements, and quadrate, together with a long temporal region, providing a large attachment area for jaw muscles.
• HABITAT *Dinilysia* was clearly terrestrial and lived on small vertebrates.
• REMARK *Dinilysia*'s skull does not support the suggestion that snakes had a burrowing stage in their ancestry.

DINILYSIA PATAGONICA
Woodward; Rio Colorado Formation; Cretaceous; Argentina.

long temporal • region

flattened • skull

eye socket •

upper jaw •

loose • upper/lower jaw articulation

• tooth sockets

Typical length 10 ft (3 m)

SKULL AND LOWER JAWS

Range L. Cretaceous	Distribution S. America	Occurrence

Order SQUAMATA	Family PALEOPHIDAE	Informal name Sea snake

PALEOPHIS

The vertebrae of this marine snake have socketed front and bulbous rear articulations, with further accessory articulations – characteristic of snakes – situated on the neural arch. The ribs are elongate.
• HABITAT Like modern sea snakes, *Paleophis* lived in shallow coastal waters and estuaries.
• REMARK Although the vertebrae of *Paleophis* are relatively common fossil finds, they provide little information about its relationships.

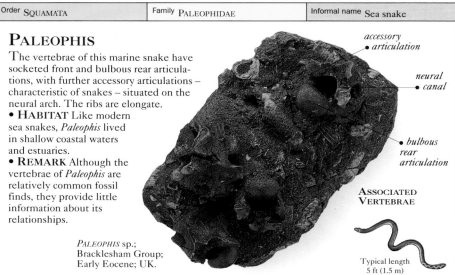

accessory • articulation

neural • canal

• bulbous rear articulation

ASSOCIATED VERTEBRAE

PALEOPHIS sp.;
Bracklesham Group;
Early Eocene; UK.

Typical length 5 ft (1.5 m)

Range L. Cretaceous–Oligocene	Distribution Europe, Africa, America	Occurrence

Order NOTHOSAURIA	Family PACHYPLEUROSAURIDAE	Informal name Pachypleurosaurid

NEUSTICOSAURUS

In Permo-Triassic times, certain reptilian groups returned to live in water, which led to a period of reptilian dominance of aquatic habitats. One such group produced the pachypleurosaurs, of which the genus *Neusticosaurus* is an example. The aquatic preference of this genus is indicated by its small, lightly built skull, long slender body, short limbs, and the simplification and streamlining of its upper limb bones. However, the hands and feet have not been transformed into paddles.

• **HABITAT** This marine genus fed on small aquatic organisms.

NEUSTICOSAURUS PUSILLUS (Fraas); Bituminous shales; Middle-Late Triassic; Italy.

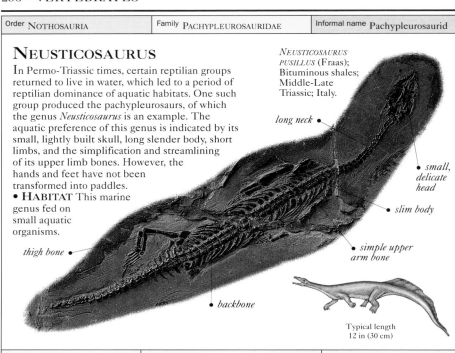

• *long neck*

• *small, delicate head*

• *slim body*

• *simple upper arm bone*

• *thigh bone*

• *backbone*

Typical length
12 in (30 cm)

Range M.–L. Triassic	Distribution Europe	Occurrence

Order PLESIOSAURIA	Family CRYPTOCLIDIDAE	Informal name Plesiosaur

CRYPTOCLIDUS

A medium-size plesiosaur, *Cryptoclidus* had a small, lightly built skull set on a long neck. The teeth were boomerang shaped, faintly ribbed, pointed, and round in cross section. The vertebrae were flat-faced, with two distinct openings (foramina) sited on the undersurface of the centrum. The ribs were single-headed, the girdle elements large and platelike, and the limbs paddle shaped, with the upper arm bone flared away from the attachment point.

• **HABITAT** The plesiosaurs hunted fish in warm seas.

CRYPTOCLIDUS EURYMERUS (Philips); Oxford Clay; Late Jurassic; UK.

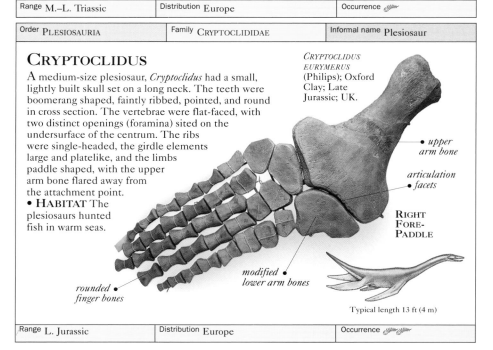

• *upper arm bone*

• *articulation facets*

RIGHT FORE-PADDLE

• *rounded finger bones*

• *modified lower arm bones*

Typical length 13 ft (4 m)

Range L. Jurassic	Distribution Europe	Occurrence

| Order PLESIOSAURIA | Family PLIOSAURIDAE | Informal name Pliosaur |

LIOPLEURODON

Liopleurodon had a large head, a short neck and tail, and long paddle-shaped limbs. The vertebral centra of the neck are compressed front to back and are flat faced, with facets that act as rib articulations. The teeth, which rise from sockets, are long and bow shaped, with some longitudinal ribbing. Large animals had heads measuring some 10 ft (3 m) in length, and held 12 in- (30 cm-) long teeth.
• **HABITAT** Pliosaurs ate fish and squidlike organisms (belemnites), which abounded during the Late Jurassic.

Typical length 33 ft (10 m)

VERTEBRAL CENTRUM

LIOPLEURODON FEROX Andrews; Oxford Clay; Late Jurassic; UK.

• *flat-faced centrum*

base with two foramina

rib articulation

NECK RIB

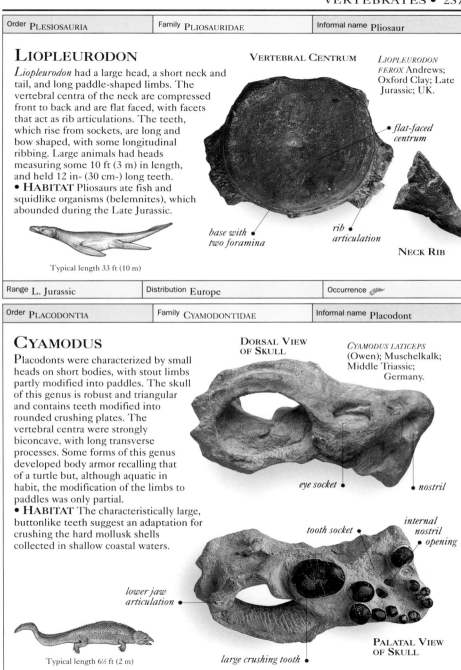

| Range L. Jurassic | Distribution Europe | Occurrence |

| Order PLACODONTIA | Family CYAMODONTIDAE | Informal name Placodont |

CYAMODUS

Placodonts were characterized by small heads on short bodies, with stout limbs partly modified into paddles. The skull of this genus is robust and triangular and contains teeth modified into rounded crushing plates. The vertebral centra were strongly biconcave, with long transverse processes. Some forms of this genus developed body armor recalling that of a turtle but, although aquatic in habit, the modification of the limbs to paddles was only partial.
• **HABITAT** The characteristically large, buttonlike teeth suggest an adaptation for crushing the hard mollusk shells collected in shallow coastal waters.

DORSAL VIEW OF SKULL

CYAMODUS LATICEPS (Owen); Muschelkalk; Middle Triassic; Germany.

eye socket

nostril

tooth socket

internal nostril opening

lower jaw articulation

Typical length 6½ ft (2 m)

large crushing tooth

PALATAL VIEW OF SKULL

| Range M. Triassic | Distribution Europe | Occurrence |

Order ICHTHYOPTERYGIA	Family MIXOSAURIDAE	Informal name Ichthyosaur

MIXOSAURUS

The body of *Mixosaurus* is streamlined and dolphinlike, with a tail
that kinks downward. The long-
snouted skull is filled with teeth
set in sockets, while the limbs
are paddle shaped, with disclike finger elements.
• HABITAT Ichthyosaurs
were adapted to a
marine existence, and
even gave birth to
live young at sea.
They were fast-
swimming
fish-eating
carnivores.

• *tail*

• *paddlelike forelimb*

MIXOSAURUS sp.;
Bituminous Shales;
Middle Triassic;
Switzerland.

• *nostril*

• *long, multi-
toothed snout*

• *round cranium
with large eye*

Typical length 39 in (1 m)

Range M. Triassic	Distribution Europe, E. Indies, USA, Asia	Occurrence

Order ICHTHYOPTERYGIA	Family ICHTHYOSAURIDAE	Informal name Ichthyosaur

ICHTHYOSAURUS

Typical ichthyosaur features are numerous teeth set in a
groove withih the long jaws, each eye held in a ring of
bony plates, the reduction of the pelvic girdle components
and associated paddle, a tail kinked downward to support
a lower tail lobe, and subdivided finger rows.
• HABITAT The ring of strengthening bones around an
ichthyosaur's eye indicates that it was capable of diving to
considerable depths in pursuit of fish.

ICHTHYOSAURUS COMMUNIS
Conybeare; Lower Lias;
Early Jurassic; UK.

SKULL

jaws •

• *teeth*

Typical length 6½ ft (2 m)

• *nostril*

• *ring of
bony plates*

Range E. Jurassic	Distribution Europe, Greenland	Occurrence

Order ICHTHYOPTERYGIA	Family LEPTOPTERYGIIDAE	Informal name Ichthyosaur

PLATYPTERYGIUS

Platypterygius had a heavy-beaked, multi-toothed head, and paddlelike forelimbs with eight to nine digital rows. As in all ichthyosaurs, the vertebral centra are short and biconcave, with no fusion of the neural arch, which has no transverse processes. The double-headed rib articulates via two indistinct bosses on the centrum.
• **HABITAT** *Platypterygius* was a marine reptile, living on fish.

PLATYPTERYGIUS AUSTRALIS (McCoy); Toolebuc Limestone; Early Cretaceous; Australia.

neural arch
• attachment

concave • vertebral centrum

Typical length 16½ ft (5 m)

bosses • for rib

FOUR VERTEBRAE

Range Cretaceous	Distribution Worldwide	Occurrence

Order RHYNCHOSAURIA	Family RHYNCHOSAURIDAE	Informal name Rhynchosaurid

HYPERODAPEDON

This rhynchosaur had a broad skull, in which the front of the upper and lower jaws had developed into curved tooth-like, bony processes. The cheek teeth are set in sockets in multiple longitudinal rows.
• **HABITAT** Rhynchosaurs were four-footed pig-sized vegetarians, living in arid regions.
• **REMARK** These lizardlike reptiles were thought to be related to the living tuatara of New Zealand, but the resemblance is only superficial and they are now placed in a separate order. Their remains are commonly found in Late Triassic rocks.

• *nostril*   • *eye socket*   LATERAL VIEW OF SKULL

bony • *projections*

• *lower jaw*

• *upper jaw*

• *lower jaw*

rows of teeth •

BASAL VIEW OF SKULL

HYPERODAPEDON GORDONI Huxley; Elgin Sandstone; Late Triassic; UK.

Typical length 6½ ft (2 m)

Range L. Triassic	Distribution Europe, Asia	Occurrence

Order THECODONTIA	Family ORNITHOSUCHIDAE	Informal name Ornithosuchid

RIOJASUCHUS

The head of *Riojasuchus* is large, but lightly built, with the upper jaw curved down over the lower. There is a skull opening just before the eye socket, and the teeth are large, bladelike, compressed sideways, and recurved. The hip joint is only partly open and the head of the thigh bone only slightly turned in. There are three pairs of sacral ribs.
• **HABITAT** All ornithosuchids were land-dwellers, mainly four-footed, and living on a flesh diet.
• **REMARK** This order is a member of the great archosaur assemblage, which includes dinosaurs, pterosaurs, and crocodiles.

RIOJASUCHUS TENUISCEPS
Bonaparte; Los Colorados Formation; Late Triassic; Argentina.

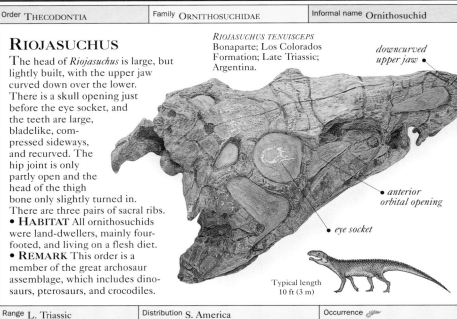

downcurved upper jaw •

• *anterior orbital opening*

• *eye socket*

Typical length
10 ft (3 m)

Range L. Triassic	Distribution S. America	Occurrence

Order THECODONTIA	Family PHYTOSAURIDAE	Informal name Phytosaurid

BELODON

Outwardly, the body of this phytosaur resembled that of our modern long-snouted crocodiles, having short legs, an ornate sculptured surface to the skull, and considerable body armor. In detail, however, the ankle joint and the platelike elements of the hindlimb girdle indicate a more primitive condition, and thus a more awkward gait. With the nostrils situated on top of the head just forward of the eye sockets, rather than at the tip of the snout as in crocodiles, *Belodon* is instantly indentifiable. These nostril

BELODON PLIENINGERI
Meyer; Keuper Sandstone; Late Triassic; Germany.

nostril • *openings*

• *eye socket*

• *long, hooked snout*

tooth row •

jaw articulation •

openings are also elevated above the other skull bones, so that they could protrude above the water when the remainder of the body was submerged.
• **HABITAT** The long snout suggests a fish-eater, but preserved stomach contents show that *Belodon* fed on a variety of reptiles.

Typical length 10 ft (3 m)

Range L. Triassic	Distribution Europe	Occurrence

Order CROCODYLIA	Family METRIORHYNCHIDAE	Informal name Marine crocodile

METRIORHYNCHUS

The metriorhynchid family is the most specialized of all known crocodiles and is perhaps the only archosaur group to become fully aquatic. Changes in its original habit are clearly reflected in its skeleton, for the forelimbs were transformed into paddles, the neck was shortened, the tail was bent downward at the end to support a large caudal fin, and the body armor lost. In contrast to their more terrestrial crocodilian cousins, the skull is long and lightly built – this was another requirement for a fully aquatic mode of life.

• **HABITAT** Species of *Metriorhynchus* were particularly common in the Jurassic seas of Europe, where they hunted for fish and squidlike animals which shared the same habitat. It may be that they only came to land to lay their eggs, in the manner of modern turtles. It is also possible that they hauled themselves onto sand banks to bask after hunting for fish.

• **REMARK** The metriorhynchids belong to the primitive mesosuchian suborder of crocodiles, which appeared in the Triassic but finally became extinct in the earliest part of the Tertiary, some 60 million years ago.

nostril

long snout

METRIORHYNCHUS LAEVE Andrews; Oxford Clay; Late Jurassic; UK.

neural spine

articulation

eye sockets

flat-faced articulation

VERTEBRA

plain bone surface

large temporal opening

jaw articulation

SKULL

Typical length 10 ft (3 m)

Range M.–L. Jurassic	Distribution Europe, S. America	Occurrence

| Order CROCODYLIA | Family GONIOPHOLIDIDAE | Informal name Crocodile |

GONIOPHOLIS

Goniopholids had strongly built low-profiled skulls with ornamented bone surfaces and patterned body armor, thus differing from the metriorhynchids. Like their marine cousins, however, they had nearly flat-faced centra to their vertebrae, which contrasts with the socket-and-ball development found in the more modern forms.
• **HABITAT** Like most unspecialized crocodiles, *Goniopholis* lived a semi-aquatic existence, feeding on a mixture of animal and plant matter.

DORSAL ARMOR

GONIOPHOLIS CRASSIDENS Owen; Wealden Beds; Early Cretaceous; UK.

• *rib fragment*

• *matrix*

• *highly ornate bony scute*

Typical length 10 ft (3 m)

| Range L. Jurassic–L. Cretaceous | Distribution Europe, Asia, N. America | Occurrence |

| Order CROCODYLIA | Family GAVIALIDAE | Informal name Crocodile |

RHAMPHOSUCHUS

Modern crocodiles are divided into three families: alligators, crocodiles, and gavials. *Rhamphosuchus* is a member of the gavial family. The Gavialidae are regarded as specialized fish-eaters, catching their prey with the aid of long, sharply pointed teeth situated in long, slender jaws. In *Rhamphosuchus*, however, the teeth are robust and conical, suggestive of a mixed diet .
• **HABITAT** This giant was an inhabitant of the larger rivers and lakes of Central Asia.

RHAMPHOSUCHUS CRASSIDENS Falconer & Cautley; Siwalik Series; Pliocene; Pakistan.

• *elongate snout*

• *nostrils*

• *conical teeth*

Typical length 50 ft (15 m)

| Range Pliocene | Distribution Asia | Occurrence |

Order CROCODYLIA	Family ALLIGATORIDAE	Informal name Alligator

DIPLOCYNODON

Alligators like the medium-size *Diplocynodon* can be distinguished from true crocodiles by the absence of a pit to house the fourth tooth of the lower jaw. In other respects, the skull anatomy of the modern families is basically similar, having a strongly buttressed skull with a highly ornate bony surface, a jaw articulation set well back to facilitate the wide opening of the mouth, and a variety of rounded to sharply pointed teeth placed in deep sockets in the jaws. The remainder of the crocodilian skeleton is even more conservative, for its basic plan has been unchanged since the Triassic.
• **HABITAT** Unlike Recent species, *Diplocynodon* had a distribution that encompassed both North America and Europe. Although alligators are now restricted to America, this genus was particularly common in the swamps of Europe in Oligocene times. It had a mixed diet of animal and plant matter.
• **REMARK** The crocodiles survived the great extinction at the end of the Mesozoic, becoming even more numerous and widespread during the warmer periods of the Tertiary. But their more primitive mesosuchian cousins became extinct at the start of this era.

DIPLOCYNODON HANTONIENSIS Wood; Lower Headon Beds; Late Eocene; UK.

NECK VERTEBRA

rear ball articulation

neck rib

eye socket

SKULL

broad snout

nostril

Typical length
10 ft (3 m)

Range Eocene–Pliocene	Distribution Europe, N. America	Occurrence

Order PTEROSAURIA	Family PTERODACTYLIDAE	Informal name Pterosaur

PTERODACTYLUS

Pterodactylus is thought to have been a small-toothed insectivore, belonging to an order of archosaurs characterized by delicate skulls with lightly built skeletons, paper-thin hollow bones, greatly extended fouth fingers supporting a wing membrane, and short legs. All family members had short tails and long skulls.

• **HABITAT** The pterosaurs were the only reptiles to develop powered flight, chasing and catching their prey on the wing, in a manner similar to that of certain birds.

PTERODACTYLUS KOCHI Wagner; Solnhofen Limestone; Late Jurassic; Germany.

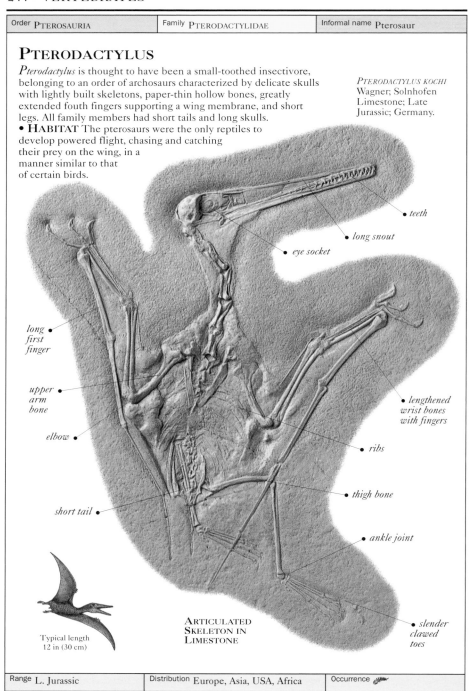

teeth

long snout

eye socket

long first finger

upper arm bone

elbow

lengthened wrist bones with fingers

ribs

thigh bone

short tail

ankle joint

Typical length 12 in (30 cm)

ARTICULATED SKELETON IN LIMESTONE

slender clawed toes

Range L. Jurassic	Distribution Europe, Asia, USA, Africa	Occurrence

DINOSAURS

T HIS SUCCESSFUL DIAPSID group, made up mainly of land-dwelling reptiles, first appeared about 225 million years ago, having evolved from the closely related thecodontian archosaurs. They are divided into two orders: the reptile-hipped Saurischia, in which the pubic bone faces forward; and the bird-hipped Ornithischia, in which it faces backward. Included in the Saurischia are the great four-footed herbivores and the two-footed flesh-eaters, while the Ornithischia contains the remaining plant-eaters. The rise to dominance of the dinosaurs has been attributed to modifications of the limbs and girdle bones, which so improved their stance and gait that they were able to adapt to new habitats. Their largely un-explained extinction at the end of the Mesozoic Era, along with most of the great aquatic reptiles, brought to an end 150 million years of domination.

Order SAURISCHIA	Family COMPSOGNATHIDAE	Informal name Compsognathid

COMPSOGNATHUS

This small, chicken-size dinosaur had recurved serrated teeth set in a lightly built skull. The limbs are long, slender, and hollow, and the pubic bone faces forward.

• **HABITAT** This highly mobile, bipedal carnivore preyed upon insects and small, lizard-like creatures, which it stalked and snatched from the ground.

• **REMARK** Its hunting habit, therefore, could have been in direct com-petition with those suggested for the similar-size bird *Archaeopteryx*.

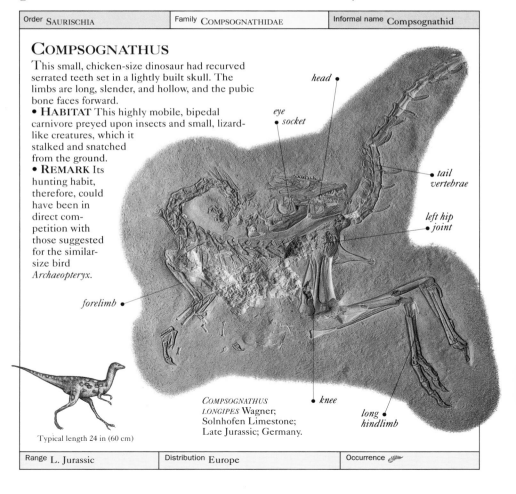

head •

eye
• socket

• tail
vertebrae

left hip
• joint

forelimb •

*COMPSOGNATHUS
LONGIPES* Wagner;
Solnhofen Limestone;
Late Jurassic; Germany.

• knee

long •
hindlimb

Typical length 24 in (60 cm)

Range L. Jurassic	Distribution Europe	Occurrence

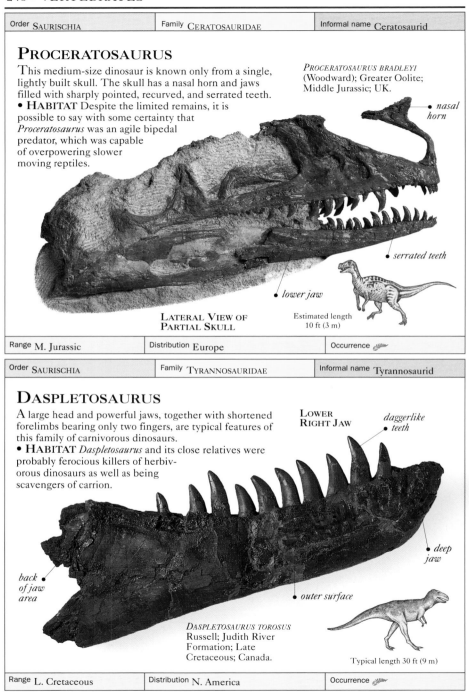

| Order SAURISCHIA | Family CERATOSAURIDAE | Informal name Ceratosaurid |

PROCERATOSAURUS

This medium-size dinosaur is known only from a single, lightly built skull. The skull has a nasal horn and jaws filled with sharply pointed, recurved, and serrated teeth.
• HABITAT Despite the limited remains, it is possible to say with some certainty that *Proceratosaurus* was an agile bipedal predator, which was capable of overpowering slower moving reptiles.

PROCERATOSAURUS BRADLEYI (Woodward); Greater Oolite; Middle Jurassic; UK.

nasal horn

serrated teeth

lower jaw

LATERAL VIEW OF PARTIAL SKULL

Estimated length 10 ft (3 m)

| Range M. Jurassic | Distribution Europe | Occurrence |

| Order SAURISCHIA | Family TYRANNOSAURIDAE | Informal name Tyrannosaurid |

DASPLETOSAURUS

A large head and powerful jaws, together with shortened forelimbs bearing only two fingers, are typical features of this family of carnivorous dinosaurs.
• HABITAT *Daspletosaurus* and its close relatives were probably ferocious killers of herbivorous dinosaurs as well as being scavengers of carrion.

LOWER RIGHT JAW

daggerlike teeth

back of jaw area

deep jaw

outer surface

DASPLETOSAURUS TOROSUS Russell; Judith River Formation; Late Cretaceous; Canada.

Typical length 30 ft (9 m)

| Range L. Cretaceous | Distribution N. America | Occurrence |

Order SAURISCHIA	Family ORNITHOMIMIDAE	Informal name Ostrich dinosaur

GALLIMIMUS

The ostrich dinosaurs were long-limbed, lightly built, small-headed reptiles, with a tendency to become toothless. In *Gallimimus*, the toothless jaws were covered by a horny beak.
• HABITAT Although presumed to be a carnivore, it has been suggested that *Gallimimus* also raided the nests of other reptiles for their eggs.

large eye
• *socket*

jaw
• *articulation*

• *toothless beak*

GALLIMIMUS BULLATUS
Roniewicz & Barsbold;
Upper Nemegt Beds; Late
Cretaceous; Mongolia.

Typical length
13 ft (4 m)

• *nostril*

Range L. Cretaceous	Distribution Asia	Occurrence

Order SAURISCHIA	Family CETIOSAURIDAE	Informal name Sauropod

CETIOSAURUS

The small head, long neck and tail, and solid limb bones of this giant show it to be a member of the reptile-footed dinosaurs. Its banjolike vertebrae are characteristic.
• HABITAT *Cetiosaurus* was a plant-eater, but it is not certain whether it inhabited the margins of lakes and rivers or was a plains wanderer. The latter suggestion is the most favored at present.

VERTEBRA

• *neural spine*

• *articulation*
process

• *neural canal*

flat-faced •
centrum

CETIOSAURUS LEEDSI
Hulke; Oxford Clay;
Middle Jurassic; UK.

• *transverse*
process

Typical length
65 ft (20 m)

Range M.–L. Jurassic	Distribution Europe	Occurrence

| Order SAURISCHIA | Family DIPLODOCIDAE | Informal name Sauropod |

DIPLODOCUS

This large herbivorous quadruped had a long
neck and tail and a small, elongate head. The
rakelike teeth, situated toward the front of the
jaws, together with the short front legs and the
beamlike chevron bones under the tail
vertebrae, are characteristic.
• **HABITAT** *Diplodocus* probably
lived close to areas of freshwater,
using its specially adapted teeth to
gather in surrounding vegetation.
• **REMARK** An adult probably
weighed up to twice as much as a
bull African Elephant.

TAIL
VERTEBRA

DIPLODOCUS LONGUS Marsh;
Morrison Formation; Late
Jurassic; USA.

*bone cavity
reduced weight of tail*

Typical length 88½ ft (27 m)

| Range L. Jurassic | Distribution N. America | Occurrence |

| Order SAURISCHIA | Family DIPLODOCIDAE | Informal name Sauropod |

JOBARIA

The basic body shape of *Jobaria* resembled
that of other sauropods, but the neck and
tail were somewhat shorter. The skull was
characteristically flat-faced with a round
profile, and the leaf-shaped teeth extended
along the length of the jaws.
• **HABITAT** Like others of its type, this
genus was a plant-eating quadruped
that lived close to well-watered areas.
The large teeth were well adapted for
shearing vegetation.

*cutting
edge*

LEAF-SHAPED
TOOTH

*JOBARIA
TIQUIDENSIS* Sereno
et al Tiourarén
Formation; Early
Creta-ceous; Niger.

root

tooth

FRAGMENT OF
LOWER JAW
WITH TEETH

Typical length
65 ft (20 m)

| Range E. Cretaceous | Distribution Africa | Occurrence |

Order SAURISCHIA	Family TITANOSAURIDAE	Informal name Sauropod

TITANOSAURUS

The titanosaurs were the last of the reptile-footed plant-eaters, but their remains are usually fragmentary. However, they appear to have followed the type in having small heads, long tails, and elephantine limbs, although the neck was shorter. Their most important distinguishing feature is the ball-and-socket articulation of the vertebrae at the beginning of the tail. Being long-faced, the most complete skull is said to resemble that of *Diplodocus*. At least one species developed bony scutes as armor.
• **HABITAT** Like others of its type, it may not have wandered far from water.

TAIL VERTEBRA

ball articulation •

Typical length
40 ft (12 m)

TITANOSAURUS AUSTRALIS Lydekker; Late Cretaceous; Argentina.

• *socket articulation*

Range Cretaceous	Distribution Europe, Africa, Asia, S. America	Occurrence

Order ORNITHISCHIA	Family HETERODONTOSAURIDAE	Informal name Heterodontosaurid

HETERODONTOSAURUS

The lower jaws of this early bipedal genus were toothless in front – a feature common to the order. However, it is unusual in that two pairs of fang-like teeth accompany the single-rowed shearing dentition of the cheek region. The presence of teeth at the front of the upper jaw is regarded as primitive.
• **HABITAT** This land-living plant-eater may also have grubbed out roots.

HETERODONTOSAURUS TUCKII Crompton & Charig; Cave sandstone; Early Jurassic; South Africa.

eye socket • *bar*

SKULL

shearing teeth •

fanglike • *canine*

Typical length
39 in (1 m)

Range E. Jurassic	Distribution S. Africa	Occurrence

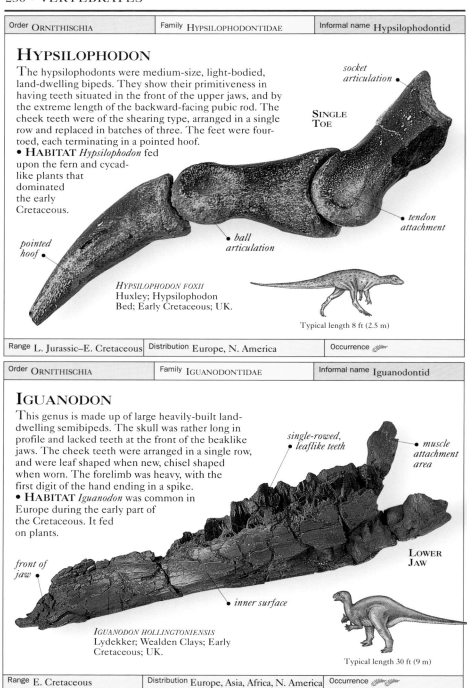

| Order ORNITHISCHIA | Family HYPSILOPHODONTIDAE | Informal name Hypsilophodontid |

HYPSILOPHODON

The hypsilophodonts were medium-size, light-bodied, land-dwelling bipeds. They show their primitiveness in having teeth situated in the front of the upper jaws, and by the extreme length of the backward-facing pubic rod. The cheek teeth were of the shearing type, arranged in a single row and replaced in batches of three. The feet were four-toed, each terminating in a pointed hoof.
• **HABITAT** *Hypsilophodon* fed upon the fern and cycad-like plants that dominated the early Cretaceous.

socket articulation

SINGLE TOE

tendon attachment

pointed hoof

ball articulation

HYPSILOPHODON FOXII
Huxley; Hypsilophodon Bed; Early Cretaceous; UK.

Typical length 8 ft (2.5 m)

| Range L. Jurassic–E. Cretaceous | Distribution Europe, N. America | Occurrence |

| Order ORNITHISCHIA | Family IGUANODONTIDAE | Informal name Iguanodontid |

IGUANODON

This genus is made up of large heavily-built land-dwelling semibipeds. The skull was rather long in profile and lacked teeth at the front of the beaklike jaws. The cheek teeth were arranged in a single row, and were leaf shaped when new, chisel shaped when worn. The forelimb was heavy, with the first digit of the hand ending in a spike.
• **HABITAT** *Iguanodon* was common in Europe during the early part of the Cretaceous. It fed on plants.

single-rowed, leaflike teeth

muscle attachment area

LOWER JAW

front of jaw

inner surface

IGUANODON HOLLINGTONIENSIS
Lydekker; Wealden Clays; Early Cretaceous; UK.

Typical length 30 ft (9 m)

| Range E. Cretaceous | Distribution Europe, Asia, Africa, N. America | Occurrence |

| Order ORNITHISCHIA | Family HADROSAURIDAE | Informal name Duck-billed dinosaur |

EDMONTOSAURUS

The body form of this duck-billed dinosaur was similar to that of the iguanodontids, being large and heavily built. However, the skull was much flatter in profile, and the diamond-shaped teeth were arranged in batteries, with as many as 700 visible at any one time. The tail, too, was more laterally flattened but retained the bony tendon support.
• **HABITAT** This plant-eater may also have been partly aquatic.

EDMONTOSAURUS ANNECTENS (Marsh); Lance Formation; Late Cretaceous; USA.

• *battery of teeth*

LOWER RIGHT JAW

• *front of jaw*

Typical length
42½ ft (13 m)

| Range L. Cretaceous | Distribution N. America | Occurrence |

| Order ORNITHISCHIA | Family HADROSAURIDAE | Informal name Duck-billed dinosaur |

PARASAUROLOPHUS

This large, semibipedal, crested duckbill is identified by the bizarre extension of the nasal bones over the skull, which forms a tubular crest over 59 in (1½ m) long.
• **HABITAT** *Parasaurolophus*, like all hadrosaurs, was a grazing herbivore.
• **REMARK** The hadrosaurian crest may have been used for visible identification between species, while the crest's tubular construction could have been used as a resonator to make warning calls to other grazing herbivores.

SKULL AND LOWER JAWS

tubular • *crest*

PARASAUROLOPHUS WALKERI Parks; Judith River Formation; Late Cretaceous; Canada.

• *eye socket*

jaw • *articulation*

• *cutting edge of teeth*

• *nostril*

Typical length
33 ft (10 m)

| Range L. Cretaceous | Distribution N. America | Occurrence |

Order ORNITHISCHIA	Family STEGOSAURIDAE	Informal name Plated dinosaur

STEGOSAURUS

This heavy-bodied quadrupedal genus can be recognized by its very small and low-profiled skull and by the double row of alternating, upward-pointing, angular plates and four tail spikes that adorned the body. The combination of blunt leaflike teeth and particularly short front legs (about half the size of the rear) also assists in identification.
• HABITAT *Stegosaurus* was a plant-eater, using its tail spikes only for defense.
• REMARK The orientation and alternating pattern of the angular back plates would have made them ideal for regulating the animal's temperature, by radiating heat from its massive body.

ANGULAR, BONY PLATE

STEGOSAURUS sp.; Kimmeridge Clay; Late Jurassic; UK.

Typical length
30 ft (9 m)

articulation facet

Range L. Jurassic	Distribution N. America, Europe	Occurrence

Order ORNITHISCHIA	Family PACHYCEPHALOSAURIDAE	Informal name Bone-headed dinosaur

STEGOCERAS

The thickened skull roof, fashioned into a solid bony dome and partly surrounded by a lumpy frill, distinguishes the bone-headed dinosaurs from the other bipedal ornithopods. Further characteristics include the presence of teeth in the front of the upper jaw, a single row of leaf-shaped cheek teeth, and an excessively shortened pubic rod, which lacks a connecting process to the ischium (pelvic bone).
• HABITAT All members of the family were herbivores, living in open country.

THICKENED SKULL ROOF

bony frill

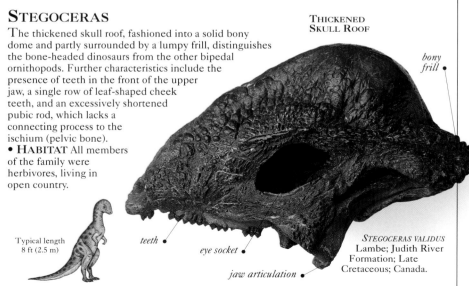

Typical length
8 ft (2.5 m)

teeth

eye socket

jaw articulation

STEGOCERAS VALIDUS
Lambe; Judith River Formation; Late Cretaceous; Canada.

Range L. Cretaceous	Distribution N. America	Occurrence

Order ORNITHISCHIA	Family ANKYLOSAURIDAE	Informal name Armoured dinosaur

EUOPLOCEPHALUS

This tanklike quadruped can be identified by its skull, protected by a series of scutes fused to its surface, and by its body, covered by a mosaic of flat and keel-shaped, interlocking, bony plates which narrow to a tail terminating in a huge club.
• **HABITAT** This genus probably lived in arid areas.

END OF TAIL

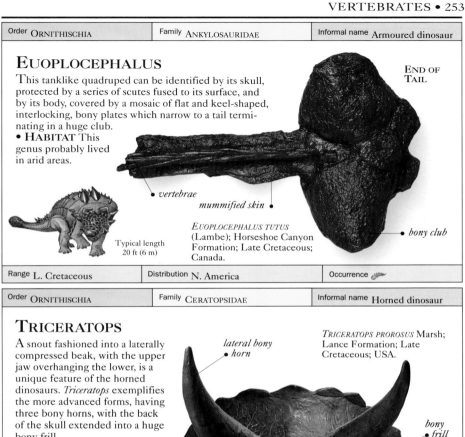

• *vertebrae*

mummified skin •

EUOPLOCEPHALUS TUTUS (Lambe); Horseshoe Canyon Formation; Late Cretaceous; Canada.

Typical length 20 ft (6 m)

• *bony club*

Range L. Cretaceous	Distribution N. America	Occurrence

Order ORNITHISCHIA	Family CERATOPSIDAE	Informal name Horned dinosaur

TRICERATOPS

A snout fashioned into a laterally compressed beak, with the upper jaw overhanging the lower, is a unique feature of the horned dinosaurs. *Triceratops* exemplifies the more advanced forms, having three bony horns, with the back of the skull extended into a huge bony frill.
• **HABITAT** This was a large, quadrupedal herbivore that used its powerful beak to slice through the tougher stems of plants. It may have lived in more open habitats, forming small herds in a fashion similar to that of many present-day plains mammals.

TRICERATOPS PROROSUS Marsh; Lance Formation; Late Cretaceous; USA.

lateral bony • *horn*

bony • *frill*

eye socket •

• *nostril*

SKULL

• *single tooth row*

toothless beak •

• *lower jaw*

Typical length 30 ft (9 m)

Range L. Cretaceous	Distribution N. America	Occurrence

Order ORNITHISCHIA	Family PROTOCERATOPSIDAE	Informal name Horned dinosaur

PROTOCERATOPS

This small, stocky quadruped is characterized by a horny beak, a small nose horn, leaflike cheek teeth set in a single line, and a much reduced neck frill containing large perforations.

• HABITAT *Protoceratops* probably lived in open areas, where it fed on plant stems which it cut off with its powerful beak. The stems were then sheared into smaller pieces by the cheek teeth.

• REMARK During the1920s, an American expedition to Mongolia discovered numerous *Protoceratops* nests and eggs, some containing partly developed young. This provided paleontologists with their first insight into the social behavior of the dinosaurs. It was evident that the eggs had been deliberately arranged in neat concentric rings, before being buried by the adults. Numerous adult bones were also encountered, suggesting that they nested in loose colonies, standing guard over their nesting sites.

ELONGATE EGG

textured eggshell

PROTOCERATOPS ANDREWSI Granger & Gregory; Djadochta Beds; Late Cretaceous; Mongolia.

SKULL

frill

skull roof

eye socket

upper jaw

Typical length 6 ft (1.8 m)

Range L. Cretaceous	Distribution Asia	Occurrence

SYNAPSID REPTILES

T HE SUBCLASS SYNAPSIDA, more popularly referred to as the mammal-like reptiles, is the third major division of the class Reptilia. It is characterized by the possession of a single opening in the skull roof, together with a unique configuration of the associated bones behind the eye socket. The first synapsids appeared during the Carboniferous, 300 million years ago. Although early examples were small and lizardlike, they were highly successful and developed numerous varieties. By the Permian they were the dominant land forms but were then unable to compete with the newly evolved and more agile thecodonts, crocodiles, and dinosaurs in the late Triassic. They became extinct at the beginning of the Jurassic, but not before they had given rise to the line that produced mammals.

Order PELYCOSAURIA	Family SPHENACODONTIDAE	Informal name Sail-backed lizard

DIMETRODON

The most spectacular feature of this genus was the huge dorsal sail, the result of the extreme elongation of the vertebral neural spines, which characteristically remain smooth along their length. The skull is deep, has daggerlike teeth, with the lower jaw articulation situated well below, and behind, the tooth row. In comparison with other sail-backs, the quadrupedal *Dimetrodon* had lightly built limbs.
• **HABITAT** This relatively fast-moving carnivorous reptile preyed on less agile species in arid environments.
• **REMARK** It was this group of pelycosaurs that acquired the adaptations that eventually developed fully in mammals.

DIMETRODON LOOMISI
Romer; Arroyo Formation; Early Permian; USA.

• *eye socket*

• *nostril*

• *daggerlike teeth*

jaw articulation •

Typical length 10 ft (3 m)

Range E. Permian	Distribution N. America	Occurrence

Order PELYCOSAURIA	Family EDAPHOSAURIDAE	Informal name Sail-backed lizard

EDAPHOSAURUS

The overall body shape of this short-limbed slow-moving quadruped was similar to that of a giant lizard, but the neural spines of the backbone extended upward to form a skin-covered sail. Individual spines have characteristic short transverse processes along their length. The short broad skull contained both marginal and palatal teeth. The vertebral centra were strongly biconcave, a typical synapsid feature.
• **HABITAT** This plant-eater lived in arid areas.
• **REMARK** The spectacular sail was probably a temperature-control mechanism.

VERTEBRA

• *extended neural spine*

process of spine •

EDAPHOSAURUS sp.; Wichita Formation; Early Permian; USA.

fragment of palate, with teeth •

Typical length
10 ft (3 m)

Range L. Carb.–E. Permian	Distribution Europe, N. America	Occurrence

Order THERAPSIDA	Family LYSTROSAURIDAE	Informal name Lystrosaur

LYSTROSAURUS

Skulls of lystrosaurs are characterized by their marked facial angles, the high placement of the nostrils, the possession of only two caninelike teeth in the upper jaw, and the massive, but toothless, lower jaw. They were heavy limbed, had short tails, and were quadrupedal in their gait.
• **HABITAT** The high position of the nostrils suggests that *Lystrosaurus* was semiaquatic. This vegetarian sheared plants with its massive jaws.

• *eye socket*

• *nostril*

• *tooth*

SKULL

LYSTROSAURUS MURRAYI (Huxley); Karoo Formation; Early Triassic; South Africa.

Typical length
6½ ft (2 m)

Range E. Triassic	Distribution Worldwide	Occurrence

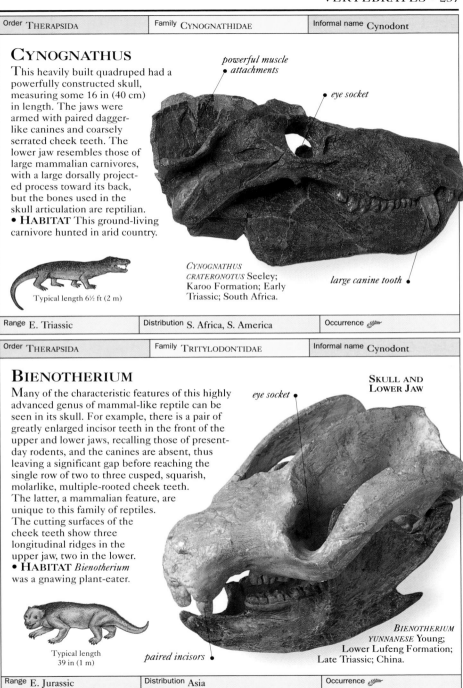

Order THERAPSIDA	Family CYNOGNATHIDAE	Informal name Cynodont

CYNOGNATHUS

This heavily built quadruped had a powerfully constructed skull, measuring some 16 in (40 cm) in length. The jaws were armed with paired dagger-like canines and coarsely serrated cheek teeth. The lower jaw resembles those of large mammalian carnivores, with a large dorsally project-ed process toward its back, but the bones used in the skull articulation are reptilian.
• **HABITAT** This ground-living carnivore hunted in arid country.

powerful muscle attachments

eye socket

large canine tooth

Typical length 6½ ft (2 m)

CYNOGNATHUS CRATERONOTUS Seeley; Karoo Formation; Early Triassic; South Africa.

Range E. Triassic	Distribution S. Africa, S. America	Occurrence

Order THERAPSIDA	Family TRITYLODONTIDAE	Informal name Cynodont

BIENOTHERIUM

Many of the characteristic features of this highly advanced genus of mammal-like reptile can be seen in its skull. For example, there is a pair of greatly enlarged incisor teeth in the front of the upper and lower jaws, recalling those of present-day rodents, and the canines are absent, thus leaving a significant gap before reaching the single row of two to three cusped, squarish, molarlike, multiple-rooted cheek teeth. The latter, a mammalian feature, are unique to this family of reptiles. The cutting surfaces of the cheek teeth show three longitudinal ridges in the upper jaw, two in the lower.
• **HABITAT** *Bienotherium* was a gnawing plant-eater.

SKULL AND LOWER JAW

eye socket

paired incisors

Typical length 39 in (1 m)

BIENOTHERIUM YUNNANESE Young; Lower Lufeng Formation; Late Triassic; China.

Range E. Jurassic	Distribution Asia	Occurrence

BIRDS

T HE CLASS AVES is divided into four subclasses: Archaeornithes, Odontornithes, Enantiornithes, and Neornithes, with only the last surviving beyond the onset of the Cenozoic Era. Most specialists now agree that birds evolved from one of the carnivorous dinosaur families. Exactly when this occurred is unclear, but the first clearly identifiable remains were found in Late Jurassic rocks. Following its appearance, the class seems to have been slow in establishing itself as an important group until the end of the Cretaceous, when many reptile types became extinct and ceased to be the dominant vertebrates. At this juncture, birds of the neorthine type quickly diversified and started the progression toward the 8,600 or so species included in the modern avifauna.

Order ARCHAEOPTERYGIFORMES	Family ARCHAEOPTERYGIDAE	Informal name Archaeopteryx

ARCHAEOPTERYX

The chicken-size *Archaeopteryx* can be readily identified by the great proportion of reptilian features in its skeleton. For example, the lightly built skull possesses true teeth, set in sockets in the jaws; the breastbone is small and lacks a keel; the forelimb skeleton retains three functional fingers and lacks the reductions and fusions present in other birds; the hindlimb girdle, although modified, is distinctly dinosaurian in character; and there is a long bony tail. Other uncharacteristic avian features include almost flat-faced vertebrae, belly ribs, and an incomplete fusion of the lower leg bones. Impressions of feathers, associated with the five known skeletons, confirm that this creature was a bird.
• HABITAT *Archaeopteryx* was certainly capable of flight, but probably chased and seized insects and reptiles on the ground, near the shores of inland seas.

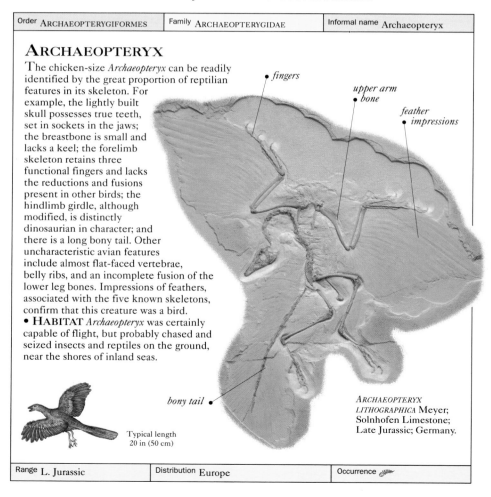

fingers

upper arm bone

feather impressions

bony tail

Typical length
20 in (50 cm)

ARCHAEOPTERYX LITHOGRAPHICA Meyer;
Solnhofen Limestone;
Late Jurassic; Germany.

Range L. Jurassic	Distribution Europe	Occurrence

Order HESPERORNITHIFORMES	Family HESPERORNITHIDAE	Informal name Dawn bird

HESPERORNIS

The dawn birds were specialized, flightless foot-propelled divers. In appearance, their bodies resembled those of modern divers and grebes, but there is no actual relationship. The skeleton possessed a skull with true teeth, a keel-less breast bone, a much reduced forelimb, and some characteristically avian, saddle-shaped vertebral centra. The aquatic modifications of *Hesperornis* included thick-walled and nonpneumatic bone, and laterally flattened lower leg bones.
• **HABITAT** *Hesperornis* was a fish-eating carnivore, living in warm seas.

HESPERORNIS REGALIS
Marsh; Kansas
Chalk; Late
Cretaceous;
USA.

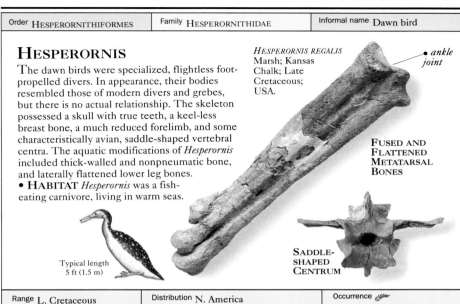

• *ankle joint*

FUSED AND FLATTENED METATARSAL BONES

SADDLE-SHAPED CENTRUM

Typical length
5 ft (1.5 m)

Range L. Cretaceous	Distribution N. America	Occurrence

Order AEPYORNITHIFORMES	Family AEPYORNITHIDAE	Informal name Elephant bird

AEPYORNIS

Aepyornis was the largest genus of this ostrichlike family, popularly known as elephant birds. It grew to an estimated weight of 1,000 lb (450 kg) – by far the heaviest bird ever to have existed. Its weight prevented any form of flight, resulting in the loss of the keel on the breast bone and the reduction of the wings. The legs, however, were relatively short and powerful, with a three-toed foot. The ovoid eggs of these birds, found buried in sand dunes, were huge, the largest examples having a liquid capacity of 2¼ gallons (8.5 liters).
• **HABITAT** Elephant birds are thought to have been browsers, feeding on fruit and leaves.

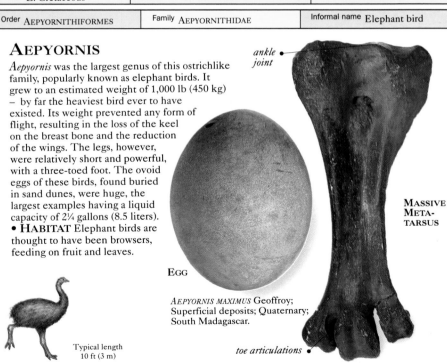

ankle joint

EGG

MASSIVE META-TARSUS

AEPYORNIS MAXIMUS Geoffroy;
Superficial deposits; Quaternary;
South Madagascar.

Typical length
10 ft (3 m)

toe articulations •

Range Pleistocene–Recent	Distribution Madagascar	Occurrence

Order SPHENISCIFORMES	Family SPHENISCIDAE	Informal name Penguin

PACHYDYPTES

This very large genus of penguin was similar in
structure to modern forms, its wings having
developed into flippers for swimming. The
modifications to the forelimb included a marked
flattening of the individual elements, the pronounced development of the head end of the
upper arm bone, and considerable thickening
of the bone walls. Except for the excessively
short and broad tarsus, the remainder of the
skeleton was similar to those of other
aquatic wing-propelled divers.
• HABITAT All penguins are marine
and feed on fish caught underwater.

• *enlarged head*

• *flattened shaft*

UPPER ARM BONE

*PACHYDYPTES
PONDEROSUS* Oliver;
Runangan; Late
Eocene; New
Zealand.

elbow joint •

• *compressed articulation*

Typical length
4½ ft (1.3 m)

Range L. Eocene–E. Oligocene	Distribution New Zealand	Occurrence

Order PROCELLARIIFORMES	Family PROCELLARIIDAE	Informal name Cory's Shearwater

CALONECTRIS

This large genus is distinguished from other
similar-size shearwaters by its relatively short-
hooked bill, more rounded
wing bones, less forwardly
projecting keel to the
breast bone, and pro-
portionally longer tarsus.
• HABITAT As Cory's
Shearwater favors warmer
waters, its breeding range
now extends no farther
north than the Medi-
terranean Sea and the
Atlantic seaboard of
Portugal. However,
100,000 years ago it is
known to have inhabited
certain sea caves of south
Wales, where remains of
nestlings and adults have
been found.

**ASSOCIATED
SKELETON**

CALONECTRIS DIOMEDEA
(Scopoli); Cave deposits;
Pleistocene; Gibraltar.

upper arm bone •

skull •

Typical length
16 in (40 cm)

Range Pleistocene–Recent	Distribution Mediterranean, Atlantic Ocean	Occurrence

Order PELECANIFORMES	Family ODONTOPTERYGIDAE	Informal name Bony-toothed bird

ODONTOPTERYX

The bony-toothed birds were long-winged seabirds, with unique toothlike projections along the cutting edge of the jaws. In the diminutive *Odontopteryx*, these projections have a distinct forward slant, and are set in a 6 in- (15 cm-) long skull, similar in form and size to that of the living gannet. The larger species are thought to have had a wingspan of about 16½ ft (5 m).
• **HABITAT** *Odontopteryx* was certainly a fish-eater, perhaps snatching its prey from the sea as it glided over the surface.
• **REMARK** *Odontopteryx* is sometimes classified with pelicans and cormorants.

*ODONTOPTERYX
TOLIAPICA* Owen;
London Clay; Early
Eocene; UK.

SKULL

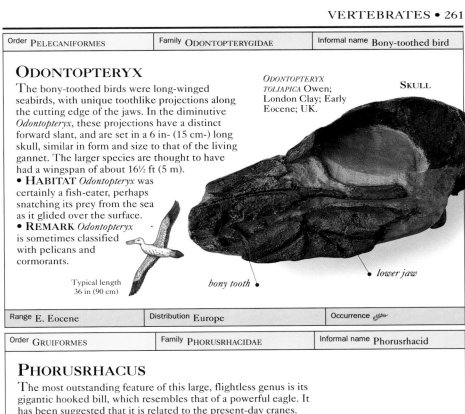

• *lower jaw*

bony tooth •

Typical length
36 in (90 cm)

Range E. Eocene	Distribution Europe	Occurrence

Order GRUIFORMES	Family PHORUSRHACIDAE	Informal name Phorusrhacid

PHORUSRHACUS

The most outstanding feature of this large, flightless genus is its gigantic hooked bill, which resembles that of a powerful eagle. It has been suggested that it is related to the present-day cranes.
• **HABITAT** It probably hunted over open plains country.
• **REMARK** The family first appeared during the Oligocene in South America, where it evolved and became the dominant carnivore. Its superiority lasted until about four million years ago, when it became extinct before the end of the Pliocene.

*PHORUSRHACUS
INFLATUS* Ameghino;
Santa Cruz Formation;
Miocene; Argentina.

Typical length
5 ft (1.5 m)

nostril •

SKULL

eye socket •

Range Miocene	Distribution S. America	Occurrence

Order APODIFORMES	Family AEGIALORNITHIDAE	Informal name Swift

PRIMAPUS

The upper arm bone of this genus exhibits structures clearly adapted for a specialized aerial mode of life. For example, it is short and stout, the head is highly developed, and the bicipital surface and deltoid crest are well formed. All these characteristics suggest a bird that had considerable powers of flight, and it is with the modern swifts that the closest match occurs.
• **HABITAT** The successful early evolution of the swifts probably resulted from the increase in flowering plants and their insect pollinators. The latter provided an ample source of food for this insect predator.

head of upper
• *arm bone*

• *deltoid crest*

• *bicipital crest*

UPPER ARM BONE

Typical length
6½ in (17 cm)

PRIMAPUS LACKI
Harrison & Walker;
London Clay;
Early Eocene; UK.

• *distal articulation*

Range E. Eocene	Distribution Europe	Occurrence

Order COLUMBIFORMES	Family COLUMBIDAE	Informal name Dodo

RAPHUS

The enormous size of this flightless pigeon makes it easy to identify its fossilized remains. Notable bone features include a 6¾ in- (17 cm-) long head, with a distinct hooked bill; reduced wing elements; a keel-less breast bone; and short legs.
• **HABITAT** *Raphus* was a ground-dweller in wooded areas. It ate mainly fallen fruit and possibly grubs.
• **REMARK** The extinction of the dodo during the 17th century was caused by the predation of humans and the animals they introduced.

RAPHUS CUCULLATUS
(Linnaeus); Superficial deposits; Quaternary; Mauritius.

nostril •

hooked beak •

SKULL AND LOWER JAW

• *eye socket*

Typical length
39 in (1 m)

Range Quaternary	Distribution Mauritius	Occurrence

MAMMALS

MAMMALS ARE A VERY successful group. From terrestrial origins they have colonized most of the habitable areas of the Earth's surface, the oceans, and the air. The main identifying features of mammals, such as the possession of hair, milk-producing mammary glands, and the details of their reproductive system, are rarely preserved as fossils. To the paleontologist, the most vital mammalian identification feature is the jaw articulation between the dentary bone (the only bone in the lower jaw) and the squamosal bone in the skull. The quadrate and articular bones, forming the articulation in other vertebrates, became associated with mammalian hearing and survive today as the incus and malleus of the middle ear.

Order MULTITUBERCULATA	Family TAENIOLABIDIDAE	Informal name Multituberculate

TAENIOLABIS

The multituberculates are an extinct order of primarily small rodentlike animals characterized by the possession of highly distinctive teeth. One of the lower cheek teeth in each jaw was often enlarged to form a massive grinding tooth. Two-thirds of the mammals found in the Mongolian Cretaceous were multituberculates.
• **HABITAT** This small rodent was a tropical forest-dweller.

enlarged grinding tooth

TAENIOLABIS TAOENSIS (Cope); Early Paleocene; USA.

mandibular bone

LOWER JAW

Typical length 24 in (60 cm)

Range E. Paleocene	Distribution N. America	Occurrence

Order EUPANTOTHERIA	Family DRYOLESTIDAE	Informal name Dryolestid

AMBLOTHERIUM

Amblotherium was a small, primitive, insectivorous mammal, known mainly from isolated jaws. The genus was characterized by having a large number of teeth behind the canines, up to 12 per jaw. The individual teeth are broad and short, resembling those of the modern Madagascan tenrec, although the tenrec is a much more advanced mammal.
• **HABITAT** *Amblotherium* was a land-dweller.

short pointed insectivorous teeth

AMBLOTHERIUM PUSILLUM Owen; Purbeck Beds; Late Jurassic; UK.

Typical length 10 in (25 cm)

ramus of mandible

LOWER JAW

Range L. Jurassic	Distribution Europe, N. America	Occurrence

Order DIDELPHIMORPHIA	Family DIDELPHIDAE	Informal name Opossum

DIDELPHIS

SKULL

Opossums are mouse- to cat-size marsupials with up to 50 teeth, a long snout, and small eyes. The pouch (or marsupium) is variably developed. Opossums have hands and feet well adapted for grasping; there are usually five digits on each foot, with the big toe acting as an opposable digit. While most species are climbers, some are not, and one is aquatic. Many species have prehensile tails.

• **HABITAT** Opossums are arboreal, feeding on a wide variety of animal and vegetable matter.

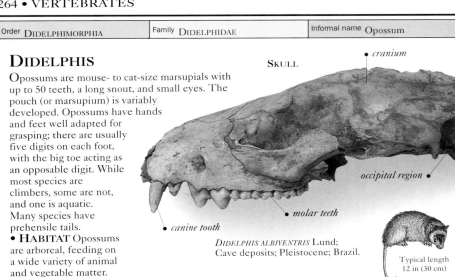

• *cranium*

occipital region •

• *molar teeth*

• *canine tooth*

DIDELPHIS ALBIVENTRIS Lund; Cave deposits; Pleistocene; Brazil.

Typical length 12 in (30 cm)

Range Pleistocene–Recent	Distribution N. & S. America	Occurrence

Order DIPROTODONTIA	Family THYLACOLEONIDAE	Informal name Marsupial lion

THYLACOLEO

sagittal crest •

RIGHT PROFILE OF SKULL

Thylacoleo was one of the more remarkable of the extinct members of the Australian marsupials, and the largest of the indigenous carnivores. Lionlike in many respects, this animal was most closely related to the living phalangers or cuscuses, a group that now consists of small to medium-size, arboreal herbivores. The wide, short-faced skull possesses large paired front incisors, which seem to have fulfilled the functions of true carnivore canines, and massive, long, bladelike, shearing carnassial teeth for cutting up animal tissue. The braincase is small.

THYLACOLEO CARNIFEX (Owen); River deposits; Pleistocene; Australia.

• **HABITAT** This land mammal preyed on a wide variety of animals, many of which are now extinct, including *Diprotodon (opposite)*, which was the largest of the native herbivores.

incomplete • *hard palate*

BASE VIEW OF SKULL

Typical length 6 ft (1.5 m)

carnassial tooth •

• *nasal opening*

Range Pliocene–Pleistocene	Distribution Australia	Occurrence

Order DIPROTODONTIA	Family MACROPODIDAE	Informal name Kangaroo

PROCOPTODON

This large kangaroo, now extinct, had notably heavy jaws and a relatively short face. Living kangaroos have smaller forelimbs than hindlimbs, adapted for a primarily bipedal gait. The hindfoot was elongate and narrow, with unequal development of the digits. The cheek teeth had two dominant transverse shearing ridges with a longitudinal connecting ridge. The paired lower incisors protruded forward. In each jaw, there was only one premolar, a shearing tooth, and this was followed by four molars which erupted over a long period, moving forward in the jaw through the animal's life.
• HABITAT *Procoptodon* was adapted for

PROCOPTODON GOLIAH Owen; River deposits; Pleistocene; Australia.

RIGHT LOWER JAW

empty tooth • sockets

molar teeth •

Typical length 10 ft (3 m)

Range Pleistocene	Distribution Australia	Occurrence

Order DIPROTODONTIA	Family DIPROTODONTIDAE	Informal name Diprotodon

DIPROTODON

Diprotodon, the largest of the extinct giant marsupials, resembled a rhinoceros. It had huge rodentlike incisor teeth and cheek teeth each with two prominent transverse ridges, that wore down to form a shearing surface. The jaws were particularly thick and heavy. Skulls of *Diprotodon* are disproportionately massive, with a high nasal opening, large facial area, and small braincase.
• HABITAT *Diprotodon* was a forest-dweller, probably browsing on low-growing trees and shrubs.

DIPROTODON AUSTRALIS Owen; River deposits; Pleistocene; Australia.

LEFT LOWER JAW

two shearing facets • on each cheek tooth

huge lower • incisor

massive jaw bone •

Typical length 10 ft (3 m)

Range Pleistocene	Distribution Australia	Occurrence

Order INSECTIVORA	Family TALPIDAE	Informal name Russian Desman

DESMANA

Desmana is an aquatic insectivore still found living in parts of the former Soviet Union. The short legs each bear five digits with deeply grooved terminal phalanges. The bones of the forelimb are massive, with large muscle attachments. A short thick clavicle is present, anchoring the limb to a prominent sternum. The dentition is typical of the insectivores, the molar teeth bearing many sharp, pointed cusps for dealing with an insect diet.
• HABITAT *Desmana* was a common member of European lake and stream fauna in the Middle Pleistocene, making nesting chambers in muddy banks. It became extinct in western Europe 250,000 years ago.

large mandibular processes

LOWER JAW

pointed cusps

strong jaw

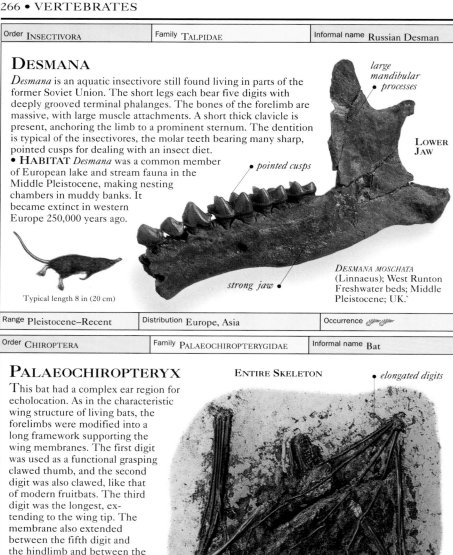

Typical length 8 in (20 cm)

DESMANA MOSCHATA
(Linnaeus); West Runton
Freshwater beds; Middle
Pleistocene; UK.`

Range Pleistocene–Recent	Distribution Europe, Asia	Occurrence

Order CHIROPTERA	Family PALAEOCHIROPTERYGIDAE	Informal name Bat

PALAEOCHIROPTERYX

This bat had a complex ear region for echolocation. As in the characteristic wing structure of living bats, the forelimbs were modified into a long framework supporting the wing membranes. The first digit was used as a functional grasping clawed thumb, and the second digit was also clawed, like that of modern fruitbats. The third digit was the longest, extending to the wing tip. The membrane also extended between the fifth digit and the hindlimb and between the hindlimb and the tail.
• HABITAT This bat lived off moths and flew close to the ground.

ENTIRE SKELETON

elongated digits

PALAEOCHIROP-TERYX TUPAIODON
Revilliod; Messel
Formation;
Eocene; Germany.

Typical length 2¾ in (7 cm)

hindlimb bones

Range Eocene	Distribution Europe	Occurrence

Order PRIMATES	Family CERCOPITHECIDAE	Informal name Macaque

MACACA

The macaques are a widespread group of medium-size monkeys living in highly structured social groups. Large males can weigh up to 29 lb (13 kg). Their teeth are rather like smaller versions of their human equivalent but the individual cusps are more prominent and more clearly defined.
• **HABITAT** Macaques live in temperate woodland on a variety of plant and animal foods.
• **REMARK** Never particularly common as fossils, they are Europe's only native Pleistocene primate, other than humans.

strong low cusps

thick dental enamel

Typical length
28 in (70 cm)

MACACA PLIOCAENA (Owen); Thames Terrace Deposits; Middle Pleistocene; UK.

UPPER MOLAR

Range Pliocene–Recent	Distribution Europe, N. Africa, N. Asia	Occurrence

Order EDENTATA	Family GLYPTODONTIDAE	Informal name Glyptodon

GLYPTODON

The body of this armadillo-like herbivore is almost completely clad in a bony armor coat, which forms a head shield, a domed carapace made up of hundreds of fused hexagonal scutes, and a dermal sheath to the tail. The forefeet bear large and powerful claws. *Glyptodon* has a short face, a very deep lower jaw, and massive zygomatic arches. The continuously erupting teeth are set very deeply into the jaw and lack an enamel coating.
• **HABITAT** This giant herbivore lived on the pampas of South America.

SKULL

massive zygomatic arch

nostril

teeth without enamel

deep lower jaw

Typical length
6½ ft (2 m)

GLYPTODON RETICULATUS Owen; Alluvium; Pleistocene; Argentina.

Range Pleistocene–Recent	Distribution S. America	Occurrence

Order EDENTATA	Family MEGATHERIIDAE	Informal name Giant ground sloth

MEGATHERIUM

CLAW-BEARING PHALANGE

This giant sloth, now extinct, had a massive but short, high skull with a high nasal opening and very deep jaws. It had very thick skin, armored throughout with small ossicles of bone, and huge powerful claws on all four feet. Its very simple teeth, lacking in dental enamel, consisted of a battery of continuously growing square columns deeply set in each jaw.
• **HABITAT** This giant sloth lived on a wide range of vegetation.

channels for blood vessels

groove from which outer part of claw grew

deep articular notch

Typical length
20 ft (6 m)

MEGATHERIUM AMERICANUM
Cuvier; Alluvium;
Pleistocene; Argentina.

Range Pliocene–Pleistocene	Distribution N. & S. America	Occurrence

Order RODENTIA	Family GLIRIDAE	Informal name Giant dormouse

LEITHIA

Dormice are a primitive group of rodents, with very low-crowned grinding teeth that suit their mixed plant-food diet. Their teeth have biting surfaces divided into transverse ridges, which grind the food as if between two files. In common with many other herbivores, there is a long gap (or diastema) between the incisor teeth and the cheek teeth, dividing the mouth into two distinct functional regions, one dealing with procurement of food, the other with mastication.
• **HABITAT** Probably nocturnal, this giant dormouse lived in woodland and dense scrub. It is likely to have hibernated in caves and holes in the ground.

UNDERSIDE OF SKULL

diastema (gap between incisors and cheek teeth)

transverse enamel ridges

cheek teeth

LEITHIA MELITENSIS
Falconer; Cave breccia;
Pleistocene; Malta.

Typical length 20 in (50 cm)

Range Pleistocene	Distribution Malta	Occurrence

Order RODENTIA	Family ARVICOLIDAE	Informal name Water vole

ARVICOLA

Like many other voles, this water vole can easily be identified by its teeth. It has an enlarged platelike zygomatic arch. Its high-crowned cheek teeth are made up of triangular prisms. The enamel pattern of the largest lower molar identifies the genus. The skull is slightly flattened, in keeping with the predominantly burrowing habits of many family members.
• **HABITAT** Voles form extensive shallow burrows for nesting and feeding.

back of skull missing

PART OF SKULL

high-crowned cheek teeth

incisor

ARVICOLA CANTIANA (Hinton); Estuarine silts; Middle Pleistocene; UK.

Typical length 2¾ in (7 cm)

Range Pliocene–Recent	Distribution Europe, Asia	Occurrence

Order CETACEA	Family BASILOSAURIDAE	Informal name Whale

BASILOSAURUS

The basilosaurid whale had a long body with little or no hindlimbs and forelimbs modified into paddles. The skull underwent relatively little modification beyond elongation of the muzzle and the development of specialized teeth. The nasal region was little modified, and the posterior part of the skull closely resembled contemporary terrestrial carnivores, with large, zygomatic arches and a marked sagittal crest.
• **HABITAT** Basilosaurids lived in warm, shallow seas.

BASILOSAURUS sp.; Mokattam Formation; Eocene; Egypt.

olfactory lobe

cerebral hemisphere

NATURAL CAST OF BRAIN

cerebellum

Typical length 53 ft (16 m)

Range Eocene	Distribution Worldwide	Occurrence

Order CETACEA	Family BALAENIDAE	Informal name Right whale

BALAENA

Balaena has developed a highly specialized filtration system to replace its dentition. The filter is composed of baleen plates – like the bristles of a huge brush – and is used to filter out small sea creatures like krill. The nasal opening has migrated to a position high on the forehead to form a closeable blowhole. There is no trace of a hind limb, and the fore limb is modified into a huge paddle articulated on a very short humerus. Whales have distinctive tympanic (ear) bones which are quite commonly found as fossils. In baleen whales, these actually resemble a large ear.

• HABITAT *Balaena* lives in temperate to Arctic seas.

EAR BONE (TYMPANIC)

BALAENA PRIMIGENIA Van Beneden; Red Crag; Pliocene; UK.

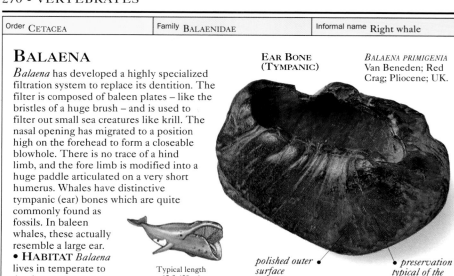

Typical length 65 ft (20 m)

polished outer surface

preservation typical of the Red Crag

Range Pliocene–Recent	Distribution Worldwide	Occurrence

Order CREODONTA	Family HYAENODONTIDAE	Informal name Creodont

HYAENODON

This large specialized carnivore was terrestrial, walking on its toes (digitigrade). It had well-developed flesh-piercing canine teeth, and the upper first and second molars, along with the lower second and third molars, developed into carnassial (meat-slicing) teeth. In modern carnivores, the carnassials are the last upper premolar and first lower molar.

• HABITAT *Hyaenodon* was a land-dwelling carnivore.

HYAENODON HORRIDUS Leidy; Fluviatile deposits; Oligocene; USA.

sagittal crest

strong neck-muscle insertions

SKULL

Typical length 6½ ft (2 m)

molar with shearing blade in upper jaw

nasal bone

canine tooth

Range M. Eocene–M. Miocene	Distribution Europe, N. America, Asia	Occurrence

| Order CARNIVORA | Family URSIDAE | Informal name Bear |

URSUS

LOWER JAW

Ursus refers to the cave, the brown, and the grizzly bear. Fossil remains are usually of the cave bear. Its characteristics include a skull with a high forehead, loss of the anterior premolars, and low-crowned cheek teeth, with many tiny cusps on the crushing surfaces.

• HABITAT They lived in temperate woodland. In winter they hibernated in caves.

• REMARK Many European caves have been found to contain extraordinary quantities of cave bear remains.

articulation with skull

cheek teeth with many low cusps

diastema

large canines

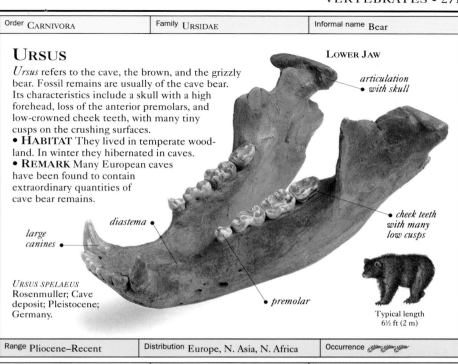

URSUS SPELAEUS
Rosenmuller; Cave deposit; Pleistocene; Germany.

premolar

Typical length
6½ ft (2 m)

| Range Pliocene–Recent | Distribution Europe, N. Asia, N. Africa | Occurrence |

| Order CARNIVORA | Family MUSTELIDAE | Informal name Clawless otter |

CYRNAONYX

The family Mustelidae was characterized by small to medium-size carnivores with short limbs, short muzzles, and particularly powerful jaws. They are not common as fossils. The largest tooth, the first lower molar, has two main components – an anterior shearing blade and a posterior concave crushing surface known as a talonid. The talonid is usually very well developed in the Mustelidae in comparison with other Carnivora.

• HABITAT These otters lived close to water and ate aquatic invertebrates, small mammals, and waterfowl.

CYRNAONYX ANTIQUA
(de Blainville); "Otter Stratum"; Middle Pleistocene; UK.

deep insertion for jaw muscles

strong pointed premolars

first molar with shearing blade and talonid

large canine tooth

Typical length
5 ft (1.5 m)

LOWER JAW

| Range Pleistocene | Distribution Europe, Asia | Occurrence |

Order CARNIVORA	Family FELIDAE	Informal name Big cat

PANTHERA

The first lower molar of this large cat has a highly efficient flesh-shearing notch that works against the blade of the corresponding last upper premolar. The canine tooth is large and conical, with two prominent parallel grooves in its enamel surface, typical of the family.
• **HABITAT** *Panthera* was an open-country predator.
• **REMARK** Fossil lions are closely associated with fossil horses. Both the horses and lions of the Middle Pleistocene were large.

PANTHERA LEO (Linnaeus); Fluviatile deposits; Middle Pleistocene; UK.

large three-cusped • last premolar

alveoli of missing premolar •

outer edge • of alveolus of canine

LOWER JAW

Typical length 6½ ft (2 m)

Range Miocene–Recent	Distribution Northern hemisphere	Occurrence

Order CONDYLARTHRA	Family PHENACODONTIDAE	Informal name Condylarth

PHENACODUS

This genus is known from the entire skeleton. The size ranged from that of a medium to a large dog. Each foot bore five toes, each with a small hoof. The teeth had low blunt cusps, suitable for a diet consisting mainly of fruit. The family is considered close to the stem of the Perissodactyla (horses, rhinoceroses, and tapirs), the Proboscidea (elephants), and the Sirenia (sea cows).
• **HABITAT** *Phenacodus* was a ground-dweller that fed mainly on fallen fruit.

low, blunt cusps •

molar • tooth

PHENACODUS VORTMANI (Cope); Willwood Formation; Early Eocene; USA.

FRAGMENT OF LOWER JAW

Typical length 36 in (90 cm)

Range L. Paleocene–M. Eocene	Distribution N. America, Europe	Occurrence

Order NOTOUNGULATA	Family TOXODONTIDAE	Informal name Notoungulate

TOXODON

This large grazing animal had the size and build of a rhinoceros, with robust limb bones and a short neck. The feet bore three hoofed toes.
• **HABITAT** The incisors and cheek teeth were continuously growing, suggesting an abrasive diet, such as grass.
• **REMARK** The notoungulates, like the litopterns *(below)*, evolved in isolation in South America during the Tertiary. *Toxodon*, like *Macrauchenia* was the last survivor of its order.

TOXODON PLATENSIS Owen; Fluviatile gravels; Pleistocene; Argentina.

eye socket

short nasal bone

SKULL

continuously growing cheek teeth •

Typical length 10 ft (3 m)

alveoli for chisel-shaped incisors •

Range Pleistocene	Distribution S. America	Occurrence

Order LITOPTERNA	Family MACRAUCHENIIDAE	Informal name Litoptern

MACRAUCHENIA

This large camel-like mammal had a long neck and three-toed feet. Its external nasal opening was in the skull roof between the eyes, instead of at the front of the skull. This has been interpreted as denoting either an aquatic mode of life or the presence of a trunk.
• **HABITAT** *Macrauchenia* is thought to have browsed on the edges of lowland forests.
• **REMARK** This specimen was collected by Charles Darwin in 1834 during the famous voyage of the *Beagle*. It still bears the registration number given by the Royal College of Surgeons.

registration number •

long toe bone

MACRAUCHENIA PATACHONICA Owen; Fluviatile gravels; Pleistocene; Argentina.

BONES OF RIGHT FOREFOOT

Typical length 10 ft (3 m)

Range Pleistocene	Distribution S. America	Occurrence

Order PROBOSCIDEA	Family GOMPHOTHERIIDAE	Informal name Gomphothere

PHIOMIA

Phiomia had short, protruding, flattened lower tusks (incisors) and longer, down-curved upper tusks. The cheek teeth are low with conical cusps arranged in three pairs (bunodont). A diastema is present between the tusks and cheek teeth. The retracted position of the nasal opening suggests that there was a short trunk.

• **HABITAT** *Phiomia* probably fed on low-growing shrubs.
• **REMARK** It is likely that the upper tusks were used for defensive purposes.

flattened lower tusks

diastema

articulates with upper jaw

cusps in three rows

low-crowned cheek teeth

PHIOMIA SERRIDENS
Andrews & Beadnell;
Jebel Qatrani Formation;
Oligocene; Egypt.

NEAR-COMPLETE, PAIRED MANDIBLES

Typical shoulder height
8 ft (2.4 m)

Range Oligocene	Distribution N. Africa	Occurrence

Order PROBOSCIDEA	Family GOMPHOTHERIIDAE	Informal name Gomphothere

TETRALOPHODON

Tetralophodon represents the stem group for the true elephants. The head was long and often lacked mandibular tusks, although those from the upper jaw were often quite long. The cheek teeth bear a series of paired, conical, "bunodont" cusps similar to the mastodon's.

• **HABITAT** *Tetralophodon* is thought to have browsed on vegetation beyond the reach of other herbivores.

TETRALOPHODON
LONGIROSTRIS Kaup;
Middle Miocene;
France.

paired, conical cusps

root

Typical shoulder height
8 ft (2.5 m)

CHEEK TOOTH

Range Miocene–Pliocene	Distribution Europe, Asia, N. America	Occurrence

Order PROBOSCIDEA	Family DEINOTHERIIDAE	Informal name Deinothere

DEINOTHERIUM

The deinotheres are an extinct group of elephantlike proboscideans. They lacked tusks in the upper jaw, but possessed a large pair of down-turned tusks in the lower jaw. The cheek teeth are characterized by having two or three simple transverse ridges (lophs). These were used to shear plant material as opposed to the crushing action that was more common in most other more primitive proboscideans.
• HABITAT *Deinotherium* was probably a forest dweller. Wear patterns suggest that the down-turned tusks were used for digging roots or stripping tree bark.

CHEEK TOOTH

transverse ridges, with enamel worn
• *through to dentine*

DEINOTHERIUM GIGANTEUM Kaup; Miocene; Germany.

• *tooth root*

Typical shoulder height
13 ft (4 m)

Range Miocene–Pleistocene	Distribution Europe, Asia, Africa	Occurrence 〰

Order PROBOSCIDEA	Family MAMMUTIDAE	Informal name Mastodon

MAMMUT

A contemporary of the mammoths, the North American mastodon was a member of a morphologically more primitive group of proboscideans, with low-crowned or "bunodont" cheek teeth covered in thick enamel, and with large rounded, crushing cusps.
• HABITAT Besides being a forest-dweller, *Mammut* was thought to have been at least partly aquatic. If so, it must have occupied the same ecological niche as the Old World hippopotamuses.

CHEEK TOOTH

low, crushing
• *cusps*

MAMMUT AMERICANUM (Cuvier); Spring deposits; Pleistocene; USA.

• *cusps arranged in parallel rows*

Typical shoulder height
8 ft (2.5 m)

Range Miocene–Pleistocene	Distribution N. America	Occurrence 〰〰

Order PROBOSCIDEA	Family ELEPHANTIDAE	Informal name Mammoth

MAMMUTHUS

Although smaller than an African elephant, mammoths must have proved a formidable prey for early human hunters. Mammoths first appeared in the African Pliocene and rapidly spread to Europe and Asia. Their evolution can be traced most readily through their tooth structure. The teeth of a mammoth consist of a series of plates composed of enamel surrounding a dentine core. These are held together in a matrix of dental cement. Each tooth erupted from the back of the jaw and slowly moved forward as it wore, to be replaced by another tooth from behind. The thickness and number of tooth plates are important identification criteria.
• HABITAT Mammoths are thought to have grazed on grasses and low shrubs. Whole frozen carcasses have been found in the Siberian Arctic. The carcasses confirm the accuracy of drawings of long-haired mammoths in European caves.

MAMMUTHUS PRIMIGENIUS Blumenbach; Permafrost deposits; Pleistocene; Siberia.

• *long auburn hair*

HAIR

MAMMUTHUS PRIMIGENIUS Blumenbach; Glacial gravels; Pleistocene; UK.

• *matrix of dental cement*

series of enamel plates •

UPPER CHEEK TOOTH

Typical shoulder height 20 ft (3 m)

flat chewing surface •

Range Pliocene–E. Holocene	Distribution Europe	Occurrence

Order HYRACOIDEA	Family PLIOHYRACIDAE	Informal name Giant hyrax

TITANOHYRAX

Resembling a very large guinea pig, *Titanohyrax* was the largest known species of hyrax, about the size of a modern tapir. The incisors were enlarged for nibbling. The cheek teeth were rhinoceroslike and quadrate, with a thick enamel coat and prominent lophs.
• HABITAT It is probable that *Titanohyrax* browsed on scrub vegetation.

TITANOHYRAX ULTIMUS Matsumoto; Jebel Qatrani Formation; Oligocene; Egypt.

UPPER CHEEK TOOTH

enamel •

• *prominent dentine lophs*

Typical length 6½ ft (2 m)

Range Eocene–E. Oligocene	Distribution N. Africa	Occurrence

Order PERISSODACTYLA	Family EQUIDAE	Informal name Dawn horse

HYRACOTHERIUM

Classically considered the "dawn horse," the genus is related to the true horses, which evolved in North America, and the paleotheres, which evolved in isolation in Europe and became extinct in the Oligocene. *Hyracotherium* had four toes on the forefeet and three toes on the hindfeet, each of which bore a small hoof. It was adapted for running, but its gait was less erect than that of a modern horse. Its teeth were low-crowned with low cusps, which enabled it to live on both fruit and soft leaves.
• HABITAT *Hyracotherium* is thought to have lived in a tropical forest environment.

HYRACOTHERIUM CRASPEDOTUM Cope; Wind River Formation; Early Eocene; USA.

MAXILLA WITH CHEEK TEETH

simple low-crowned tooth •

• *fragment of upper jaw*

Typical shoulder height 16 in (40 cm)

Range L. Paleocene–E. Eocene	Distribution Europe, N. America	Occurrence

Order PERISSODACTYLA	Family EQUIDAE	Informal name Horse

EQUUS

Among the best known of all the mammals, the horse is nearly extinct in the wild – but survives in domestication. A grazing terrestrial herbivore, the horse has square, high-crowned cheek teeth with complex enamel patterns. The feet are heavily modified, being reduced to a single elongate metapodial with a short phalange terminating on a prominent hoof, thus adapting them for rapid forward movement on hard ground. The anatomy and physiology of the digestive system includes a large cecum and colon, which permits horses to subsist on high-fiber diets with a low protein content.

• **HABITAT** Modern horses and their relatives have teeth and limbs that are adapted for a grazing, plains-dwelling life.

• **REMARK** The genus *Equus* first appeared in North America in the Pliocene and rapidly spread to every continent except Australia and Antarctica. Cave paintings dating from the Paleolithic period indicate that the Late Pleistocene forms resembled the extant Przewalskii's horse, with a mane of short, stiff, upwardly pointing hair.

HOOF BONE (THIRD PHALANGE)

articular surface

tendon insertion

EQUUS FERUS Boddaert; Cave earth; Late Pleistocene; UK.

MAXILLA

molars

premolars

Typical shoulder height
5 ft (1.5 m)

Range Pliocene–Recent	Distribution Worldwide	Occurrence

Order PERISSODACTYLA	Family HYRACODONTIDAE	Informal name Giant hornless rhino

PARACERATHERIUM

Together with the closely related *Indricotherium*, *Paraceratherium* was the largest land mammal ever to have lived. It could be described as a gigantic long-legged hornless rhinoceros. The absence of a horn has been deduced from the long slender nasal bones that are too weak to have supported a horn. Its teeth bear a similar pattern to that of modern rhinoceroses.

• **HABITAT** This land mammal was adapted for tree-top browsing.

FRAGMENT OF MAXILLA

dentine exposed by wear

cheek tooth

hard palate

PARACERATHERIUM BUGTIENSE Cooper; Bugti Beds; Oligocene; Pakistan.

Typical shoulder height 16½ ft (5 m)

Range Oligocene–E. Miocene	Distribution Asia	Occurrence

Order PERISSODACTYLA	Family RHINOCEROTIDAE	Informal name Woolly rhinoceros

COELODONTA

The most striking features of the woolly rhinoceros were its prominent shoulder hump, shaggy coat, and two horns arranged in tandem. The cheek teeth are high-crowned, with thick, rugose enamel and a heavy covering of dental cement.

• **HABITAT** The woolly rhinoceros was a grazer, feeding on tundra grasses and low-growing shrubs.

• **REMARK** European cave paintings show a similar animal, with two horns and a shaggy coat.

thick rugose enamel

square in occlusal outline

high-crowned cheek tooth

SECOND UPPER MOLAR

COELODONTA ANTIQUITATIS Blumenbach; River gravels; Pleistocene; UK.

Typical length 13 ft (4 m)

Range Miocene–Pleistocene	Distribution Europe, Asia	Occurrence

Order ARTIODACTYLA	Family GIRAFFIDAE	Informal name Giraffe

SAMOTHERIUM

This relatively short-necked giraffe had a pair of horns just behind the eyes. The muzzle was elongated with a long diastema and a rounded end. The cheek teeth are high-crowned and adapted for sideways chewing, much like those of a sheep or cow.
• **HABITAT** The rounded muzzle is regarded as an adaptation to grazing, so it is likely that *Samotherium* inhabited open grasslands. By contrast, the modern giraffids (the giraffe and okapi) are browsers.

SAMOTHERIUM BOISSIERI Major; Tuffs; Late Miocene; Greece.

medium-crowned cheek teeth •

sharp, crescentic • ridges

Typical length 10 ft (3 m) **FRAGMENT OF LOWER JAW**

• *jaw bone*

Range Miocene	Distribution Europe, Asia, Africa	Occurrence 〰〰

Order ARTIODACTYLA	Family HIPPOPOTAMIDAE	Informal name Hippopotamus

HIPPOPOTAMUS

Hippopotamuses are principally short-legged, stocky, aquatic herbivores. They have long, protruding lower incisors, huge canine teeth (tusks,) a short diastema, and a battery of high-crowned cheek teeth. They can exceed three tons in weight, although the dwarf species illustrated here was the size of a small pig.
• **HABITAT** Because of their great bulk, hippopotamuses are cumbersome on land but are surprisingly agile in water. They graze on grasses, reeds, and other aquatic plants.
• **REMARK** The illustrated specimen is a dwarf species. Dwarf and giant forms are typical of island faunas.

HIPPOPOTAMUS MINOR Demarest; Cave deposits; Pleistocene; Cyprus.

• *alveolus (socket) of tusk*

• *sockets of premolars*

• *high-crowned molars*

INCOMPLETE SKULL

Typical length 39 in (1 m)

Range E. Pliocene–Recent	Distribution Europe, Asia, Africa	Occurrence 〰〰〰〰

| Order ARTIODACTYLA | Family MERYCOIDODONTIDAE | Informal name Oreodont |

MERYCOIDODON

This genus, formerly known as *Oreodon*, is distantly related to the camels, although this was not reflected in its outward appearance. It was a short, stocky animal the size of a sheep. It looked like a short-legged deer or horse, but had four toes on each foot. It had medium-crowned, crescentic cheek teeth, and no diastema.
• HABITAT During the Oligocene, herds of *Merycoidodon* roamed the woodlands and prairies of North America, browsing on leaves.

MERYCOIDODON CULBERTSONII Leidy; Brule Formation; Oligocene; USA.

• eye socket

SKULL

Typical length 5 ft (1.5 m)

deep, robust mandible •

• *medium-crowned, crescentic teeth*

| Range Oligocene | Distribution N. America | Occurrence |

| Order ARTIODACTYLA | Family BOVIDAE | Informal name Bison |

BISON

Bison have true horns comprising a core of bone covered by a horn sheath in a single, upright curve. These are found in both sexes. Mature bulls use their horns both for fighting and display. The lower incisor teeth are spatulate, the uppers are absent. The cheek teeth are high-crowned.
• HABITAT Herds of bison have roamed temperate grasslands in North America and Europe from the Pleistocene to the present day.

BISON PRISCUS Bojanus; Floodplain terrace; Late Pleistocene; UK.

horn core •

SKULL ROOF

frontal bone •

• *eye socket*

Typical length 10 ft (3 m)

| Range Pliocene–Recent | Distribution Europe, N. America | Occurrence |

Order PRIMATES	Family PONGIDAE	Informal name Gigantopithecine

GIGANTOPITHECUS

This was an enormous, gorillalike ground-living ape, possibly the largest primate ever to have lived. Estimates of its weight are in excess of 602 lb (273 kg). This primate had robust canine teeth and huge cheek teeth with thick enamel, high crowns (for a primate), and low cusps.
• **HABITAT** The degree of wear on the teeth suggests that they were used heavily in mastication of a specific kind of plant food, perhaps seeds.
• **REMARK** The genus survived in China at least until 500,000 years ago.

- *extensive occlusal surfaces*
- *peglike incisors*

GIGANTOPITHECUS BLACKI von Konigswald; Cave deposits; Early Pleistocene; China.

Typical height
6½ ft (2 m)

- *canines worn flat*

LOWER JAW

Range Miocene–Pleistocene	Distribution Asia	Occurrence

Order PRIMATES	Family HOMINIDAE	Informal name Australopithecine

AUSTRALOPITHECUS

These australopithecines were characterized by robust skulls with powerful lower jaws and bipedal locomotion. Their canines were smaller than those of their presumed ancestors, but the cheek teeth were large with thick enamel, suitable for a tough, herbivorous diet.
• **HABITAT** They lived in open country and woodland environments in tropical and subtropical areas.

AUSTRALOPITHECUS BOISEI Tobias; Shungura Formation; Pliocene; Ethiopia.

molars with expanded occlusal surfaces

LOWER JAW

premolar

Typical height
4 ft (1.4 m)

Range Pliocene–E. Pleistocene	Distribution Africa	Occurrence

| Order PRIMATES | Family HOMINIDAE | Informal name Early man |

HOMO HABILIS

Homo habilis had a larger and more rounded skull than any earlier hominid. The incisor teeth were relatively large; the premolars were small. The molars were narrow, with thick enamel.
• **HABITAT** *Homo habilis* lived in the open savannah.
• **REMARK** The dental features combined with evidence of toolmaking point to a possible dependence, for the first time in hominids, on meat-eating and hunting.

large, rounded vault

SKULL

short face

Typical height
4 ft (1.2 m)

HOMO HABILIS Leakey, Tobias & Napier; Pleistocene; Kenya.

canine tooth •

| Range L. Pliocene–E. Pleistocene | Distribution Africa | Occurrence |

| Order PRIMATES | Family HOMINIDAE | Informal name Neanderthal Man |

HOMO SAPIENS NEANDERTHALENSIS

The neanderthals were short and heavily muscled, with prominent brow ridges and a receding forehead and chin. The body shape probably resulted from a long process of climatic adaptation. They had a brain size similar to that of modern humans, were hunters, fashioned complex wood and bone tools, used fire, and buried their dead. They inhabited Europe and western Asia during the last ice age.
• **HABITAT** Neanderthal Man lived in temperate and cold climates.

HOMO SAPIENS NEANDERTHALENSIS King; Cave earth; Pleistocene; France.

gap behind third molar •

edge-to-edge bite •

LOWER JAW OF YOUNG ADULT

poorly developed chin

Typical height
5½ ft (1.6 m)

| Range L. Pleistocene | Distribution Europe, Asia | Occurrence |

| Order PRIMATES | Family HOMINIDAE | Informal name Modern man |

HOMO SAPIENS SAPIENS

Modern humans are taller than the neanderthals, with more gracile bones, more prominent chins, and more domed foreheads. Their teeth are similar, though the incisors are less protruding.
• **HABITAT** Although once restricted to warm climates, the acquisition of the skills to make clothing and construct shelters allowed modern humans to colonize more hostile environments. Co-operative hunting, armed with simple stone and wood weapons, allowed them to exploit prey that would otherwise have eluded them.
• **REMARK** Modern humans manufactured a variety of tools with specific functions, as distinct from the multipurpose axes of their forbears. The bone, flint, and antler tools shown opposite are often found associated with fossil human remains, although not strictly speaking fossils themselves. Although of different ages and degrees of sophistication, they indicate a level of culture rather than a specific date.

SKULL CAP

well-rounded skull

absence of prominent brow ridges

HOMO SAPIENS SAPIENS Linnaeus; Cave earth; Late Pleistocene; UK.

fully modern dentition

small teeth

UPPER JAW OF YOUNG ADULT

Typical height
5½ ft (1.8 m)

| Range L. Pleistocene–Recent | Distribution Worldwide | Occurrence |

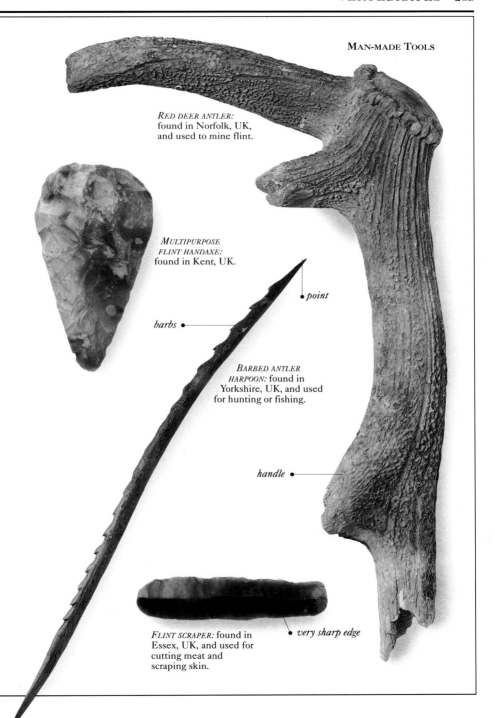

RED DEER ANTLER: found in Norfolk, UK, and used to mine flint.

MULTIPURPOSE FLINT HANDAXE: found in Kent, UK.

point

barbs

BARBED ANTLER HARPOON: found in Yorkshire, UK, and used for hunting or fishing.

handle

FLINT SCRAPER: found in Essex, UK, and used for cutting meat and scraping skin.

very sharp edge

PLANTS

ALGAE

T HE ALGAE HAVE A fossil record that extends from the Precambrian to the present day. Some algae are important age indicators and are used extensively in the oil industry. They present a wide range of form, from simple unicells to complex multi-cellular plants. Fossil remains are usually limited to those that produce structures impregnated with silica or forms of calcium carbonate, or which developed tough-walled cysts. As algae released oxygen into the atmosphere, they were responsible for a critical change in atmospheric composition during the Precambrian.

Order CYANOPHYTA	Family Unclassified	Informal name Stromatolites

COLLENIA

Part of the stromatolite group, this genus has a conical to cylindrical structure composed of limestone and/or silica. This structure is always layered, sometimes with alternating light and dark bands. The minute algal threads of which it is composed can be seen under the microscope. These threads bound to-gether detrital sands and muds in a bed of lime produced by the algae.
• HABITAT Like living stroma-tolitic algae, *Collenia* inhabited tropical intertidal zones.

COLLENIA sp.;
Stromatolitic Limestone;
Precambrian; USA.

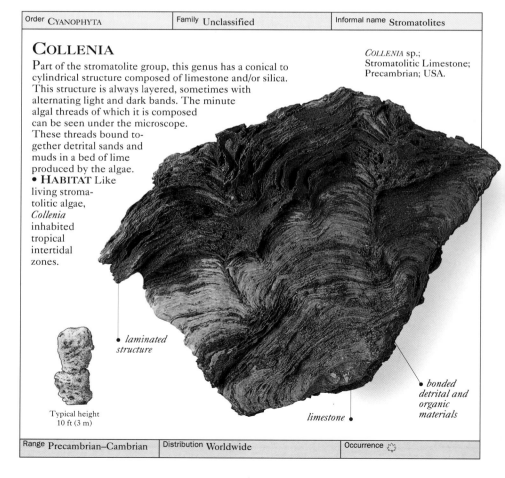

• *laminated structure*

Typical height
10 ft (3 m)

limestone •

• *bonded detrital and organic materials*

Range Precambrian–Cambrian	Distribution Worldwide	Occurrence

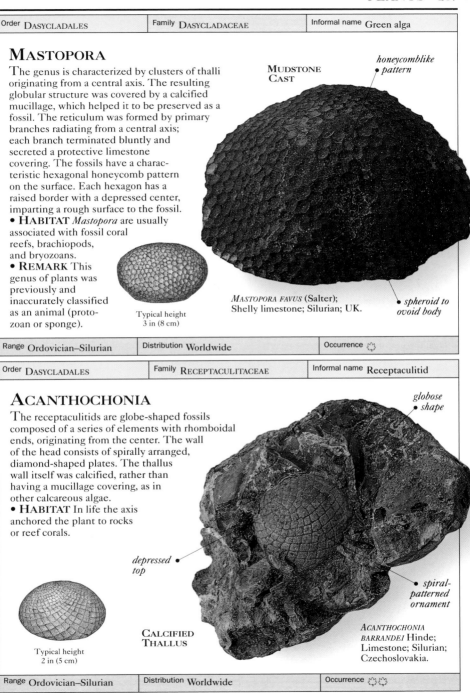

| Order DASYCLADALES | Family DASYCLADACEAE | Informal name Green alga |

MASTOPORA

The genus is characterized by clusters of thalli originating from a central axis. The resulting globular structure was covered by a calcified mucillage, which helped it to be preserved as a fossil. The reticulum was formed by primary branches radiating from a central axis; each branch terminated bluntly and secreted a protective limestone covering. The fossils have a characteristic hexagonal honeycomb pattern on the surface. Each hexagon has a raised border with a depressed center, imparting a rough surface to the fossil.
• **HABITAT** *Mastopora* are usually associated with fossil coral reefs, brachiopods, and bryozoans.
• **REMARK** This genus of plants was previously and inaccurately classified as an animal (protozoan or sponge).

MUDSTONE CAST

honeycomblike pattern

spheroid to ovoid body

MASTOPORA FAVUS (Salter); Shelly limestone; Silurian; UK.

Typical height 3 in (8 cm)

| Range Ordovician–Silurian | Distribution Worldwide | Occurrence |

| Order DASYCLADALES | Family RECEPTACULITACEAE | Informal name Receptaculitid |

ACANTHOCHONIA

The receptaculitids are globe-shaped fossils composed of a series of elements with rhomboidal ends, originating from the center. The wall of the head consists of spirally arranged, diamond-shaped plates. The thallus wall itself was calcified, rather than having a mucillage covering, as in other calcareous algae.
• **HABITAT** In life the axis anchored the plant to rocks or reef corals.

globose shape

depressed top

spiral-patterned ornament

CALCIFIED THALLUS

Typical height 2 in (5 cm)

ACANTHOCHONIA BARRANDEI Hinde; Limestone; Silurian; Czechoslovakia.

| Range Ordovician–Silurian | Distribution Worldwide | Occurrence |

Order PHAEOPHYTA	Family Unclassified	Informal name Brown alga

BYTHOTREPHIS

These soft-bodied algae were small to moderately large plants of simple, purely vegetative structure, with "Y"-fork branches. The fossils are present as impressions or carbonaceous films on the rock surfaces. There is often no detailed preservation, although linear striations, which indicate the remains of tube structures within the body of the plant, may be present on the branches.
• HABITAT *Bythotrephis* can be found in shallow (or shoreline) to deep-water sediments.
• REMARK Care is needed when identifying these fossils as they are similar to burrow systems of small marine invertebrates. The presence of carbonaceous or similar minerals is the only certain guide to a correct identification.

BYTHOTREPHIS GRACILIS Hall; Clinton Group; Late Silurian; Canada.

WHOLE PLANT

• *impression*

• *simple branching structure*

Typical height
12 in (30 cm)

Range Silurian–Miocene	Distribution Worldwide	Occurrence ☼☼

Order CHLOROPHYTA	Family Unclassified	Informal name Green alga

PARKA

The liverwort-like thallus or plant body of *Parka* had a thick outer covering or cuticle. The plant body itself sometimes had a simple "Y" branch, and was only tens of cells thick. It nearly always bore distinct rounded bodies or spore capsules, which contained numerous small spores.
• HABITAT The protective outer covering to both plant and spores may indicate that *Parka* was, in fact, a land plant.

PARKA DECIPIENS Flemming; Carmyllie Beds; Early Devonian; UK.

FRAGMENT OF THALLUS

Typical diameter
1½ in (4 cm)

spore capsules •   *mudstone* •

• *carbonaceous layer*

Range L. Silurian–E. Devonian	Distribution Europe, N. America	Occurrence ☼☼

EARLY LAND PLANTS

THE FIRST INDISPUTABLE land plants are characterized by a mechanical supporting tissue which provided rigidity, a perforated cuticle that allowed the plant to "breathe," and spores resistant to desiccation, because of a tough spore coat, which helped them survive and germinate on land. Spore-bearing capsules were borne either at the ends of thin branches, singly or in bunches, or along the side. These plants ranged from small, scrambling types to spiny-stemmed varieties 3 ft (1 meter) tall.

Order RHYNIALES	Family RHYNIACEAE	Informal name Cooksonia

COOKSONIA

These small plants were characterized by "Y" branches. The simplest consisted of one or two branches, but some had five to six levels of branching. Typically, each branch had a spore capsule at the end, which was oval or kidney-shaped and contained spores with resistant coats.
• **HABITAT** The earliest known land plant, its remains are usually associated with shallow marine or fluvio-deltaic deposits.

Typical height 3 in (7.5 cm)

• *spore capsule*

• *"Y" branch*

shelly mudstone •

COOKSONIA HEMISPHAERICA Lang; Shelly mudstone; Early Devonian; UK.

Range L. Silurian–Devonian	Distribution Worldwide	Occurrence

Order ZOSTEROPHYLLALES	Family ZOSTEROPHYLLACEAE	Informal name Zosterophyll

ZOSTEROPHYLLUM

Zosterophyllum is a genus of plants that had spore capsules placed near the end of the stem, but always on the side, never at the extremity. The spore capsules were oval shaped and on short stalks. The branching was a mixture of "Y" type (these were less pronounced) and "H" type.
• **HABITAT** *Zostero-phyllum* grew mainly on the margins of lakes.
• **REMARK** It is probable that plants like this gave rise to the giant lycopods of the coal swamps, such as *Lepidodendron (see p.294).*

spore capsules on • *stem side*

ZOSTEROPHYLLUM LLANOVERANUM Croft & Lang; Senni Beds; Early Devonian; UK.

mudstone •

Typical height 10 in (25 cm)

• *stems*

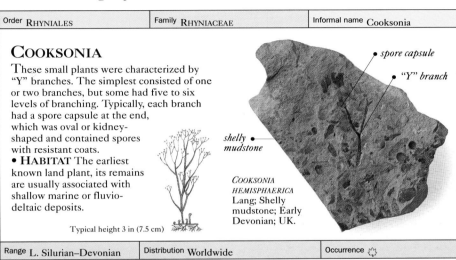

Range L. Silurian–M. Devonian	Distribution Worldwide	Occurrence

HEPATOPHYTES

HEPATOPHYTES OR LIVERWORTS are small plants, with flat (thalloid) or leafy bodies. They reproduce by spores contained in capsules borne on wiry stems. They usually have either prone growth (thalloid liverworts), or only limited vertical growth (leafy liverworts). They have a poor fossil record. Today these plants are found in damp environments worldwide.

Order MARCHANTIALES	Family MARCHANTIACEAE	Informal name Liverwort

HEXAGONOCAULON

This small creeping plant had a noticeable "Y"-branch pattern every one or two centimeters. The plant body was flat and broad. Small rootlike structures were present on the under-side in life. This plant sometimes produced simple spores.
• **HABITAT** *Hexagono-caulon* lived in damp, humid conditions.

Typical height
3 in (8 cm)

HEXAGON-OCAULON MINUTUM Lacey & Lewis; Williams Point Beds; Triassic; Antarctica.

carbon-aceous film

simple branching plants

Range Triassic–Cretaceous	Distribution Southern hemisphere	Occurrence

SPHENOPSIDS

THE FOSSIL HISTORY of sphenopsids can be traced back to the Late Devonian. Commonly known as horsetails, these plants have jointed stems and leaves produced in whorls about the stem. The spores are produced in spore capsules, which are tightly grouped into cones.

Order EQUISETALES	Family EQUISETACEAE	Informal name Horsetail

EQUISETITES

These small horsetails had ribbed stems, with spores present in terminal cones. Individual leaves were jointed, linear, or grasslike, with up to 30 per whorl. Scale leaves clothed the base of the leaf. The plant spread by underground stems and tubers.
• **HABITAT** *Equisetites* lived in wetland conditions. Its tubers are often found in fossil soils.

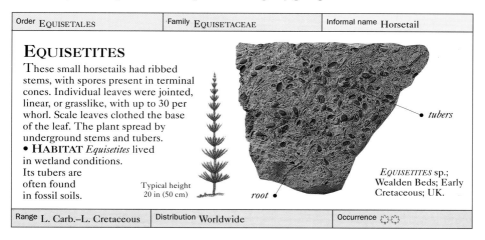

Typical height
20 in (50 cm)

root

tubers

EQUISETITES sp.; Wealden Beds; Early Cretaceous; UK.

Range L. Carb.–L. Cretaceous	Distribution Worldwide	Occurrence

Order EQUISETALES	Family CALAMOSTACHYACEAE	Informal name Horsetail

ASTEROPHYLLITES

This horsetail was actually tree sized. The stem was ribbed and derived its strength from an outer cylinder of woodlike tissue (as seen in bamboo), protecting a spongy interior. The branches were arranged in whorls about the thick main stem. The leaves were sword shaped, with a single, central vein, and arranged in whorls about the branch, which gave a dense, almost ornamental conifer look to the mature plant. It spread by underground runners, or by spores produced in terminal cones formed from tight aggregations of whorled spore capsules and cone leaves.

ASTEROPHYLLITES EQUISETIFORMIS (Brongniart); Coal Measures; Late Carboniferous; UK.

• **HABITAT** *Asterophyllites* was one of several plant groups to reach gigantic sizes in the Late Carboniferous swamps.

• **REMARK** *Asterophyllites* is the name applied to the foliage of the giant horsetail *Calamites*.

branch •

jointed stems •

• *leaves in whorls*

• *carbonized leaves*

• *shale*

Typical height
33 ft (10 m)

Range L. Carb.–E. Permian	Distribution Worldwide	Occurrence ✿✿✿

FERNS

THIS LARGE GROUP of plants has a fossil record extending back to the Middle Devonian. Ferns have leaves, called fronds, which usually consist of leaflets, although some have entire or undivided fronds. Reproduction is by spores produced in a variety of spore capsule types found either on the underside of fronds or, more rarely produced on specialized fronds. Sizes vary from large tree ferns to minute filmy ferns. They live in a wide range of habitats, ranging from the tropics to cold temperate regions.

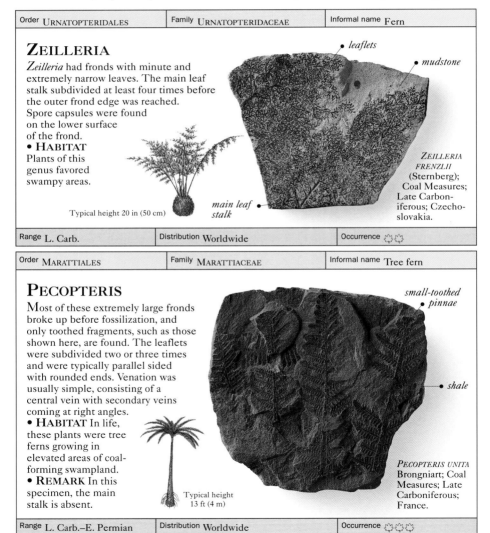

Order URNATOPTERIDALES	Family URNATOPTERIDACEAE	Informal name Fern

ZEILLERIA

Zeilleria had fronds with minute and extremely narrow leaves. The main leaf stalk subdivided at least four times before the outer frond edge was reached. Spore capsules were found on the lower surface of the frond.
• **HABITAT**
Plants of this genus favored swampy areas.

Typical height 20 in (50 cm)

• *leaflets*

• *mudstone*

main leaf stalk

ZEILLERIA FRENZLII (Sternberg); Coal Measures; Late Carboniferous; Czechoslovakia.

Range L. Carb.	Distribution Worldwide	Occurrence

Order MARATTIALES	Family MARATTIACEAE	Informal name Tree fern

PECOPTERIS

Most of these extremely large fronds broke up before fossilization, and only toothed fragments, such as those shown here, are found. The leaflets were subdivided two or three times and were typically parallel sided with rounded ends. Venation was usually simple, consisting of a central vein with secondary veins coming at right angles.
• **HABITAT** In life, these plants were tree ferns growing in elevated areas of coal-forming swampland.
• **REMARK** In this specimen, the main stalk is absent.

Typical height 13 ft (4 m)

small-toothed • *pinnae*

• *shale*

PECOPTERIS UNITA Brongniart; Coal Measures; Late Carboniferous; France.

Range L. Carb.–E. Permian	Distribution Worldwide	Occurrence

Order OSMUNDALES	Family OSMUNDACEAE	Informal name Royal fern

OSMUNDA

This is a fern with a short stem, large ordinary fronds, and specialized spore-bearing fronds. The stem, when present, has a fibrous structure with many leaf bases passing through it to the outside. The ordinary fronds bear large leaflets with complex netted venation. Spore-bearing fronds either have no leaflets or are only present at the leaf stalk end.

• **HABITAT** It is probable that, like its modern counterpart, fossil plants of this genus were to be found near water, often in tropical or warm, temperate, wetland areas.

OSMUNDA DOWKERI (Carruthers); Thanet Formation; Paleocene; UK.

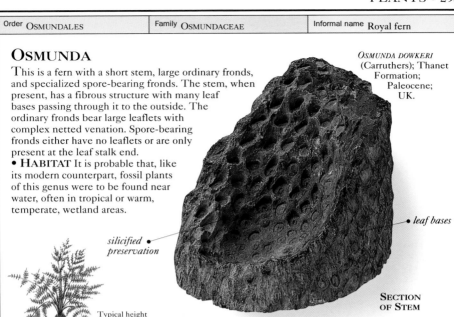

• *leaf bases*

silicified preservation

SECTION OF STEM

Typical height 6½ ft (2 m)

Range Cretaceous–Recent	Distribution Worldwide	Occurrence

Order FILICALES	Family DICKSONIACEAE	Informal name Fern

ONYCHIOPSIS

This plant is known only from its fragmentary fronds. These appear as very delicate-looking feathery toothed leaves. The leaflets are extremely narrow and join the stem at an angle of about 30 degrees. Spore capsules have been found on fronds from Britain and the USA.

• **HABITAT** *Onychiopsis* grew near lakes, probably in forest-edge habitats, among other ferns, cycads, and cycad-like plants. All ferns require a moderately damp habitat for reproduction.

• **REMARK** At one time this plant was regarded as a club moss or lycopod, but it is currently thought to be a fern. This specimen is preserved in siltstone.

ONYCHIOPSIS PSILOTOIDES (Stokes & Webb); Wealden Beds; Early Cretaceous; UK.

• *siltstone*

• *delicate frond structure*

Typical height 20 in (50 cm)

FROND

Range Cretaceous	Distribution Northern hemisphere	Occurrence

LYCOPODS

T HE LYCOPODS OR CLUB MOSSES have a long fossil history stretching back to the Late Silurian. They reached their peak in the Late Carboniferous, and today they are represented by only a handful of genera. All plants have spirally arranged leaves with spore capsules in the leaf axil, or aggregated into distinct terminal cones. In the Carboniferous, many lycopods were tree sized, with branches clothed in long, grasslike foliage and cones containing spores. Today, lycopods are small herbaceous plants.

Order LEPIDODENDRALES	Family LEPIDODENDRACEAE	Informal name Giant club moss

LEPIDODENDRON

These tree-size lycopods or club mosses are notable for their scalelike bark. From the base upward the plant was anchored in shallow soil by several "Y"-branch rooting organs called stigmaria. These had spirally arranged, finger-size roots coming from them. A polelike trunk, unbranched for most of its length, and up to 130 ft (40 m) or more in height, supported a crown of simple branches. Much of the trunk was covered in diamond-shaped leaf bosses, the familiar *Lepidodendron* fossil. Grasslike leaves, spirally arranged, clothed the upper branches, terminating in cigar-shaped cones (*Lepidostrobus*). These contained, depending on the species, only small spores, large spores, or both.
• **HABITAT** *Lepidodendron* grew in hot and humid swampland.

LEPIDODENDRON ACULEATUM Sternberg; Coal Measures; Late Carboniferous; UK.

BARK

• *scalelike surface*

ironstone nodule •

diamond-shaped • pattern

• *cast*

Typical height 100 ft (30 m)

LEPIDOSTROBUS VARIABILIS Lindley & Hutton; Coal Measures; Late Carboniferous; Locality Unknown.

CIGAR-SHAPED CONE

Range Carb.	Distribution Worldwide	Occurrence ✿✿✿✿

Order DREPANOPHYCALES	Family DREPANOPHYCACEAE	Informal name Club moss

BARAGWANATHIA

These were prostrate or low-growing, soft-bodied (herbaceous) plants, with a simple "Y"-branch structure. The stems were always entirely clothed in fine leaves about ⅜ in (1 cm) in length. Spore capsules were present where the leaf joined the main stem (axil). The capsules were organized into zones up the stem, but not into cones.
• **HABITAT** *Baragwanathia* grew in lowland areas and floodplains.
• **REMARK** Much debate has arisen from *Baragwanathia* appearing in the fossil record as early as the Late Silurian, given that it is such an "advanced" plant as compared with its contemporaries.

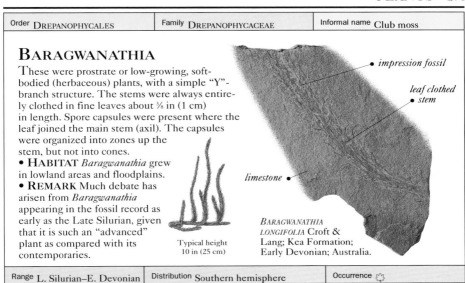

impression fossil

leaf clothed stem

limestone

Typical height 10 in (25 cm)

BARAGWANATHIA LONGIFOLIA Croft & Lang; Kea Formation; Early Devonian; Australia.

Range L. Silurian–E. Devonian	Distribution Southern hemisphere	Occurrence

PTERIDOSPERMS

T HIS DIVERSE GROUP of plants was at its height during the Late Paleozoic and most of the Mesozoic. Pteridosperms were popularly called seed ferns, after the Carboniferous forms whose foliage was seemingly indistinguishable from some ferns. Evidence of seed association discovered earlier this century has now placed them within their own group.

Order MEDULLOSALES	Family MEDULLOSACEAE	Informal name Seed fern

PARIPTERIS

The illustrated pollen-bearing organ of *Paripteris* is called a potoniea. Bell-shaped, it was produced upon separate candelabralike structures at the base of the frond. Each potoniea had many fingerlike pollen-producing structures.
• **HABITAT** *Paripteris* was an inhabitant of elevated regions of hot, humid swampland.

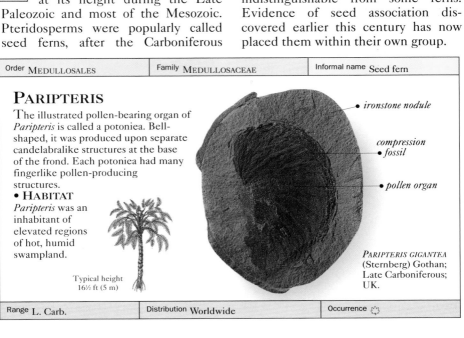

ironstone nodule

compression fossil

pollen organ

Typical height 16½ ft (5 m)

PARIPTERIS GIGANTEA (Sternberg) Gothan; Late Carboniferous; UK.

Range L. Carb.	Distribution Worldwide	Occurrence

Order MEDULLOSALES	Family MEDULLOSACEAE	Informal name Seed fern

MEDULLOSA

These were seed-bearing plants, growing up to 16½ ft (5 m) in height. The stem or trunk consisted partially of old leaf bases, similar to the sago palm (cycad), with prop roots coming off near the base. They bore enormous fronds of various types: some toothed, others with rounded leaflets. All reproduced by seeds, which were often quite large.
• **HABITAT** This was a typical plant of Late Carboniferous swamps.
• **REMARK** The genus *Medullosa* may, in fact, represent a number of similar genera.

MEDULLOSA NOEI Steidtmann; Coal Measures; Late Carboniferous; USA.

COAL BALL
SECTION

preservation of fine detail

Typical height
16½ ft (5 m)

Range L. Carb.–E. Permian	Distribution Worldwide	Occurrence ✿✿✿

Order MEDULLOSALES	Family MEDULLOSACEAE	Informal name Seed fern

ALETHOPTERIS

This plant was characterized by large fronds with toothed leaflets. Typically, the thick, robust individual leaflets were not separated from one another but connected by leaf tissue running between them. Venation was simple: a central vein with smaller veins coming off it at, or near to, right angles.
• **HABITAT** *Alethopteris* grew in elevated areas of hot swamps.
• **REMARK** This genus name applies to the foliage, which was was borne on *Medullosa* stems. The name *Alethopteris* is used for a number of plants with a similar frond shape, which may not, in fact, be closely related.

cast

thick, strong-veined leaflets

ironstone nodule

Typical height
16½ ft (5 m)

ALETHOPTERIS SERLII Brongniart; Coal Measures; Late Carboniferous; USA.

frond part

Range L. Carb–E. Permian	Distribution Worldwide	Occurrence ✿✿✿

Order GLOSSOPTERIDALES	Family GLOSSOPTERIDACEAE	Informal name Gondwana Tree

GLOSSOPTERIS

These were tree-size pteridosperms with rosettes of small to very large leaves. The leaves varied in shape from very narrow to broad, and were similar in shape to banana leaves. The venation consisted of a broad central vein which was made up of many smaller veins. From this a fine reticulum (or net) of minor veins, spread, dividing the leaf surface into small lozenge shapes. The wood was of softwood type, with evidence of growth rings, indicating a seasonal climate. Fructifications were borne on specialized leaves, such as pollen-bearing capsules or seed-bearing structures.
• **HABITAT** *Glossopteris* grew in warm, damp lowlands.

SLAB OF
LEAF BED

GLOSSOPTERIS
sp.; Red beds;
Permian; India.

• *shale*

• *net venation*

• *sword-shaped leaves*

• *straight leaf margins*

Typical height
26 ft (8 m)

Range Permian	Distribution Southern hemisphere	Occurrence

Order MEDULLOSALES	Family Unclassified	Informal name Seed fern

MARIOPTERIS

The large fronds of *Mariopteris* had a distinct organization, the pointed leaflets being distributed on a frond divided into four areas. Although not usually found whole, part of one quadrant may be found with a typically reduced basal set of leaflets. Individually, the leaflets had a single central vein, from which secondary veins were given off at an angle of about 60 degrees. The stem consisted in part of old leaf bases, with strongly marked striations along its length.

• HABITAT An inhabitant of Late Carboniferous swamps, some species of *Mariopteris* may have been scrambling or climbing plants.

small carbonized leaflets

MARIOPTERIS MARICATA
Schlotheim; Coal Measures; Late Carboniferous; Czechoslovakia.

Typical height 16½ ft (5 m)

COMPRESSION FOSSIL

Range L. Carb.–E. Permian	Distribution Worldwide	Occurrence

Order MEDULLOSALES	Family MEDULLOSACEAE	Informal name Seed fern

TRIGONOCARPUS

Casts and compressions of seeds from a variety of pteridospermous plants are found as fossils. This seed had three ribs, dividing it into equal sections (and internally into valves). The outside of the seed was usually covered in longitudinal striations representing fibrous or woody bands that strengthened the seed wall. The seeds were attached terminally or beneath a frond, but are rarely found *in situ* in fossil form.

• HABITAT *Trigonocarpus* inhabited the less wet areas of hot, humid swamps.

"plumb-bob" shape

ISOLATED SEEDS

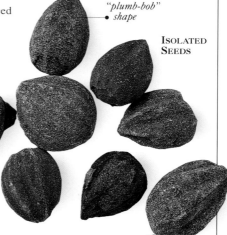

TRIGONOCARPUS ADAMSI Lesquereux; Coal Measures; Late Carboniferous; USA.

Typical height 16½ ft (5 m)

seeds strongly ribbed

Range L. Carb.	Distribution Worldwide	Occurrence

Order CAYTONIALES	Family CORYSTOSPERMACEAE	Informal name Seed fern

DICROIDIUM

This large plant, a notable constituent of some Triassic flora of the southern hemisphere, was actually of shrub to small tree stature. The fronds had unusual "Y"-forked branches, with opposite leaflets along the complete length. Paleobotanists know little about the plant as a whole; however, by association with other plant fossils, they believe it was likely to have been seed bearing.
• HABITAT *Dicroidium* was an inhabitant of tropical tree-fern forests.

DICROIDIUM sp.; Ipswich Series; Triassic; Australia.

• *opposite pairs of leaflets*

mudstone •

"Y"-forked • *leaf*

Typical height 13 ft (4 m)

Range Triassic	Distribution Southern hemisphere	Occurrence

Order PELTASPERMALES	Family UMKOMASIACEAE	Informal name Seed fern

PACHYPTERIS

A common constituent of many Jurassic flora, *Pachypteris* had small fronds with a regularly or irregularly lobed appearance. It possessed an extraordinarily thick, waxy outer covering, which is often preserved in fossils. It was one of the last of the pteridosperms and became extinct during the Cretaceous period.
• HABITAT *Pachypteris* grew in salt marshes.

shale block •

LEAF BED

PACHYPTERIS sp.; Shemshak Formation; Jurassic; Iran.

Typical height 6½ ft (2 m)

smallest • *lobed leaflets*

• *compression fossil*

Range Triassic–Cretaceous	Distribution Worldwide	Occurrence

BENNETTITES

T HE BENNETTITES or cycadeoids were very similar in appearance to sago palms or cycads. They were distinguished by their star-shaped flowers, of which several types are known. The form of the plants varied from globular stumps to branching trees, all with palmlike foliage.

Order BENNETTITALES	Family Unclassified	Informal name Cycadeoid

WILLIAMSONIA

This plant resembled a shrub or small tree with diamond-patterned bark and palm like leaves. Its most interesting aspect was its large star-shaped flowers. One type contained spore capsules, while the other pro-duced seeds.
• HABITAT
Williamsonia grew in tropical tree-fern forests.

Typical height 10 ft (3 m)

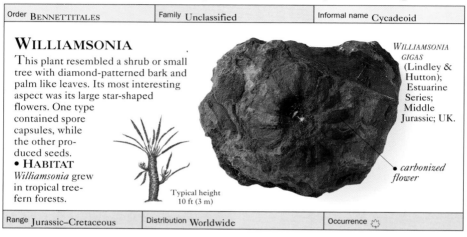

WILLIAMSONIA GIGAS (Lindley & Hutton); Estuarine Series; Middle Jurassic; UK.

• *carbonized flower*

Range Jurassic–Cretaceous	Distribution Worldwide	Occurrence

PROGYMNOSPERMS

T HIS GROUP IS BELIEVED to be ancestral to all seed plants. Appearing in the Devonian, some were moderately large trees, while others were like tree ferns. They began to produce both small and large spores, and determined spore and seed repro-duction during the Late Devonian.

Order ARCHEOPTERIDALES	Family ARCHEOPTERIDACEAE	Informal name Archeopteris

ARCHEOPTERIS

Archeopteris was one of the first trees on Earth. Trees of this genus were small to medium in size, with leafy foliage reminiscent of some conifers. The leafy shoots occurred in opposite arrangement in a single plane. The leaves overlapped one another and were subcircular to nearly wedge shaped. Leaves were replaced by spore capsules on fertile branches.
• HABITAT This genus grew in flood-plain woodland.

Typical height 33 ft (10 m)

compression fossil

leafy shoots off axis

• *limestone*

ARCHEOPTERIS sp.; Kiltorcan Beds; Late Devonian; USA.

Range Devonian	Distribution Worldwide	Occurrence

CORDAITALES

MEMBERS OF THIS GROUP of plants were distinguished by long leathery leaves, spirally arranged, with many parallel veins. Their reproductive structures were loosely aggregated cones, producing flat seeds with a membranous outer "skirt."

Order CORDAITANTHALES	Family CORDAITACEA	Informal name Cordaite

CORDAITES

An ancestor of the true conifers, *Cordaites* was a tree-size plant that bore huge, strap-shaped leaves in tight spirals about the stem. The leaves have distinctive linear venation. The cones were loose terminal aggregations of spore capsules or seeds. Some members of the genus were thought to be mangroves, with arching stilt roots.

• **HABITAT** *Cordaites* was an inhabitant of mangrove swamps and elevated hummocks.

CORDAITES ANGULOSTRIATUS Grand Eury; Coal Measures; Late Carboniferous; UK.

straplike leaves

Typical height 33 ft (10 m)

Range L. Carb–E. Permian	Distribution Worldwide	Occurrence

CONIFERS

THESE ARE USUALLY shrubs or trees distinguished by the production of woody cones of various shapes and sizes. The leaves are often needle shaped in temperate and subtropical genera, but are flat and broad in tropical podocarps. The seeds are produced mainly in cones.

Order CONIFERALES	Family PINACEAE	Informal name Pine

PITYOSTROBUS

The form genus represents the cones of various pinelike trees common in the Jurassic and Cretaceous periods. They were about three times longer than broad. The cones were woody, with the curved to reflexed cone leaves or bracts arranged helically about a central axis. Seeds were attached to the bract bases and fell out of the cone when mature.

• **HABITAT** *Pityostrobus* grew in sub-tropical forests.

CARBONIZED CONE

curved cone leaves

PITYOSTROBUS DUNKERI (Mantell) Seward; Wealden Beds; Early Cretaceous; UK.

Typical height 65 ft (20 m)

Range Jurassic–Cretaceous	Distribution Worldwide	Occurrence

Order CONIFERALES	Family TAXODIACEAE	Informal name Coast Redwood

SEQUOIA

This genus includes very large trees, also known as coast redwoods. Small, very globular cones are a feature of these plants. The woody cone leaves (or bracts) are arranged helically about a central axis, and have a seed with a scale leaf on the upper surface, near the base or point of attachment. The cones do not often disintegrate (as disassociated bracts), even as fossils, but open to let the seeds fall out.
• **HABITAT** Redwoods once formed extensive forests in subtropical regions of the world. These forests, as found today in California, are of an open nature, with few other tree species present.

globular shape

PINE CONES

ironstone

carbonized interior

SEQUOIA DAKOTENSIS Brown; Hell Creek Formation; Late Cretaceous; USA.

Typical height 230 ft (70 m)

Range Jurassic–Recent	Distribution Worldwide	Occurrence 🍁🍁

Order CONIFERALES	Family TAXODIACEAE	Informal name Wellingtonia

SEQUOIADENDRON

These giant redwood trees are not as tall as *Sequoia*, but are distinguished by the huge diameter of the trunk. They have small leaves or needles, in common with many other conifers. The leaves are scalelike, arranged alternately along either side of the twig. They are very small, with a blunt, toothlike shape, and are pressed closely to the stem. Wood from the tree is of softwood or gymnospermic type, with no conducting tubes but often with growth rings.
• **HABITAT** Trees of this genus grew in the same subtropical forest habitats as the *Sequoia*.
• **REMARK** Counting the rings shows that the plants can live to impressive ages. More than 1,000 years is by no means uncommon for the larger examples seen growing in California, USA.

compression fossil

leaves in opposite pairs

small leaves

shale

SEQUOIADENDRON AFFINIS (Lesquereux); Oligocene; USA.

Typical height 200 ft (60 m)

Range Jurassic–Recent	Distribution Worldwide	Occurrence 🍁🍁

Order CONIFERALES	Family Unclassified	Informal name Softwood

CONIFER WOOD

Conifer wood is distinguished by its very uniform appearance and is commonly called "softwood." Growth rings can often be seen, as can resin canals or ducts. The bulk of the tissue is made up of a single type of woody cell called a tracheid. Generic and species distinctions between softwoods is difficult and can usually only be made at the microscopic level from the study of ground sections. Similar wood is produced by *Ginkgo*, and by some progymnosperms and pteridosperms.

• **HABITAT** Conifer wood is found in a wide selection of plant community types, including tropical to temperate forests, woodlands, parklands, and mangroves.

dark stained outer layer

SILICIFIED CONIFER WOOD; Lower Greensand; Early Cretaceous; UK.

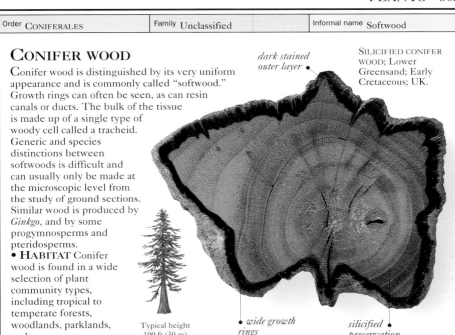

Typical height 100 ft (30 m)

wide growth rings

silicified preservation

Range Permian–Recent	Distribution Worldwide	Occurrence

Order CONIFERALES	Family TAXODIACEAE	Informal name Dawn redwood

METASEQUOIA

These are large trees with small leaves in the form of flattened needles, in opposite pairs along the twig. Seed cones are produced on long stalks and the cone leaves or bracts are in cross-pairs. At the base of the tree, where it joins the roots, vertical growths of wood called "knees" are produced.

• **HABITAT** *Metasequoia* grows in subtropical swampland, thriving in very wet areas with its roots immersed in water.

• **REMARK** The plant was known only as a fossil until 1941, when it was found growing in Szechuan, China – a remarkable example of a "living fossil."

METASEQUOIA OCCIDENTALIS (Newberry) Chaney; Shale; Oligocene; Canada.

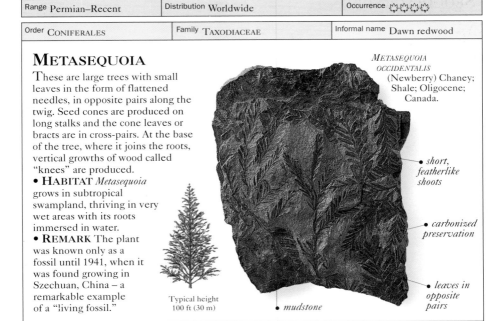

short, featherlike shoots

carbonized preservation

leaves in opposite pairs

Typical height 100 ft (30 m)

mudstone

Range Cretaceous–Recent	Distribution Northern hemisphere	Occurrence

Order CONIFERALES	Family ARAUCARIACEAE	Informal name Monkey Puzzle

ARAUCARIA

This genus of large trees includes the Monkey Puzzle Tree and Norfolk Island Pine. The leaves are small and toothlike, spirally arranged and closely pressed to the twig, hiding it completely. The cones are large, almost spherical, and very spiny. The surface is formed of the closely packed woody ends of cone leaves or bracts. Seeds are present at the base of the bracts.
• **HABITAT** This genus grew in subtropical mountain forests. Recent genera are restricted to the southern hemisphere.
• **REMARK** The famous fossil forest buried by volcanic ash at Cerro Cuadrado, Patagonia, is made up of *Araucaria* trees. Silicified twig, cone, and wood remains from there are common.

CUT SECTION
OF CONE

all tissues
• preserved

• seeds
within
cone

• silicified
preservation

woody surface

SIDE VIEW

broken
• surface

• interlocking
diamond
pattern

TOP VIEW

rusty •
color

Typical height
100 ft (30 m)

*ARAUCARIA
MIRIBILIS* (Spegazzini)
Windhausen; Cerro Alto
Beds; Early Cretaceous;
Argentina.

• seeds in
diamond-
shaped cavities

Range Jurassic–Recent	Distribution Worldwide	Occurrence

Order CONIFERALES	Family Unclassified	Informal name Softwood

SILICIFIED WOOD

Petrification of wood involves the replacement of the original tissue by minerals in solution, usually silica or calcium carbonate. Recrystallization of silica, due to pressure and heat, together with impurities in the solution, causes new forms of this mineral – usually agate or, more rarely, opal – to grow. It also results in the destruction of the wood anatomy.

• **HABITAT** Silicified wood is found in a very wide variety of habitats.

• **REMARK** It is often impossible to attribute silicified or similarly preserved woods to particular plants or trees. All that can be said is that the wood is of a broadly soft-wood type (as illustrated). Silic-ified wood is often attractive and multicolored.

SILICIFIED CONIFEROUS WOOD; Red beds; Triassic; USA.

• *wood structure destroyed*

• *no growth rings*

Estimated height 100 ft (30 m)

Range Permian–Recent	Distribution Worldwide	Occurrence 🍂🍂

Order CONIFERALES	Family PINACEAE	Informal name Spruce

PICEA

This is a large group of mainly tall, narrowly conic trees that today is confined to the northern hemi-sphere. Many spruce trees have characteristic drooping branches, giving a distinctive tiered effect to the whole plant. The stiff, needlelike leaves are arranged spirally about the stem, and are ¾ to 1¼ in (2 to 3 centimeters) long. They grow from small pegs, which remain if the leaves are shed. The woody cones are pendulous, ovoid, or cylindrical, and often have strongly recurved bracts that open to shed seeds as the cone matures.

• **HABITAT** The wood is of softwood type, often with strongly marked growth rings, in keeping with the seasonal montane climate found in most pine habitats.

CARBONIZED CONE

PICEA sp.; Thanet Formation; Late Paleocene; UK.

• *woody bracts*

• *diamond pattern*

Typical height 130 ft (40 m)

Range E. Cretaceous–Recent	Distribution Worldwide	Occurrence 🍂🍂

Order CONIFERALES	Family Not applicable	Informal name Amber

AMBER AND COPAL

Amber is fossilized resin or gum produced by some fossil plants. The earliest recorded fossil resins are of Carboniferous age, but ambers do not occur until the Early Cretaceous. Famous amber deposits include those from the Baltic region and the Dominican Republic. It is likely that ambers were mainly ancient gymnosperm (probably conifer) resins, but today such gums are also produced by flowering plants. Baltic amber occasionally contains insect and plant remains. It is supposed to have been formed in forests of a primitive species of pine, *Pinus succinifera*. Recent and semifossil copal resins differ from amber, in that they are still readily soluble in organic solvents. Resins are exuded from within the tree when it is traumatized by attack or growth splits. Today they are gathered commercially, one example being the copals derived from Kauri pine in New Zealand. Baltic amber is used in jewelry; copals in varnish manufacture.

KAURI GUM;
Pleistocene;
New Zealand.

MIXED
CLEAR AND
CLOUDY
AMBER

• *cloudy
area rich
in succinic
acid*

• *stalactitic
flow*

BALTIC AMBER
(Succinite); Late
Eocene; Denmark.

CLEAR, GEM-
QUALITY AMBER

ROLLED
AMBER
PEBBLE

• *red
patina*

TREE
(*PINUS* sp.)

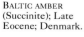

Typical height
100 ft (30 m)

Range E. Cretaceous–Recent	Distribution Worldwide	Occurrence

GINKGOS

THIS WAS FORMERLY an extensive group of plants, but it is now represented by a solitary relict genus, the *Ginkgo*, or maidenhair, tree. The group appeared during the Early Permian and was at its height during the Jurassic. All members had a characteristic fan-shaped leaf architecture.

Order GINKGOALES	Family GINKGOACEAE	Informal name Maidenhair tree

GINKGO

These very tall trees have a distinctive fan- or wedge-shaped foliage. The leaves may be notched or almost entire. The trees produce spherical seeds.
• **HABITAT** A "living" fossil, the *Ginkgo*'s natural habitat is China, but it has been introduced as an ornamental tree in many parks and gardens.

Typical height 115 ft (35 m)

GINKGO sp.; Ardtun Leaf Bed; Paleocene; UK.

fan-shaped leaf

compression fossil

mudstone

Range L. Triassic–Recent	Distribution Worldwide	Occurrence

DICOTYLEDONOUS ANGIOSPERMS

THESE FLOWERING PLANTS are distinguished by having two seed leaves. Ordinary leaves have a variety of simple to compound shapes. Plants range from herbaceous to tree types. All reproduce sexually by seeds. The earliest record of the group is from Early Cretaceous pollen.

Order HAMAMELIDALES	Family BETULACEAE	Informal name Birch

BETULITES

The leaves of this genus have some similarity to those of *Betula* or the birch family. They were round, oval, or heart shaped, and always had teeth along the margin. Venation consisted of a central vein, with secondary veins coming off at about 45 degrees. They are usually found disassociated from twigs, which indicates that at least some were dropped seasonally.
• **HABITAT** This genus grew in temperate climates and usually damp habitats.

Typical height 33 ft (10 m)

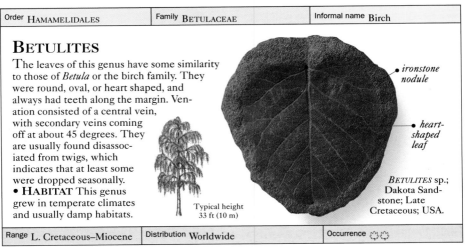

ironstone nodule

heart-shaped leaf

BETULITES sp.; Dakota Sandstone; Late Cretaceous; USA.

Range L. Cretaceous–Miocene	Distribution Worldwide	Occurrence

Order APIALES	Family ARALIACEAE	Informal name Ginseng

ARALIOPSOIDES

This genus is characterized by large leaves. Typically, they were coarsely three-lobed, but were sometimes of very variable appearance. The leaf margins were smooth with no teeth or serrations. The venation was simple – a central vein with straight secondary veins coming off at about 45 degrees. They were very thick and resilient, which explains their survival in sandstones.

• **HABITAT** *Araliopsoides* grew in warm, temperate to sub-tropical, deciduous forests.

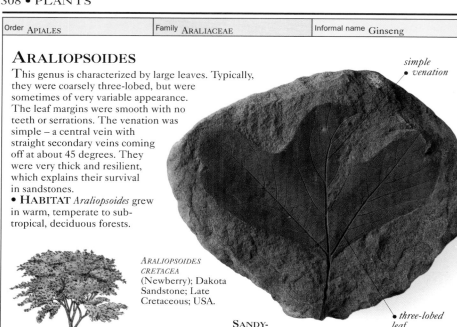

simple venation

ARALIOPSOIDES CRETACEA (Newberry); Dakota Sandstone; Late Cretaceous; USA.

Typical height 33 ft (10 m)

SANDY-IRONSTONE CAST

• *three-lobed leaf*

Range L. Cretaceous	Distribution Worldwide	Occurrence ☼

Order SAPINDALES	Family ACERACEAE	Informal name Maple

ACER

These are small to large trees of temperate regions, popularly called maples. The leaves are usually of a basic three-lobed appearance, toothed, with a long stalk, shed in the autumn. The wood is zoned, with noticeable spring wood composed of large conducting tubes. Flowers are produced in drooping clusters, followed by the distinctive winged fruits. These are always produced in pairs, but can become separated when they fall to the ground.

• **HABITAT** This genus is an inhabitant of temperate, deciduous forests.

ACER sp.; Freshwater limestone; Miocene; Croatia.

• *single wing with venation*

limestone •

Typical height 80 ft (25 m)

WINGED FRUIT

Range Oligocene–Recent	Distribution Worldwide	Occurrence ☼

Order HAMAMELIDALES	Family MORACEAE	Informal name Fig

FICUS

A large genus of shrubs and trees, the figs have thick, oval to fiddle-shaped leaves, with a noticeable central vein. The fruit is a globular, flat-topped, and stalked structure, with seeds embedded in a fleshy surround. One species, the Strangler Fig, is a parasite of other trees. Germinating in a branch crook, it gradually constricts its host until it dies.
• **HABITAT** This is a tropical to temperate genus.

Typical height
100 ft (30 m)

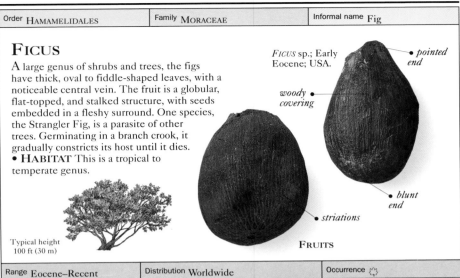

FICUS sp.; Early Eocene; USA.

• *pointed end*

woody covering

• *blunt end*

• *striations*

FRUITS

Range Eocene–Recent	Distribution Worldwide	Occurrence

Order HAMAMELIDALES	Family FAGACEAE	Informal name Oak

QUERCUS

A genus of large trees with distinctive foliage and fruits, the leaves of *Quercus* are a variety of shapes, from lobed to fiddle-shaped or hollylike. The leaves may be shed in autumn or they may be evergreen. The fruit is the familiar acorn, with the ornament of the cup varying from species to species. Usually the wood has very large conducting tubes and distinct growth rings.
• **HABITAT** *Quercus* grows in temperate, deciduous to semi-evergreen forests and woodlands.

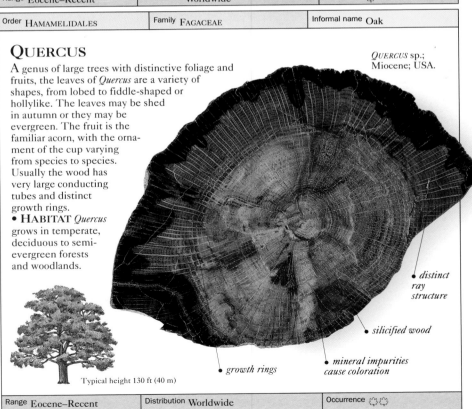

QUERCUS sp.; Miocene; USA.

• *distinct ray structure*

• *silicified wood*

• *mineral impurities cause coloration*

• *growth rings*

Typical height 130 ft (40 m)

Range Eocene–Recent	Distribution Worldwide	Occurrence

Order HAMAMELIDALES	Family HAMAMELIDACEAE	Informal name Sweetgum tree

LIQUIDAMBAR

These small to large trees are often called sweetgum. The twigs sometimes have corky flanges or wings, and the leaves are distinctively lobed or star shaped, with five to seven points and toothed margins. Leaf venation consists of a single central vein for each lobe, with nets of veins on either side. Leaves are shed in the autumn. Fruits are aggregates of woody, burrlike capsules, borne on a long stem. The wood is fine grained, with small conducting tubes.
• **HABITAT** They grow in temperate, deciduous to semi-evergreen forests and woodlands.

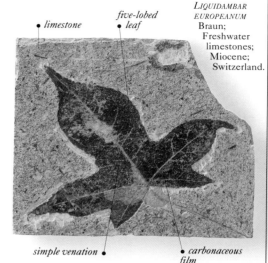

limestone • *five-lobed leaf* •

LIQUIDAMBAR EUROPEANUM Braun; Freshwater limestones; Miocene; Switzerland.

simple venation • • *carbonaceous film*

Typical height 80 ft (25 m)

Range Oligocene–Recent	Distribution Worldwide	Occurrence

Order HAMAMELIDALES	Family BETULACEAE	Informal name Birch

BETULA

This is a small tree, with bark that is often distinctively patterned or colored in modern representatives. The leaves are usually small with toothed margins, and they are shed during autumn. Trees of this genus reproduce with catkins and seeds, with seed leaves or bracts. The wood is fine-grained with very small conducting tubes and sometimes with complex wood rays.
• **HABITAT** *Betula* was a common component of northern ice-age forests. Today it is found in temperate climates, often in waterside habitats.

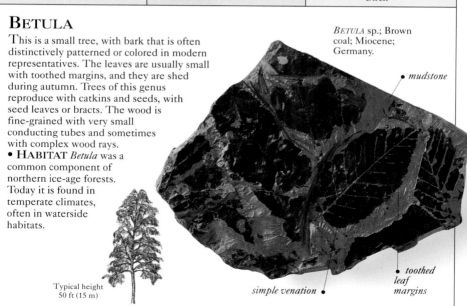

BETULA sp.; Brown coal; Miocene; Germany.

• *mudstone*

• *toothed leaf margins*

simple venation •

Typical height 50 ft (15 m)

Range Miocene–Recent	Distribution Worldwide	Occurrence

MONOCOTYLEDONOUS ANGIOSPERMS

THIS IMPORTANT GROUP of plants is characterized by their mode of germination – with a single seed leaf – and by leaves with parallel venation. Included in this group are grasses, narcissi, sedges, rushes, orchids, lilies, irises, and palms – all having a bewildering range of flowers and reproduction strategies. Fossil forms are recognized from the Late Cretaceous as palms and rushes, while grasses do not appear until the Early Cenozoic Era. A possible monocot is recorded from the Triassic of America.

Order ARECALES	Family ARECACEAE	Informal name Palm tree

PALMOXYLON

Fossil palm tree wood is quite homogeneous, and typically has many round, dark spots on a lighter background in cross section. These spots are conducting or vascular tissues, and distinguish the genus from dicotyledonous angiosperms and conifer woods. There are no growth rings.
• **HABITAT** *Palmoxylon* grew in subtropical, semi-evergreen forest and woodland.

Typical height 65 ft (20 m)

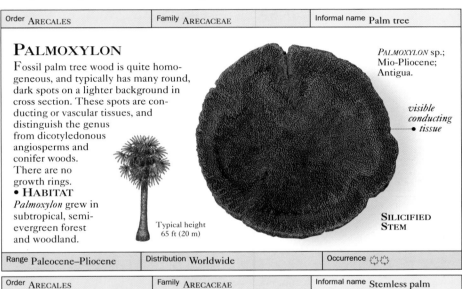

PALMOXYLON sp.; Mio-Pliocene; Antigua.

visible conducting tissue

SILICIFIED STEM

Range Paleocene–Pliocene	Distribution Worldwide	Occurrence 🍁🍁

Order ARECALES	Family ARECACEAE	Informal name Stemless palm

NIPA

This is a palm with little or no stem. The leaves or fronds are large, with long, pointed, subopposite leaflets. Coconut-like fruits are produced near the base of the frond, and within the fibrous husk are several seeds.
• **HABITAT** Stemless palms grow in mangrove swamps and are restricted to Southeast Asia.
• **REMARK** These plants were a distinctive feature of some Early and Middle Eocene plant communities.

Typical height 5 ft (1.5 m)

NIPA BURTINII Brongniart; Sables de Bruxelles; Middle Eocene; Belgium.

subspherical shape

woody outer layer

FRUIT

Range L. Cretaceous–Recent	Distribution Northern hemisphere	Occurrence 🍁🍁🍁

GLOSSARY

THE USE OF SOME technical expressions is unavoidable in a book of this nature. Commonly used technical words are often defined in the text itself, and many terms are explained by the annotated illustrations. The definitions given below have been simplified and generalized, and are appropriate for this book only. Words in bold type are explained elsewhere in the glossary.

- **ADDUCTOR MUSCLES**
The muscles controlling the valves of bivalves and brachiopods.
- **ADIPOSE FIN**
In fish, a fleshy **dorsal** fin.
- **ALATE PLATE**
A flaplike extension on the interior hinge line of the **brachial valve** of a brachiopod.
- **ALVEOLUS**
A tooth socket in vertebrates; a cavity containing **phragmocone** in belemnites.
- **AMBULACRA**
The plated zones of echinoderms associated with tube feet.
- **ANAL FIN**
An unpaired **posterior** fish fin.
- **ANAL TUBE**
The projecting part of the arm that carries the anus in crinoids.
- **ANTENNULES**
The sensory appendages toward the front of a trilobite.
- **ANTERIOR**
Toward the front.
- **APERTURE**
The opening surrounded by the shell margin in mollusks.
- **APICAL DISC**
The upper central disc of a sea urchin, from which the **ambulacra** radiate.
- **APTIAN STAGE**
The fifth out of the six stages in the Early Cretaceous.
- **ARAGONITE**
A crystalline form of calcium carbonate.
- **ARISTOTLE'S LANTERN**
The five-sided feeding and locomotor structure sited around the mouth of sea urchins.
- **ARTICULAR BONES**
The bones incorporated in the articulation between the skull and lower jaw in some vertebrates.
- **AURICLES**
The earlike structure on a bivalve shell.
- **AVICULARIA**
The defensive individuals in a bryozoan colony.

- **AXIAL BOSS**
The raised node at the center of the **corallites** in corals.
- **AXIS**
In trilobites, the ridge that runs from **anterior** to **posterior**, down the midline; in vertebrates, the first or second element of the backbone.
- **BARBEL**
A slim, sensitive process near the mouth of some fish.
- **BASAL**
At, or pertaining to, the base.
- **BEAK**
A prominent curved structure: in bivalves, the extremity of the **umbo**; in cephalopods and vertebrates, a part of the jaw structure.
- **BENTHONIC**
Living on the sea floor.
- **BICIPITAL SURFACE**
A bulbous surface at the **proximal** end of the upper arm bone in vertebrates.
- **BICONIC**
Pointed at both ends.
- **BOREAL**
Suggesting a fauna with preference for a cold climate.
- **BOSS**
A protuberance.
- **BRACHIAL VALVE**
One of the two valves that form the brachiopod shell.
- **BRACHIOLE**
An armlike appendage to a brachiopod.
- **BRACT**
A modified leaf associated with plant reproductive structures.
- **BUNODONT**
A condition in which molar teeth possess rounded **cusps** and **tubercles**.
- **BYSSAL NOTCH**
The notch near to the **hinge** of some bivalve shells, associated with attachment threads.
- **BYSSUS**
The attachment threads of a bivalve.

- **CALICE**
The upper portion of a coral skeleton.
- **CALLUM**
The dome of calcite in mollusks.
- **CALCAREOUS**
Made of calcium carbonate; chalky.
- **CALYX**
In crinoids, a cup-shaped structure to which the arms are attached; in plants, the outer circle of a flower made up of sepals.
- **CAPITILUM**
A portion of a crustacean or chelicerate, usually composed of armored plates, protecting the food-gathering organs.
- **CARAPACE**
In crustaceans and chelicerates, the external shield covering head and trunk; in vertebrates, the upper shell.
- **CARDINAL TEETH**
The articulating structures on the **hinge** of a brachiopod.
- **CARINA (pl. CARINAE)**
A ridge- or keel-shaped structure.
- **CARNASSIAL TOOTH**
A molar or premolar specialized for cutting.
- **CARTILAGE**
Highly specialized tissue that is hard but flexible.
- **CAST**
The filling of a **mold**.
- **CAUDAL FIN**
The tail fin of a vertebrate.
- **CENOZOIC**
The fourth era of time in the history of the Earth, 65 to 2 million years ago.
- **CENTRUM (pl. CENTRA)**
The main body of a **vertebra**.
- **CEPHALON**
The head of a trilobite.
- **CEPHALOTHORAX**
The combined head and trunk region of an arthropod.
- **CERCI**
The sensory appendages at the **posterior** of the abdomen of insects.

- **CHELA** (*pl.* **CHELAE**)
The pincerlike end of limb of crustaceans or chelicerates.
- **CHELICERAE**
The biting appendages of spiders.
- **CHEVRON BONES**
In reptiles, the pair of bones, often fused to form a Y, that hang below the tail **vertebrae**.
- **CHITIN**
A horny substance, forming all or part of the skeleton of arthropods.
- **CILIA**
Tiny, hairlike structures on a cell.
- **CIRRI**
A tendril-like animal appendage; the jointed **thoracic** appendages of barnacles.
- **CLASPERS**
The specialized pelvic fins of sharks, rays, and ratfishes.
- **COENOSTEUM**
The **calcareous** skeleton of a bryozoan and some corals.
- **COLONY**
An assemblage of connected organisms that have grown from an individual.
- **COLUMELLA**
The column that surrounds the shell's **axis** in gastropods.
- **COLUMNAL**
The stem **ossicles** in crinoids.
- **COMMISSURE**
The line along which two valves of a shell meet.
- **COMPRESSION FOSSIL**
A flattened fossil.
- **CORALLITE**
In corals, an individual **polyp's** skeleton.
- **CORNUA**
A hornlike structure in fish.
- **COSTAE**
Fine, concentrically arranged ribbing.
- **COXA** (*pl.* **COXAE**)
The **proximal** or base region of a limb, which articulates with the body in insects and some other arthropods.
- **CRANIUM**
The part of the skull enclosing the brain.
- **CUSP**
A projection of the chewing surface of a tooth.
- **CUSPLET**
A small **cusp**.
- **CUTICLE**
The hardened outer surface of the external skeleton of arthropods.
- **CYST**
A thick-walled cell in plants.

- **DEGENERATE**
Not fully formed.
- **DELTOID**
A V-shaped plate in the cup of a blastoid.
- **DELTOID CREST**
The projection of the upper arm bone for the attachment of muscles in vertebrates.
- **DEMOSPONGE**
A sponge with a skeleton possessing one- to four-rayed sponge fibers.
- **DENTARY**
The bone of the lower jaw in vertebrates.
- **DENTICLE**
A small, toothlike structure.
- **DENTICULATE**
Serrated; housing **denticles**.
- **DENTINE**
The bonelike substance that makes up the bulk of a tooth.
- **DERMAL ARMOR**
The bony plates situated in the skin of some vertebrates.
- **DERMAL DENTICLE**
A toothlike structure found in the skin of sharks.
- **DETRITUS**
Fine particles of organic matter.
- **DIAGENESIS**
The process involved in turning sediment into a rock.
- **DIASTEMA**
The space between two types of teeth.
- **DISCOIDAL**
Disc shaped.
- **DISSEPIMENT**
In corals, a vertical plate sited between **septa**.
- **DORSAL**
The upper surface or back.
- **DORSAL FIN**
A midline, unpaired, vertical fin sited on the back of aquatic vertebrates.
- **DORSOVENTRALLY FLATTENED**
Compressed from top to bottom.
- **ELYTRA**
The modified **anterior** wings that act as protective covers for the membranous hindwings in beetles.
- **ENTOPLASTRON**
The **anterior**, median bony plate of the lower shell in turtles.
- **EPIDERMIS**
The bloodless, nonsensitive portion of the skin in vertebrates.
- **EPIPLANKTONIC**
The area of the sea from the surface to about 100 fathoms.

- **EPIPLASTRON**
One of the **anterior** pair of bony plates of the lower shell in turtles.
- **EPISTOME**
The area covering the mouth and second antennae, and the plate covering this region, in crustaceans.
- **ESCUTCHEON**
A depression found behind the **umbones** of a bivalve shell.
- **EVOLUTE**
Loosely coiled.
- **EXOSKELETON**
The hard outer casing of arthropods.
- **EXTERNAL MOLD**
An impression of the outside of an organism.
- **FACIAL SUTURE**
A line on the head of a trilobite along which splitting occurred during molting.
- **FENESTRULE**
An opening located between the branches of a bryozoan colony.
- **FILTER FEEDER**
An organism that gains nutrition by filtering particles from the water.
- **FLAGELLUM**
A whiplike appendage.
- **FOOT**
In invertebrates, the base from which the organism grows, or by which it is cemented to the substrate.
- **FORAMEN** (*pl.* **FORAMINAE**)
A small opening or perforation in brachiopods.
- **FORM-GENUS**
A genus containing many similar species but that may not actually be related.
- **FRONTAL BONE**
In vertebrates, one of a pair of bones situated in the skull.
- **FUSIFORM**
Tapering at each end.
- **GENAL ANGLE**
The angle between the back and lateral margins of a trilobite's head.
- **GENAL SPINE**
A trilobite's cheek spine.
- **GIRDLE**
In chitons, the outer portion of the **mantle**; in vertebrates, the hoop-like group of bones that support the limbs.
- **GLABELLA**
In trilobites, the central region of the head; in vertebrates, the prominent front bone that joins the ridges above the eyes.

• GLAUCONITIC
Containing the mineral glauconite, the presence of which indicates that a sediment was deposited in marine conditions.

• GONADS
Sex glands.

• GRACILE
Lightly built.

• GROWTH LINES
The dividing lines between periods of growth.

• GUARD
A massive, bullet-shaped calcite structure in belemnites.

• HADROSAURIAN CREST
A bony crest found on the skulls of hadrosaurian dinosaurs.

• HALTERES
The pair of structures representing hindwings in flies.

• HETEROCERCAL TAIL
The tail of a fish with unequal-sized lobes.

• HINGE
The linear area along which a mollusk shell articulates.

• HINGE PLATE
In mollusks, the portion of valve that supports the hinge teeth; in brachiopods, the socket-bearing portion of the dorsal valve.

• HINGE TEETH
Articulating structures in mollusk shells.

• HOLDFAST
A basal structure that attaches a plant to the substrate.

• HOMOCERCAL TAIL
A symmetrical fish tail.

• HYOPLASTRON
The paired, second lateral, bony plate of the lower shell of a turtle.

• HYPOCERCAL TAIL
A type of fish tail in which the notochord ends in the extended lower lobe.

• HYPOPLASTRON
The paired, third lateral, bony plate of the lower shell of a turtle.

• INCUS
The central of the three bones of the inner ear of vertebrates.

• INTERAMBULACRAL
The area between two radial plates, along which the tube feet of echinoids are arranged.

• INTERAREA
The flat area on a brachiopod shell between the hinge line and beak areas.

• INTERNAL MOLD
An impression of the inside of an organism.

• LABIAL
Pertaining to the lips.

• LABIAL SPINES
Spines sited at the aperture of certain gastropod shells.

• LIVING FOSSIL
An animal or plant species that has remained almost unchanged for millions of years.

• LOCALLY OCCURRING
Found only at certain, specific localities.

• LOPH
A crest or ridge.

• LUNULE
A crescent-shaped structure or mark in the test of some sea urchins.

• MACROCONCH
The larger form of a shell in a species in which males and females differ.

• MALLEUS
The outermost bone of the inner ear in vertebrates.

• MANDIBLE
In vertebrates, the lower jaw; in invertebrates, the various mouth-parts that hold or bite food.

• MANTLE
The external body wall, lining the shell of some invertebrates.

• MANTLE CAVITY
The space between the body and mantle of a bivalve.

• MARINE INDICATORS
Characteristics denoting saltwater conditions.

• MARL
A calcareous mudstone.

• MATRIX
The material on which an organism rests or is embedded.

• MAXILLARY LOBES
A part of the mouth of an arthropod.

• MEDIAN TOOTH
A tooth placed in the midline of the mouth.

• MESIAL TOOTH
A tooth placed near the middle of the jaw.

• MESOPLASTRON
In turtles, one of a pair of bony plates forming the lower shell.

• MESOSUCHIAN
A primitive crocodile.

• MESOZOIC
The second era of the Phanerozoic aeon, from 248 to 65 million years ago.

• METAMORPHISM
A change in an organism's structure during development.

• METATARSAL
Pertaining to the bones in the ankle.

• MICROCONCH
The smaller form of a shell in a species in which males and females differ in size.

• MICROSCULPTURE
Small patterns of ornamentation.

• MONTANE CLIMATE
Hilly areas below the timberline.

• MONTICULE
A hummock on the surface of a bryozoan colony.

• MORPHOLOGY
The structure and form of plants and animals.

• MOLD
An impression obtained from an original form.

• MUCILLAGE
A carbohydrate found in certain plants, which can be secreted.

• MUCRON
A short tip or process.

• MUCRONATE
Ended by a short tip or process.

• NACRE
An iridescent internal layer of a mollusk shell.

• NACREOUS
Made of nacre.

• NEMA
The attachment thread found in some graptolites.

• NEOTONY
A condition in which development is terminated at a pre-adult stage but sexual maturity is reached.

• NEURAL ARCH
The upper portion of a vertebra.

• NEURAL CANAL
The channel through which the spinal cord passes.

• NEURAL PLATE
A series of bony plates sited in the midline of the upper shell of turtles.

• NEURAL SPINE
The blade- or pronglike structure located on the dorsal aspect of a vertebra.

• NODES
Bumps or protruberances; in plants, the attachment point of leaf stem.

• NOTOCHORD
A skeletal rod located above the nerve chord of fish.

• NUTRITIVE GROOVE
Food channel.

• NYMPH
An immature insect, or, in bivalves, the narrow ledge on the hinge behind the umbo.

- **OCCIPITAL**
A bone at the rear of the skull that articulates with the spinal column.
- **OCCLUSAL**
The cutting or grinding surface of a tooth.
- **OPERCULUM**
The structure attached to a gastropod's foot, used to close the shell's **aperture**.
- **ORAL TEETH**
Teeth situated in the mouth, as opposed to on the rostrum.
- **ORBIT**
An eye socket.
- **ORNITHOPOD**
A group of dinosaurs with bird-like feet.
- **OSSICLES**
In invertebrates, the **calcareous** bodies that make up the skeleton.
- **OSSIFIED**
Turned to bone.
- **OTOLITH**
A **calcareous** concretion in a vertebrate's ear.
- **PALEOZOIC**
The first era of the Phanerozoic aeon, 545 to 248 million years ago.
- **PALLETS**
The burrowing structure of mollusks.
- **PALLIAL LINE**
In bivalves, an impressed line inside the valve, parallel to the margin, caused by the attachment of the **mantle**.
- **PECTORAL FIN**
One of a pair of forward-pointing fins in fish.
- **PEDICLE**
A **cuticle**-covered appendage for the attachment of a brachiopod shell to the **substrate**.
- **PEDIPALPS**
The first pair of post-oral appendages in chelicerates.
- **PEDUNCLE**
In some invertebrates, the stalk that supports most of the body.
- **PELVIC FIN**
In fish, one of a pair of fins placed toward the back.
- **PEN**
The horny internal skeleton of squids.
- **PERIDERM**
A horny, cuticular covering.
- **PHRAGMOCONE**
In belemnites and other mollusks, the conelike internal shell that is

divided into chambers by **septa** and perforated by a **siphuncle**.
- **PINNAE**
Small leaflets on plants.
- **PINNULE**
A part of the fanlike structure of the arms of a crinoid.
- **PLANISPIRAL**
Coiled in one plane.
- **PLANKTON**
Weak-swimming or passively floating animals or plants.
- **PLASTRON**
The lower bony shell of turtles.
- **PLEOTELSON**
In crustaceans and chelicerates, the plate formed by the fusion of tail plates with abdominal segments.
- **PLEURAL LOBES**
The lateral parts of the **thoracic** segments of trilobites.
- **PLEURAL SPINE**
The body spine of a trilobite.
- **PNEUMATIC BONE**
In birds, the bones connected by canals to the respiratory system.
- **POLYMORPHIC**
A species with more than one form.
- **POLYP**
An individual member of a coral colony.
- **POSTERIOR**
Toward the rear.
- **PRESACRAL VERTEBRAE**
Part of the backbone in front of the hindlimb girdle.
- **PRISMATIC**
A shell structure of minute, columnar prisms.
- **PROBOSCIS**
In insects, a tubular feeding structure; in mammals, a flexible, elongated snout.
- **PROCESS**
An extension or appendage to a organism.
- **PUSTULE**
A small, rounded protuberance, smaller than a **node**.
- **PRONOTUM**
The back of the first body segment in insects.
- **PRO-OSTRACUM**
The thin, tonguelike extension in front of the **guard** in belemnites.
- **PROPARIAN**
A form of **suture** in trilobites that reaches the edge in front of the **genal angle**.
- **PROP ROOT**
A root that helps support a plant.
- **PROXIMAL**
At or toward the near, inner, or attached end.

- **PSEUDOPELAGIC**
Refers to the life-style of organisms that live attached to floating objects in the sea.
- **PUBIC BONE**
One of the paired girdle bones in vertebrates.
- **PUSTULE**
A small, raised mound or **tubercle**.
- **PYGIDIUM**
The tail of a trilobite.
- **PYRITE**
Gold-colored mineral composed of iron sulfide.
- **QUADRATE**
The bone that produces the **articulation** of the skull and lower jaw in some vertebrates.
- **RADIAL**
Diverging from the center.
- **RADULA**
A horny or toothlike structure located in the mouth of all mollusks, except bivalves.
- **RAMUS**
A **process** projecting from a bone.
- **RECURVED**
Curved backward.
- **REFLEXED**
Turned backward.
- **RETICULUM**
A fine network.
- **RIBS**
In invertebrates, raised ornamental bands; in vertebrates, part of the **thoracic** skeleton.
- **ROCK FORMER**
Animals that occur in sufficient abundance and frequency as to form the major bulk of a rock.
- **ROSTRAL PLATE**
One of the plates covering a barnacle (also known as a rostrum).
- **RUGAE**
Wrinkles on a shell surface.
- **SACCULITH**
The largest **otolith** in the inner ear.
- **SACRAL**
Associated with the hip girdle.
- **SAGITTAL CREST**
The median crest sited on the posterior portion of the skull.
- **SANDSTONE**
A rock made from coarse mineral grains, principally quartz.
- **SCALE LEAF**
A tough, membranous leaf that often has a protective function.
- **SCLEROSPONGE**
A calcified **demosponge**.
- **SCLEROTIC RING**
A ring of bony plates around the eye socket in reptiles and birds.

- **SCULPTURE**
Ornament on bone surface.
- **SCUTE**
The bony, scalelike structure found in reptiles.
- **SELENIZONE**
A groove in a gastropod shell.
- **SEPTUM** (*pl.* **SEPTA**)
A thin dividing wall.
- **SEXUAL DIMORPHISM**
A condition in which the sexes differ in form.
- **SHELF SEA**
Shallow seas around land masses.
- **SICULA**
The cone-shaped skeleton of a graptolite colony.
- **SILTSTONE**
A rock formed from silt deposits.
- **SINUS**
A cavity or recess in gastropods.
- **SIPHON**
A tubular element used for the intake of water in mollusks.
- **SIPHUNCLE**
A tubular extension of the **mantle** passing through all chambers of shelled cephalopods.
- **SOMITE**
A body segment of a crustacean.
- **SPICULE**
A spikelike supporting structure in many invertebrates, especially sponges.
- **SPINNERET**
An organ that spins fiber from the secretion of silk glands.
- **SPINULE**
A small, spinelike **process**.
- **SPIRE**
A complete set of **whorls** of a spiral shell.
- **SPRING WOOD**
The part of an annual ring formed mainly in the growing season in plants.
- **SQUAMOSAL**
A skull bone situated behind the ear in many vertebrates.
- **STERNITE**
The **ventral** plate in an arthropod segment.
- **STERNUM**
The breast bone of vertebrates.
- **STILT ROOT**
The aerial roots that help support trees such as mangroves.
- **STIPE**
A branch supporting a colony of individuals.
- **STRIAE**
Minute lines, grooves, or channels.
- **STROMATOLITE**
A cushionlike, algal growth.

- **SUBCHELATE**
Having a claw without a fixed finger, and a movable finger operating against a short outgrowth of the hand.
- **SUBSTRATE**
The base on which an animal or plant lives.
- **SULCUS**
A depression on a shell's surface.
- **SUSPENSION FEEDER**
An organism that derives its nourishment from food particles suspended in water.
- **SUTURE**
A line on gastropod shells where **whorls** connect.
- **SYMBIOSIS**
The mutually beneficial inter-relationship between two differ-ent species.
- **SYMPHYSEAL TOOTH**
A tooth located in the midline, near the apex of the jaw.
- **TABULA**
A transverse **septum** that shuts off the lower region of a **polyp** cavity in some extinct corals.
- **TABULATE**
Flat, tablelike.
- **TALONID**
The posterior part of the lower molar tooth in certain mammals.
- **TEGMEN** (*pl.* **TEGMINA**)
The thickened forewing of certain insects, such as beetles.
- **TELSON**
In crustaceans, the last segment of the body, containing the anus and/or spines.
- **TERMINAL MOUTH**
Mouth placed at the front in fish.
- **TEST**
A hard external covering or shell.
- **TETHYS OCEAN**
An ancient seaway that stretched from Europe to eastern Asia.
- **THALLUS**
A plant body consisting of a single cell or a complex multicellular structure.
- **THECA**
In graptolites, the organic-walled tubes housing **zooids**.
- **THORACIC**
Pertaining to the **thorax**.
- **THORAX**
In certain arthropods, the middle of the three main divisions of the body; in vertebrates, the chest region.
- **TRACHEID**
An elongate plant cell with thickened secondary walls.

- **TRITORS**
Specialized dentine in certain fish.
- **TUBE FEET**
Tentaclelike structures found in sea urchins.
- **TUBER**
A thickened underground stem or root of a plant.
- **TUBERCLE**
A raised mound or bump.
- **TUMID**
Raised, swollen.
- **TYMPANIC BONES**
Bones of the ear.
- **ULNA**
In vertebrates, one of the lower arm bones.
- **UMBILICUS**
The first-formed region of a coiled shell.
- **UMBO** (*pl.* **UMBONES**)
The beaklike first-formed region of a bivalve shell.
- **UROPOD**
A limb on the sixth trunk segment of crustaceans; generally fanlike.
- **VENTER**
In arthropods, the undersurface of the abdomen; in mollusks, the external, convex part of a curved or coiled shell.
- **VENTRAL**
Toward the underside.
- **VERTEBRA**
(*pl.* **VERTEBRAE**)
One bone in the series that makes up the backbone in vertebrates.
- **VISCERA**
The organs within the body cavities of an animal.
- **WATER COLUMN**
Water depth from surface to bed.
- **WEBERIAN OSSICLES**
A chain of three to four bones that connect the swim bladder to the inner ear of some fish.
- **WHORL**
One complete turn of a shell.
- **XIPHIPLASTRON**
A paired, bony plate of the lower shell of a turtle.
- **ZONAL MARKER**
See Zone Fossil.
- **ZONE FOSSIL**
A fossil species that characterizes a particular layer of the Earth's crust and is restricted to it in time.
- **ZOOID**
An individual of a colonial animal, such as corals, graptolites, and bryozoans.
- **ZYGOMATIC ARCH**
In mammals, a bony bar located on the side of the face below the eye.

INDEX

A

Acadagnostus 56
Acanthochirana 70
Acanthochonia 287
acanthodians 208
Acer 308
Acidaspis 63
Acrodus 199
Acrosterigma 108
Acroteuthis 161
Actinoconchus 85
Actinocrinites 169
Actinocyathus 52
Actinostroma 35
Aepyornis 259
agnathans 194
Ailsacrinus 174
Alethopteris 296
algae 286
Alveolina 32
Amaltheus 146
amber 306
Amblotherium 263
ammonites 145
Ammonoidea 141
Ampakabastraea 53
amphibians 221
anapsid reptiles 225
Ancistrocrania 92
Andrias 223
Apateon 222
Aphaneramma 222
Apiocrinites 173
Araliopsoides 308
Araucaria 304
Archaeocidaris 176
Archeogeryon 72
Archaeopteris 300
Archaeopteryx 258
Archeria 224
Archimediella 120
Archimylacris 76
Arctica 108
Arvicola 269
Aspidorhynchus 213
Astarte 106
Asteroceras 154
asteroids 186
Asterophyllites 291
Atrypa 84
Aturia 140
Aulacophoria 86
Australiceras 152
Australopithecus 282
Australorbis 133
Aviculopecten 98

B

Baculites 160
badlands 17

Balaena 270
Balanus 66
banded flint 10
Baragwanathia 295
Basilosaurus 269
Batrachosuchus 223
Belemnitella 163
belemnite limestone
  164
belemnites 161
Belemnotheutis 165
Bellerophon 115
Belodon 240
bennettites 300
Betula 310
Betulites 307
Bibio 78
Bienotherium 257
Bifericeras 150
birds 258
Birgeria 211
Birkenia 195
Bison 281
bivalves 94
Blapsium 78
blastoids 190
Bostrychoceras 159
Bothriolepis 197
Bourguetia 119
brachiopods 79
Brotia 120
Bryozoa 36
bryozoan
  limestone 39
Bulla 132
buying fossils 23
Bythotrephis 288

C

Calliostoma 118
Calonectris 260
Calymene 61
Campanile 121
Cancellothyris 93
Carbonicola 103
Carcharocles 203
Cardinia 107
Cardiola 94
carpoids 193
Cassis 126
cast 11
Cenoceras 138
Cenoceras
  simillium 139
Centroberyx 219
Cephalaspis 195
Ceratodus 209
Ceratites 144
Ceriocava 37

Cetiosaurus 247
Chama 105
Charniodiscus 43
Cheiracanthus 208
Cheirolepis 210
Chelicerata 73
Chione 109
chitons 114
chondrichthyans 198
Chondrites 42
Chonetes 83
Cimochelys 230
Cirsotrema 127
classification 7
Clavilithes 129
cleaning 20
Cleithrolepis 213
Clifton black
  rock 168
Clymenia 141
Clypeaster 180
coastal sites 16
Coccosteus 196
Coelodonta 279
Coleopleurus 179
collecting 18
Collenia 286
Colpophyllia 54
Compsognathus 245
Concoryphe 17
conifers 301
conifer wood 303
Constellaria 36
Conulus 180
Conus 130
Cooksonia 289
copal 306
coprolite 10
corals 50
cordaitales 301
Cordaites 301
Cothurnocystis 193
Crassatella 107
Crepidula 124
crinoids 166
Crioceratites 151
Crustacea 66
Cruziana 42
Cryptoclidus 236
Cucullaea 95
Cupressocrinites 167

Cyamocypris 68
Cyamodus 237
Cyathocrinites 167
Cyclosphaeroma 68
Cyclothyris 84
Cylindroteuthis 163
Cynognathus 257
Cyrnaonyx 271
Cyrtina 88
Cyrtoceras 134
cystoids 191

D

Dactylioceras 149
Dapedium 212
Daspletosaurus 246
Deinotherium 275
Deltoblastus 190
Dentalium 114
Derbyia 89
deserts 17
Deshayesites 158
Desmana 266
diapsid reptiles 231
Dicellopyge 211
Dicoelosia 80
dicotyledonous
  angiosperms 307
Dicroidium 299
Dictyothyris 87
Didelphis 264
Didymograptus 48
Digonella 90
Dimerocrinites 166
Dimetrodon 255
Dinilysia 235
dinosaurs 245
Diodora 116
Diplacanthus 208
Diplocaulus 221
Diplocynodon 243
Diplodocus 248
Diplomystus 216

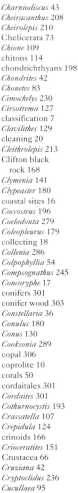

Diprotodon 265
Discinisca 92
Discitoceras 136
Dolomedes 75
Douvilleiceras 152
dung 10

E

early land plants 289
Echinocorys 182
echinoids 175
Echioceras 155
Ecphora 128
Edaphodon 207
Edaphosaurus 256
Edmontosaurus 251
Elginia 226
Elrathia 64
Enchodus 217
Encope 181
Encrinurus 62
Encrinus 171
Eocyphinium 65
Eosurcula 131
Epithyris 87
equipment 18
Equisetites 290
Equus 278
Eryon 69
Estonioceras 135
Euhoplites 156
Euomphalus 115
Euoplocephalus 253
Euproops 73
Eutrephoceras 139
Exogyra 101
Expansograptus 46

F

family 8
Favosites 51
Fenestella 37
ferns 292
Ficopsis 126
Ficus 309
Fimbria 105
finding fossils 16
footprint 10
Foraminifera 32
fossilization 11

G

Galeocerdo 204
Gallimimus 247
Gastrioceras 143
gastropods 115
genus 8
Geochelone 230
Geocoma 189
geological time 14
Gervillaria 96
Gigantopithecus 282
Ginkgo 307
ginkgos 307
Glomerula 41
Glossopteris 297
Glycymeris 95
Glyptodon 267
Goniatites 143
Goniopholis 242
Goniophyllum 50
Goniorhynchia 90
Graeophonus 75
Granosolarium 131
graptolites 45
Gryphaea 101
Gunnarites 155
Gyrodus 212

H

Halysites 53
Hardouinia 182
Harpoceras 149
Helicoprion 198
Heliobatis 206
Heliophyllum 50
Helminthochiton 114
Hemiaster 183
Hemicidaris 178
Hemicrinus 170
Hemipristis 204
hepatophytes 290
Hesperornis 259
Heterodontosaurus 249
Hexagonocaulon 290
Hibolithes 161
Hildoceras 150
Hipponix 123
Hippoporidra 39
Hippopotamus 280
Hippurites 112
Homeosaurus 231
Homo habilis 283
Homo sapiens neanderthalensis 283

Homo sapiens sapiens 284
Hoplopteryx 219
Huntonia 62
Huronia 135
Hyaenodon 270
Hydnoceras 33
Hydrophilus 77
Hymenocaris 66
Hyperodapedon 239
Hypsilophodon 250
Hyracotherium 277

I

Ichthyosaurus 238
identification key 24
Iguanodon 250
indexing 20
insects 76
invertebrates 32
Ischyrhiza 205

JK

Jobaria 248
Kingena 91
Kosmoceras 148
Ktenoura 59
Kuehneosuchus 232

L

labeling 20
Laosciadia 33
Leiodon 233
Leithia 268
Leonaspis 61
Lepadocrinites 192
Lepidodendron 294
Lepidotus 214
Leptaena 80
Leuciscus 218
Lingula 79
Linthia 183
Linuparus 71
Liopleurodon 237
Liquidambar 310
Loganograptus 46
Lovenia 185
Luther, Martin 6
lycopods 294
Lystromycter 232
Lystrosaurus 256
Lytoceras 145

M

Macaca 267
Macrauchenia 273
Macrones 217

Macropoma 209
mammals 263
Mammut 275
Mammuthus 276
Mantelliceras 156
Mariopteris 298
Marsupites 173
Mastopora 287
Mawsonites 43
Medullosa 296
Megalania 233
Megalocephalus 221
Megatherium 268
Meiolania 228
Melonechinus 175
Meristina 85
Merocanites 142
Merycoidodon 281
Mesoleuctra 77
Mesolimulus 74
Metaldetes 35
Metasequoia 303
Metopaster 188
Metriorhynchus 241
Micraster 185
mineralization 11
Mixosaurus 238
Modiolus 96
monocotyledonous angiosperms 311
Monograptus 48
Mortoniceras 157
Mucrospirifer 86
mummification 10
Murexsul 127
museums 22
Myliobatis 205
Myophorella 104

N

Natica 125
national parks 17
nautiloids 134
Neithea 100
Neohibolites 162
Neptunea 128
Nerinea 132
Neusticosaurus 236
Nipa 311
Nipponites 158
Notorynchus 202
Nuculana 94
Nummulites 32

O

Odontopteryx 261
Ogygopsis 64
Olenellus 56
Onnia 58
Onychiopsis 293
Ophiuroidea 189
order 8